CW01184302

THE BMC/BL COMPETITIONS DEPARTMENT

THE BMC/BL COMPETITIONS DEPARTMENT

25 years in Motor Sport ~ the cars, the people, the events

BILL PRICE

Foulis

Haynes

A **FOULIS** Motoring Book

First published 1989

© W. R. Price 1989

All rights reserved. No part of this book may be reproduced or transmitted in any form or by any means, electronic or mechanical, including photocopying, recording or by any information storage or retrieval system, without permission of the publisher.

Published by:
Haynes Publishing Group
Sparkford, Nr. Yeovil, Somerset
BA22 7JJ, England.

Haynes Publications Inc.
861 Lawrence Drive, Newbury Park,
California 91320, USA.

British Library Cataloguing in Publication data
Price, W.R.
BMC/BL Competitions Department.
(General motorsport).
1. British Leyland competition cars.
Racing, to 1981.
I. Title. II. Series.
796.7'2

ISBN 0-85429-677-8

Library of Congress catalog card number
88-82503

Editor: Mansur Darlington
Layout design: Mike King.
Printed in England by: J. H. Haynes & Co.

Contents

Introduction	6
1 The B.M.C. Competitions Department **1955**	9
2 Enter the Mini **1959-61**	37
3 Stuart Turner Incumbent **1961-63**	83
4 Monte Magic **1964-67**	119
5 Marathon Year **1968**	201
6 Triumphs at Abingdon **1969**	223
7 16,000 Miles to Mexico **1970**	249
8 Special Tuning Department **1964-74**	275
9 Leyland Returns to Motor Sport **1975**	295
10 V8 Power **1978-80**	337

Appendices

A Competitions department letter headings	367
B Works Drivers' Significant Results **1955-80**	368
C Event Results **1955-80**	369
Index	388

INTRODUCTION

I had the fortune of being a small cog in the BMC/BL Competitions Department wheel from 1960–1970 and then for a second time from 1974–1981. Despite being made redundant twice from the same department I decided during my second period of unemployment that I would like to try to write in one volume the story of the whole 25 year existence of the department, if only for historical reasons.

One or two very good books have already been published concerning various aspects of the life of the Abingdon team but this is my attempt to cover the full story. Inevitably, space limitations must be contended with so I have concentrated on the events entered officially by the factory but have also included some which were 'works' entries in everything but the entrant's name. My apologies to those works-assisted drivers who feel that they have not had a mention.

The Competitions Department at Abingdon saw many changes in its 25 years. Below is listed a brief resume of the persons in charge of the day-to-day running of the department over that period:

1955–1961 Marcus Chambers – BMC Competitions Manager

Worked in the motor trade before the Second World War. Served in the RNVR Coastal Forces from 1939–46. Engineer in Africa after the War. Appointed BMC Competitions Manager in 1955.

I hope I will be forgiven for mentioning several of my own experiences but feel that they represent a cross-section of the sort of things that could (and did) happen to many members of the staff, particularly when representing the Company on events.

I am most grateful for the assistance given to me by a considerable number of the drivers, co-drivers and staff of the department too numerous too mention individually, but I would like to thank particularly Marcus Chambers, Peter Browning, Paul Easter, Sandy Lawson, Stuart Turner, Basil Wales, Richard Seth-Smith, Doug Watts, Tommy Wellman, Cliff Humphries, Den Green, Brian Moylan, Gerald Wiffen, Pat Moss, Paddy Hopkirk, Kevin Best, Brian Culcheth, David Wood, Don Moore, Bill Burrows, Simon Pearson, Alan Zafer and Norman Higgins. My apologies for those not mentioned but all the help I have been given has been most appreciated.

1961-67 Stuart Turner – BMC Competitions Manager

Experienced navigator and co-driver on National & International rallies. Completed two years National Service. Trained as an accountant. Sports Editor of Motoring News. *BMC Competitions Manager in 1961 leaving to join Castrol in 1967.*

1967-70 Peter Browning – BMC Competitions Manager

Freelance journalist. RAC timekeeper. Later became General Secretary of the Austin Healey Club at Abingdon. Assistant Editor of Safety Fast *magazine. Appointed BMC Competitions Manager in 1967. Title changed to British Leyland Competitions Manager with the BL merger in 1968.*

1970-74 Basil Wales – Manager, British Leyland Special Tuning Department

Left: *Morris Motors Engines Branch apprentice at Coventry. Completed two years' National Service in the RAF. Worked as sports car specialist in the Product Problem Liaison department at BMC Service Ltd, Cowley. Appointed BMC Special Tuning Department Manager at Abingdon in 1964. With closure of the Competitions Department, continued as Manager of the British Leyland Special Tuning Department until 1974.*

I am proud to have been a member of such a memorable team, but feel sad that once again it has been disbanded. Competing in motor sport events seems a natural way for a motor manufacturer to promote the product but there are only one or two manufacturers who can claim to have had a long term commitment to the sport. Interest in motor sport seems to come and go with new chairmen or managing directors.

I think the number of ex-works Abingdon cars which still exist, lovingly cared for, reflects an indefineable magic created by Abingdon.

1974–76 Richard Seth-Smith – Manager, Leyland ST

Right: *Trained as an engineer at de Havilland. Worked in publicity for a trailer company. Press Officer for Standard-Triumph. Overseas PR Manager for BL. Manager of the Public Relations Department of Leyland Truck & Bus Division. Appointed Manager of the relaunched department, Leyland ST in 1974. Retained overall control until 1977 after being promoted to Manager of Product Affairs, BL, Redditch.*

1976–77 Bill Price – Manager, Leyland ST

Left: *Apprentice with BMC at Morris Commercial Cars Ltd. Completed two years' National Service in REME. Appointed assistant to BMC Competitions Manager in 1960. Appointed BL Special Tuning workshop supervisor 1974. Appointed Manager, Leyland ST in 1976. Competitions Manager reporting to John Davenport until 1981.*

1977–81 John Davenport – Director of Motor Sport, British Leyland

Right: *Motoring journalist. Rallies Editor of Autosport magazine. Experienced international rally co-driver. Press Officer of the RAC Motor Sport Division. Appointed Director of Motor Sport responsible for all BL motor sport activities in 1977. Moved to Cowley with the Department when MG closed.*

1
The BMC Competitions Department
1955

THE MG CAR Company was involved extensively in racing before the Second World War but officially the MG Competitions Department had been closed for some years. In 1954 John Thornley was general manager of MG and he had been plugging for an official re-entry into racing for some time. The formation of the British Motor Corporation had brought the Nuffield and Austin organisations together and Leonard Lord was persuaded to agree to the opening of an official competitions department.

The BMC directors under George Harriman gave instructions to form the new department at Abingdon which, to quote John Thornley, 'was to legitimise competitions'. Prior to this, John Thornley had authorised various racing outings with MG cars 'off my own bat with no questions asked'. The go ahead for the production of a new car (the MGA) had been authorised and this seemed to be an appropriate time to come back officially.

Early in December 1954, George Harriman directed Reg Bishop, BMC publicity chief, to make plans to get BMC to the top in motor sport, stating that the money to achieve that goal would be made available. The existing Nuffield competitions committee was to be dissolved and a new BMC committee formed with representatives from the Austin and Nuffield organisations, John Thornley as Chairman and including Reg Bishop and Bob Grice, Chief Road Test Superintendent from Austin.

John Thornley realised that he would not have the time to involve himself in the running of the new department and therefore would require a full time manager. Coincidentally at this time Marcus Chambers, who had not been back in England long, after working in East Africa on the Ground Nuts Scheme, was thinking of ways of resuming his connections with motor sport. Marcus wrote to an old friend, Jack Emmott of British Automotive Products, for a list of the most likely companies to contact. Marcus wrote a number of letters and one reply – which was to have a significant effect on the story of BMC Competitions – was a letter from John Thornley asking him to come along for a chat. Marcus duly arrived for his appointment and soon learned that John had already persuaded the BMC Directors to embark on an ambitious programme of races, and also to do some rallies.

John and Marcus both knew Sammy (SCH) Davis who was motor sport consultant to the Austin Motor Company. Marcus had met Sammy a number of times before the War when he was racing HRG's at Le Mans and elsewhere. No advertisment had been placed for the new post but Mort Morris-Goodall was one of the other applicants considered.

However, John Thornley was satisfied with his chat with Marcus and as they parted he told him that if he could convince Sammy Davis he could do the job, it was his. Marcus met Sammy at Bagshot that evening and it was not long afterwards that his appointment was confirmed as the first BMC Competitions Manager.

In January 1955 Marcus was nominated a member of the Competitions Committee and was soon given the go ahead to call the new department 'The British Motor Corporation Competitions Department' with note paper to suit.

Some people remarked cynically that there was no one with racing or rallying experience at Abingdon but they had, of course, forgotten names like Cecil Cousins, Alec Hounslow. Henry Stone and Syd Enever to mention a few, plus, of course, John Thornley and newcomer Marcus with his racing experience with HRG cars at Le Mans, Brooklands, Montlhéry and Spa in the late thirties. Not much rallying experience but a tremendous racing expertise to call upon.

It was agreed that the Committee would have the authority to enter any BMC car, including Austin Healeys. The Committee would also deal with the already planned MG 'racing programme' and the programme run by the Donald Healey Motor Company. Austin cars would be prepared in the Experimental Dept at Longbridge, work load permitting; all other models were to be prepared at Abingdon. A tentative maximum expenditure of £100,000 split between Austin and Nuffield was agreed, to cover all motor sport activities including record breaking.

The first event Marcus inherited was the 1955 Monte Carlo Rally in which an entry of three MG Magnettes and three Austin A90s had already been made. In addition, four of the new MGs, known only by the code EX182, were being built for the Le Mans 24 Hour race. They were, of course, MGAs, prototypes of the model to replace the MG TF in June. Other plans for the BMC model programme included the fitting of the 6-cylinder Austin A90 engine in the Austin Healey 100.

At the BMC Competitions Committee meeting in January, the BMC model range was discussed and they came to the conclusion that the most promising cars to choose from were the Austin A90 Westminster, Wolseley 4/44, Wolseley 6/90, Riley Pathfinder, MG Magnette and MG TF 1500. With new models on the way, Marcus felt he had the opportunity to build a team which could eventually make a good showing against the best in Europe.

Where was all the car preparation and administration going to be housed at MG, which was already short of

BMC Competitions Department

accommodation? The MG racing cars of earlier years had been built in the development shop at the end of A Block (the Assembly Building) which was eventually to become the Apprentice Training School. The development shop had a single engine test-bed protected by railway sleepers, with one or two broken windows which, according to legend, were caused by flying con-rods! However, the original hangars which comprised B block, numbering 1, 3, 5 and 7 were being joined up by building hangars 2, 4, 6 and 8 in between and the extra space would be used to house a paint shop, drawing office and rectification department as well as a new experimental/development shop. The building work was not scheduled to be completed until April 1955.

Hinged Lucas Flame-thrower hoods on the J. Shaw MG Magnette, 1955 Monte Carlo Rally

On his arrival at Abingdon, Marcus was allocated an office in A block on the first floor, some distance from the Development workshop, at the top of the stairs next to the MG tool stores. It was said that this gave Marcus a slight tactical advantage when dealing with difficult customers as they were breathing heavily when they arrived at his door, but it was not very convenient to be some way from the car preparation workshop.

To cope with the full time re-entry into motor sport, particularly the new venture into rallying, the Department had to set up an organisation to make entries, travel bookings, hotel reservations, sort out passport and visa problems and arrange customs documents and carnets for the movement of cars and spares across the continent.

Soon after settling into his office, Marcus was fortunate to be able to find a secretary who was keen on motor sport, and had some knowledge of French, Gillian Jinks. She soon started to sort out the paperwork inevitable in any organisation.

While all this was going on the Monte Carlo Rally had taken place and the BMC cars that had participated in this much publicised event had achieved little success despite being crewed by such names as John Gott, Mrs Tommy Wisdom and the Holt brothers. The Austins had been built at Longbridge and the Magnettes at Abingdon. Marcus recalls that the Westminster lacked traction on ice and snow and the Magnettes had a very poor power/weight ratio with rear springs which were much too stiff. The highest placed finisher was one of the A90s driven by Mrs Wisdom and Joan Johns with fifth place in the Ladies and 68th overall – not a very auspicious beginning.

First Rally for 'Stirling's sister'

The Monte was followed in March by the major British rally of the year, the RAC. Prior to 1955, a young lady usually referrred to by the press as 'Stirling's sister' had been doing a few rallies. One of her cars was a Morris Minor side-valve model and this was getting a little tired and using a lot of oil. When her father borrowed the Minor one day to go to London he was horrified with the state of it and when he came home he told his daughter to go and order a Triumph TR2, the car that she really wanted most of all. There was a long waiting list for new cars in the fifties and it took about a year to get the TR2. In the meantime, Mr Moss bought half his daughter's current horse to help her pay for this new car. You will have guessed by now that the young lady in question was of course, Pat Moss.

The Triumph eventually arrived and, because Pat was to compete in the RAC Rally, she contacted Triumph Competitions at Coventry and asked them if they would be prepared to assist her with her expenses. The answer was that they would loan her a car but she would have to pay her own expenses. This was the wrong way round for Pat who already had a car.

However, as the result of this reply, Mr Alf Moss contacted John Thornley at Abingdon. The two had already met at race meetings and, following the request for assistance, Marcus agreed not only to loan Pat an MG TF 1500 but to pay her expenses as well. The car arrived completely standard, with disc wheels, no heater and no extra lights, in fact none of the basic extras one would normally expect on a rally car. It was red with the registration number KRX90; Pat Faichney was asked to navigate. In addition to the TF with its inexperienced crew, the other BMC entries comprised three Austin Westminsters, three MG TF 1500s and a trio of Magnettes (the Three Musketeers) for Messrs Holt, Holt and Shaw.

I think it would be reasonable to suggest that Pat Moss is a little superstitious and she became rather uneasy about competing in the RAC – her first major rally – when she realised that her rally number, 193, added up to thirteen! Her two main superstitions were the number thirteen and the colour green; at one stage during her association with Abingdon a loan car was delivered to her and she nearly had a fit when she saw that it was green and the registration number was 13! The number of the car and the colour were changed.

An accident on the way to start of the RAC did not inspire confidence, as if to confirm her belief that '13' was unlucky. The car skidded off the road on some ice and broke the fog lamps, but after having them replaced in Chester she made the start in Blackpool.

On the rally her navigator, who was also inexperienced, made a number of errors which hardly helped their progress. Pat did well on the driving tests, however, and remembers that Sheila Van Damm admitted to her at the finish that she had got a bit ratty during the rally when having been asked after each special test who had been the fastest lady so far, she was repeatedly told, 'Pat Moss'. This made Shelia all the more

1955

The crew posing with the J. Shaw MG Magnette in Glasgow before the start, 1955 Monte Carlo Rally

determined and she eventually beat Pat into third place in the Ladies. Not a bad result for Pat on her first big rally.

The Circuit of Ireland followed in April, with the MG TF 1500 of Ian Appleyard, another famous name, coming fourth overall.

Six cars were entered in the Tulip Rally: once again three Magnettes and three Westminsters. Pat had made a favourable impression on Marcus and she was asked to drive one of the Magnettes, named *Athos*, this time with Sheilagh Cooper navigating, but unfortunately with rally number 139 (adding up to thirteen)! This was Pats' first time on the Continent and on the way to the start at Nordwijk she managed to have a head-on collision with a local driver after forgetting to return to the right-hand side of the road after reading a signpost. The car was not badly damaged but the fan was hitting the radiator. A phone call to Marcus and some late night work by the mechanics saw the car in one piece for the start. Unfortunately, during the first day of the rally a big-end went at Frankfurt and that was that. The other cars in the team were not much more successful, Gerry Burgess also retiring with a blown core plug in the Westminster.

Pat was still heavily involved in show jumping during this period and only managed a few rallies during the remainder of 1955. In November she crashed the TR2 on a rally, but fortunately Marcus did not cross Pat off his list of promising drivers.

Marcus was still considering the problems of which drivers to use. In June, the entry on the Scottish Rally had consisted of three TF's and three Westminsters. This was a little more successful, with Joan Johns winning the Ladies and the three TF's coming first, second and third in class.

Fateful Le Mans

No one will forget the 1955 Le Mans 24 Hour race which was the début of the prototype MGAs in racing trim.

The chassis for these cars were built by hand by Doug Watts, Tommy Wellman and Harold Wiggins from sheet metal, much of it waste material from the MG press shop. The flat bed in the development shop was used to jig up the sections for final assembly and they were welded up mainly by Harold. The B-type cylinder block did not have oil galleries suitable for the fitting of a full flow oil filter so Doug and Tommy had to take the blocks down to the tool room where they were set up on the radial drill and carefully drilled with the extra holes. Twelve engines were built, so they had plenty of late nights completing the various tasks in time. The engines were built without head gaskets and this entailed plugging the waterways in the head and blocks with dural plugs which then had to be refaced. Adaptor plates and hose connections had to be fitted to the rear of the block/heads to take the coolant between the two.

The aluminum bodies were made by the Morris Bodies Branch at Coventry and the cars were covered-in underneath with a full-length undershield. There was no passenger door, and an aluminium tonneau cover was fitted to improve the aerodynamics. To assist cooling of the rear axle, a small oil cooler, without a circulation pump, was piped to the differenti-

BMC Competitions Department

G. Holt, MG Magnette during a driving test at Hastings, 1955 RAC Rally

Pat Moss, MG TF swings through the pylons, 1955 RAC Rally

Pat Moss, MG TF at speed, 1955 RAC Rally

al casing, but with cold air directed through it by an air scoop in the undershield.

On 28 April Dick Jacobs and Ken Wharton went to Silverstone to test the cars, along with Alan Foster with his Magnette and Harold Grace with his Riley Pathfinder. Alec Hounslow did three warming-up laps before Dick Jacobs did a few laps at race speed on a damp track, making fastest time in 2m 18.5s. Ken Wharton continued the running and after a number of stops for minor adjustments, recorded a time of 2m 7s. After removing the rear check straps he did a further two laps, one flying lap being timed at 2m 6.8s. Marcus was taking notes of the jobs to be done prior to the race and the main items were:

Heat in the cockpit
Move the pedals 3 inches nearer the driver
Footrest for left foot needed
Arm catches on drivers door pocket
Lower steering gear ratio
Door does not open wide enough

Dick Jacobs did a few laps in the Magnette completing a lap in 2m 27.5s compared with Alan Fosters best lap of 2m 32s. Best lap in the Pathfinder was 2m 20s.

The new BMC transporter was used for the Le Mans trip although it had already seen service at Silverstone race meetings. It was well equipped with bunks, kitchen, work-

1955

Final preparations for the 24 Hour race, Le Mans 1955

bench etc, but with a fuel consumption of only 10 mpg the petrol engine was proving a mistake.

The three race cars were driven to Le Mans by Doug Watts, Jimmy Cox and Alec Hounslow with the spare car travelling in the transporter driven by Dickie Green accompanied by Cliff Bray and Gerald Wiffen. Marcus led the convoy in a Riley Pathfinder with Mrs Chambers and Harold Wiggins. As with any convoy, the 'tail-end charlie' was having to travel the fastest to keep up and at one stage Marcus was stopped by a gendarme who tactfully suggested that if he was leading the group perhaps he would slow down and wait for the rest. The team stayed in a Hotel outside Le Mans where John Thornley soon had an MG banner flying over the entrance.

Sammy Davis was with the team and proved to be a great help with general advice on race tactics and general organisational problems. He kept a fatherly eye on the drivers and after practice had been completed he discussed their respective performances with Marcus and John Thornley. He commented that they all seemed to be OK except one, who did not take kindly to advice, indicating Dick Jacobs. The third car was in fact on the reserve list until the day before the race, but was included in the final list of starters. The MG line-up was:

Dick Jacobs/Joe Flynn No 42
Ken Miles/John Lockett No 41
Ted Lund/Hans Waeffler No 64

In the race itself, on lap 28 at about 18.30 hours Dick Jacobs crashed at White House corner owing to what was believed to be an error of judgement, not mechanical failure. The car was badly damaged and caught fire, but happily Dick was rescued, although with serious chest, hip and facial injuries. Dr King was acting as a chartkeeper in the MG pits and was able to help sort out the medical arrangements.

Unfortunate as the accident to Dick was, it was overshadowed by the terrible accident which befell the Pierre Levegh Mercedes only about half an hour later. It is of course now history that 80 people were killed when the Mercedes ploughed into the crowd in front of the pits following a collision with an Austin Healey 100. Gerald Wiffen was on duty in the pits at the time, with Doug Watts among others, and witnessed the crash. He still has a vivid recollection of the horror of the pieces of car spraying amongst the crowd and although many people did not realise how bad it had been for some hours, anyone in the pit area was aware that it was very serious owing to the number of bodies being carried away.

The race carried on without the rest of the Mercedes team who withdrew as a mark of respect, and eventually came to a sad and subdued end with the two remaining MG's finishing twelfth and seventeenth overall. During the race the Miles/Lockett car recorded the fastest MG lap with a speed of 93.72 mph. It is interesting to note that the leading MG recorded a faster race average than the Ferrari driven by Chinetti which won in 1949.

Despite the tragedy, the MG team had made a good showing and there were many favourable comments concerning their performance. One point which received press coverage was the fact the cars were driven to and from the circuit.

Dick Jacobs was in a serious condition at Coulaines and Dr King stayed on in France to keep an eye on his progress.

BMC Competitions Department

Within 24 hours he became aware that Dick was not doing too well so he contacted Mr Woodcock at Longbridge and in conjunction with Laurie Pyle, Chief Thoracic Consultant at Oxford, Dick was flown to England.

John Thornley had gone on his planned holiday straight from Le Mans after everything had been sorted out and on his return called at Coulaines to see how Dick was getting on. He was concerned to see that the window of the room where Dick had been confined was shuttered and feared the worst. The staff inside were not very helpful and John had quite a row before he found out that Dick was back in England. It seemed that the hospital staff were a bit put out that their patient had been removed. During the confusion of the Mercedes accident, it had been difficult for anyone in England to obtain accurate information and at one stage an English newspaper reported that Dick had been killed.

Checking the spares in the pits, 1955 Le Mans 24 Hour race

Tommy Wellman did not go to Le Mans and was given the job, along with Henry Stone, of moving the Department from A block into the new B8 hangar at the top of the B block. This included moving the test-bed into it's new building close to B block, opposite Cemetery Road gate.

A small office was allocated for the use of Marcus just inside the door of B8, the bay being split into roughly three equal size sections; Development, Competitions in the middle, and the section nearest the door for the customer tuning workshop. Another person to join the Department at about this time was Brian Moylan who had been working in Service

K. Miles/E. Lund pass under the Dunlop bridge after the start, 1955 Le Mans 24 Hour race

14

1955

E. Lund, MG 182 being chased by a Triumph TR2, 1955 Le Mans 24 Hour race

Repair under Bill Lane. Bill had told Brian that a racing section was being formed and asked if he wanted to get in to it. Brian did manage to get a transfer just before the cars left for Le Mans, and soon earned the reputation of the 'thinking man's mechanic'. Brian was one of the staff who was to stay at Abingdon for longer than most in Competitions.

The Department was now settling down and it was at this time that John Thornley asked Doug Watts and Tommy Wellman up to his office to ask them if they would be prepared to become Foreman and Chargehand respectively of the Department, pointing out that this would involve time away abroad and a lot of overtime. They both agreed. During Le Mans another person to join the staff was Johnny Organ who was soon to rival Marcus as a bit of a gourmet, always being ready to sample a new foreign dish.

Mechanics struggle with the damaged wing on E. Lund's MG 182, 1955 Le Mans 24 Hour race

One good point to come out of the Le Mans trip was an improvement in liaison between Abingdon and the Medical Centre at Cowley. Marcus arranged to send Doc White copies of all event movement sheets and this gave the Medical Centre time to prepare for any emergencies. First Aid kits for the rally and service cars were supplied and restocked for each event and Doc White made sure that key members of his staff had valid passports.

As soon as his appointment had been announced Marcus found that he was receiving a steady stream of letters from budding 'works' drivers including some of the HRG team such as Bill Shepherd, John Williamson, John Gott and Nancy Mitchell. On the racing side there were, of course, people like Ken Wharton, Ron Flockhart and even Jack Brabham.

One person in particular, John Gott, was an old friend of both Marcus and John Thornley and he was invited down to Abingdon for a chat. John had seven years experience as a private owner competing in international rallies and was impressed by the methods that John Thornley and Marcus were planning to use to construct the team. In John Gott's own

15

BMC Competitions Department

The pit team with sad remains of Dick Jacob's MG 182, 1955 Le Mans 24 Hour race

words written in *Autosport* magazine, 'I was delighted to find that as I had expected, both abhorred the things which I had observed with distaste in various other "works" teams: petty jealousy towards team-mates, a couldn't care less attitude about damaging factory cars and, above all, an apartheid policy by the drivers towards the mechanics, without whose devoted work no success would be possible'. It was not long before John Gott was driving Abingdon-built cars officially.

One battle John Thornley did not win was his effort to get Longbridge to build a tuned version of the Austin A90 Westminster. Ken Wharton had been achieving some first class results on the circuits with this model and John discussed the possibility of such a car with George Harriman. However, when he suggested that the new car should be called the Austin Abingdon the idea was quietly shelved. One of the mods that John wanted to incorporate, already tried on the race cars, was stiffening of the chassis to prevent the steering box's moving, thus improving the handling.

Alpine Test Session
The Le Mans disaster had naturally caused a public outcry against motor sport, particularly in France, and a number of events were cancelled including the Alpine Rally. This event was on the Abingdon programme and Marcus was hoping to gain some useful experiences with the MGA in Alpine conditions. All the reservations had been confirmed including space on the Silver City Airways car ferry to Le Touquet. It was decided that a test session would be undertaken, using existing bookings, from 3 to 13 July. The drivers included John Gott, Bill Shepherd, John Milne and John Williamson plus the two Swiss drivers, J. Keller and H. Zweifel. The cars for the test were:

1. Austin Westminster. Tuned single carburettor engine, lowered rear springs, high rate front springs and 4.1 axle.
2. Austin Cambridge. MGA Le Mans engine, oil cooler, rear-mounted battery, E242 brake linings and Michelin X tyres.
3. MG Magnette. Le Mans engine, remainder of spec. as Production Car Race car.
4. MG EX182. As prepared for Alpine Rally.
5. MGA. Production car, standard in all respects.

In addition to the rally testing in the mountains, tests were carried out at Nürburgring and Montlhéry and the hill climbs of the Col de la Faucille, Col des Aravis, Col de la Forclaz, Col du Galibier and Col de l'Iseran, a round trip of over 2300 miles. Chief Engineer from MG, Syd Enever, accompanied the team and I think it is interesting to record some of the problems highlighted during the testing.

The Westminster was used as baggage car and suffered with brakes boiling and a difficult column gearchange.

The Austin Cambridge performed well but also had brake problems. Suspension was too soft and gearchange from third to second difficult. The oil cooler pipes fractured during the Montlhéry test, thought to have been partly caused by the use of Castrol R. Seats needed more lateral support and the gear ratios were too wide. The wear rate on the Michelin tyres was considerably less than on the Dunlop racing tyres, this being 1.5mm compared with 2.5mm over the same distance. In the wet at Nürburgring, the lap times differed only marginally between wet and dry conditions on the Michelin tyres.

The MG Magnette also had trouble with the oil cooler pipes and excessive brake fade. This was with the E242 linings and the drums had been ventilated as on the Le Mans car.

The Le Mans car suffered severe overheating in the cockpit. This was caused by the undershield, and accentuated by the lack of heat absorbent material. Oil consumption was heavy due to the three-ring pistons. The oil cooler pipes also gave trouble.

The production MGA was fitted with DM12 linings and although suffering from brake fade, pedal loss was less. The main trouble with the Le Mans car was a number of the tonneau and hood fasteners coming adrift from the body. The Bodies Branch were to look at this for production. The Magnette was only 8 seconds slower than the MGA Le Mans car at Nüburgring, but the Le Mans car was fastest at Montlhéry at 101.79mph compared with the production car at 96.61mph. This was useful preparation for the Liège-Rome-Liège in August, the last year the rally was to visit Rome.

Later, back at Abingdon, Marcus received a visit from George Eyston, past holder of the Land Speed Record and involved with the MG and Austin Healey records at Bonneville, Utah in 1954. George was a director of Castrol and apparently had quite a say in the Castrol Competitions budget. After one of his visits, George Williams, Castrol Competitions Manager, called and handed over a cheque for £10,000, Castrol's contribution towards the Abingdon budget. Castrol were to have a long association with Abingdon and their service personnel worked alongside Abingdon mechanics on many International events.

Harry Weslake was a consultant to the Austin Motor Company and was a regular visitor to Mr W. V. Appleby in Engineering at Longbridge. He also visited Marcus and through these meetings many items of common technical interest were discussed.

The Liège-Rome-Liège was scheduled to take place from 17–21 August, and consisted of approximately 3000 miles of non-stop driving over 90 hours, through five countries. As Marcus commented in his own book, it was John Gott who sold BMC the idea of competing in the 'Liège' and it was to be his first event as an official member of the BMC team. It was to be something of an exploratory effort in which three rather different cars were to be entered: an Austin Healey 100S for Peter Reece/Dennis Scott, an Austin A50 with a Le Mans MGA engine for John Gott/Bill Shepherd, and a modified Westminster for Gerry Burgess/Sam Croft-Pearson.

The plan was to get the two saloons to the finish and let the Austin Healey see what it could do against the foreign opposition. In his report of this rally, Marcus was a little ashamed at the service support on the rally, but the days of the 'service umbrella' had not yet arrived. Marcus spent most of the rally in Liège with Peter Morrell of Castrol sampling some of the local gastronomic delights. They were not completely out of touch because Maurice Garot, the Liège organiser, had a most efficient scoreboard kept up to date by telephone from his officials along the route.

The Austin Healey only got as far as Idar Oberstein, in Germany when it crashed and landed in a wood. The A50 was more encouraging, but the crew did not like the gear ratios. Although not finding much time to get a meal for over twenty-four hours, John Gott and Bill Shepherd finished tenth in class and 36th overall. Gerry Burgess had dynamo trouble at Brescia but managed to buy a battery to keep going, finishing 31st overall. This was a modest success, suggesting that the team were starting to find their way.

Dundrod TT

There was some doubt over the future of the racing programme after the Le Mans accident but the go ahead was given to compete in the Tourist Trophy at Dundrod in Northern Ireland over the 7 mile circuit on closed roads near Belfast. This was to be the last official MG race entry for some time and was made up of three MGA prototypes.

Before the race, one car, looked after by Tommy Wellman and Henry Stone, was taken over to the circuit for a test session. They drove the car up to Preston where they were met by Ted Lund who was to do some of the driving. The party carried on to the docks where the ferry, an old tank landing ship, was waiting. They soon discovered that there was no beer on board for passengers, so they nipped ashore for a few bottles for the voyage. The cabin was very cold with pulldown bunks, and meals were taken with the captain in the wheelhouse which helped break up the rather long crossing.

Ronnie Adams assisted with the testing which produced no major problems, and was carried out on the actual race course which was conveniently closed by Mercedes-Benz for their own testing.

The three cars entered were originally to be of different specification. One MGA was fitted with the Morris Engines-designed twin-cam engine with the 80 degree cylinder head, the second MGA had the Austin designed 66 degree cylinder head while the third was to be a Le Mans car with the 1500 cc OHV pushrod engine.

Eddie Maher was behind the development of the Morris engine and was rather upset when he found out that there was to be an Austin engine in one of the cars. The rivalry between Austin and Nuffield was still quite strong. His dismay soon changed to smiles.

During testing, the twin-cams were found to have a fuel surge problem with their twin-choke Solex carburettors. The cars were finally tested down the Bicester straight by Doug Watts and in the meantime Engines Branch were busy making up some new manifolds to take Weber carburettors. The night before leaving for Liverpool, the cars were finished, and the mechanics went home to get ready for an early start. Later that evening Tommy Wellman was surprised to see Alec Hounslow at his front door. Hounslow had received a call from Syd Enever instructing him to arrange to remove the Austin twin-cam engine from the race car and replace it with a 1500 cc Le Mans pushrod engine. The twin-cam was to be placed in a crate and the lid nailed down for return to Longbridge. As far as one can tell that is the last that was seen of the compact, good looking Austin twin-cam engine. A

BMC Competitions Department

political decision had been made that the engine was not to be seen in public.

After burning the midnight oil the cars were once again ready for an early start. Driving the cars up to Liverpool on Dunlop racing tyres in the pouring rain, with tonneau covers and aero screens was no joke. Near Preston, Tommy was horrified to see one of the cars gyrating down the road. Jimmy Cox had aquaplaned into a spin and was fortunate to end up backwards down a smooth grass verge, without any damage.

The cars travelled across from Liverpool but the transporter had to cross from Holyhead and the team were put up in Bob Porter's garage in Belfast. The new Weber carburettors and manifolds were flown over to Belfast in time to be fitted for practice which was completed without further trouble. The twin-cam-engined car was driven by Ron Flockhart/John Lockett with the two other cars crewed by Jack Fairman/Peter Wilson and Ted Lund/Dickie Stoop. In the race the twin-cam developed a serious misfire which was found to be caused by splits in the manifold. This car was externally different to the other two cars as it had modified front wings fitted with 5 inch headlamps. It managed a fastest lap average of 79.46 mph before it was retired at about half distance. The Jack Fairman car, which was fitted with disc brakes, completed the race at an average speed of 71.07 mph finishing fourth in class behind three Porsche's. Unfortunately the third car retired on the eight lap when the experimental aluminium alloy fuel tank split; the 20 gallon tank had objected to the humps and bumps of this road circuit, the same tank having been used at Le Mans.

In previous years John Thornley had accompanied the team to races, but he felt that now Marcus had settled in to the job he should be allowed to get on with team management without interference.

This race was also beset with tragedy when two competitors were killed in separate accidents, and this following on so closely to Le Mans brought an edict from George Harriman at Longbridge to withdraw from 'works' participation in racing.

Production Cars at Montlhéry

The year ended for Competitions with a successful high speed publicity run at the Montlhéry circuit using five standard BMC production cars with the object of achieving 100 miles in the hour with each one. The engines were prepared by Morris Engines and the cars were tested at MIRA by Doug Watts and Tommy Wellman to make sure they could achieve their targets.

During the test runs the Westminster's engine went sick with Tommy driving and they were obliged to limp down to Coventry with the car where Eddie Maher supplied the parts and Doug and Tommy rebuilt the engine. A piston had failed, but after some running-in the car completed the full test. By the end of the day, Doug and Tommy had completed over 500 miles at 100 mph. One car of the original six, a Morris

Ken Wharton in the MGA during the Montlhéry 100 mph runs, October 1955

1955

L-to-R: Bob Porter, John Gott, Marcus Chambers, Ron Flockhart, Henry Stone (MG), Doug Watts (MG) and Alec Hounslow (MG) with the Austin Healey 100 1955 100 mph Record runs at Montlhéry

Isis (christened the 'Crisis'), could not achieve the magic 100, reaching only 98 in the hour, so was withdrawn from the trip.

Despite atrocious weather conditions with gales and driving rain, all the cars achieved 100 miles in the hour. John Gott had a worrying moment when a tyre burst while he was at the wheel of the Westminster with only 15 minutes to go during his first run with the car. The Riley did the run four-up. The figures achieved by each car were:

Riley Pathfinder	108.03 mph	Bob Porter
Austin Healey 100	104.32 mph	Ron Flockhart
MGA 1500	102.54 mph	Ken Wharton
Austin Westminster	101.99 mph	John Gott
Wolseley 6/99	101.20 mph	John Gott

Three of the cars were sealed after the runs for later verification by the RAC, but the MGA had a 3.7 final drive fitted together with aero screens and an undershield after

BMC advertisement, 1955 Montlhéry Production Car Run

removal of the windscreen, hood, side windows, and bumpers. In this trim John Gott managed 112.36 miles in the hour with a best lap of 114.3 mph. The Publicity Department made full use of these results with full page adverts in the National press and other publications.

November 2, 1955 — *The Motor*

Sensational Test of B.M.C. Engineering

Five B.M.C. models achieve

100 miles in one hour

AUSTIN A90 WESTMINSTER
MG SERIES M.G.A.
AUSTIN-HEALEY 100 'M'
Riley PATHFINDER
WOLSELEY 6/90

Each of these models was officially timed on the Montlhéry track on 21-23 October 1955 at over 100 m.p.h. for one hour. B.M.C. are the only manufacturers to offer you five 100 m.p.h. models yet there is no increase in the price of any of these superbly engineered cars.

THE BRITISH MOTOR CORPORATION LTD

19

BMC Competitions Department

Marcus was now looking forward to the next season (1956) with the help of John Gott's great experience of continental events. His knowledge and assessment of which drivers from the disbanded HRG team would fit in to the BMC team, assisted Marcus when considering who to approach for next year. It was felt an experienced Ladies' crew would be a great asset to the team because, for one thing, lady drivers always seemed to attract interest from the press. Nancy Mitchell was invited to join and as she was very particular about her choice of co-driver; this was left to her to sort out.

1956

1956 – Team Captain

Early in 1956 Marcus appointed John Gott as Team Captain, having also considered Ken Wharton for the position. Ken had declined saying that the position could affect his driving and adding that he felt he would slave his guts to give people an easy ride only to get few thanks and many moans. John Thornley was not very happy about a Team Captain appointment and he registered his disapproval with Marcus on the grounds that to raise one driver to a position above the others was unecessary. However, John Gott himself said after he had retired from the team that he had found the job most rewarding if extremely exacting.

The Team entered the 1956 Monte Carlo Rally in its first serious attempt for an outright win. As Marcus commented afterwards, 'We probably overstepped the mark with the number of entries'. This may not have been a record, but no less than twelve cars were entered from various points as far apart as Lisbon, Glasgow and Rome.

Pre-event preparation did not go to plan; the Austin A90 to be driven by Raymond Baxter and Reg Phillips was destroyed by a fire which gutted the Export Despatch Block at Cowley where the car was awaiting shipment to Stockholm. The only other car with the right equipment was Marcus's service car which was prepared as a replacement rally car in thirty-six hours. Because the last boat had sailed for Stockholm, a Bristol Freighter from Silver City Airways was hired to fly the car to the start. Rather an expensive exercise, but one which was felt to be justified bearing in mind the publicity value of supplying a car for the BBC commentator on the rally. All efforts were in vain as this car retired in Germany with electrical trouble.

J. Sears/A. Scott-Brown/K. Best, Austin A50 comes into Monte Carlo showing signs of some damage! 1956 Monte Carlo Rally

The other cars fared a little better despite freezing fog over the Col de Granier and Col de Rousset. As a result of the weather only 36 cars arrived in Monte without penalty and, of the ninety qualifying for the final Mountain Circuit, eight of the twelve BMC entries were included. On the Mountain Circuit several cars suffered with boiling brake fluid, Joan Johns (A90) had gone over the edge and Jack Sears (A50) had rolled on to its roof without serious injury to the crew. Ken Wharton had asked Marcus to arrange for the mechanics to throw a bucket of water over the brakes on the descent of the Col de Braus, and in the absence of mechanics, Bill Shepherd had slackened the brakes of his car instead of adjusting them up. There were other minor accidents but some consolation at the finish when Mike Couper was awarded the Concours de Confort. John Gott was highest finisher, being 55th overall, and Nancy Mitchell was third in the Ladies' Prize.

Of the twelve starters, four had accidents and two retired with electrical trouble.

Following this experience, it was decided to make entries of quality rather than quantity and mechanics would be stationed along the route to adjust brakes etc. when necessary!

It is interesting to note that John Gott, in talking about the three most important rallies in 1956 (Monte, Alpine and Liège) described the RAC as one of the lesser events. It had not yet achieved the status it has today.

K. Wharton/G. Shanley, Austin Westminster, 1956 Monte Carlo Rally (Motor)

BMC entries in the RAC for 1956 included Pat Moss in an MGA (the first 'works' entry for this model in a rally), Nancy Mitchell in a Magnette, two Austin A90s for Joan Johns and Gerry Burgess, an A50 for Jack Sears, and Ken Wharton in a Riley Pathfinder. Pat Moss was allocated number 79, so no worry about '13' this time.

Despite a number of incidents including jumping a ditch, on arrival at the finish in Blackpool Pat was leading the Ladies' class by seventy points. The last test, known as the Monte Blackpool, was a driving test on the promenade. Marcus was all set to announce her win in the Ladies but Pat unfortunately passed a pylon on the wrong side and was penalised 100 points, pushing her down to third. The Team prize was won by the A90 team and the husband/wife crew of Douglas and Joan Johns was sixth overall.

Also in March, Nancy Mitchell accompanied by Doreen Reece, did the Lyons Charbonnières Rally in a Magnette and won the Ladies' Prize.

Towards the end of 1955, Marcus had been approached by Peter Scott-Russell who wanted to drive one of the Le Mans MGAs in the Mille Miglia the following year but was told that there were no plans to compete in the race. This decision

1956

was in fact reversed with an entry confirmed of two MGAs.

The two MGAs were driven by Peter Scott-Russell/Tom Haig and Nancy Mitchell/Pat Faichney. Marcus went out to Italy in a Morris Oxford Traveller with Doug Watts and Alec Hounslow and they were able to see the cars twice, at Florence and Brescia. It was very wet and Alec Hounslow had a very large tool box which seemed to take up rather a lot of the luggage space. Although outclassed, the two MGs went well with the girls winning the Ladies' prize and Peter coming in fourth in their class just in front of the other car. This entry had been contrary to Marcus's wishes because he was worried that Nancy might jeopardize her chances in the European Championship if she had an accident.

Preparations were in hand for the Tulip Rally and the

Joan Johns, Pat Moss (helmet), and Doreen Rich pick up the pieces after crashing their Austin Westminster, 1956 Monte Carlo Rally (Motor)

BMC Competitions Department

Ken Wharton at speed in a Riley Pathfinder, 1956 RAC Rally

Nancy Mitchell with her MG Magnette after winning the Ladies Cup, 1956 Lyons Charbonnières Rally (M. Chambers)

May Touring Car Race at Silverstone. Ken Wharton drove an Austin A90 at Silverstone and, in what was considered to be one of the best races ever seen at the circuit, came in second overall.

For the Tulip, a car had been promised to the *Motor* magazine for their correspondent, Dickie Bensted-Smith to drive. The Magnette for Nancy Mitchell was fitted with aluminium alloy panels, of which twelve sets had been made for sale to any competitors who wanted them. Unfortunately, at scrutineering, the alloy panels were ruled to be contrary to the regulations and the car was excluded. However, Sid Henson finished second in class in an Austin A90 with Joan Johns fourth in the same class.

Marcus had sent over three mechanics in the transporter on the Tulip but they did not go out of Holland and did quite a bit of sightseeing with Marcus, including a visit to the model town at Madurodam. They did see the cars near the finish and Tommy Wellman was asked by Marcus to see if the Brookes father and son crew in an Austin A30, who were leading the rally overall, on handicap, required any assistance. This offer was rejected with the comment, 'Marcus didn't offer any assistance before we started winning, so you can tell him to piss off!'

Nancy Mitchell was having a busy time going for Championship points, and it seemed inevitable that some more events might have to be fitted in. The Geneva Rally was next, held in France owing to the policy of the Swiss Government not to allow motor sport, but it was a relatively small-scale effort with Nancy driving a Magnette with Patsy Burt, and two A90s and an A50 also taking part. Marcus drove one of the A90s with Peter Wilson and between them they collected three class places and Nancy was second in the Ladies.

In Sweden Nancy was joined by Doreen Reece again to come fourth in the Ladies driving a Magnette, this time in the Midnight Sun Rally.

Alpine MGAs

Despite some post-Le Mans jitters, the Alpine Rally organisers decided to go ahead with the rally in July. It was to be the first outing for the MGA 1500s (with hardtops), in an international

1956

rally. Marcus had brought together a strong team comprising Messrs Gott, Milne, Shepherd and Sears, with Nancy going for the Ladies' Prize.

The engines were running on the new Castrol R vegetable-based oil and serious leaks developed in the oil cooler pipes. The same type of pipe had been used on the Mille Miglia, so it looked like a bad patch, anyway; new pipes were sent for from Abingdon. In the end, on the recommendation of Alec Hounslow, the oil coolers were removed from the cars and they did the event without any bearing trouble or loss of oil pressure.

The mechanics brought the transporter out to Marseilles with spares to look after the four red cars and John Gotts' white one. Sid Henson of Ferodo was present, keeping a watchful eye on his company's new VG 95 anti-fade brake material which several of the cars were using. During the rally he was asked to drive one of the BMC film cars when the crew found difficulty in keeping to schedule.

It was very hot in Marseilles for the start as the cars set off on the route which wound its way to Aix-en-Provence, Gap, Briançon and across the Col de Montgenevre down to Turin and Monza in Italy. No penalties had been incurred by the cars at Monza where Jack Sears was fastest of the MGs with a lap of 2 m 34 s (83.2 mph). In a class of fourteen cars, Jack was lying third behind two Porsches.

Later on, in the dust of the Giovo and Pennes passes, both John Milne and John Gott had accidents when trying to overtake slower cars. John Gotts' car moved the axle back, breaking the spring, and bending the axle casing; this unfortunately caused their retirement, despite the mechanics changing the spring in 26 minutes, when the axle shaft decided it was not designed to act as a flexi-drive! During the hectic spring change, Doug Watts put his knee out, and after a local doctor could find nothing wrong, he was transported to Cortina where a specialist at the sanatorium set his leg in plaster, from where he was taken to Geneva to be flown home. Jack Sears rolled his car over and Marcus was dismayed to see the car coming down the road minus screen and hardtop, but with the crew otherwise unhurt.

The rally eventually arrived back at the finish in Marseilles and Marcus was pleased to learn that Nancy had

John Gott/Ray Brookes with MGA 1500, 1956 Alpine Rally (M. Chambers)

BMC Competitions Department

1956

maintained her clean sheet (winning a Coupe des Alpes) to win the Ladies' Prize, and be placed fifteenth overall. The John Milne and Bill Shepherd cars were fourth and fifth in class respectively.

Left: *Service stop for Bill Shepherd MGA 1500, 1956 Alpine Rally (M. Chambers)*

Below left: *L-to-R: J. Milne, R. Bensted-Smith, G. Burgess, S. Croft-Pearson, Nancy Mitchell, Anne Hall, J. Gott, C. Tooley with their MGA 1500s, 1956 Liège-Rome-Liège rally (M. Chambers)*

Right: *Nancy Mitchell, MGA 1500 at Cortina, 1956 Liège-Rome-Liège rally (M. Chambers)*

Below: *Team line-up, 1956 Viking Rally (M. Chambers)*

The BMC film crew collected enough footage to make a full length film which was later to become popular in the Nuffield film library.

The third major event on the agenda for 1956 was the Liège, and the MGA 1500's were once again in action. The event brought mixed fortunes, with second place in the Manufacturer's Team Prize to the first place of the PV 544 Volvos, and Nancy Mitchell came runner-up in the Ladies.

Nancy Mitchell MG Magnette, 1956 Viking Rally (M. Chambers)

John Gott commented after the rally that we probably lost the Team Prize by being too sporting when the mechanics repaired the leading Volvo's throttle. Whether a factory team should stand back when a rival was in trouble, when the mechanics had the time and means to help, is a matter of opinion, but Marcus and John Thornley had always made it

25

BMC Competitions Department

clear that the team as a whole should always act in a sporting manner and help others when possible.

In August, the modified version of the Westminster (A105) was put into production and as a test run for the Monte in January, three of the new model, plus a Magnette, were entered in the Viking Rally in Norway. The big cars were a little two wide for the narrow roads and all three cars suffered radiator and core plug problems. Nancy, however, maintained her finishing record coming home 64th overall.

The Suez crisis now blew up and it came as quite a blow to the programme when the government announced petrol rationing on 17 December. Petrol was short on the Continent, and resulted in the cancellation of the Monte Carlo rally. Although 1956 ended on a low note, Nancy Mitchell gave the company something to shout about by winning the European Ladies Rally Championship, using an MG on all her points scoring events.

The Suez war badly affected the 1957 programme with the RAC and the Alpine rallies being cancelled, the Alpine at such short notice that the crews were already on their way to the start when the telegram arrived from the organisers.

1957

1957 – Competitions Moves to B1

Space was cramped in the MG Development department and it was with some relief that Alec Hounslow saw Competitions move down to the end of B block to take over the end bay, B1 early in 1957. This bay had been used during the war for the assembly of tanks, among other things, and to lift the turrets and other heavy parts, a 20 ton travelling crane had been installed. As it was very useful for lifting cars etc, a number of staff signed up as crane drivers.

With the move, Tommy Wellman was appointed deputy foreman and Marcus had a change of secretary when he took on Margaret Hall to replace Gillian Jinks. Margaret was a Canadian by birth, and soon learned the ropes in the busy competitions atmosphere. She became a very popular member of the team with her charming personality and was well respected by both team drivers and private owners alike. Her husband, a Wing Commander in the RAF, had been killed in a flying accident in 1947.

Some continental events survived the petrol shortage and Marcus decided to enter the Sestrière Rally to give the team some practice. The rally was to be decided on speed tests rather than tight navigational sections on open roads which suited the drivers better, and was safer. Marcus supplied Ray Brookes with a Morris Minor for the event as a thank you for winning the Tulip, and he made a good showing coming third in class in NJB 277. Nancy Mitchell, this time with Anne Hall co-driving, was second in the Ladies but Jack Sears with Ken Best managed only sixth in class.

Marcus took along the motoring journalist, Joe Lowrey in his service car, and with Brian Moylan making up the crew, they went to San Marino during the rally to buy some postage stamps of the Principality. On their way back to Sestrière, they hit a tree and wrecked the car, having to catch a train to get back to the finish at Sestrière. One of the mechanics had to return to Italy later in the year to collect the car.

1957 Tulip Rally

Marcus had been planning to give Pat Moss another drive but with the cancellation of the Monte, her next outing was the Tulip Rally. This time her car was a grey Morris Minor 4-door (NJB 277), with John Gott also entered in a Morris Minor 1000, a green 2-door (NMO 933), the car Pat would soon nickname 'Granny'.

Part of the route of the Tulip Rally ran through Germany but the German authorities cancelled many of the timed tests and the team were unable to achieve better than third in the Ladies (Nancy Mitchell, Magnette) and fourth in class by Jack Sears/Ken Best driving an Austin A105. The rally did not experience the best May weather and Pat Moss well remembers the snow, and the way that her breath froze on the inside of the windscreen. Her own achievement was sixteenth in class and 90th overall.

Cancellation of the Alpine left the Liège as the main rally on the calendar. Once again four MGAs with hardtops were entered, one for Harris/Hacquin who had impressed Marcus with their drive in a Volvo the previous year. John Gott, John Milne and Nancy Mitchell were in the other cars, and with the shortage of events, Pat Moss nagged Marcus to let her do another continental rally and he agreed for her entry in the Minor 1000 (NMO 933).

On the event, Harris crashed, as did Bill Shepherd who went off the road when grabbing hold of his co-driver when the passenger door flew open. Pat did not have a trouble-free run in coming second in the Ladies, losing a shock-absorber and then the gearbox drain plug, but still managing to finish. Mrs Moss was naturally very worried that her daughter was competing in this tough event for the first time, and tried to get Marcus to retire them before half distance. Pat would not hear of it and persevered to achieve a great result in the smallest car ever to finish the Liège.

The two remaining cars finished eighth and ninth in class with Nancy winning the Ladies yet again.

Marcus did not travel on this Liège because of domestic problems at home but kept in touch by telephone with John Williamson and John Valentyne who were helping with the service.

Afterwards, Pat admitted that that first Liège was tiring both physically and mentally and by the time they had reached Yugoslavia they were very tired and starting to see 'black cats' and then later on 'burning cars in the road'. It was fairly common in the fifties and early sixties for drivers and co-drivers to take some form of 'wakey-wakey' pills in the form of benzedrine or caffeine tablets. Pat occasionally used them on the longer events and found that if she had forgotten them or run out, there was always another driver who could let her have some. Pat also found that black tea was a better stimulant than black coffee.

Saloon car racing was still attracting entries from BMC and at the *Daily Express* May Meeting at Silverstone, Harold Grace in a Pathfinder and Jack Sears in an Austin A105 were first and third in the 2000–3000 cc class respectively, with Alan Foster winning his class in the MG Magnette.

Austin A35 Records

A mention must be made of the record attempt at Montlhéry with an A35. It was back in the autumn of 1956 that Gyde Horrocks, secretary of the Cambridge University Car Club came to see Marcus to ask if BMC would be prepared to loan a car for an attempt on the International Class G record for cars from 750–1,000 cc. It was agreed that the car would be prepared by Abingdon, but all other arrangements regarding drivers, pit organisation, timekeeping etc, would be handled by the Club, the pit crew being supported by mechanics from Competitions.

The existing record stood at an average of 67.0 mph over a period of 4–6 days. Gyde Horrocks suggested a target of 4, 5, 6 and 7 days; 10,000 miles, and 15,000 and 20,000 kilometres. Marcus consulted with Syd Enever concerning the spec of the car and after preliminary tests at MIRA a spec was decided upon using a 3.9:1 final drive which the 948 cc engine proved to be able to pull round the high speed circuit at a comfortable 80.0 mph. The main differences from the standard car were a 30 mm Zenith carburettor, oil cooler, 50 litre fuel tank, balanced propshaft and Dunlop D2/103 special compound tyres. The engine ran with Castrol XL oil lubricating the Vandervell Thin Wall bearings. To save weight, a number of items were removed such as bumpers, wheel trims and heater while a radio, windscreen washers and a fairing under the front bumper location were added.

The driver line-up consisted of Gyde Horrocks, Peter Riviere, Tom Threlfall, Ray Simpson and John Taylor with Marcus doing a spell at the wheel during the run. The weather was quite hot, remaining between 80–90°F until the last day when it rained. It proved to be a fine team effort under Pit Manager John Aley, with the 4, 5 and 6 day records together with 10,000 miles and a new record at 20,000 kilometres being attained.

The car covered 20,250.512 km in seven days at an average speed of 74.90 mph using fuel at the rate of 28 mpg and oil at 128 miles per pint (56 litres). The battery was topped up seven times and the steering greased 39 times while the only repair was one of the spring shackle pins which had to be replaced with a bolt carried on the car. Seven tyres were changed including three offside front ones. The engine when stripped down was found to be in perfect condition after the run with little measurable wear, and Vandervell were happy to have the big-end and con-rod bearings to put in their museum.

So ended the frustrating year of Suez, but once again Nancy Mitchell became Ladies European Rally Champion.

1958

1958 – Monte Carlo Snow

The team held out much more hope for a successful Monte, with the Austin A105 becoming more competitive and after the recent introduction of the Riley One Point Five. Three 105's and two Rileys were included in the ten BMC entries. The Riley had suffered production delays and insufficient numbers had been built for it to be homologated in the Touring Category so it had to run with the Grand Touring cars. As part of the continuing brake development, the A105 of Shepherd/Williamson was fitted with special Ferodo brake recording equipment to record temperatures and the number of times the brakes were applied. Pat Moss and Wiz (Ann Wisdom) were back in 'Granny' with Nancy Mitchell and Joan Johns in an MG Magnette. John Sprinzel and Tommy Wisdom were in Austin A35 and Austin Healey 100/6 respectively.

The Paris start was chosen for a number of reasons such as its closeness to Abingdon, fewer frontier crossings and relative ease of getting the mechanics to service points. Weather forecasts were not too accurate in 1958 but there was no prediction of any serious snow falls in Northern Europe.

However, the 91 starters soon found a very different situation developing. Through the Gerardmer and Chaumont area John Gott was glad of his experience on the Police Skid Pan at Hendon as the snowfall became severe. With only 20 miles to go to reach the control at St Claude, and with snow and ice clogging the wipers, John was pushed off the road by a Triumph TR3. They managed to dig out only to be shunted back off again by another car, into retirement.

Pat Moss who had been running in close company with John Sprinzel, came down a hill into a village and slid off into a snowdrift, which unfortunately concealed a concrete post. The Minor stopped rather abruptly, with the fan in the radiator. Pat cut her head and poor Ann was unhurt until she slipped on the ice when getting out of the car, and suffered slight concussion. They were given first aid by monks from the local monastery who took them to the dentist where Pat's cut was cleaned up and they were sent on their way. They managed to get the car repaired and although out of the rally, motored down to Monte to see the finish. They were amazed to find that only one of the Paris starters had reached Monte within the time allowance; this was Edward Harrison in a Ford. The entire BMC entry had been wiped out!

Marcus was, among others, critical of the organisers for haphazard and sometimes unecessary rerouting during the snow. The Glasgow starters had been allowed insufficient time to disembark from the Channel ferry, and some runners were up to 37 minutes late before leaving the docks. From the BMC point of view, it was a lesson learned the hard way. Don't put all your eggs in one basket!

The RAC rally was still run in March in 1958, and it was at this time that all BMC rally car preparation was centralised at Abingdon, with the Donald Healey Motor Company at Warwick, under Geoff Healey concentrating on racing.

There were two starting points for the RAC, Blackpool and Hastings, but all the Abingdon entries started from Hastings which was also the finish. This was more convenient and took away the added worry of moving the crews baggage from the start. The weather was mild at the start but a change to colder weather was forecast, causing some crews to carry chains and even snow tyres. Without a comprehensive tyre service Marcus would have to arrange tyre movements in the event of a dramatic change in the conditions.

Pat was in her favourite car, 'Granny', and was pleased to be running in the class for Improved Series Production Cars with a more powerful tuned engine. It was noticed that one

BMC Competitions Department

Minor in her class had telescopic rear shock-absorbers fitted, which helped keep the car on four wheels, but no one seemed to protest in those days. The Minor was running on Michelin tyres which were not very good on snow and ice and when the weather turned, the girls only got up one hill in Wales by fitting chains.

After Prescott Hill climb the cars carried on north to Carlisle where the unfortunate John Sprinzel hit a telegraph pole in his A35. Worst still, Nancy Mitchell overshot a corner on the Otterburn Ranges in her Riley and went through a dry stone wall and then down a slope fifty feet end-over-end. The crew were both shaken with Nancy suffering a suspected broken rib. A Dr Penny was first on the scene and took the girls to the Bowes control where they were taken to the Darlington Hospital, being kept in overnight. Their safety harness had saved them from serious injury.

One footnote to the 1958 RAC; Nancy Mitchell received a bill from the owner of the dry stone wall: £1 for the repair of 12 yds of wall, and £12 for the recovery of the stones. Nancy had to miss the Lyons Charbonnières Rally while her broken rib mended.

On the Circuit of Ireland, Pat Moss won the Ladies, despite Ann Wisdom having trouble with 1929-vintage maps. Ann Wisdom was now Pat's permanent co-driver, the daughter of a famous racing and rally driver, Tommy Wisdom.

The Tulip Rally did not provide any spectacular results (Pat was second in the Ladies) but John Gott in his report to Marcus after the event commented on an incident which reflected the natural ability of a certain lady driver. In his own words, 'On a particularly tight section, in driving rain, we caught up Pat in her One Point Five and managed to get past. She tucked in behind, turned off her lights and hung on for 20

The finish at Hastings was arranged as usual with the manoeuvering test the morning after the rally. Pat Moss had driven magnificently to come fourth overall and win the Ladies' Prize and her class. Doug Watts reckons he took Pat Moss's car to scrutineering so that Marcus could keep out of the way in case the exhaust manifold, which had been modified, was queried by the scrutineer. Pat's three awards brought her the princely sum of £130, which was quite important to her as she was not being paid by Marcus. It became a recognised policy that the crews paid 10 per cent of the prize money into a Mechanics Fund, which in later years brought the staff in the shop a nice Christmas bonus.

Pat Moss/Ann Wisdom with rally stained MGA 1500, 1958 Midnight Sun Rally

kilometres, during which time I was driving at ten-tenths without her being left behind'. This convinced John that they had in the team one who was surely to set new standards for a lady driver.

Pat's position in the Tulip had added some more points to her European Championship total and Marcus was persuaded that Pat should do some more events with a view to, perhaps, winning the Ladies section. So, over she went to Stockholm for the Midnight Sun Rally with just one mechanic

1958

to look after her MGA 1500. The choice of car was not ideal because she found that there were a lot of Porsches in her class. On the event, while 'yumping' over a particularly bad brow, they put the car off the road, but the strength of the car kept them in the rally. It was on this rally that the girls met Eric Carlsson for the first time when he offered them an orange to eat while waiting at a control. The rally finished at Ostersund near the Arctic Circle but unfortunately no Championship points this time, only fifth in class.

In July the much awaited MGA Twin Cam was announced to the public with the 80 degrees Morris Engines-designed cylinder head. Marcus had hoped to enter a team of Twin Cams in the 1958 Alpine but for various reasons this proved impossible.

Austin Healey 100/6 Joins the Fray

Rather a last minute decision was made to enter a team of Austin Healey 100/6 cars in the Alpine. Production of the 100/6 had started at Longbridge in August 1956 and was transferred to Abingdon when BMC decided to move all sports car production to the MG factory. In June, the 2/4-seater was made available in addition to the 2-seater version.

Pat Moss shows a leg before the 1958 Alpine Rally

Service check for Jack Sears, 1958 Alpine Rally

No less than five cars were entered in the Alpine which caused Marcus a problem in finding enough. The Department had three cars, one was borrowed from the Donald Healey Motor Company and the fifth car, in use by BMC Vice-Chairman, George Harriman, was sent down from Longbridge. This car was red and black and was allocated to Nancy Mitchell. The car from Warwick was green and was taken over by John Gott who quite liked the colour. Pat Moss

BMC Competitions Department

found that she could not reach the pedals, so the mechanics solved this by fitting wood blocks. In addition to the Healeys there were fourteen private owners in BMC cars, including an A105 which had been loaned to Frank Grounds.

This was one of the first events in which a member of the MG Development staff accompanied the team in one of the service cars, for Marcus had been able to persuade Syd Enever to let Terry Mitchell, Chief Chassis designer, go. This arrangement was repeated when other engineering people such as Roy Brocklehurst and Don Hayter made similar trips. It was no bad thing for the designers of the cars to see just what sort of punishment could be inflicted by international drivers in their search for a win.

During the Alpine, John Gott crashed his car and found that he had lost a wheel; in fact, while he and his co-driver were still sitting in the car, the wheel landed on the roof after bounding some way up the mountainside. The splined hub had sheared and the wheel had come off. The offending parts were taken back to Abingdon by Terry Mitchell and as a result modified hubs were eventually fitted in production. One of the first-hand results of 'rallying improving the breed'.

During the rally, after the second rest halt at Megeve, Pat Moss suffered from some well intentioned 'outside assistance' from a motoring journalist. The car had been losing some of its performance and the mechanics had suggested that the air cleaners should be removed. There had not been time owing to the tight schedule, but at one control Pat had a few minutes to spare and in the absence of the mechanics at that spot, got out the tool kit and took off the air cleaners herself. She finished just in time, but left the breather hanging loose, as instructed by the mechanics. As she leapt back into the car, she asked a watching journalist to close the bonnet. Not many miles later, the clutch started to slip, with also a loss of oil pressure. They arrived in Gap five minutes late where the mechanics discovered that the crankcase breather pipe had been tied in a knot. It was discovered later that the person responsible was none other than Joe Lowrey, Technical Editor of *Motor* magazine who had 'tied it up because it looked untidy', before closing the bonnet. Pat said after the rally that at the time she could have done the person responsible a mischief, but on reflection, decided that with an unfamiliar car, anyone could have done the same thing. The problem was that the crankcase pressure had built up and oil had been pumped through into the clutch. Luckily the contamination was not too bad and after the breather was untied, though the clutch slipped a bit, they were able to finish and were first in the Ladies and fourth in class. Nancy Mitchell was second in the Ladies and John Williamson won a coveted Coupe des Alpes for a penalty-free run. Private owners did well with John Sprinzel leading a 1, 2, 3, in class.

Nancy Mitchell/Gillian Wilton-Clarke with their bouquets, 1958 Alpine Rally

The Austin Healey 100/6 was proving to be a strong car so this was to be the model for the Liège. Four 100/6 cars were entered with what is probably a record – five ladies in the total of eight crew members. In addition, the Liège was the first official entry of an MG Twin-Cam in an international rally by Abingdon. The Liège was a really fearsome test of man (or woman) and machine, being 96 hours over some of the roughest roads in Europe and many of the toughest Italian passes.

Ninety-eight cars left Spa at minute intervals and on the section before Rijeka, Pat Moss was faster than the three Mercedes Benz 300 SL's and was going well. The heat was fierce, and the Healey with its low ground clearance took a terrible beating on the rough roads. Heat in the cockpit was excessive and the dust poured in through the sidescreens and every other hole and crack. As the cars ran down through Yugoslavia, John Gott found that his Twin Cam was losing power which at first was put down to the very poor petrol. At the next point where the mechanics were waiting, they took some time to discover that the trouble was caused by the distributor clamp bolt coming loose allowing the timing to retard. When this was fixed the car went like a bomb!

Austin Healey 100/6 cars of Gerry Burgess, Pat Moss & Nancy Mitchell pause on the 1958 Liège-Rome-Liège Rally

Joan Johns and Sam Moore retired when they damaged the steering near Tarvisio, but continued after repairs, helping the mechanics and supplying food and drink to the rest of the team. Only 22 cars finished and when the results had been sorted out Marcus found that they had achieved their best result so far, and was very pleased to receive a telegram from Sir Leonard Lord.

Pat Moss was highest placed British driver, coming fourth overall, and winning the Ladies, while Nancy was fifteenth and second in the Ladies. Gerry Burgess was tenth and made up a winning Manufacturers' Team. Not to be outdone, John Gott, despite his early loss of power was ninth overall, a very good advertisement for the new model. John was very enthusiastic about the cars' ability to hold off the Porsches, something he had been dreaming about for some time.

Ray Brookes/John Gott contemplate the result with their MGA Twin Cam, 1958 Liège-Rome-Liège Rally

1958

BMC Competitions Department

Ann Wisdom and Pat Moss with their trophies after winning the Ladies Cup, 1958 Liège-Rome-Liège Rally

Bouquets for Nancy Mitchell, 1958 Liège-Rome-Liège rally

G. Burgess/S. Croft-Pearson Austin Healey 100/6 on Col St Roche, 1958 Liège-Rome-Liège Rally

Austin Healey 100/6 at Montlhéry

Unfortunately Marcus was unable to attend the Liège prizegiving because he was scheduled to attend another Cambridge University Automobile Club project at Montlhéry. Following the successful run with the Austin A35 the year before, Castrol had invited the CUAC team to a little celebration, presided over by George Eyston. Gyde Horrocks had not wasted any time in researching further record possibilities and suggested to Marcus that the Class D 2000–3000 cc Record, held by Citroen could be taken with an Austin Healey 100/6. It was decided that the two main objectives would be to put the records up over the 100 mph mark, and at the same time, of course, beat the existing figures.

The car was a left-hand drive version, and after some consultation with Eddie Maher at Morris Engines, a final drive

1958

Den Green fits Pat Moss's rally plate to John Gott's MGA Twin Cam at Abingdon

Sorting out spares before the Austin Healey 100/6 Record Run at Montlhéry 1958 (A. G. Goodchild)

ratio was settled at 3.9:1 with overdrive also fitted and Dunlop racing tyres. This gearing was calculated to keep the engine out of the potentially harmful vibration period, and extra power would be provided by larger SU carburettors as used by the Warwick racing Healeys at Sebring.

Doug Watts took Doug Hamblin and Gerald Wiffen from Abingdon and Derek Lowe from Engines Branch, travelling in the transporter. Pye of Cambridge had supplied a two-way radio for car-to-pit communication, and after some difficulty obtaining the necessary permit this proved to be very useful during the run.

Four drivers from the A35 Run were included in the team plus Rupert Jones, John Clark and Bill Summers. The latter made a name for himself during one of his stints when he had a heart-stopping 400 yard spin after hitting flood water on the track. No serious damage was done but soon after that, the run was curtailed by a slipping clutch. Not oil on the plate this time, but a strip down revealed that the special linings had not fully bedded-in.

The attempt was restarted but after 30 hours the rear springs succumbed to the pounding from the rough concrete track. New springs were fitted and bound with tape by Doug Watts and his crew and by 11 September the 2-day record at 98.73 mph had been taken. Once again the clutch started to slip, but at the suggestion of Marcus, each restart after a driver change was made in second gear and that seemed to sort it out. Later, while Marcus was doing a spell of driving, Marcus hit a piece of concrete which must have been dislodged on the previous circuit, the impact being described as 'like a bomb going off', but luckily the sump was not damaged.

Despite the delays, the 15,000 kilometer and 10,000 mile records were gained; not a bad effort. When the car was

BMC Competitions Department

returned to Abingdon, it was found that the front engine mountings and one of the new springs were broken. Incidentally, one lap was completed at an average speed of 124 mph and the oil consumption was a bit better than the Austin A35 at 1000miles/pint.

Pat Moss had accumulated a good points lead in the European Championship, helped further by coming second in the Ladies in the Viking Rally in Norway driving a Morris Minor 1000. This gave the girls outright victory in the European Ladies Championship.

Checking the two-way radio before the Montlhéry Austin Healey 100/6 Record Run (A. G. Goodchild)

Driver line-up before the Austin Healey 100/6 Record Run, 1958 (A. G. Goodchild)

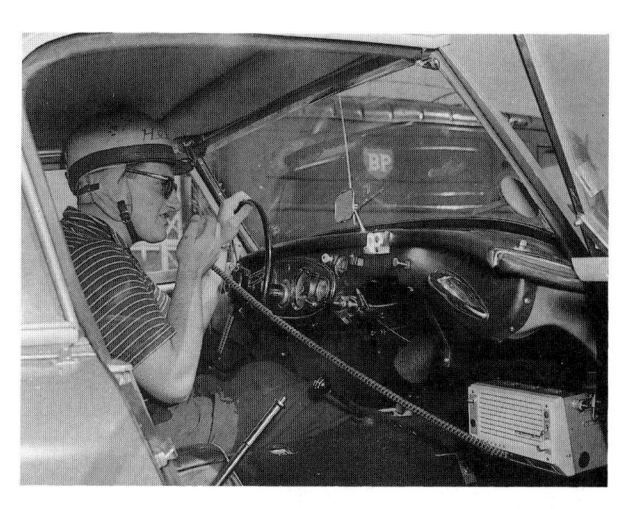

Nineteen Fifty Eight was the first year that 'Thornley's Party' was held. This was to become an annual event to which were invited members of the team plus some of the private owners who had done particularly well during the year. A member of the 'hierarchy' from Longbridge usually attended and Reg Bishop, Publicity Chief and Syd Enever would also attend. John Thornley would make a brief speech summarising the achievements of the team during the year and present the drivers with a token of the Company's appreciation, all guaranteed to keep up team morale.

The Austin Healey 100/6 had shown itself capable of beating the continental opposition and this had given Marcus another problem. He received many more requests for works drives than previously and decided that the policy for 1959 would be to give the established drivers a reasonable number of drives in events in which experience had been gained, but also to try out some new blood in other rallies. Pat Moss and Ann Wisdom were to have another go at the European Ladies Championship, following their success this year.

Austin Healey 100/6 at speed on the circuit during Montlhéry Record Run 1958 (A. G. Goodchild)

1958

Enter the Mini

2
Enter the Mini
1959–61

ELIMINATION OF the entire entry by severe snow conditions during the 1958 Monte resulted in a reduced entry for 1959 with half the team starting from Paris, including Pat Moss in the first international rally outing for the Austin A 40 Farina. The car was registered XOE 778, and Pat christened it 'Zoe', and it was also entered in the Concours de Confort fitted with a number of extras including extra carpets, seat head-rests and a rear window wiper. The extra weight did not please Pat but when she realised that the engine was uprated and had a Weber carburettor fitted, she was not so unhappy.

Left: *John Gott, MGA Twin Cam in preparation for the 1959 Monte Carlo Rally*

Pat's rally was not without its problems, for just after leaving the control at Chalons, the engine stopped. Ann got out to look under the bonnet and took a few moments to convince Pat that the carburettor had fallen off. The manifold had fractured, but as they were only a few yards from a garage, they pushed the car up to the entrance. They got on the phone to Marcus and asked him what they should do to be told, 'get it welded'. Amazingly, the owner of the garage was an English woman and she got her chief mechanic out of bed, and he made a first class job of welding the aluminium alloy casting back into one piece. As a precaution Marcus had a new manifold sent out to Cambrai to meet up with the rally but, although the girls carried it in the car, they finished with the repaired unit.

Left: *Tommy Wisdom and Douglas Johns at a control on the 1959 Monte Carlo Rally (E. Eves)*

One other stroke of fortune was that this section had been cancelled and this gave them an extra 1½ hours to carry out the repair. Apart from the manifold, the car went well and they finished tenth overall, first in the Ladies and second in class, not to mention winning the RAC Challenge Trophy for the best equipped car. John Gott had not been so lucky, as his car skidded on some ice and crashed off the road requiring two cranes to recover it later. This had been the best result on the Monte after four years of trying and with it Pat took an immediate lead in the Championship.

As reigning Ladies Champions, the girls were in much demand by BMC Publicity Dept and their next trip was to Canada to take part in the Canadian Winter Rally as well as make numerous appearances on radio and TV. Their Austin A40 Farina was locally prepared and part of the compulsory equipment included self-igniting flares in case of breaking

Ian Paterson, BMC Canada greets Ann Wisdom and Pat Moss arriving for the Canadian Winter Rally 1959

Icicles on the Austin A40 Farina after 600 miles of the Canadian Winter Rally 1959

down in the sub-zero temperatures.

By European standards the rally was slow and boring and on top of that they had to contend with a car which was difficult to start, to such an extent that they had to resort to leaving the engine running even when filling with petrol and

Enter the Mini

at controls. On one section they ditched the car but a man following them in a Borgward pulled them out again. They did win the Ladies and, as if to add insult to injury, they were presented with a Trophy inscribed with the words 'Corps des Dames'!

On their return to Europe, the next event was the Sestrière Rally in Italy in which they drove a Riley One Point Five and won the Ladies despite a slipping clutch.

They were really in the winning ways now with further victories in the Ladies on the Lyons Charbonnières with 'Zoe' and on the Circuit of Ireland with 'Granny'.

MGA Twin Cams at Sebring

With the success of BMC sports cars sales in North America, Hambro Automotive Products of New York and BMC Canada combined to place entries for three MGA Twin Cams, prepared at Abingdon, and three Sprites from Warwick in the Sebring 12 Hour Grand Prix of Endurance in Florida. The weather turned out to be rather unseasonable with heavy rain for almost five days during the race period.

Just before Marcus and Doug Watts left for Sebring an urgent call was received from Eddie Maher at Morris Engines. He had discovered that there was a problem with a batch of pistons amongst which were those fitted to the race cars which had already been shipped to Sebring for the race. He had a new batch of pistons set aside for the race cars and had just caught Marcus in time before he flew out.

Pat and Ann getting ready to start the 1959 Sestrières Rally (M. Chambers)

Above right: *Jack Sears, Johnny Organ and Doug Watts discuss one of the 1959 Sebring MGA Twin Cam during testing at Silverstone*

Right: *Jack Sears testing an MGA Twin Cam at Silverstone, 1959 Sebring 12 Hour Race*

Peter Millard of BMC Canada had everything organised when Marcus and Doug arrived, with the cars already trailered from the docks. Doug was pleased to see that the engines had already been stripped in readiness for the new pistons but was horrified at the working conditions with sand and dust blowing about the workshop area.

John Thornley had combined a business trip to coincide with Sebring and was present to give Marcus moral support. The Twin Cams were in more or less standard trim and started the race in good order. In the first hour the car driven by John Dalton/Jim Parkinson developed a faulty starter as the result of its staying engaged for three laps. Doug attended to the car when it came into the pits and was slightly burnt by hot engine oil when removing the oil filter to gain access to the starter. One of the other cars had some mechanical trouble, dropping it out of the results but cars number 28 and 29 finished second and third in class.

The last two rallies for the Austin Healey 100/6 were to

1959

Enter the Mini

be the Tulip and Acropolis. In the Tulip two cars were driven by Jack Sears and Pat Moss with an MGA Twin Cam for John Gott, this rally giving the chance for Marcus to bring his newly promoted assistant, Margaret Hall, along to a Continental event. The rally started from Paris, but the start proper took place at the Montlhéry Autodrome, the scene of many motoring epics.

John Sprinzel/Stuart Turner in their MGA Twin Cam during the 1959 Tulip Rally

The rally was quite eventful, starting off with a lot of rain which made the speed tests very slippery. Pat was driving a red and black 100/6 and was not very happy with the handling or braking. Near St Agreve the car skidded off the road head-on into a bank. The starter motor shorted out and was making an awful noise until Pat and Ann disconnected the battery. The Twin Cam teams made rather uncharacteristic navigational errors, and then, later, John Sprinzel crashed during the Zandvoort race while lying third. Jack Sears had been going well and on the test at Chamrousse he was fastest in the class by 19 secs beating a Ferrari into second place. The usual

Jack Sears/Peter Garnier Austin Healey 100/6 on the banking at Montlhéry during the 1959 Tulip Rally

Zandvoort races were held after the rally finished and Jack Sears was fastest in winning his race. Jack left immediately for Silverstone where he was driving his own Healey in the Grand Touring car race, returning in the nick of time to collect his prize for winning Class J. The rally was won by Donald Morley, a Suffolk farmer, in a Jaguar; he was later to become involved in the Abingdon team.

The Acropolis Rally was attracting more interest from overseas crews and for a first time entry Marcus decided to enter two cars, an Austin Healey 100/6 for Pat and an MGA Twin Cam for John Sprinzel. The cars were using a new version of the Dunlop Duraband tyre, described at the time as Dunlops answer to the Michelin X, both using steel cords in their construction.

Unloading the Pat Moss Austin Healey 100/6 for the 1959 Acropolis Rally

The cars were driven down to Brindisi to catch the MV *Miaoulis* to Piraeus, the port for Athens. Marcus took only one mechanic, Johnny Organ, and used as a service car the A40 Farina (XOE 778) which had been used by the girls as a recce car. The Austin dealer in Athens, Ducas Brothers, offering workshop space.

The rally turned out to be rather a disaster for the crews. First the Healey came unstuck, crashing down a bank about twenty feet and rolling over. Ann Wisdom was in some pain from suspected cracked ribs, but some other crews stopped to render assistance. Although the car was manhandled back onto the road and initially started, it could not be fully resuscitated and their rally was over. They were eventually rescued by Marcus and after a check-up at the local hospital, which was heavy with the aroma of garlic, they were soon thinking about getting home.

A little later in the rally, John Sprinzel put the Twin Cam off the road and that was the end of the BMC challenge for that year. The cars were made fit with help of Ducas Brothers and on the return journey a recce of the most important Alpine rally stages was made. This was most useful because John Gott used the information to calculate whether GT cars or Touring cars would have the best chance of a good result.

1955

Two MGA EX 182 cars in front of the pits, 1955 Le Mans 24-Hour Race. (Marcus Chambers)

MGA Prototype parked on the Col du Galibier during the Alpine test, 1955. (Marcus Chambers)

1956-57

MGA 1500's en route to the start of the 1956 Alpine Rally. (Marcus Chambers)

Drivers group stop on Mont Ventoux en route to Marseilles, 1956 Alpine Rally. L-to-R: John Milne, John Gott, Nancy Mitchell, Jack Sears, K. Best. (Marcus Chambers)

Above right: Marcus Chambers and Doug Watts in the original Competitions Department with the J. Gott/C. Tooley Tulip Rally Minor 1000, 1957. (C. Tooley)

The MGA driven by John Gott and Chris Tooley at a control during the 1957 Liège-Rome-Liège Rally (C. Tooley)

1958

Austin Healey 100/6 team before the 1956 Alpine Rally. L-to-R: W. Shepherd/J. Williamson, Pat Moss/Ann Wisdom, J. Sears/S. Croft-Pearson, Nancy Mitchell/Gillian Wilton-Clarke, J. Gott/C. Tooley. (Marcus Chambers)

Above left: Pat Moss and Ann Wisdom refuelling during the 1958 Alpine Rally. (Marcus Chambers)

Above: John Sprinzel and Pat Moss seem amused by the photographer. (Marcus Chambers)

Liège-Rome-Liège Rally 1958. Two Austin Healey 100/6s disembark from the train at Avignon. Terry Mitchell (left) talks to John Gott while Anne Hall supports the boot lid. (Marcus Chambers)

1959

Special toolkit in the Pat Moss Austin A40 Farina, Monte Carlo Rally 1959. (Marcus Chambers)

Assistance for Tommy Wisdom (bending) to change a wheel, 1959 Sestrières Rally. (Marcus Chambers)

Right: *Austin Healey 3000 line-up at la Ciotat, Alpine Rally 1959. L-to-R: W. Shepherd/J. Williamson. J. Sears/S. Moore, J. Gott/C. Tooley. (Marcus Chambers)*

Below: *Pat Moss on the way home with her damaged Austin Healey 3000, 1959 Acropolis Rally. (Marcus Chambers)*

1959

45

1959

Pat Moss and her Austin A40 Farina, 1959 Alpine Rally. (Marcus Chambers)

John Gott's Alpine Rally plate (6).

Ann Wisdom clocks in at a control, 1959 Alpine Rally. (Marcus Chambers)

1960

Tommy Wisdom with his Mini, 1960 Monte Carlo Rally. (Marcus Chambers)

Above left: *Tony Ambrose and Alec Pitts outside the White Cliffs Hotel, Dover, 1960 Monte Carlo Rally. (Marcus Chambers)*

Above: *RAC Rally 1960. Doug Hamblin 'doctors' the clutch on the David Seigle-Morris Mini 850 at Brands Hatch.*

BMC plaques awarded to succesful private owners.

47

1961

Bill Shepherd stands beside the Austin Healey 3000 after retiring from the 1961 Liège-Sofia-Liège rally. (M. Chambers)

Pat Moss/Ann Wisdom leaving a service point during the 1961 Alpine rally. (M. Chambers).

1959

John Sprinzel/Richard Bensted-Smith MGA Twin Cam leaves the start ramp, 1959 Acropolis Rally

Enter the Mini

Ann Wisdom beside the Austin Healey 100/6 as they wait for a level crossing, 1959 Acropolis Rally

Peter Riley/Rupert Jones during the 1959 Liège-Rome-Liège Rally

1959

Austin Healey 3000 Announced

On 1 July 1959 the Austin Healey 3000 was announced, fitted with an enlarged version of the 2.6 litre C-type engine, taking it up to 2.9 litres. Marcus was keen to test the new car under rally conditions as soon as possible, and despite the time schedule for GT cars, three of the new cars were entered in the Alpine together with an MGA Twin Cam for John Milne and an Austin A40 Farina for Pat. This car was registered XOK 195 and Pat had soon christened it 'Zokky'.

The Healeys were in more or less standard tune with side outlet exhausts to give some extra ground clearance, and had the consecutive numbers SMO 744, 745 and 746, numbers which were to become quite famous in the future.

The first stage of the rally was from Marseilles to Cortina d'Ampezzo, over 800 miles including three laps of the Monza circuit where the only cars to achieve the time were the two Healeys of John Gott and Jack Sears and the Mercedes of Walter Schock. John Gott felt that the 'hot' A40 would surprise a few people while it was running and he was proved right at Monza where it was faster than all the Sunbeam Rapiers and

Engine compartment of the Pat Moss Austin A40 Farina, 1959 Alpine Rally

had got up to fifth overall. Unfortunately Jack Sears suffered a holed radiator on the Vivione Pass, John Milne went off the road in the Twin Cam and John Gott's car lost all its water when a rock almost tore the drain tap out of the bottom of the radiator. Various temporary repairs were ineffective but eventually the tap was removed and a plate brazed over the hole in a local garage. The Healey driven by Bill Shepherd cracked its sump and ran the bearings but it was John Gott who battled on to salvage a second in class for the team. Looking back on the event did not give Marcus much pleasure, but the lessons learned had been invaluable for future rallies.

This year the Liège had a split classification, one category for GT cars and one for Touring, with no overall general classification. Four Healey 3000's were entered plus an A40 for Pat to have a go at the Ladies prize. Fatigue always played a part in the Liège and with their fog lamps out of

Enter the Mini

Liège-Rome-Liège Rally 1959, Jack Sears/Peter Garnier Austin Healey 3000 on the Stelvio Pass (Motor)

Liège-Rome-Liège Rally 1959, Pat Moss/Ann Wisdom Austin A40 Farina on the Stelvio Pass (Motor)

action, Pat and Ann ran out of time in the foggy conditions. They had already retired, when just after leaving a control, the engine put a con-rod through the crankcase. Ken James was co-driving John Gott and after overshooting a junction by 30 km were OTL (Over Time Late) at the next control. Gerry Burgess crashed leaving Peter Riley/Rupert Jones to bring home a result with first in class, one of only thirteen finishers.

The Mini

On 26 August 1959, BMC launched the Austin Seven and Morris Mini Minor, at the time a most unlikely competition car.

On the Viking Rally Pat was second to Ewy Rosqvist driving 'Zoe', after a timing error by the organisers, gaining more Championship points. This rally was also the first international event in which a Mini was entered, Marcus himself driving the car with Peter Wilson as co-driver. The ruts made by the Saabs were too deep for the little 10 inch wheels (always a Mini problem) but even so, Marcus finished 51st overall.

To give Pat some experience in the new AH 3000, she was sent off on the German Rally which brought a rather unusual result. Pat found that the 3000 was much quicker than the 100/6 at Monza and on the Mont Ventoux hill climb, but the results were decided on how well each competitor did in his respective class. Pat had been fastest in her class on each test

but a large Swedish driver had done similarly well and this resulted in a tie. As the regulations stated that in the event of a tie, the smaller capacity car would be declared winner, Pat had to settle for second overall behind Erik Carlsson.

At this time John Gott was appointed Chief Constable of Northamptonshire which was to reduce the time he had available to participate in rallies for the team.

Just before the RAC rally, Pat Moss with Stuart Turner co-driving, entered the Mini Miglia National Rally in a Mini 850 (TJB 199), winning by ten minutes. This is believed to be the first rally win by a Mini. If anyone can prove an earlier victory the author would be pleased to know.

November RAC

The 1959 RAC Rally, for the first time, was moved to the end of the year, in November. However, the RAC could hardly have wished for the snow and ice which beset the event this November and cause such chaos.

Above Right: *L-to-R: Marcus Chambers, Willy Cave, Jack Sears, Donald Morley, Erle Morley with Jack Sears's Austin Healey 3000, 1959 RAC Rally (A. G. Goodchild)*

Right: *Tish Ozanne and Noreen Gilmour with blue Morris Mini Minor, 1959 RAC Rally (A. G. Goodchild)*

1959

Enter the Mini

Three Healeys, three Minis (on their first major outing) and 'Granny' for Pat were entered. It was to be a fairly good result for Abingdon. The main problems occurred in Scotland, and one in particular became known as the Braemar Incident. Heavy snow blocked many roads and competitors found that the Nairn to Braemar road was also blocked, but the organisers had not authorised the local control officials to re-route the cars. Some tried the route south only to get stuck or have to turn back, while others took the decision to go west and join the A9 south of the Boat of Garten. Those competitors who took the latter route went on to take the top positions in the results.

Pat Moss was one who unfortunately spent too long trying to get through with the help of chains, shovels and even some pushing from Erik Carlsson, the time lost dropping them down the list to finish third in the Ladies. Marcus had given the Morley brothers a drive for the first time and they did particularly well to come fourth overall and win their class with Jack Sears second in the same class. The blockage in Scotland had caused quite an upset and when Gerry Burgess was declared winner, the German DKW driver, Wolfgang Levy, put in a protest requesting that the blocked section be scrubbed from the results. This was turned down, went to the FIA on appeal but was finally rejected some weeks later, and Burgess confirmed as winner.

The three (TMO) Minis driven by Tish Ozanne, Ken James and Alec Pitts all retired with slipping clutches; not unknown on early 850s! The Ladies Championship had not yet been decided, but a win by Pat on the last qualifying event, the Portuguese Rally, would clinch the title. Pat was entered in the 100/6 (PMO 203) converted to 3000 spec and two Minis

Pat and Ann in 'Granny' on the 1959 RAC Rally (A. G. Goodchild)

were also entered, as a try out for the Monte in January, for Nancy Mitchell and Peter Riley.

Marcus entered a Wolseley 6/99 which he was to drive with Den Green, acting as baggage/service car. It was a chapter of accidents from the time the crews left England, with passports left behind, Pat having an accident with a cyclist at Cahors, and Marcus finding that the front wheel nuts on his car had been mysteriously loosened. The most disappointing aspect of the whole event was finding out that Annie Soisbault in her Triumph was a non-starter, despite arriving in Portugal. This meant that with only two starters in the Ladies' class, points could not be scored for the Championship.

Jack Sears (No 6) and Donald Morley (No 9) wait at the start of the Crystal Palace test, 1959 RAC Rally (A. G. Goodchild)

Pat and Ann just beat Nancy Mitchell for the Ladies, making spectacularly fast times on the speed tests. The organisers penalised most of the foreign entrants for not having black competition numbers on a white circular background on the side of the cars. Pat's red Healey had white numbers on the doors and Erik Carlsson with his blue Saab also had white numbers. This penalty cost Erik the European Championship. Marcus and Den finished 58th overall in the Wolseley despite Den falling over a low wall in his excitement to reach the control table at Estoril.

John Gott, as always, kept an accurate record of all the Championship points scored during the year and when Annie Soisbault was announced as 1959 Ladies Champion, he wrote to the FIA pointing out that, at best, she should be joint Champion with Ewy Rosqvist, as she had scored her points in fewer events. John felt that there was not much point in protesting about Annie Soisbaults' 'rallymanship' at the time of

1959

the Portuguese Rally, as BMC had, after all, 'won the Ladies Championship four times in the last six years, and any protest would have been regarded as 'sour grapes'.

1960

1960 Monte Minis

The year 1960, was described by John Gott as the Zenith. It was certainly to turn out to be the most successful season by any British rally team and it started with the traditional Monte Carlo Rally. The handling and amazing cornering speed of the underpowered Mini 850 had encouraged Marcus 'to put all his eggs in one basket' and enter six on the Monte, three in the standard class and three in the class for Improved Touring cars, plus Pat Moss driving an A40 (947 AOF) 'Alf'.

After the three Stockholm Minis had arrived for the start one of the mechanics, Brian Moylan, was sent to Stockholm to carry out a primary gear modification. Brian changed the primary gears in the BMC Sweden workshop with some assistance from the local mechanics. While he was working on the third car which happened to be Nancy Mitchells', Nancy turned up to see how the work was progressing. She indignantly asked why her car had been left to last and

Nancy Mitchell in her Austin Seven at the start of the 1960 Monte Carlo Rally

remained unconvinced by Brians reply that he had taken the cars in the order in which they were parked.

The Monte again came up with some weather problems for many crews, including Pat Moss who ran into snowstorms in Germany and had to run the gauntlet of jack-knifed lorries

Enter the Mini

Pat and Ann in 'Alf' on the 1960 Monte Carlo Rally

on the autobahn. At Chambery, they were one of only 63 unpenalised crews but ran into further ice as they reached the Col de Granier which made progress impossible as they had no studded tyres. It was dawn and as soon as the sun came up and started to melt the ice they were able to continue, but it

Left: *Tommy Wisdom/Jack Hay during the 1960 Monte Carlo Rally – note the studded Dunlop Duraband tyres.*

Right: *The damaged Mini of Alec Pitts and Tony Ambrose on the 1960 Monte Carlo Rally*

was a rather dispirited crew that arrived in Monte in 64th position. The Mountain Circuit was still to come and this year an unusual marking system had been adopted. Competitors could choose an average speed between 40 and 60 kph; this may seem a fairly low average speed but try doing it in the French Alps on sheet ice! The girls were so poorly placed that they chose the higher average, made more difficult by the fact that the time taken on the first lap had to be maintained on the second lap within five seconds to avoid penalty. Ann did a fantastic job on the clocks and despite a glancing blow from a wall, their times were right, moving them up the General Classification to seventeenth overall and first in the Ladies.

Meanwhile the Minis had their troubles with Alec Pitts being plagued with clutch slip, despite liberal doses of fire extinguisher fluid. In the fog Alec collided with another competitor, then near Monte hit a milk float so hard that the car had to be tied together with string. To finish 73rd overall after all that was a sterling effort. Both Nancy Mitchell and Tish Ozanne retired but the other three Minis finished which was some encouragement to Marcus and the lads, for all their hard work.

MG Accountant

There has not been much mention of money, but as far as Competitions was concerned, the MG Accountant normally looked after the books. When the Department had been formed, Mr A. E. (Alf) Smith was Accountant at MG but in 1960 he was transferred to Cowley. Norman Higgins was appointed as his replacement with responsibility for Competitions as well as MG accounts plus the MG Car Club and Riley Motor Club finances.

Before long Norman became heavily involved in the affairs of Competitions, liaising with Longbridge concerning the motor sport budget. .This theoretically was agreed to cover all motor sport activities including Record Attempts, Donald Healey Motor Co Ltd expenditure, and all the expenses incurred by the various factories in the Corporation.

In practice, Norman received very few invoices from the other factories and was rarely asked how much had been spent over a specific period or on a particular event.

Works drivers were not paid much during the fifties, a retained driver possibly getting up to £1000 a year, plus expenses. As an example of event expenses paid, John Gott's entitlement for the 1959 Monte was:

Petrol	£96	10s	0
Subsistance – 13 days @ £7/ day	91	0	0
Agreed fee	40	0	0
Total	227	10	0

There was also prize money, which was rarely very much, and the bonus payments from companies with whom contracts had been signed such as Champion, Castrol, Ferodo and Dunlop. It was BMC Competitions policy that these bonus payments were shared by driver and co-driver of the successful car.

At the beginning of 1960 an International Bonus Scheme was introduced whereby successful private owners of BMC cars could win cash awards. The highest award was for overall victory in any one of the more prestigious international rallies such as Monte, Tulip, Alpine and Liege amounting to £500, with lesser prizes for class wins and successes in international races.

Marcus also introduced the BMC Competition plaques which were in the form of an enamel BMC rosette with the marque names across the centre. These were suitably engraved and sent out to successful private owners.

Margaret Hall

Next event planned was the Sestrières Rally in Italy in which Pat was to drive an Austin Healey 3000 and Peter Riley and Tish Ozanne were also in the team. The weather had been particularly bad over the proposed route just before the event, and a sudden thaw had left the roads in such bad condition that the organisers were forced to cancel the rally at the last minute. Entry fees were returned together with a share of the prize money and Pat and some of the others decided to go off to do some skiing. Marcus returned to the hotel to find a telegram waiting for him with the news that his assistant Margaret Hall had been killed in a road accident while returning home from a party; her MGA skidded on some ice and overturned near Wendover. This was a terrible shock to everyone in the Department, especially Marcus, who returned by road immediately to Abingdon with Tony Ambrose sharing the driving.

Margaret had been a great success at her job and was admired and loved by everyone who met her. Fortunately her two sons were looked after by the RAF Benevolent Fund and a trust which was contributed to generously by many of her friends. Marcus was particularly sad that Margaret did not live to see how the Department had gone from strength to strength in the following years. This sad event was to have a considerable bearing on my own career.

Enter the Mini

I had completed an Apprenticeship with the Nuffield Organisation at Morris Commercial Cars Ltd in Birmingham, and was called up for National Service in 1958 spending my two years with REME. I kept in touch with my Apprentice Supervisor, Bert Bibb at Adderley Park and looking ahead to employment at the end of National Service, I mentioned my interest in motor sport. To cut a long story short, in June 1960 during transit leave, I attended an interview with Marcus at Abingdon. I remember particularly the speed that Marcus drove the Austin Westminster to the Dog House Hotel at Frilford Heath for lunch.

The main point which sticks in my memory concerning the interview, was the question 'Have you any ambition to become a rally driver?' Marcus made it quite clear that there was no room in the Department for someone who wanted to use his position to further a career in rallying. I had done some Club rallies in my Morris 8 Series E tourer and could even claim to have competed against Pat Moss in the Clacton Rally. My reply must have convinced Marcus that I was not aiming to emulate Pat Moss and others, because I eventually received a letter from Marcus offering me the job of assistant to the BMC Competitions Manager.

I still had a few months to do in the army and eventually arrived at Abingdon to start my new job in October 1960. I shared the small outer office with Jane Derrington, now secretary to Marcus, and Jean Stoter the junior typist. The letter confirming the new job stated that I would be on the junior staff, weekly paid, with overtime payments for any hours worked over 38. My starting salary would not be less than £13 per week, which seemed a fortune after National Service pay of about thirty bob a week!

Pat's Solitude Accident

Cancellation of the Sestrières Rally gave the opportunity for Pat to compete in the Lyons Charbonnières Rally. Unfortunately, the rally car for this event, the Austin Healey 3000 SMO 745, was involved in an accident just before the rally and the mechanics had to work all night preparing SMO 746, changing over the registration and identification plates to make it look like 745. Pat described the car as a little worn, probably because it's last event had been the RAC rally.

The Lyons Charbonnières was run in France and Germany and one of the special tests was at the circuit at Solitude. Pat was in a class including Triumphs, AC's and Porsches and on a very wet slippery circuit with no co-drivers on board, Pat was going to have a go for a good time. She soon passed all the other cars but on the last corner the car started to spin. Unable to control the car on the greasy surface it hit the barrier made of railway sleepers at about 90 mph and somersaulted high into the air to land on its wheels in a field. On impact, one of the sleepers had penetrated the passengers door and broke off with most of its length inside the car. Afterwards, Pat recalled thinking that she was going to be killed and when it hit the barrier, said to herself, 'you bloody nit!'. Apart from a nose bleed and a bump on her leg, miraculously Pat was unhurt. Ann Wisdom was watching the test from the window of the restaurant and had seen the car go high into the air but did not recognise the Healey. The car was shipped back to Abingdon with the sleeper still inside and it took some time to cut it out before repairs could begin.

As soon as she got back to England, Pat did a club rally in 'Alf' (A40) with Stuart Turner which they won, a good tonic after the Solitude accident and a confidence-restorer for the forthcoming Geneva Rally.

SMO 745 was rebuilt for the Geneva and there were also three Minis in the entry list, the sister cars AOG, to be driven by Donald Morley, Alec Pitts and Tish Ozanne. The Minis had all seen service on the Monte and it was Donald Morley who did particularly well to beat Erik Carlsson (Saab) and the factory DKWs to win the class with Tish coming second in the same class. Pat took a little time to settle to the Healey again, but encouraged by Ann Wisdom, the stage times improved and they won the Ladies, their class and a very nice clock as one of the prizes.

After the Geneva, it was the third Healey (SMO 744) in as many rallies for the Circuit of Ireland, described by Pat as a pig of a car, retiring with a slipping clutch and then gearbox failure.

Ecurie Safety Fast

Earlier in the year Marcus had taken out a Team Entrants licence in the name 'Ecurie Safety Fast'. Decals with Ecurie Safety Fast superimposed on a BMC rosette were also made and it became normal practice to attach them to the front wings of all the works cars, varnished over to prevent their removal by the weather or souvenir hunters. Although many requests were received from competitors for these decals, they were restricted to team cars and were removed before cars were sold.

John Sprinzel and Mike Hughes in a Morris Mini Minor on the 1960 Tulip Rally

A change of fortune for Pat came on the Tulip Rally driving the Healey 3000 URX 727, a car which Pat would eventually buy, and which was yet to achieve its best result. The Tulip went right down to Monte in 1960 and there was a stage on the famous Col de Turini where Pat made an excellent time to win the Ladies, their class and eighth overall. The Morley brothers drove the original Austin Healey 3000 press car, SJB 471, finishing in the same class as Pat. Marcus was persisting with the Mini and the three cars all finished this time.

Having already had a taste of the Acropolis, a larger team was put in this time with two big Healeys, and three Minis for Tish Ozanne, Mike Sutcliffe and John Milne. The Trieste start was chosen and Marcus had Den Green as co-driver/mechanic in his Westminster service car.

The route covered some of the roughest roads in Yugoslavia and it was at Belgrade that Marcus caught a glimpse of Tish going away from the control on the wrong road but could not catch her. Later Tish had a broken shock-absorber, and then a broken front suspension ball-joint forced her retirement. At Larissa, Pat's Healey was very battered and, on inspection, it was discovered that the chassis was cracked and because it was not possible to effect a safe repair, they were retired.

Peter Riley had no better luck when one of his Dunlop Duraband tyres threw a tread at speed. They had to change the wheel, and failed to do up their seat belts in their excitement to make up time. The car shortly left the road and

Peter and Tony Ambrose were thrown out, the car carrying on down the mountainside, but the crew suffering only minor injuries. The car was later recovered by the BMC dealer in Athens, the recovery truck requiring a 265 ft rope to reach the car.

The Durabands had suffered tread failure previously, and Marcus lost no time in sending a telegram to Fort Dunlop advising them of the problem and saying that he would be looking for an improved tyre for the Alpine. The other two Minis reached the finish, although John Milne's car was brakeless when collected from the *parc fermé* for the traditional Tatoi circuit race. Marcus suggested to John that he better not do the race but Mike Sutcliffe brought applause from the big crowd with the way he hurled his Mini round the test. Once again the rough roads of Yugoslavia and Greece had defeated cars and crews. At the end of 1959 Jack Sears had retired from rallying having become frustrated with the regulations which often prevented drivers achieving good results. Racing was more straightforward and in June 1960 Jack and Peter Riley drove an Austin Healey 3000 (UJB 143) in the Le Mans 24 Hour Race, the car being one of the original cars raced at Sebring earlier in the year. The car was privately entered and had been prepared by the Donald Healey Motor Co., although the Department did help with the event by sending Den Green over to assist in the pits. The car retired during the race with big-end failure and Den recalls finding the cause of the failure when he stripped the engine after the race. A modification to the oil filter had resulted in a felt sealing washer being cut and a small piece of the felt had passed round the oilways eventually blocking off one of the big-end journals, the offending felt being found jammed in the oilway.

Pat did one more event before the Alpine with 'Alf' but found the engine down on power and finished third in the Ladies. When the engine was stripped, the cylinder block was discovered to be cracked.

Pat and Ann refuelling during the 1960 Tulip Rally (E. Eves)

1960

Donald and Erle Morley at speed on the 1960 Tulip Rally (E. Eves)   *The three works Minis lined-up, 1960 Acropolis Rally*

Enter the Mini

Pat rummages through her handbag, 1960 Acropolis Rally (M. Chambers)

Peter Riley and Rupert Jones on a stage in the 1960 Midnight Sun Rally

Successful Alpine Rally

The 1960 Alpine Rally was to prove to be one of the Department's best events so far. The entry comprised four big Healeys and three Minis. The rally started from Marseilles where the team, including a strong team of mechanics under Doug Watts, were staying at the Hotel Mediterranée at La Ciotat. There were no prestart problems apart from a slight hiccup concerning the interpretation of Appendix J, and a clutch change on Marcus's service car. The large Healey class

Service stop for the Austin Healey 3000 of Pat Moss/Ann Wisdom, 1960 Alpine Rally

included Alfa Romeos, Ferraris and some hot Ford Zephyrs, and it was obviously going to be some battle. At the service point at the Col de Montegenevre, Ronnie Adams arrived in his Healey with virtually no gears and had to retire, and the Morley brothers were missing third gear and had no overdrive. At Monza, Pat was second fastest and Donald Morley equalled Oreiller's Alfa Romeo despite no third gear. At the rest halt at Chamonix, fifteen of the remaining 49 cars were still penalty-free including Pat, the Morleys and John Gott. Near Die, an Alpine Renault crashed, caught fire and this in turn set the entire forest alight, temporarily halting the rally.

The Tommy Gold Mini was running but John Sprinzel and Rupert Jones had both retired with gearbox and suspension damage respectively. At Comps the Healeys were still unpenalised and the Morley brothers were determined to reach Cannes with their poorly gearbox now only having top gear. Marcus followed the rally route in the hope that if the Morleys became stranded on one of the many hairpins they might be able to help them. It was a hair-raising ride with Marcus having to pull over a number of times to let competitors overtake, but they never saw the Morleys who scraped in with only four minutes to spare. When the results were announced, everyone was delighted to see that Pat was second overall, first in the Ladies, winner of a Coupe and a member of the winning Manufacturer's team. The Minis were not disgraced with Tommy Gold winning his class. Pat's result was the highest position ever attained in an international rally by a ladies crew – a wonderful achievement.

Unlike in some other teams, Marcus did occasionally release his drivers to drive other makes of car. This could, of course, backfire if the driver should have an accident putting him/her out of action for a period. Pat drove a Saab in the 1000 Lakes rally after the Alpine and in fact did roll the car, luckily without injury.

Pat Wins the Liège

The success of the Austin Healey 3000 in the Alpine gave the team new confidence for their attack on the toughest event of all, the Liège. The Morley brothers were unable to compete

1960

Pat Moss/Ann Wisdom at speed in the Alps on the 1960 Alpine Rally

Alec Pitts and Tony Ambrose in a Morris Mini Minor on the 1960 Alpine Rally

Enter the Mini

because of the harvest in Suffolk, but four cars were entered with newcomers David Seigle-Morris and Vic Elford making up for the absence of the Morleys.

The gearbox problems on the Alpine had resulted in some splendid cooperation from Charles Griffin at Longbridge who had some stronger gears made in time for the Liège but not with ideal ratios. The service 'umbrella' was much more extensive with Eric Carlsson and Bob Domei in the Minor 1000 'Granny' assisting the team.

Rupert Jones and John Gott pause briefly during the 1960 Liège-Rome-Liège Rally (E. Eves)

From the start, the Healeys were recording top ten times but near Tarvisio, Peter Riley, whose car had been troubled with a sticking throttle, lost a fan blade which unfortunately went through the radiator and he was out. In Yugoslavia, Pat's clutch was slipping and she was rather dejected at the repeat of this problem, believing that her lower final drive ratio could have contributed. At Verona, Syd Henson was servicing for Ferodo and he discovered that the drain plug was missing from Pat's gearbox. He removed the plug from his Westminster service car and Pat continued, but the damage was already done. To cure the clutch slip a new seal was despatched from Nice but did not arrive at Barcelonette in time. Meanwhile Doug Hamblin had borrowed a garage lift to carry out repairs to Pat's car, and after a heroic effort the mechanics changed the gearbox, fitted a French oil seal and got the car away in just under the hour. Eric Carlsson drove Doug Hamblin's A99 service car in a follow-up operation carrying the parts they had not had time to fit, and with Pat putting up consistently good times, despite their tiredness, arrived back in Liège, to find they had won the rally. There were only thirteen finishers but three Healeys were amongst them; David Seigle-Morris came fifth and John Gott tenth. This

Pat and Ann in the winning Austin Healey 3000 speed through a village on the 1960 Liège-Rome-Liège (E. Eves)

64

BMC advertisement, 1959 Monte Carlo Rally — AUTOSPORT — SEPTEMBER 16, 1960

LIEGE-ROME-LIEGE

OUTRIGHT WIN
and COUPE DES DAMES

AUSTIN-HEALEY '3000'

(Driven by Miss P. Moss & Miss A. Wisdom)

Also MANUFACTURERS' TEAM PRIZE

(P. Moss/A. Wisdom) (D. Seigle-Morris/V. Elford) (J. Gott/R. Jones)

1ST   5TH and 10TH

in GENERAL CLASSIFICATION

850-1000 c.c. CLASS

1ST AUSTIN-HEALEY SPRITE (J. Sprinzel & J. Patten)

3RD also IN GENERAL CLASSIFICATION

2500 c.c. — 3000 c.c. CLASS

AUSTIN-HEALEY '3000'

1ST   2ND   3RD

P. Moss / A. Wisdom   D. Seigle-Morris / V. Elford   J. Gott / R. Jones

These cars secured 4 places out of the first 10. In this gruelling contest only 13 cars finished out of 82 entrants.

Subject to official confirmation

B·M·C BUILDS TO WIN

THE BRITISH MOTOR CORPORATION LIMITED
BIRMINGHAM AND OXFORD

Enter the Mini

was a sensational win, being the first time that a ladies crew had won an international event, and the first British win on the Liège.

This was the highlight of Marcus's career as BMC Competitions Manager and it also meant a lot to John Gott who was responsible for much of the event planning. John recalled with pride the National Anthem playing as the now clean Healeys were shepherded into *parc fermé* in Spa.

The Viking Rally in Norway still put a restriction on outside assistance, so to give Pat some 'unofficial' service, Marcus entered a Wolseley 6/99 for himself with Den Green as co-driver. Den had joined the Department in August 1957 and had already sampled the role of co-driver on the 1959 Portuguese Rally. On the Viking Marcus, who was no mean driver, had cause to get too close to the rock face in the big car, and one of Dens' vivid memories was the glow as the sparks showered from the door on his side of the car. Soon after this event, Den developed a white patch in his hair, believed by some to have been caused by his Viking rally experiences! However, Pat won the Ladies, was twentieth overall and fourth in class.

In the German Rally which followed, the Healeys continued their winning ways with a class 1, 2, 3.

I arrived at Abingdon to start my new job on 10 October. I had a lot to learn and soon found that there was a large postbag to deal with, among other things. The bulk of the correspondence was from owners of BMC cars wanting information on how to make them go faster, prepare them for rallies etc, Marcus also handed over the task of preparing the FIA Homologation Forms for all BMC cars, the forms themselves being quite simple sheets before the FIA introduced a more comprehensive form. It was not generally realised that unless a car was recognised by the FIA it could not compete in international competitions; some manufacturers kept their cars out of international motor sport by a deliberate policy of not homologating their cars.

The Homologation Form was the specification sheet or

Marcus Chambers and Den Green in a Wolseley 6/99 on the 1960 Viking Rally

'passport' of the car which was used by scrutineers to check that the car was what it was supposed to be. A certificate of production had to be submitted with the FIA Homologation form which determined in which Group the car could run, stating that the required number of cars had been manufactured in twelve consecutive months. A certain amount of rule bending in the early days caused a tightening-up of the checking of the production numbers, with members of the FIA homologation committee visiting manufacturers to check that cars had, in fact, been built.

The Tour of Corsica is known as the rally of the ten thousand corners, and for the first time Pat Moss and Ann Wisdom were entered to drive, in an Austin Healey Sprite (WJB 707). The car had the optional wire-spoke wheels fitted, a hardtop and the engine was tuned and fitted with larger carburettors.

The Tour of Corsica was only about 24 hours in length but each section was just about impossible to achieve on time. Unfortunately for the girls the gearbox in the Sprite was the weak link and after about 10 hours it broke and they were stranded on a mountain top. It looked like a long night but Photo Junior (the professional motor sport photographer) was nearby and heard them stop, so they were able to get a lift back to the hotel.

1960

Pat Moss in her Austin Healey 3000 heads the queue on the 1960 German Rally (S. Turner)

Pat and Ann negotiate a hairpin in Corsica only to retire with a broken gearbox, 1960

Enter the Mini

The Mini Wheels

Soon after I started at Abingdon, the Department became involved in the saga of the Mini wheels. At the Six Hour Relay Race at Silverstone a number of Minis were racing and several cars lost wheels due to fracture of the wheel hub. They were all called off the track on safety grounds with the resulting publicity stirring Longbridge into action. Before long a new and stronger wheel had been designed and produced, at first in limited quantities for motor sport use.

There were two suppliers of the original wheel, Dunlop and Rubery Owen; the new wheel had a hub of 11 swg material, the wheel itself being of 9 swg thickness. The first supplies were sent to Abingdon and Competitions was made responsible for their distribution. So that scrutineers could identify the stronger wheel, without which no one could race, they were stamped with an MG octagon stamp. I dealt with the requests for wheels with the assistance of Neville Challis in the stores, the new wheel eventually going into production (part no. 21A559). This was probably the first component on the Mini which was modified as the direct result of the car's competing in a motor sport event.

The mechanics of supplying these wheels highlighted another problem which was not solved until the Special Tuning department was formed. The MG Service Department had all the paperwork for invoicing customers, but Competitions was not allowed to sell standard parts to the public. This contravened the agreement with BMC dealers, so we were forever getting into trouble with Service for selling parts to competitors who for one reason or another could not get that particular part for the next race or rally in time.

In the interests of good public relations we were forever bending the rules and, in the case of the Mini wheels most were given away to bona fide competitors because it was just about impossible to raise the paperwork to do it legally.

During the last week in October, two Austin Healey 3000 cars and a Mini (TMO 559) were taken to the Club Circuit at Silverstone for testing. Both the Healeys were fitted with triple 2 inch SU carburettors, but the inlet manifold pipes on SJB 471 were longer by 2 inches. Both Healeys had 4.1 final drives with straight-cut close ratio gearboxes, and the Dunlop Durband tyres were set at 40 psi front/rear. The track was wet but with a strong wind was beginning to dry.

Three Healeys on the front row at Brands Hatch. L-to-R: Donald Morley, Peter Riley, Ronnie Adams, 1960 RAC Rally

1960

Peter Riley and Donald Morley both achieved times of 1 m 18.3 s on a wet track, with David Seigle-Morris doing 1 m 19 s. Peter and David did some laps in the Mini which was fitted with Duraband 5.5 × 10 tyres and the best lap time was 1 m 32.8 s; heavy wear was observed on the shoulders of the nearside tyres.

Donald and Erle Morley leave the start ramp, 1960 RAC Rally

The 1960 RAC Rally was again to see two Championships being decided, both the European Men's and Ladies' titles being at stake, with Pat and Ann needing to finish in front of Ewy Rosqvist in her Volvo to gain their title. This year the rally started in Blackpool, went up to Inverness and then returned south to finish up with races for the surviving competitors round Brands Hatch after a nights rest in London.

We had an entry of eight cars, made up of three Healey 3000s, three Minis and two Austin Healey Sprites. The weather was wet and foggy and it was at Inverness that Pat and Ann ran into a bit of trouble; but not mechanical, this time. After the night halt, Marcus had arranged to use the premises of Macrae & Dick, the BMC dealer, to service the cars in the 90 minute period allowed between booking out of *parc fermé* and the official restart. It only required one crew member to collect the car from *parc fermé* but it was not until Pat arrived at the control that she realised that their Time Card had been

Enter the Mini

left in the hotel. Marcus immediately made a lightning dash back to the hotel causing some traffic chaos, collected the card from a startled Ann, and shot back to Pat. He did not quite make it and Pat and Ann were penalised 5 minutes which dropped them down to third in the Ladies.

The Morley brothers were well placed, and as far as Pat and Ann were concerned, their luck changed when Ewy Rosqvist lost seven minutes in Yorkshire owing to a navigational error, ensuring Pat of the title. There were several tests to complete before Brands Hatch and on the skid pan at Wolvey Mike Sutcliffe made fastest time in his Mini. Tommy Gold retired the Sprite with gearbox problems and Tom Christie also retired his Mini.

After a night recovering, the crews tackled the tests at Brands Hatch. The Healeys driven by Donald Morley, Peter Riley and Ronnie Adams were up against the Aston Martin of John Rhodes. Donald wanted to finish in front of his team mates to get second overall, and on a slippery track it became quite a race. Two of the cars slid off the track and Donald finished fourth in his race, even so managing to finish third overall. I felt very honoured to be allowed to go down to Brands in one of the company cars to see the races and could not quite believe that I was now part of the team running these very competitive cars.

The Mini of David Seigle-Morris had clutch slip and, although technically in *parc fermé* while waiting for his race, Doug Hamblin and the lads made a crowd round the car while a little fire extinguisher fluid was applied through the flywheel housing. In his race, despite being forced onto the grass by Erik Carlsson at one stage, David finished third, and a fine fifth overall in the rally, an excellent result for the 850 cc car. The three Healeys won the Manufacturers' team prize and the girls were second in the Ladies. Their 7 minutes penalty had cost them a certain fourth overall.

Apart from winning the Ladies European Championship, the award which gave Pat and Ann the greatest pleasure was to be chosen as joint Drivers of the Year by the Guild of Motoring Writers, previous winners including Juan Manuel Fangio, Mike Hawthorn and Stirling Moss. Not bad; two winners from one family.

At another ceremony, Donald Healey presented the girls each with a painting of their Liège winning Healey in action to commemorate the victory.

Nineteen Sixty had been a good year for the team, so Marcus was justified in signing the Brothers Morley and David Seigle-Morris, with everything looking good for 1961.

Pat Moss at speed at Brands Hatch, 1960 RAC Rally

1961

Taxi to Monte Carlo

The closing date for entries on the Monte Carlo Rally was 26 November, with the organisers producing a handicap system, based this time on a separate factor for each car, known as the 'r' factor. It took into consideration the Group in which the car was entered, the cubic capcity, and the weight of the car in units of 100 kg. The following is an example of one of the formulae:

Cars with four stroke engines, $r = 1.0 \times \dfrac{\text{cubic capacity}}{\text{weight}}$

Once the various formulae had been calculated, it became clear that heavy cars with small engine capacities would have a distinct advantage. In the end Marcus decided on three Group 2 Minis, two Group 2 Austin A40 Farinas and one Group 3 A40, the Minis starting from Paris and the Austin A40s from Stockholm.

One additional entry, for the publicity, was, of all things, an Austin FX3 taxi in black, crewed by Tony Brooks, Peter Dimmock of the BBC, with Willy Cave on the maps. The car had to be homologated and preparation took place in the MG show shop, the Department specialising in show cars and building cut-away engines for display etc. BMC Publicity Dept made considerable mileage out of this rather unusual entry and when the Press pack was sent out, on the reverse side of the photo of the car was the following.

> They were three from the BBC
> Who said, 'let us see, let us see'
> Since we enter a rally just once in a while
> We must get down to Monte in comfort and style
> So let's trundle along in a taxi!

Pat was in 'Alf' which had been prepared to take full advantage of Group 3 with much lightening of the body with holes being drilled and metal being removed from less obvious places, front disc brakes and the stronger Austin Healey Sprite road wheels were fitted. The car was fitted with a much hotter engine using $2 \times 1½$ inch SU carburettors,

The three Austin A40 Farina cars loaded at Abingdon ready for shipment to Stockholm, 1961 Monte Carlo Rally

Enter the Mini

Peter Dimmock drives the Austin Taxi with MG Show Shop Manager Tim Binnington on board, 1961 Monte Carlo Rally

Gerald Wiffen checking the rear wheel Halda drive on a Monte Carlo Rally Mini, 1961

1961 Works Minis drive out of the Marcham Road Gate at Abingdon on route for the Paris start, Monte Carlo Rally

9.55:1 compression ratio, special exhaust manifold, the whole being put together by Nobby Hall, one of Pat's favourite mechanics.

The other cars were less extensively modified, but one interesting feature of the Minis was the rear wheel drive for the Halda mileage recorder. Tommy Wellman designed and built this piece of equipment which had to allow for quick wheel changes during the event. Like all good designs it was simple, consisting of extending the stub axle with a modified hub carrying a Smiths angle gearbox which could be removed by taking out a single split pin. Co-drivers were still concerned about navigation on some internationals, and this mod was to reduce the inaccuracy of the distance recorder due to wheel spin from the small front wheels.

Dunlop were looking after the teams' tyre requirements

1961

and the studded Duraband was available for ice and snow conditions. Oliver Speight was on the rally for Dunlop as he was shortly to take over from David Hiam as rally manager. David had been in the job since 1959 and was to open his own garage at Minworth hoping to continue to compete in rallies, already having made a bit of a name for himself in his famous Mini 16 BOJ.

Despite early expectations, the event was not a great success with the Minis all running into trouble. Peter Garnier was involved in an accident with a French farmer in a Peugeot at a crossroads near Rheims and, although the car was still driveable, Peter received a broken rib and they were out. Tom Christie retired with food poisoning, while the Derek Astle Mini was struck by a falling rock and the co-driver, Saville Woolley, was hit in the face and was lucky to escape serious injury.

The Taxi started from Glasgow and caused some

Rupert Jones waits for the Gendarmes after being put out of the 1961 Monte Carlo Rally

recording the following times:

    0–50 mph   9.0 secs
    0–60 mph   15.0 secs
    0–70 mph   18.5 secs   Max rpm in top gear 6,900 = 91 mph

After attention to the plugs, points and carburettors the tests were repeated with no improvement except that the maximum rpm the engine would pull in top was 7,100, equalling 94 mph.

Pat was never very keen on the Mini and her first international event in one was on the Lyons Charbonnières rally. The car was the red 850 Mini TMO 560 which had already seen service on the RAC. Pat was a little apprehensive about doing the rally after the accident in 1960 but although the Mini was a bit slower, at Solitude she was pleased to find that she was able to keep up with Erik Carlsson in his Saab.

Unfortunately a problem developed in the transmission (reported as crankshaft) when the idler gear bearings col-

amusement when the crew arrived at the start dressed in black overcoats, bowler hats and with rolled umbrellas under their arms. They started the meter in Glasgow and when the car arrived at St Cloud it was reading £102 4s 9d. However, the snowy conditions and the Taxi's lack of performance dropped them out of the running and they eventually retired having missed a control.

Meanwhile the A40s were keeping the flag flying with Pat coming third in the Ladies and second in class, the other two not doing so well, finishing 28th and 39th overall.

When 'Alf' returned to Abingdon after the Monte, Doug Watts tested the car on the road against the stopwatch

lapsed and they were forced to retire. I remember this quite well because although I had not been out on an event in any official capacity, Marcus asked me to fly to Frankfurt to collect TMO after it had been repaired by the local dealer.

Two MGA 1600 Coupés were prepared by the Department for Sebring, to be driven by Jim Parkinson/Jack Flaherty and Peter Riley/John Whitmore, with Bob Olthoff from South Africa acting as spare driver and mechanic. Bob had come over to work in England and had got himself a job at MG working in the Show Shop, and racing a Twin Cam in his spare time. Doug Watts went out with Marcus to this event which turned out to be a triumph for the MGAs. The cars were in

Enter the Mini

more or less Stage 6 Tuning Book tune with the optional centre-lock disc wheels, Dunlop discbrakes all round and 17 gallon fuel tanks. Extra air ducts were fitted each side of the radiator grille and the car driven by the two Americans had the front valance painted white to make identification from the pits easier.

Marcus Chambers holds out a pit signal to the Flaherty/ Parkinson MGA 1600 Coupé, 1961 Sebring 12 Hour Race

After practice, an estimate of tyre wear suggested that the two cars would probably go through the race with only one tyre change. The race went according to plan and after an early challenge from the Sunbeam Alpines, the two MG's finished first and second in class, a very welcome result for Rob Learoyd and BMC North America. Incidentally, Pat Moss was also at Sebring, not as a works driver but driving at the request of John Sprinzel in one of his locally-owned Sebring Sprites in a race for GT cars before the main 12 Hour Race. Brother Stirling was also in a Sprite, finishing fifth; Pat came seventh after a clutch problem. She was very worried that she might have damaged the gearbox because the owner of the car, Cyril Simpson, was entered in the big race. Before the end she came in and handed over to him so that he could have the privilege of risking the gearbox further. Pat enjoyed the trip to Florida but was less than impressed with the 'boring airfield circuit'.

Stirling Moss was behind the wheel of a BMC car again at the end of March when he tested two of the Liège Austin Healey 3000s, one fitted with Duraband tyres and the other with Dunlop racing rubber. The weather was dry and Stirling did a number of laps of the Silverstone Grand Prix circuit in both cars, recording a best time of 2m 2s on Durabands and 1m 57.8s on the racers. Stirling did not like the Durabands and commented that he would like to try the cars on the new German Dunlop SP tyre. Henry Taylor was also there, and he did a few laps before the front shock absorbers faded, managing a best lap in 2m 4s.

The Monte had been a triumph for the handicap system, and on the Tulip class improvement system was again used, pushing Pat and Ann down to twelfth overall. There was some consolation when the two Healeys, making up a team with Tommy Gold in his Sprite, won the Manufacturer's Team Prize.

Both the Healeys suffered with fading shock absorbers, but after some further testing, Armstrong produced shock absorbers with remote reservoirs, which cured the problem.

The Morley brothers Austin Healey 3000 on the 1961 Tulip Rally

Marcus was determined to get a result in Greece so an entry of three Minis and a single Austin Healey 3000 was made, this being the last entry of 848 cc Minis from Abingdon in an international rally. Once again the Minis could not stand the rough terrain, one car retiring with broken front suspension ball-joints; the other two crashed, the car being driven by Donald Morley having Ann Wisdom unusually as co-driver.

This was to herald the end of Vic Elfords career as a codriver with BMC, doing only one more event, the Alpine. (He had crashed the Mini on the Acropolis.) Vic was driving his rally car home but managed to miss the ferry at Piraeus. He decided to drive to Patras to catch the ferry but was short of

1961

Marcus Chambers and his new headgear causes some mirth at the Tulip Rally prizegiving, 1961

money and had to sell a gallon of Castrol oil so he could buy some petrol. As the ferry was passing along the Corinth canal some members of the team who were on deck were surprised to hear someone calling to them in English from above. It was Vic who was crossing the bridge on the way to Patras. As you can imagine, there was some leg-pulling when he finally caught up with the ferry. It was generally felt that Vic had aspirations to become a driver, but I don't think anyone forecast what a wonderful record of rally and race wins he would achieve as a driver in later years.

Midnight Sun

During a recce of the Alpine rally route using 'Alf', Peter Riley had to get some welding done to the car when the steering idler-box broke away from the chassis, the work being carried out at Montreux in Switzerland where Peter's parents lived. Peter was scheduled to compete in the Midnight Sun Rally before the Alpine, and the plan was to drive up to Dusseldorf with the A40 and meet up with the Austin Healey 3000 (UJB 143) and then travel on to Sweden in the Healey.

As the A40 was still being repaired, Peter drove up to Dusseldorf in his fathers' Citroen ID19 with Tony Ambrose. Marcus asked me to take the Healey to Dusseldorf and to collect the A40, having crossed the Channel on a Bristol Freighter of Silver City Airways from Lydd to Ostend. As the A40 was still in Montreux I had a longer trip than expected, taking the Citroen back to Mr Riley and returning to Abingdon with 'Alf'.

As for Peter and the Midnight Sun, the almost expected run of class wins was not to be when they were beaten by Walter in a Porsche, but still achieved the best result by a British crew with twelfth overall.

In June two new models were announced, the Austin Healey 3000 Mk2 and the Austin Healey Sprite Mk2. The Sprite lost its bug-eyes and had an opening lockable bootlid, but still had the 948 cc engine.

The main effort now was again concentrated on the Alpine and Liège rallies with Marcus and John Gott leaving no stone unturned in their efforts to repeat the 1960 results. John was very concerned about the choice of tyres for the test at Monza, the recent Duraband tread failures had not instilled confidence in either drivers or management. The answer for

Enter the Mini

Peter Riley waits for the Tatoi Race, 1961 Acropolis Rally

Monza must surely, it was felt, be racing tyres. Four service cars were sent out including the two Westminsters, a Wolsley 6/99 and a Morris Oxford Traveller in which Terry Mitchell and Ann Clayton, Competitions Press officer, would travel.

Just before the rally the organisers announced some route amendments which the crews had not had a chance to recce, so Marcus went out himself and made notes of the 'new' section, handing copies to each of our crews before the start. This was very worthwhile as our cars were on average five minutes early on this part of the route while some other teams found themselves as much as five minutes late. A number of protests were submitted by other teams who had not had the forethought to do a recce, and much to the dismay of Marcus and the crews, the organisers 'scrubbed' the section from the results.

Ann Wisdom does a spell at the wheel as Pat Moss sleeps, 1961 Alpine Rally

At the halfway halt at Chamonix, the Healeys were lying first and third and leading the team award, but both David Seigle-Morris and Peter Riley had crashed. Peter's accident occurred after he lost his brakes and he dropped down a 20 ft drop to sustain broken ribs. Pat crashed on a road section when she had a lapse of concentration, the car ending upside-down with a crushed hardtop. The girls were trapped in the car with petrol dripping about, until Ann managed to squeeze

1961

Peter Riley/Tony Ambrose near the snow line on the 1961 Alpine Rally

Enter the Mini

```
                    ALPINE RALLY NOTES

      The team will cross from Dover to Boulogne on Tuesday, 20th June.
  The latest time alongside at Dover is 1500, the boat sails at 1600.

      On arrival at Boulogne cars will be loaded into the train straight
  away and passengers should remove any light luggage they require for the
  night before locking their cars. Proceed to your Wagon-Lit and deposit
  your luggage before going to the Station Restaurant for the evening meal.
  It is advisable to buy some mineral water to take on the train before
  leaving the station, as supplies are doubtful.

  Luggage
      All crews should carry as much of their own luggage as possible as
  the Service cars will have very little spare room. The shooting brake
  will be able to carry one suitcase per rally car in excess of its own
  load. This is the absolute maximum. Dunlops will ferry baggage from La
  Ciotat to Cannes as in previous years.

  Hotels
      Monza              Hotel Ville - Tel. No. 3441
      La Ciotat          Rose The - Tel. No. La Ciotat 223
      Chamonix           Les Alpes - Tel. No. 0 - 27
      Cannes             Mediterranee - Tel. No. 918 - 52

  Note  If your car is placed in the public car park opposite the Mediterranee
  at Cannes after it is removed from parc Ferme, please remove your clocks and
  any other valuables as they are certain to be stolen otherwise.

  Return
      The team and tender cars have been booked ex-Lyon Sunday July 2nd.

  Service
      There will be three service cars during the event.

  Service Points                          Approx time    Est. time
                                          of 1st car     available
  1.  St. Maximin        24th June        11. 31         20'
  2.  Bedoin                "             14. 18         40'
  3.  Malaucene             "             15. 10         15'
  4.  Die i. Dunlop Service "             19. 40         10'
  5.  Die ii.  "    "       "             23. 07         30'
  6.  Thones             25th June        06. 17         10'
  7.  Chamonix Dunlop Service "           08. 05         10'
      (We may not be able to make this before the
      Healeys)

  2nd Stage
  8.  Chanomix           26th June   Dep 10. 00          -
  9.  Aosta                 "             12.16          20'
      At Supercorte Station on Right leaving town
  10. Monza with Dunlop Service "         16.32          30'
  11. Saronno            27th June        09. 32         30'
  12. Briancon              "             17. 35         20'
      With Dunlop Service
  13. Comps                 "             22. 29         30'
      Dunlop
  14. Cannes             28th June        01. 24         5'

  Note for service cars, you should be at all service points at
  least 30 minutes before the arrival times given above.

  Service Cars         Crews during Rally      Service Points
  Car No. 1            D. Watts                3. 4. 5. 6.
  Austin A.99          J. Organ                10. 11. 12. 13.
  681.AOH              E. Giles

  Car No. 2            T. Wellman              2. 3. 5. 6. 9.
  Austin A.99          G. Wiffen               10. 11. 12. 14.
  243. BOA

  Car No. 3            M. Chambers             1. 3. 4. 5. 6.
  Wolseley             Mrs. Chambers           8. (10). 11. 12. 13
  TBL. 698             J. Lay

  Car No. 4  Press (freedom of movement)
  Oxford Traveller     T. Mitchell
  WMO.66               Miss A. Clayton
                       J. Lovesey
                       A. N. Other
```

out, despite her well developed chest, to release Pat. They managed to get the car going again but the gearbox had lost too much oil and seized, putting them out for good. The farmers from Suffolk drove magnificently to arrive at the finish as winners, the only crew with a penalty-free run, to be awarded a coveted Coupe de Alpes. This was the first British car and crew to win the Alpine Rally; a fantastic result.

Service crew notes, 1961 Alpine Rally

Marcus Chambers Decides To Leave

Very few people realised at this time that Marcus was about to give up his job at Abingdon. On 4 August, the BMC Press Office put out a press release headed 'New Competitons Manager for BMC'. It went on to say that Stuart Turner, 28-year-old Sports Editor of *Motoring News* and an experienced rally co-driver would be taking over at the end of September. John Thornley was responsible for selecting Stuart; in his own words, 'I liked the look of him, and as I had always done in the past, used my own judgement and intuition'.

Marcus was opting for a more sedate form of life which would not involve so much time away from home. Marcus was not totally aware of the Mini developments going on at Longridge and although the Austin Healey 3000 had a few more seasons of life left, he could not see a big future for the Mini. Even if Marcus had been aware of the plans for the Mini Cooper it is unlikely to have changed his mind. There was not much chance of getting a salary increase in the near future, so he had decided to join Appleyards of Bradford as Service Manager.

Marcus had been given the nickname 'Chub' by the mechanics and had an eye for a good restaurant, whether in England or on the Continent with a reputation with the mechanics for being a bit of a gourmet.

He was often referred to as the 'Poor Mans Neubauer', referring of course to the famous Mercedes racing manager who was of similar build and deportment. John Thornley did not agree with this likeness as he reckoned that Marcus did not have the 'bark' of Neubauer; he was more the gentleman's Competitions Manager. There is no doubt that without his determination and diplomacy, BMC Competitions would not have achieved the same success in the period from 1955. As John Gott commented at the time Marcus announced his retirement, the loyal support of Doug Watts, Tommy Wellman, Doug Hamblin and the boys and girls in the department for whom no hours were too long to turn out a perfectionist job, was no small contribution to the success of the team.

To Pat Moss, Marcus was like a favourite uncle, the person who did everything to make one's path easy.

Liège Problems

To give Stuart a chance to see the team operating from the inside, he was invited to accompany the service crews on the forthcoming Liège rally. Three 'barges', the nickname given to the Westminster service cars, plus a Morris Oxford Traveller, were sent out on the rally. Stuart travelled in one of the 'barges' with Doug Hamblin and Gerald Wiffen, their schedule taking them to Dubrovnik.

Once again the Morley brothers were tied up with the

1961

```
                LIEGE-SOFIA-LIEGE 1961      Austin Healey 3000
                Spares to be carried in Tender Car

1 Reverse Lamp                   1 Triangle sign
1 Fan Belt Healey                1 Speedo cable 5'/6" MGA
1 R/Counter Healey               1 Speedo dual drive
1 Complete 3000 gasket set       1 R/Counter Cable 1B9140
1 Set front hub shims            1 Safety Gauge
1 Accel. Cable Healey            1 Trip Recorder
2 Front Hub Seals Healey         1 Fuse Box
2 Rear    "    "    "            1 Relay
1 At. Tin Amber Brake Fluid Top  1 Control Box
1 Soldering Iron & solder        1 Dynamo brkt.
1 Hand Drill                     1 Oil Gauge pipe
  Tools                          1 "       "   flex pipe
1 Front Hub R/H & L/H complete   1 Tapered dolly
1 Rear Hub complete              1 water pump
  576 Fog Lamps                  2 Wiper motors
1 SLR    "    "                  1 Welding Kit
1 Coil Electric Wire             1 1lb. Tin BNS Grease
1 Squirt Gun                     1 Special G/Box Oil Seal
1 Kit Mec. Tools                 1 Sponge
1 Hand Soap                      1 Leather
  Nuts, Bolts, Washers, Split Pins 1 Tyre Gauge
1 Roll insulating tape           1 Brake Master Cylinder
1 Roll masking tape              1 Clutch    "       "
2 off every type bulb in each car 1    "   Slave cylinder
1 Yellow jack                    2 U bolts
1 Tow rope                       1 Clutch plate
1 Tow bar complete               1 Marchal Lead Lamp
1 Roll mutton cloth
1 Foot pump
2 Eolopresses
6 N9Y Plugs
1 5.50 x 15 Inner Tubes
  Assorted Petrol Flexes
  Carb. return springs
2 Stop & tail lamps - Healey
1 Clutch flex hose - Healey
1 Overdrive solenoid - Healey
1    "      switch Healey G/Box
12 Rear Hub nuts - Healey
1 Dynamo 22724A
3 Galls. XL
  Grease Gun filled
1 Clutch oil seals
  Tools (special)
  Box selected switches etc.
1 HT 12 Coil
2 7lb. Rad. caps
1 Coil Locking wire
1 First Aid Kit
1 Healey King Pin
2 Headlamps 700 LHD
2 Track Rods - Healey
1 Petrol Can
1 Set brake pads 421
1 Set water hoses - Healey
1 Healey rocker
1 Push rod
1 Distributor Top Plate - Healey
1 Set brake flex pipes - Healey
```

1961 Liège-Sofia-Liège service car spares list

John Gott negotiates the Yugoslavian border on the 1961 Liège-Sofia-Liège Rally

Pat Moss looks apprehensive as she adjusts her helmet, 1961 Liège-Sofia-Liège Rally

harvest, but this did not stop Marcus entering four cars, the fourth being driven by Don Grimshaw, with Rupert Jones co-driving. Don had been making a name for himself in smaller rallies driving an ex-works Austin Healey 3000 (SMO 745), this car having been damaged in a fire on the Mercury Rally in England, but survived to fight another day.

Pat Moss, John Gott and David Seigle-Morris were driving the other three cars on this tough 5,500 kilometre event.

The roads were to take their toll again this year, with Pat and Don both retiring with broken suspension, and John Gott with a split sump. One problem lay with the rear springs, which suffered considerable wind-up on acceleration which, coupled with the rough roads, broke the front spring eye, the spring then rubbing its' way through the floor to come up under the seat.

Before Pat's car was in trouble she had come across the Mercedes of Bohringer and Aaltonen in a ditch; pleadingly holding an already attached tow rope. The girls obligingly pulled them out only to find themselves in a similar situation a few miles later when one of their front shock-absorbers fell off. Bohringer stopped and gave them a box of spare bolts when what they really wanted was the right size spanner. A local villager helped tighten the bolts and then to their consternation, decided to test the car, only to go off the road on the first corner putting them out of the rally for good.

The girls spent a very frustrating four days in the village waiting to be rescued, having endured a rather unpleasant time with little money, no spare clean clothes and with no one speaking English. Erik Carlsson eventually rescued them, and with the car temporarily repaired they made it back over the border into Italy, the car to be collected later.

One of the service crews had been waiting at the Italian border to see the cars through but with their visas used up and unable to return, they continued to Liège. Marcus was scheduled to sweep up the route but made a detour and

Enter the Mini

David Seigle-Morris refuels during the 1961 Liège-Sofia-Liège Rally

missed the girls which explains why they were missing for so long.

Meanwhile, David Seigle-Morris was still going, having been pulled out of a ditch at one stage, arriving back at the finish covered from head to foot in dust. They were sixth overall, one of only eight finishers out of 85 starters; not as good as last year, but a brave effort.

About a week later I had to fly to Klagenfurt to collect Pat's Healey from Tarvisio.

The MG Midget was announced in July being the first small MG since the TF went out of production. The car was criticised for being 'just an Austin Healey Sprite with an MG badge', and was only £30 dearer. The MGA 1600 MkII was also announced fitted with the 1622 cc version of the reliable B series engine.

The Mini Cooper

In September, the 'Ten Foot Tornado' was launched; that, at any rate, was how Wilson McComb described the Mini Cooper in *Safety Fast* magazine. There were two versions, an Austin Mini Cooper and a Morris Mini Cooper, both mechanically identical with a 977 cc twin-carburettor engine developed by BMC in cooperation with Charles and John Cooper of the Cooper Car Co Ltd. The main differences between the Mini Cooper (AD050) and the original Mini (AD015) were the larger twin-carb engine with three-branch exhaust manifold, disc front brakes, close-ratio gears with a remote control housing taking the gear lever nearer the driver, and improved seats. The Press launch was held at the MVEE track at Chobham where a number of Grand Prix drivers were on hand to put the cars through their paces. The price was £679 7s 3d for the only mass-produced production saloon car in the world to be fitted with disc crakes.

As a result of the success of the Austin Healey 3000 we received quite a number of requests from private owners wanting replicas or at least some of the proven modifications for their cars. Doug Hamblin put together a list of the parts necessary to build a replica with help from Neville Challis in the stores, and the total for parts and labour came to £835 12. 5d.

We had lists run off to supply competitors headed 'Liège-Rome-Liège Replica', resulting in some parts sales.

While testing her own Mini at Silverstone, a young music teacher suffered a broken fan belt. The mechanics who were attending a test session, always ready to help a damsel in distress, soon had it fixed. Later, Marcus put his stopwatch on this particular Mini and found that it was doing some very fast times, the driver in question being Christabel Carlisle.

This chance encounter resulted in some assistance going Christabel's way in July. She had crashed her Don Moore Mini in practice for the BE Trophy Meeting at Copse corner at Silverstone, and to get her into the race she was loaned one of the old Abingdon rally cars, 619 AOG. The car was rebuilt in time and she finished sixth in class behind the winner, Linge in a BMW 700. This was the start of a successful association between Christabel and Abingdon.

1961

David Seigle-Morris

Liège-Rome-Liège Austin Healey 3000 parts/labour estimate prepared for customers

Tommy Wellman, Deputy Foreman BMC Competitions Department

Austin Healey G.T. and Liège-Rome-Liège Replica

	MATERIAL	LABOUR	TOTAL
Polish cylinder head		£20. 18. 6	£20. 18. 6
Valve springs	5. 0		5. 0
Camshaft	£12. 15. 0		12. 15. 0
Balanced crank etc.	56. 5. 0		56. 5. 0
Strip engine and rebuild		15. 10. 0	15. 10. 0
2 x 2" carburettors	35. 0. 0	3. 2. 0	38. 2. 0
Engine mounting rubbers	3. 16. 8	15. 6	4. 12. 2
Exhaust system	20. 0. 0	2. 6. 6	22. 6. 6
Chassis and body modifications		16. 7. 6	16. 7. 6
Rear shocker brackets	7. 0	3. 2. 0	3. 9. 0
Race battery carrier	2. 0	1. 3. 3	1. 5. 3
Anti-roll bar, brackets and links	4. 10. 6	9. 13. 6	14. 4. 0
Special stub axles	7. 0. 0	2. 6. 6	9. 6. 6
Front sprints	4. 2. 2	1. 3. 3	5. 5. 3
Rear Road Springs 14 leaf	14. 0. 0	1. 11. 0	15. 11. 0
U bolts	17. 0		17. 0
6 spring packings	15. 0		15. 0
2 front shockers	2. 0. 0	15. 6	2. 15. 6
2 DAS/10 rear shockers	15. 15. 0	15. 6	16. 10. 6
Wire grille and scoops	1. 2. 6	7. 0. 0	8. 2. 6
Modified gearbox tunnel	10. 0	4. 13. 0	5. 3. 0
Modified rear bumpers	2. 6. 6	3. 5. 4	5. 11.10
Special seats	24. 0. 0	33. 0. 0	57. 0. 0
Rear discs	50. 0. 0	15. 10. 0	65. 10. 0
Brake master cylinder	1. 18. 6	15. 6	2. 14. 0
Motor Vac booster	17. 10. 0	15. 6	18. 5. 6
Brake pads	4. 14. 8		4. 14. 8
Brake fluid	16. 0		16. 0
2 speed wiper motor and switch	4. 0. 0	1. 11. 0	5. 11. 0
1 tank cover	1. 10. 0	1. 11. 0	3. 1. 0
1 set pipes		15. 6	15. 6
1 SU pump	5. 0. 0	1. 3. 3	6. 3. 3
1 dynamo 22290	11. 0. 0		11. 0. 0
Pulley and fan belt	1. 10. 0		1. 10. 0
1 ammeter	1. 15. 0	15. 6	2. 10. 6
1 RB310 regulator box	2. 10. 0	7. 9	2. 17. 9
1 race type battery	20. 0. 0		20. 0. 0
1 coil	1. 16. 0	15. 6	2. 11. 6
5 x 60 spoke wheels	21. 0. 0		21. 0. 0
		Total G.T. car	£501 18. 8

Liège-Rome-Liège Replica (additional equipment required)

1 H carburettor, inlet manifolds, special gearbox, 4.3-1 differential modified boot lid, air box, Fiamm horns, trip recorder and dual take off, speedo to suit, 20 gall. tank etc   Total   £836. 12. 5

Notes

These charges are additions to the cost of an ordinary AUSTIN HEALEY 3000 2 seater Sports car, type BN7, with or without hardtop, purchased at the price ruling in the country concerned. Allowances have been made for exchange of parts where special equipment is fitted, and any superceded parts can remain the customers property by arrangement.

Stuart Turner Incumbent

3
Stuart Turner Incumbent
1961–63

Stuart Turner started at Abingdon on 1 September 1961 and it was not long before he introduced what were to become frequent driver test sessions. He was on the look out for new blood and was keen to see drivers compete against the clock, often in a selection of cars. One of the first of these tests was at Finmere Airfield, a wartime RAF station near Bicester. The drivers invited for the session were Elizabeth Jones, Christabel Carlise, David Seigle-Morris, Ian Walker and Bob Olthoff with the Austin Healey 3000 (DD 300) owned by David Dixon,

Pat Moss changes her racing shoes during the 1961 RAC Rally

but virtually works spec, and a tired 850 Mini rally car (363 DOC) to drive. The weather was unkind, with a surface that changed frequently between wet and dry, so that the times were rather inconclusive. The fastest lap times were:

		Times
AH 3000	D. Seigle-Morris	1 15.6 (dry)
	D. Seigle-Morris	1 17.2 (wet)
	I. Walker	1 16.4 (wet)
	R. Olthoff	1 16.2 (wet)
	E. Jones	1 16.9 (dry)
	C. Carlise	1 20.0 (dry) after tuition from I. Walker
	R. Olthoff	1 29.6 (dry)
Mini	I. Walker	1 29.8 (wet)
	E. Jones	1 30.7 (dry)

Following the introduction of the MG Midget, it was planned to enter the new model in the RAC Rally. To gain some experience with the car the first one which the Department got hold of (YRX 747) was used on two test sessions, at Finmere and Oulton Park.

A view of the busy BMC Competitions Department workshop in B1 hangar at the MG Car Co Ltd

Pat had one more event to do before the RAC, this time the Tour of Corsica, which the girls were quite looking forward to. This time their car was an Austin Healey 3000 (ex-racer UJB 143), but all this power proved to be an embarrassment. Unfortunately for them, the rally did not run to form because for the first time in fifty years, snow fell on the island of Corsica.

Erik Carlsson drove the single Westminster service car accompanied by Doug Watts and one mechanic – and for the whole time it was driven, *quickly*! At one stage this was almost too much for the mechanic in the back who had the rear door open ready to jump out. The storms were terrible, with trees blocking the roads, and it was so cold that the Healey's brakes froze! The organisers were forced to abondon the rally when Pat was lying first in class and second in the Ladies.

RAC Rally

The last rally for the team in 1961 was the RAC Rally of Great Britain with an entry of three big Healeys and three MG Midgets. Four Midgets were prepared, the three RAC cars, one of which was Tommy Golds own car, and a fourth car for the Monte Carlo rally in January.

Mike Sutcliffe waits while Roy Fidler consults the Road Book, 1961 RAC Rally

The organisers had made a special effort to include as many forestry special stages as possible, following the success of this format the previous year. These had been kept secret until just before the start which was from Blackpool. There were 200 miles of stages, which were to inflict a heavy toll on the entry of 161, with only 81 reaching the finish.

This was my first rally with a service crew; it was wet and cold and I wondered what I was really supposed to be

Stuart Turner Incumbent

doing. At the hotel in Inverness the accomodation had been overbooked by the management which meant that a number of spare beds had to be brought into use. My most vivid memory was the volume of Doug Watts' snoring only a few feet away from my ears!

The cars went well with the Midgets, fitted out with factory optional hardtops, maintaining positions at the head of their class. Tommy Gold had sustained some damage to the nearside front suspension of his car and at Inverness, at the restart, it was decided to change the wishbone in the one hour allowed to take cars from the *parc fermé* to the start control. The mechanics were waiting in the workshop of the local BMC dealer and only discovered after removing the offending parts that the chassis was bent, and it took the combined efforts of Doug Hamblin and four mechanics to get the new wishbone back into position.

Later in the rally Mike Sutcliffe swiped a gate post but was able to continue to finish second to Derek Astle in the class: he was also a member of the second-placed Manufacturer's Team. The Morleys retired and Pat once again demonstrated what a wonderful driver she is by coming home second overall behind the one and only Erik Carlsson. David Seigle-Morris was fifth overall giving the team a good result, the first with Stuart at the helm.

After the RAC the annual John Thornley party was held and John Gott decided that he would spring a surprise himself this time. The Morley brothers made a presentation to John Thornley in recognition of all his work and support behind the scenes on behalf of the team. John Gott had also written to John offering his resignation as team leader because he felt that it was only fair that Stuart should have a free run. Bill Shepherd also retired from the team, so that the last of Marcus's original drivers had now bowed out.

The Mini Cooper initially inherited some of the knowledge gained from the development of the 850 in the chassis department, and Cliff Humphries was busy developing the power unit with the enthusiastic help of Eddie Maher and Derek Frost at Morris Engines in Coventry.

Although the first rally in the season was the Monte Carlo in January, planning for such an event has to start back in October at the latest, when the regulations are released and the initial notice of intention to enter have to be sent in.

1962

Mixed Bag on the Monte

Nineteen Sixty-two saw a mixture of cars entered for the Monte Carlo Rally, with no less than six different models, plus works assistance for one other. One entry which attracted a lot of publicity was the Mini 850 (363 DOC) driven by the Reverend Rupert Jones and fellow parson, Phillip Morgan.

1962

The car was suitably decorated at Abingdon with a dog-collar painted on the bonnet and a halo painted on the roof!

Another publicity-inspired entry was the Austin Westminster driven by Robert Glenton of the *Sunday Express* with two experienced crew members, Derek Astle and Mike Sutcliffe. Pat Moss and Ann Wisdom were in a Mini Cooper (737 ABL) the first entry for this model and only the second Mini drive for Pat. The remaining three cars were all sports cars, one from each capacity class, including an MGA Coupé 1600 MkII, an MG Midget and a Healey 3000, still running on the three 2 inch S.U. carburettors.

The 'supported' car was the Mini Cooper of Geoff Mabbs who was accompanied by the first of the 'Flying Finns', Rauno Aaltonen.

This was my first Monte and Stuart sent me out with Den Green and Cliff Humphries, the latter on his one and only trip with a service crew outside UK. Towards the end of the rally,

Pat and Ann push 'Able' through the snow, 1962 Monte Carlo Rally

The three sports cars which were entered in the 1962 Monte Carlo Rally

BMC Competitions Department staff 1962. L-to-R: standing B. Moylan, R. Whittington, T. Eales, C. Humphries, J. Lay, P. Bartram, H. Carnegie, J. Organ, R. Brown, D. Green, W. Price, E. Giles, mid-row N. Challis, Jean Stoter, Jane Derrington, front row A. Hall, T. Wellman, D. Watts, D. Hamblin, G. Wiffen

on a particularly long run to our next service point, we were pressing on through the mountains with light snow falling, and Den driving, when headlamps started to catch us up. Soon a Morris Oxford Treveller went by: it was one of the BMC Press fleet being driven very enthusiastically. There was now a light covering of snow on the road, and within about a dozen corners the Oxford went off on a tight left-hander, luckily onto a flat pull-off area. We hooted with mirth as we passed and were not surprised when the lights did not catch us up again.

In Monte, I was introduced to the delights of the restaurant near the Hotel du Helder called the Bec Rouge, which had already received the 'seal of approval' from the BMC team on previous visits.

We were very fortunate to have the use of the Sporting Garage, also near the Hotel, run by Madame Jacquin, and it became a tradition to be invited to her lounge above the garage to take afternoon tea in typical English style. In the same street as the Sporting Garage was a small restaurant run by a little old lady called Madame Pascal. This was always a popular eating place for the mechanics who were always made welcome by the owner and her daughter. Any new members of the team had to go through a form of initiation ceremony much to the amusement of those who had been

Stuart Turner Incumbent

David Seigle-Morris shows his studs in the Austin Healey 3000, 1962 Monte Carlo Rally

before. Madame Pascal was quite a practical joker and any newcomer would inevitably end up with a joke cheese or fruit made of plastic with a squeaker inside.

The team had a fairly successful rally, all of the cars finishing in the results except the Westminster which Robert Glenton put through a wall on a downhill hairpin when the brakes overheated.

The Mabbs/Aaltonen car crashed on the last stage, turned over and caught fire. The car came to rest with the passengers door against a low wall and as Rauno was semi-conscious, Geoff had to clamber over him to open the drivers door and then struggle to undo his seat belt. They were both burnt, but happily not seriously, Rauno having to spend some days in hospital in Monte.

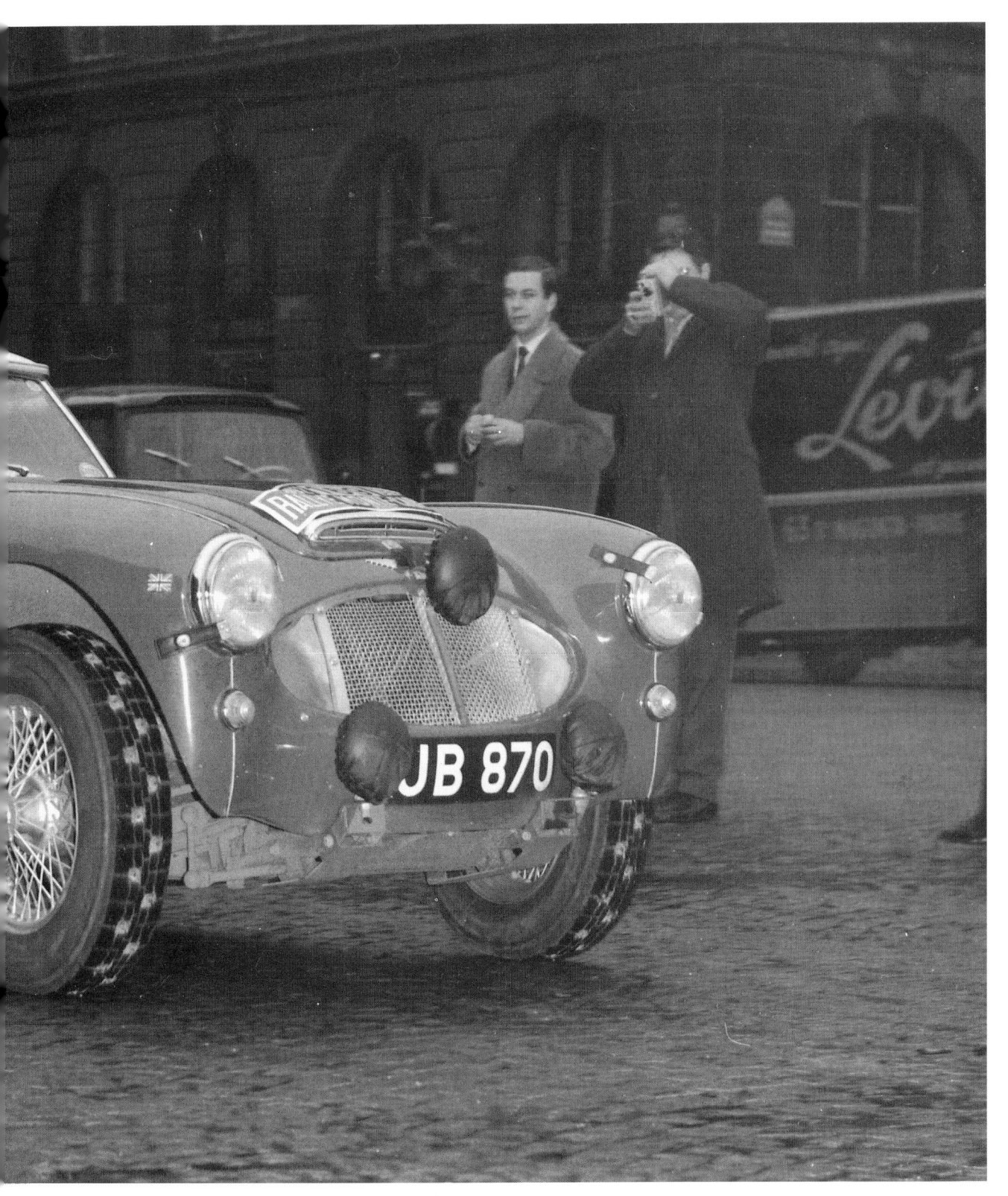

The three sports cars each won their respective classes, Pat Moss winning the Ladies Prize for the third time and thus keeping the trophy. She had not been too happy initially about the preparation of the car after the throttle cable came adrift and she had to drive quite a way using a hand held wire.

During the final race round the Grand Prix circuit, John Sprinzel driving his privately entered Austin Healey Sprite blew up spectacularly, completing a lap followed by a dense cloud of white smoke. Johns' co-driver was Christabel Carlisle who was being given some experience of rallying. As the result of this engine failure, we offered to tow the John Sprinzel's car back to England.

There was an extra job to do before leaving Monte; one of the private owners in a Mini Cooper had broken his

Stuart Turner Incumbent

Donald Morley swings the MGA 1600 Coupé round the GP circuit at Monte Carlo, 1962

Austin A110 with Derek Astle at the wheel on the 1962 Monte Carlo Rally

1962

gearbox and asked Stuart for assistance. A 'box was sent out to Nice from Abingdon and the 'supervision' – Den, Tommy, Cliff and Doug – set-to in the Sporting Garage and changed the unit. The only other thing left was to recover the burnt-out Mini from the stage where it lay. It was gutted and the molten remains of the carburettors and inlet manifold could be seen lying on the underside of the bonnet before we put it on a trailer to be brought home.

The MGA 1600 Coupé team lined up in the pits at Sebring 1962

There was a happy event on 10 March uniting two well known families; this was the marriage of Ann Wisdom to Peter Riley. Part of the service at Ferring in Sussex was taken by the Reverend Rupert Jones and a suitably decorated Austin Healey 3000 was loaned for the occasion (UJB 143).

Cars were once again being prepared for the Sebring 12 Hour race, with entries being made by BMC North America. Three MGA 1600 MkII Coupés were built with J. Flaherty/J. Parkinson in one car and two crews from this side of the water, Jack Sears/Andrew Hedges and John Whitmore/Bob Olthoff driving the other two. Meticulous preparation and good organisation on both fronts brought an excellent result with the three cars finishing 16th, 17th and 20th overall.

Tommy Gold and Mike Hughes, MG Midget, in typical Alpine terrain on the 1962 Tulip Rally

Pat was released by Stuart to compete in the East African Safari in a Saab because we did not have a car for her. She was joined by her usual co-driver, Ann Riley. Interestingly, they used Standard Vanguard recce cars which apparently stood up to the job quite well. When the girls returned to England they learned that Stirling had been involved in a serious accident at Goodwood and was in a critical condition. This, of course, caused the Moss family a great worry until he was off the critical list and was eventually on his way back to

Stuart Turner Incumbent

full health. Sadly, though, he was out of racing for good, a blow to the sport to lose one of the greatest drivers of all time. At this time Stirling and Ian Appleyard were the only two drivers to have won a Gold Cup for three consecutive Coupe des Alpes in the Alpine rally.

As the year gathered momentum the Tulip Rally attracted another mixed bag of entries from Abingdon. Pat was in her Monte Mini Cooper, 'Able' and David Seigle-Morris drove the Mini 850 363 DOC. The entry was completed by two Healey 3000s, an MG Midget and the Monte MGA 1600 Coupé, 151-ABL, to be driven by the Flying Finn, Rauno Aaltonen in his first full 'works' drive, with co-driver Gunnar Palm.

The rally was decided on the class improvement system and, although Pat was fastest in her class on every stage, the girls were delighted to find that they had in fact won outright, the first big win for the Mini Cooper. Both Donald Morley and Peter Riley went extremely well, defeating two Jaguar E-types and a Mercedes Benz 300SL to take first and second in class. Rauno, under the watchful eye of Stuart, kept his car on the road this time, to win his class to make it two in a row for the MGA Coupé.

Webers For the Big Healey

The programme of development continued with further work being done on the Austin Healey 3000 carburation, supervised by Doug Hamblin. We had managed to get some space on one of the three MG test-beds, thanks to Syd Enever, and a comparison was made between three 2 inch SUs and three Webers. The basic engine spec included the latest Servais exhaust manifold, a compression ratio of 10:1 and the Engines Branch-designed camshaft Part No 704/417. A number of runs were made to optimise the settings and the best bhp figures obtained were:

RPM	3000	4000	5000	5500
Weber	103	149	189	201
SU	102	139	182	192

This was quite a useful improvement, and a little later, Doug with Gerald Wiffen, took one of the Healeys to the Weber factory at Bologna in Italy for further development work on the installation by the experts. On the way back from Bologna, Doug and Gerald called at Monza to rendezvous with John Gott who was able to test the car in anger with the latest carburettors.

Pauline Mayman Joins Pat Moss

Soon after the Tulip Rally was over, Ann Riley advised Pat that she was pregnant and was retiring from rallying. This was a blow to Pat, who had done all her serious rallying with Ann by her side, and was to see the end of a very successful partnership. Because someone had once tried to coax Ann away from Pat to drive in another team, Pat decided that she was not going to try to pinch someone for herself. Stuart told Pat that he could get her a new co-driver, Pauline Mayman. Pat already knew Pauline who was known for her rapid driving of a Morgan on the circuits, but Pat's comment was, 'but she's a driver, she can't navigate'. Stuart contacted Pauline and it was decided that they would do one rally together to see how they got on in the confines of a rally car, with the opportunity for Pauline to demonstrate her expertise on the maps.

Their first rally was 'in at the deep end' for Pauline, for it was the Acropolis in an Austin Healey 300 (XJB 877). The Acropolis was not Pat's favourite event but nevertheless, Pauline was full of enthusiasm; despite a handicapping system, they finished eight overall, first in the Ladies and class winners.

Rauno Aaltonen/Gunnar Palm on Mont Ventoux, 1962 Alpine Rally

The result confirmed the start of a new partnership and it was not long before Pauline agreed to go with Pat regularly.

We had won the Alpine in 1961 so it was with some degree of confidence that for this event Stuart entered four big Healeys and, for a first try at the Alpine, a Mini Cooper for Rauno Aaltonen. The Brothers Morley drove extremely well again to win for the second year running, while Pat, not to be outdone, came third and David Seigle-Morris eight, these three winning the Manufacturer's Team Prize; a very satisfying result all round.

Gerald Wiffen checks the brakes on '77 Sunset Strip', 1962 Alpine Rally

The Mini Cooper retired, not able to cope with the heat and mountains, a problem which was to cause all sorts of development headaches in the future.

The lone entry of a Mini Cooper for Rauno in the 1000 Lakes rally also met with mechanical failure but the single entry of Pat Moss, in an Austin Healey 3000 in the Polish rally was more successful. The car was the same one that Pat had used in the Alpine (77 ARX) and some joker had added a

Donald Morley Austin Healey 3000 at Monza, 1962 Alpine Rally

sticker beside the rear number plate with the words 'sunset strip'. They had a fairly eventful rally, running out of petrol at one stage (not difficult in Poland), only staying in the rally after being able to scrounge some from the owner of a moped. The tarmac roads were very bumpy and full of potholes, and the problem of the rear springs' breaking occurred again. It was

1962

Stuart Turner Incumbent

the nearside one this time and after it made a hole in the floor, Pauline was made a little uncomfortable with the heat of the exhaust warming up her behind.

There was a ten-lap race to finish the rally, but the girls were able to jam two tyre levers into position to secure the spring, aided by verbal encouragement from the mechanics who were not allowed to touch the car in *parc fermé*. The race was unusual in having a Le Mans-type start with co-drivers aboard, but with only ten cars left running the only real competition was from the jovial German driver, Eugen Bohringer. Following a poor start when the car did not fire instantly, Pat soon overtook the field with the exception of the Mercedes of Bohringer. Although worried that the tyre levers might fall out Pat Moss managed eventually to get past the German to win the race. When the results were published, the Mercedes was declared winner with Pat second and first in the Ladies.

Paddy in the Team

Stuart was in the process of introducing some new names to the team. One of these was Paddy Hopkirk who had been hired on the instigation of John Thornley who was convinced that he was a better driver than his position at No 2 in Rootes team suggested, and should be given a chance. Paddy was born in Belfast and had started competition motoring while studying engineering at Trinity College, Dublin. He had driven for the Triumph team but had been sacked for driving up the Stelvio Pass with a puncture. His opportunity to move came when a chance conversation in a hotel in Monte Carlo between Norman Garrard and Basil Cardew introduced Paddy to the Rootes team where he had a successful spell.

His first BMC drive was to be a hard one with an entry on the Liège with another Irishman, Jack Scott as co-driver. Paddy had rallied with Scott in Ireland on several occasions previously.

Earlier in 1962 the Morris 1100 saloon was introduced featuring the revolutionary Hydrolastic suspension. When some of the team drivers had had the opportunity of trying the new car, there was some enthusiasm to try the new suspension on rough rally stages.

Bohringer Tries A/H 3000

Eugen Bohringer asked Stuart if he could borrow an Austin Healey 3000 for an event in Germany. It was while he had been doing the Polish Rally with Derek Astle that Stuart had noted how quickly Bohringers' co-driver, Rauno Aaltonen, had driven on the loose surface stages.

As a one-off, Stuart arranged for Eugen to drive a car in a race in Germany. The car was destined to do a recce of the Liegè route and Rauno Aaltonen and Tony Ambrose would collect it after the race. Tommy Wellman drove the car over to Bohringer's hotel near Stutgart with just the normal rally spares kit and two spare wheels. The car was entered in a GT race at the Solitude circuit but during practice the clutch failed. To save the day, Tommy phoned Abingdon and Rauno and Tony were able to fly out early with a clutch and flywheel as hand baggage. Tommy changed the clutch on his own, finishing at 4 am on race morning, and then had to get some racing tyres fitted by the Dunlop Racing crew, supervised by Morris Torlay. Bohringer drove the car very competitively finishing third in class behind two Ferraris, covering nine laps of the 9.1 mile circuit at an average speed of 135.2 kph. After the race Tommy did a quick service and new brake pads were fitted in readiness for the recce, Rauno and Tony leaving as soon as the car was ready.

Titograd Fuel Bowser

The Liège is a tough rally for any car, let alone a new untried model, but it was decided to enter two Morris 1100s, one for Pat and the other for Peter Riley. The mainstay of the entry was four Austin Healey 3000s plus the MGA 1600 Coupé to be driven by John Gott, who had come temporarily out of retirement for this one occasion.

Peter Riley/Tony Nash and the Morris 1100 climb through the mountains just before the engine failed, 1962 Liège-Sofia Liège

Morris Engines at Coventry produced two twin-carburettor engines for the 1100s and because the regulations were flexible, the cars were stripped of all excess weight and fitted with perspex windows. A large sump shield protected the gearbox casing and the cars looked quite racy with white roofs and the bumpers removed.

This was to be my first Liège, joining two mechanics in one of the Westminsters. The team's experience on this event had highlighted a particular problem in Yugoslavia, refuelling quickly. Even in the larger towns, petrol stations were very scarce and when one could find one there would normally be only one Super pump which it was imperative to use owing to the very low octane rating of the other grades.

A critical section ended at Titograd and our solution to the fuel problem was to provide our own supply. Dunlop in Manchester made a special 100 gallon flexible fuel tank and the carpenters's shop at MG made a flat wooden platform for it to fit the roof of a Westminster. The plan was that we would arrive at Titograd well before the rally was due and fill up the flexible tank. We would then drive to the control site and set up our own 'filling station', the petrol being transferrerd to the rally cars by gravity through a normal filler nozzle and hose.

Three service cars travelled down to the south of Yugoslavia to set up service points at Pec, Titograd and Dubrovnik. Roy Brocklehurst from MG Design Dept riding in one car with Brian Moylan and Mac Carpenter. Mac had been out in East Africa, had competed in the Safari in an Austin A60 and was invited to join the team as a 'thank you' for services rendered.

Paddy Hopkirk and Jack Scott take a breather during the 1962 Liège-Sofia-Liège Rally

The lads inevitably nicknamed him 'Mombassa Mac'. We travelled down in convoy, stopping the night near Munich at a country inn, and then crossing the Grossglockner Pass to get into Italy. The climb over the Pass caused some overheating in the car with the trailer so that we had to do a shuttle service with the trailer spares over the steepest bit.

It took about an hour to pass through the Italian/Yugoslavian border because we had Carnets de Passage for the cars, including lists of spares, which took the Customs some time to process. We then had the long trek down the coast road to Dubrovnik, stopping at Rijeka for the night.

1962

Stuart Turner Incumbent

The road was tarmac to Sibenik but from that point on the surface deteriorated. At Sibenik there was a choice of routes, the chosen one being the coastal road which used a ferry to cross the estuary. Leaving Sibenik the tow-bar broke on the car with the trailer so we had to hook it on to my car. At one stage we took a right turn, keeping on the tarmac, only to be confronted by a military sentry pointing a rifle at us after about 300 yards; it was the entrance to a naval dockyard. He pointed us on our way, on to a track which we could hardly believe was the main coast road.

The journey to Dubrovnik was very hot and dusty but with little traffic, which was just as well because the dust made overtaking very hazardous. While I was driving, a knock developed in the steering and despite stopping twice to investigate, the RH front wheel locked up. The shock-absorber had fallen off, luckily while the car was over to the side of the road, so no blockage was caused. One bolt had sheared but we were soon on our way with the three remaining bolts well tightened. The crews of the three cars were very glad to see the Hotel Petka in Dubrovnik, for a welcome bath, meal and cold drink.

In the morning, leaving Peter and Roy at Dubrovnik to service the rally cars, I set off with Johnny Lay in company with Brian and Mombassa Mac for Titograd where we would get our 'bowser' ready and Brian would go on to Pec. It was a spectacular road negotiating many hairpins near Kotor reaching Titograd without further incident.

Brian carried on to Pec and after a night in a hotel, next morning we took our flexible tank, now strapped down with a nylon harness, to the local petrol station to fill up. As one can imagine, we had a bit of difficulty persuading the attendant to fill this 'thing' but eventually managed to get 80 gallons in it through the 2 inch union; best customers that day.

We drove gingerly to find the control site on the other side of town where eventually the Belgian officials arrived, set up their table on the pavement, and we agreed a position where we could work on our cars.

The first car did not arrive until 22.00 hrs, but our refuelling device worked well, and we hoped we would not run out. As it happened, Peter Riley (Morris 1100) retired near Trieste with engine trouble, and Rauno Aaltonen was excluded when his Road Book was stolen near the Belgrade control. John and I had a hectic time particularly when Pat Moss arrived with the outer rear suspension brackets broken and then John Gott with a leaking petrol tank. Johnny welded the brackets, well away from the petrol while I took off the MGA tank shield in order to apply some plastic metal on an aluminium patch to the hole. As soon as our last car had gone we cleared up, repacked the spares and tools and then gave away or sold-off some of our left-over petrol to grateful private entrants.

Pat Moss and Pauline Mayman take their Morris 1100 through the Yugoslavian border, 1962 Liège-Sofia-Liège

1962

John Gott and Bill Shepherd pass the BP refuelling point at the border, 1962 Liège-Sofia-Liège

We returned to Dubrovnik in convoy, having to make a detour over a very mountainous track when we found the road closed. Collecting the other car, we continued on up the coast to Split where we had learned that Pat had retired with a blown engine. On this section we came across Erik Carlsson, long since retired from the rally, effecting temporary repairs to the rear suspension of his Saab. At Split we located the girls, had a snack meal with the chief Saab mechanic, Pelle, who had a Camping Gaz stove going on the windowsill of his hotel room, and then left with Pat's 1100 on a rigid bar behind our Westminster.

It was quite a convoy: three Westminsters, one towing a trailer, one 1100, Erik Carlssons' rally car and a Saab service car. A few miles up the road we came across an English family with a Standard Ten stopped beside the road at the end of an ominous oil slick! They were on holiday and had holed the sump only a few miles from the tarmac road. They could

Stuart Turner Incumbent

hardly believe their eyes when the mechanics got out the plastic metal, repaired the hole and left them with a gallon of oil to put in the engine when it was hard. They were featured on Womans Hour a few weeks later where they recounted their tale.

Christabel Carlisle with her Don Moore prepared Mini, Brands Hatch 6 Hour Race 1962

Apart from Pat getting some sea urchin spines in her foot when we stopped for a dip in the Adriatic, the remainder of the journey back to Abingdon was fairly uneventful. Leaving Dover, we were stopped by a police car and reminded that there was still a speed limit in England. It was quite a long way to tow a car – around 2000 miles from Split to Abingdon.

There had been some consolation with Logan Morrison coming fifth and David Seigle-Morris eight, but no joy for Paddy who retired with a broken rear spring which tried very hard to puncture his posterior! Paddy admitted afterwards that he was praying that the mechanics would not be able to repair the car because he was so tired. John Gott had also retired despite our repair when the tank guard was completely ripped off and he ran out of fuel.

This event saw the end of the works competition history of the MGA, a model which was soon to be followed by its replacement, the MGB with a 1798 cc engine. It is interesting to note that the failure of the engine in Pat's car was fracture of a piston gudgeon pin. This proved to be a weakness in

Pat Moss/Pauline Mayman, 997cc Mini Cooper on the 1962 Geneva Rally

production engines and later twin-carburettor versions had to have new gudgeon pins introduced with increased wall thickness. The Peter Riley 1100 had broken its crankshaft but a new engine was sent out from Abingdon and fitted by the local dealer in Trieste. I flew out to drive the car home with the old engine on the back seat.

Pat Moss continued her run of success on the German Baden-Baden Rally where she drove the Mini Cooper 'Able' again with Pauline Mayman. The Mercedes team had entered

1962

along with several of the other top continental drivers and the results were to be based on the class improvement system. This was one of the best results for Pat in a Mini Cooper and despite being fourth on scratch against much more powerful cars she felt sure the Mercedes had engineered a certain win. However, the last special stage was wet and Eugen Bohringer could not achieve the margin of difference to gain victory, which went to Pat and Pauline, a very popular win.

Timo Who?

With its place now firmly established at the end of the season the RAC Rally was normally our last big event of the year. One of my tasks before the RAC this year was to go into London to collect a Finnish chap from the Kensington Palace hotel and bring him back to Abingdon for an appointment with Stuart. The tall Finn had a rather limited English vocabulary while my Finnish was nil, so we had rather a quiet ride down through

Rauno Aaltonen and Roy Fenner (Automotive Products Competitions Manager) at scrutineering, 1962 RAC Rally

Pat Moss looks happy as they prepare to start the 1962 RAC Rally

David Seigle-Morris/Rupert Jones leave the start of the 1962 RAC Rally in their MG 1100

Stuart Turner Incumbent

1962

Henley to Abingdon. As you may have guessed, this person was non-other than Timo Makinen, one of the most incredible natural rally drivers of all time.

Service halt during the 1962 RAC Rally

In his search for new blood, Stuart had asked Timo to drive a Mini Cooper on the RAC, having made a name for himself already in Finland with sponsorship from his employer, the Morris Importer, Oy Voimavauu Ab. In Finland Timo naturally drove a Morris-badged car and this was to be the case during his spell with BMC, although to achieve this we often had to change Austin badges to Morris ones on his car to keep him happy.

A large entry of four big Healeys, three Mini Coopers and an MG 1100 gave the lads many a long night of preparation. The organisers were continuing their policy of extending the forest stage mileage and announced a total distance on Forestry and War Department land of 300 miles. The rally started in Blackpool and ended in Bournemouth, (the first RAC rally after the war had also finished there in 1951).

Tony Ambrose

The damaged Austin Healey 3000 of the Morley brothers, 1962 RAC Rally

Pat Moss and Pauline Mayman head towards the Ladies Prize, 1962 RAC Rally

Logan Morrison/Ross Finlay in their Mini Cooper 997cc start the 1962 RAC Rally

The MG 1100 was driven by David Seigle-Morris but did not last long, retiring with a broken piston in Scotland. The Morley brothers went out after rolling their car just in front of Pat and, although they got it going, Donald had dislocated his shoulder and Erle drove straight to the nearest hospital to get it fixed. With the inclusion of more rough stages, the RAC was changing its shape and giving the Scandinavian drivers every opportunity to show what they could do. Stuart had arranged for John Steadman to co-drive for Timo. To overcome the language problem, they had adopted a form of 'Finglish' to communicate in the car, which seemed to work, because they finished a creditable seventh overall. Paddy made up for his Liège disappointment to come home second with Jack Scott. Added to Pat's third and Rauno's fifth place, this was a good result. This was Pat's last drive for the team, ending on a high note with a Ladies prize, first place in the European Championship and an amazing third overall on points in the men's Championship.

1963

1963 – Pat Moss Joins Ford

It was only natural that other teams were keen to have Pat driving their products, but it was Ford who made an offer which, in Pat's words 'I could not refuse'. Pat was being paid a retainer of £1500 by BMC but with an offer of £5000, a chassis/cab for a new horse box and the Lotus Cortina to drive in the Ford team, she decided to make the move. The staff were very sorry to see her leave, having had a very happy relationship over a number of years, and on leaving she gave everyone a present. Pat's habit of leaving her handbag behind had not been forgotten so among the gifts to her was a plaque engraved with the word 'Handbag' to put on her next rally car (or to go on the mantlepiece).

With Pat leaving, Stuart promptly gave Pauline the driver's seat and signed Val Domleo as co-driver. This was a way of weakening the Ford effort, and a successful tactic judging by the language she used on the phone to Stuart later!

Sebring was now an annual event for the Department, 99

Stuart Turner Incumbent

1963 Monte Carlo Rally meeting at Abingdon. L-to-R: Tommy Wellman, Henry Liddon, Paddy Hopkirk, Jack Scott, Stuart Turner, Brian Moylan

and the new MGB was selected for the forthcoming race. Stuart arranged another driver test session to give Pauline, Liz Jones and Christabel Carlisle a try out; one of the first MGB's we got hold of, in standard trim, was used. Paddy came along to Silverstone to set a standard and the best times recorded on a very wet track were:

Christabel   2 m 16.8s
Liz   2 m 19.8s
Pauline   2 m 26.8s
Paddy   2m 15.2s

That gave Stuart something to think about!

The 1962/63 winter at home was one of the worst on record with heavy snowfalls in many areas including Abingdon, but this did not slow up preparation of the Monte cars. Four Mini Coopers, an MG Midget for the rallying parsons and an Austin Healey 3000 for Christabel Carlisle were in build, but it was not until after the RAC that Stuart announced that Timo Makinen would be the second crew member in the Healey.

As Christabel recalled, the four day recce that she set off on with Timo started with her wanting to jump on the next flight home after a three hour drive over the mountains in the snow. After surviving another day of terror, Christabel decided that perhaps the car was not going to fly off the road after all.

This Monte saw another new name on the BMC entry list

Paddy Hopkirk/Jack Scott in their Mini Cooper, 1963 Monte Carlo Rally

100

1963

Raymond Baxter/Ernie McMillen sweep through the snow, 1963 Monte Carlo Rally

when Brian Culcheth joined Logan Morrison as co-driver in a Mini Cooper.

It was a good Monte for the team with Rauno coming third overall and Timo managing to keep the powerful Healey on the road to win his class and finish thirteenth overall. His brave co-driver, Christabel, breathed a sigh of relief when the car was finally switched off and stillness and peace once more descended. I think she deserved a medal for the effort!

The Midget won its class and Raymond Baxter also finished driving one of our MG 1100s. The same could not be said of the MG 1100 loaned to John Cuff who had his rally terminated near Troyes when another competitior ran into the rear of the car totally wrecking it. I was sent out to Troyes with a trailer to collect the wreck, taking my wife, thanks to Stuart. The success of British cars on the Monte prompted the BBC to organise a competitive event on television soon after the rally, with invited drivers using, where possible, their Monte rally cars.

The first of these 'rallycross' type events, called a Mini Monte, was held at Brands Hatch using parts of the access roads and grass near the main grandstand. There was snow on the ground and the track soon became very muddy. Timo drove the Healey 3000 and Paddy had fun chasing Pat in a Ford Anglia. These 'Mini Montes' became a regular feature with venues as far apart as Prescott Hill Climb and a country estate owned by Saab in Sweden.

Snow At Finmere

Agreement had been reached to run two MGBs at Sebring in March and work was proceeding to get them ready for shipping. As sometimes happened when the build programme got behind schedule, the cars were subject to running-in overnight. It was done on a rota basis, with volunteers from the workshop, who were prepared to give up a couple of hours of beauty sleep, driving the cars through the night, locally in Berkshire. As this was the first time out for the model the spec was fairly mild, but unfortunately, the weather was preventing proper track testing. The snow was now carpeting Silverstone and on checking round the country we found no circuit clear enough for race testing.

The BMC Advanced Driving School at Abingdon, run by Harry Shillabeer, used Finmere Airfield for driver instruction, and they reported that the circuit was partly clear. We

Testing the Sebring MGBs at Finmere, 1963

Stuart Turner Incumbent

resorted to driving one of the BMC Service Training Units round and round the track to break up the snow and ice and this made it possible to take the Sebring cars there for testing. Christabel was among the drivers who did a spell in really awful conditions, the thawing snow making the track very bumpy.

This belated testing on a slippery track failed to reveal an oil surge problem which was to be the downfall of the 1963 Sebring effort. Both cars retired with loss of oil pressure due to oil surge. As one can imagine, the next job was to design a sump with special baffles which immediately became normal wear on competition MGBs and was sold as a Special Tuning part.

Now The Mini Cooper S

A most significant event for the Competitions Department was the introduction of the Morris/Austin Mini Cooper S with the 1071 cc power unit, larger discs and a brake servo. One of the main criticisms of the 997 Mini Cooper was the brakes which had a very high pedal pressure for a car of its size. The new S had ventilated steel wheels with a rim width of 3½ inches, 4½ inch rims being offered as an option. The power output of the new model was increased to 70 bhp compared with the 55 bhp of the Mini Cooper, the engine spec including an EN40 crankshaft, redesigned con-rods and a modified oil pump.

Pauline Mayman and Val Domleo in the Mini Cooper 'Able' on the 1963 Tulip Rally

The first outing of the new car was planned for the Alpine Rally, but for the Tulip, two Mini Coopers were back in action, together with two big Healeys. Paddy showed what a versatile driver he was by coming second overall with the Morley brothers winning their class and taking second position in the GT Category.

The Mini Cooper that Paddy drove on the Tulip was 17 CRX. It is interesting to note some of the modifications carried out to this car: Engine – Weslake cylinder head, 9.5:1 compression ration, 2 x 1½ inch carburettors.

Transmission – Austin built spur-cut gearbox with 4.1:1 final drive ratio. Suspension – 3/16 inch spacers at front, Mini van struts at rear with 0.08 inch spacers.

Body – twin petrol tanks, quick-release filler caps, RAF sump guard, woodrim steering wheel (Imagine that today).

The RAF sump guard had been developed for the Ministry of Defence for use on the Mini Moke and was available through BMC Service Ltd under a BMC part number.

Dunlop SP Sport and D7 racing tyres were used on the Alpine but the car suffered from overheating, a problem which was to beset the model, particularly on the hotter Continental rallies. Pauline Mayman had a trouble-free run with the exception of a broken co-drivers seat, and finished fourth in class. Tragically, the Tulip claimed the life of Derek Astle on the Trois Epis hill climb while driving his ex-works Austin Healey 3000. This was a sad loss to the department of a friend who had driven our cars on a number of occasions.

Pauline was finding the Pat Moss act a difficult one to follow, but her run on the Trifels Rally in 737 ABL saw a change of fortune. With her regular co-driver Val Domleo, they won the Ladies, were first in class and won an award for the best foreign entrant.

Le Mans 24 Hour Race

The same weekend at Silverstone, Alan Hutcheson drove one of the Sebring MGBs to win the 2½ litre sports car race. Alan had received support from Abingdon previously with his Riley 1.5 race car and his win with the MGB brough him an invitation to join Paddy in an MGB in the Le Mans 24 Hour Race.

Cockpit of the Le Mans 24 Hour Race MGB

The car prepared for the race was 7 DBL and was fitted with a special nose cone designed by Syd Enever which was claimed to be equivalent to an extra 6 bhp. The engine was more or less Stage 6 tune with a single Weber carburettor and to cope with the long Mulsanne straight, final drive of 3.307:1 was made. It was a privately entered in Alan Hutcheson's name because the factory was still adopting a 'no-racing' policy.

Paddy and Alan had a bit of a binge the night before the race, not the best preparation for a 24 hour race, with Alan in the company of his blond girl friend. Peter Browning was looking after the MG pit and after the Le Mans start, he was very concerned when his charge did not come round again. Alan had started the driving and in the chaos of the start, had been jostled into the sand at Mulsanne corner. Many drivers would have given up, but Alan managed to extricate the car after digging for 1 hour 25 minutes using his hands, his crash helmet and even the passengers seat to get it free. He managed to get the car back to the pits just in time to avoid being disqualified for falling behind the minimum race average.

Paddy Hopkirk driving the Le Mans 24 Hour race MGB – note the streamlined nose

After this calamity the two drivers settled down to some steady lapping with the rpm limit set at 6500. On Mulsanne straight the car was timed at 132 mph during the race and finally finished winner of the 2 litre class at an average speed of 92 mph. The car had lost 16 laps in the sand reducing the average speed by about 5 mph, but nevertheless it was a very good result which Wilson McComb, the Competitions Press Officer, made the most of.

The next two outings did not bring good news with Timo being disqualified on the Midnight Sun Rally because the Healey was not fitted with bumpers. and Logan crashing on the Scottish.

1963

Stuart Turner Incumbent

1071 S On The Alpine

This rally was the first event for the S type which was accompanied by four Austin Healey 3000s and three 997 Mini Coopers. The Morley brothers were eligible for a rare Gold Cup following their Coupes of 1961 and 1962. They were using an intercom in the car for the first time, with communication between co-driver and driver only at this stage. Another new feature was the No-Spin differential fitted to their car which was to prove a costly experiment.

The weather was very hot when the 78-strong entry left Marseilles, the first stage claiming Paddy who made fastest time only to slide off the road to retire. Rauno pulled out an early lead in the S which he was not to lose, while Logan Morrison hit a bank in his Healey, retiring with a broken radiator.

At Entrevaux Doug Watts was supervising a hectic service point where the mechanics frantically changed tyres and brake pads while the crews snatched bottles of orange juice and water before racing off again. Denise McCluggage, a journalist from the USA, driving an Abingdon Mini Cooper retired when the rubber driveshaft couplings broke miles away from the nearest service point. Before Monza, Timo also was out when the front wheel bearings failed.

John Sprinzel and Willy Cave with their Mini Cooper before retiring with steering failure, 1963 Alpine Rally

The retirement rate was high but Rauno was still impressive in the S assisted by an unorthodox modification to the cooling system. Doug and Tommy had devised a way of keeping the engine cooler, and had modified the heater so that when fully on, the hot air produced was piped out through two holes in the floor. Not strictly according to the rules but enough to keep the engine from boiling.

While still in with a great chance of winning a Coupe, the Morleys' Healey broke its differential at the start of the Col d'Allos stage, a cruel piece of luck. This was one of the penalties which could arise from using untried components.

John Sprinzel was driving a Mini Cooper and was doing well in his class when he crashed near the finish when the steering column became disconnected from the rack. Though this was due to human error, I am pleased to say that this was a very rare instance of a car letting the driver down due to carelessness in the preparation. The individual mechanics were naturally very proud of their workmanship and one of the reasons that there was such a competitive spirit in the workshop was that Doug Watts insisted that each man prepared the complete car, whenever possible. There was always friendly competition between the lads to build the next winner.

Although unusually all the Healeys retired, Pauline won the Ladies and with Terry Hunter and Rauno Aaltonen, was a member of the winning Manufacturer's Team.

1963

Doug Hamblin (Deputy Foreman) listens to Pauline Mayman's problems

The Austin Healey 3000 cars of Donald Morley and Timo Makinen at a control, 1963 Alpine Rally

Rauno Aaltonen emerges into the sunlight, 1963 Alpine Rally

1961

Right: *Peter Riley/Tony Ambrose Austin Healey 3000 arrive for prize-giving, 1961 Acropolis Rally. (Marcus Chambers)*

Far right: *UJB 143 being loaded on board a Bristol Freighter at Lydd Airport, 1961 Midnight Sun Rally.*

Main picture: *Pat Moss's own car (URX 727) near Grenoble, en route for Milan for the 1961 Mille Miglia.*

Above right: *Morley brothers at tyre service, 1961 Alpine Rally. (Marcus Chambers)*

1961

1961-63

The mechanics struggle to repair Tommy Gold's MG Midget in Inverness, 1961 RAC Rally.

BMC Titograd refuelling point, 1962 Liège-Sofia-Liège.

Doug Hamblin photographs the burnt-out shell of the Rauno Aaltonen/Geoff Mabbs Mini Cooper, 1962 Monte Carlo Rally.

The damage sustained by the Austin Healey 3000 driven by Timo Makinen/Geoff Mabbs, 1963. (P. Easter)

Mechanic John Lay sits at a remote service point (fuel tank in trailer), 1963 Spa-Sofia-Liège Rally.

1964

Top left: Service crew loading the apricots. L-to-R: Brian Moylan, Don Hayter (MG Design), Den Green, Tommy Wellman. (P. Easter)

Top: Robin Vokins and Brian Moylan relax after a hectic service point at Sigale, 1964 Alpine Rally.

Above: 1964 Monte Carlo Rally. The winning Mini Cooper S 1071 cc driven by Paddy Hopkirk/Henry Liddon.

Left: Rauno Aaltonen at the moment of retirement during the 1964 Tour de France Automobile. (P. Easter)

109

1965

Main picture: *Mini rescue. Nobby Hall fits a new driveshaft to the Morley brother's Mini abandoned during the 1965 Monte Carlo Rally.*

Above: *Monte Carlo Rally 1965, the John Fitzpatrick/Raymond Joss Austin 1800 lies in a ravine.*

Top right: *Paul Easter/Timo Makinen, winners of the 1965 Monte Carlo Rally in their Mini Cooper S 1275.*

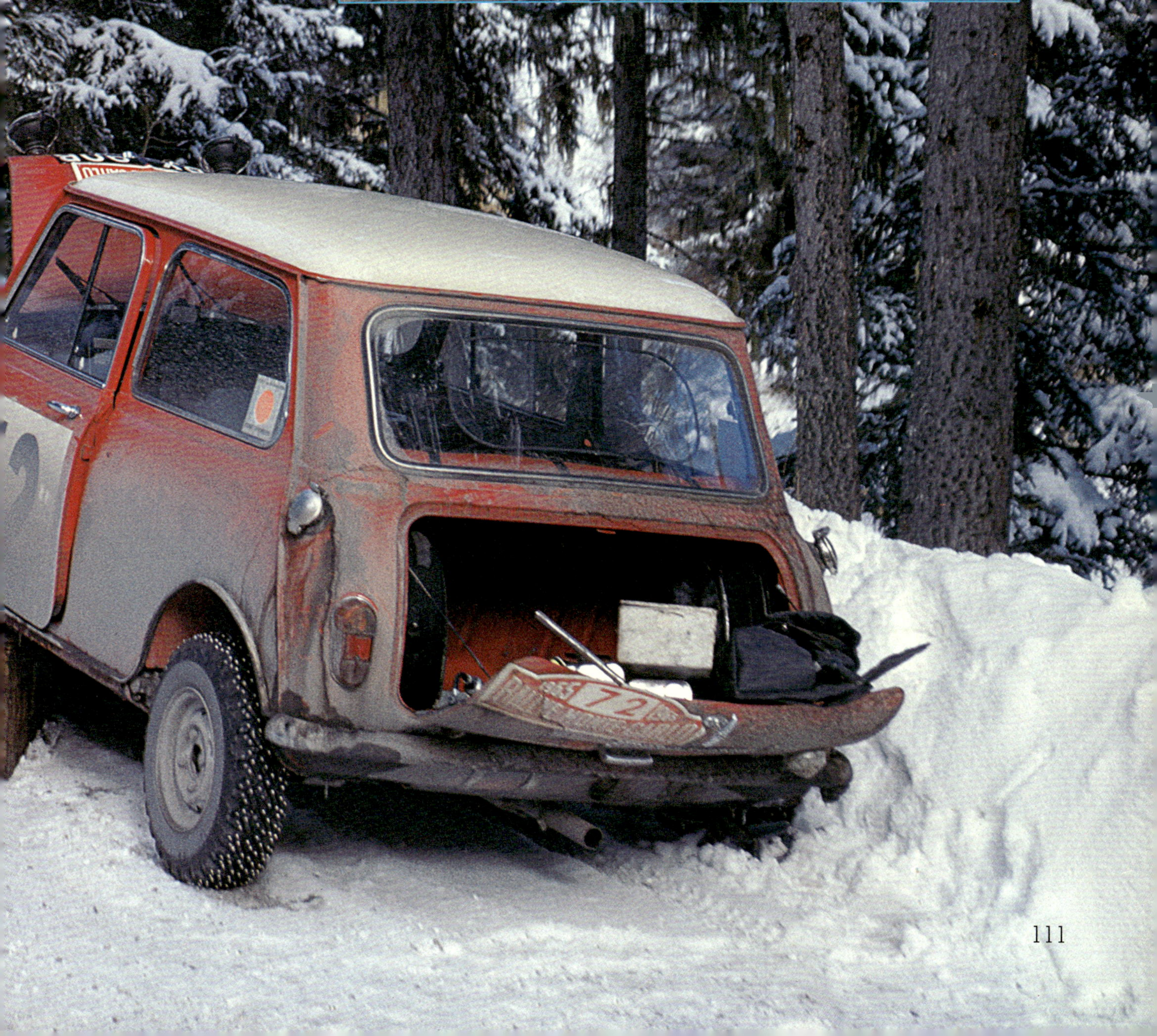

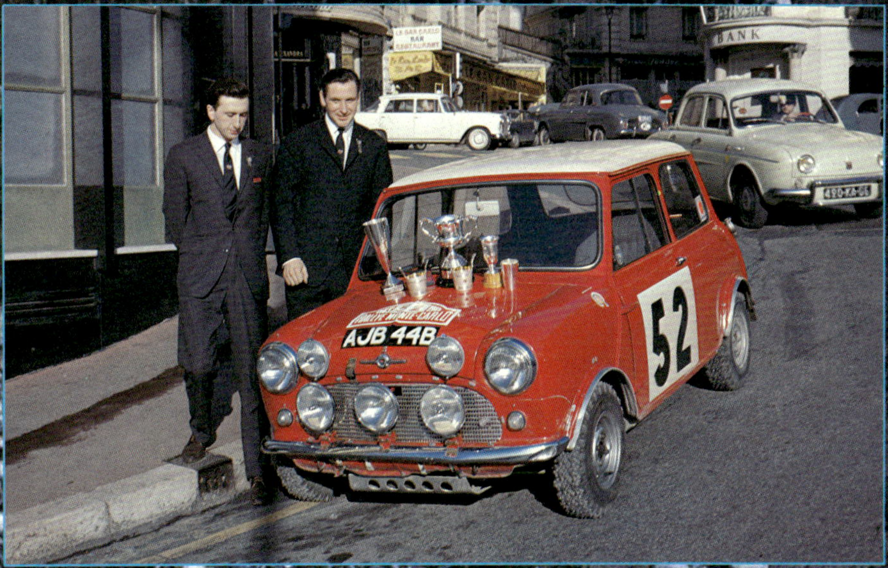
BANK
AJB 44B
52

1965

Testing in Wales. Geoff Mabbs (sports jacket) and Stuart Turner (wellies). (P. Easter)

Timo poses at scrutineering with the Mini Cooper S 1275, 1965 Rallye Vltava.

1963

Spa–Sofia–Liège Rally

Following on fairly closely after the Alpine was the Spa–Sofia–Liège. The Mini Cooper was considered to be too fragile for the Liège at this stage of its development so with the experience gained with the Austin Healey 3000, it was Healeys again for the event.

Although the Morris 1100 had retired last year with piston failure the suspension had performed well on the rough roads so an MG 1100 was also entered for Pauline Mayman and Val Domleo. As always, servicing was a problem because of the straight line distances which prevented the service crews from doing much leap frogging, and of course fuel supplies were again important. As I had been to Titograd last year, I think that was why Stuart scheduled me to do a refuelling stop this year, again with Johnny Lay. Tommy Wellman had modified the refuelling system by mounting the flexible tank in a trailer, with the petrol pump hand-driven using Mini final drive gears. The petrol service point was down almost as far as Split, but inland on a narrow road away from any town or village. After an uneventful journey from Abingdon, we managed to get the tank filled and made our way about 30 km to the scheduled control site. After some hours, the Belgian controller arrived in his Volvo and, because the road was so narrow, we agreed a parking position next to his car. It was hot and dusty but before the cars arrived a heavy thunderstorm started to come over our position. There was sheet lighting outlining the hills and we had visions of our fuel tank going up in flames, although when the rally started to come through the storm had moved on and it had stopped raining.

Timo had Geoff Mabbs as co-driver this year but unfortunately they were running as No 2, right at the front of the field, the position that everyone dreaded when running on public roads at high speed. The worst happened soon after arriving in Yugoslavia when they came round a corner and could not avoid a large truck – it caused their immediate retirement.

At Kranska Gora the mechanics had a most unpleasant service point in the heavy rain, recounting graphically afterwards how the rain was running into the necks of their overalls and out at the feet as they sorted out some damage under Paddy's car.

At our refuelling stop only Rauno and Paddy came through so once again we had surplus of petrol. Logan Morrison had crashed and on the Vivione Pass Rauno lost control and put his car almost over the edge. Paddy came along and tried desperately but unsuccessfully to tow Rauno back on to the road. This was particularly frustrating because

Val Domleo boards the MG 1100, 1963 Spa-Sofia-Liège Rally

113

Stuart Turner Incumbent

Paddy and Henry at a refuelling point, 1963 Spa-Sofia-Liège Rally

Paddy Hopkirk on the Mont Ventoux, 1963 Tour de France Automobile

they were leading Bohringer's Mercedes by over a minute. Paddy saved the day for the team by getting his car back to Liège in sixth place and first in class.

We were still with Dunlop and this year Oliver Speight, Rally Manager, produced a small brochure outlining the service points where they would have trucks or vans stationed, at Tarvisio, Belgrade, Split and Gorizia, with the Italian truck at Trafoi. The Liège was still one of John Gott's favourite events and he had found time to compete with Douglas Johns this time in a new Mini Cooper S 1071, but unfortunately the car did not finish.

Tour de France Automobile

One event which had been gaining in popularity in France was the Tour de France Automobile, consisting of a series of races and hill climbs, sponsored by Shell and the sporting newspaper *L'Equipe*. At each circuit five-course meals were laid-on and even the service crews were catered for. All of the races were at least one hour, and it really was a fearsome test for the cars.

We entered three Mini Coopers and one Mini Cooper S plus the Le Mans MGB. All the service cars had hard schedules but the crews had the consolation of several nights' sleep during the course of the 3,600 mile event. I was in a car with Brian Moylan and Gerald Wiffen and after leaving the start town of Strasbourg, our first stop was at the Nürburgring where amongst the activity, the mechanics welded the cylinder head on the Mini Cooper of Terry Hunter, a private entrant.

On the faster circuits the 7 litre Ford Galaxies were

1963

heading the 3.8 Jaguars but the Minis were doing well with Paddy leading the Touring Category on handicap. The MGB was surprising everyone, only being beaten by the Ferrari GTOs and Porsche Carreras but beating many more powerful Continental cars.

At Rouen we had to search for a replacement Woodruff key for one of the Mini Coopers which we located in the attic of the local BMC dealer. To keep cars in the event, it was permitted to work on one's car instead of racing, with penalties of course, and Timo and Logan Morrison replaced their front pulley which had come loose, with advice from the mechanics outside the work area.

At Le Mans the Minis looked spectacular as they came round nose to tail looking as if they were tied together. The two surviving Ford Galaxies were using a lot of oil and Sir Gawaine Baillie had to stop for more oil; the excitement of the American team manager, shouting instructions to his driver from the pit roof, was a sight to see. Doug Hamblin had

Timo had retired with mechanical troubles. At Pau, Paddy brought the crowd to its feet by leading all the big saloons for the first ten laps before easing off to save the car, his efforts earning front page pictures in the papers next day. His car was so reliable that he did not have one pit stop in 12 hours of racing.

At the end of the third Stage the MGB was lying fourth behind two Ferrari GTOs and a 2 litre Porsche. This was tremendous, but it all came to nought when on the Col de Jau, Andrew Hedges crashed to retirement, a disappointing end to a great drive.

Paddy won the Touring Car Handicap Category and was third on scratch behind the winning Jaguar of Bernard Consten. The end-of-event party was held at La Fiesta, an open air complex near Nice Airport, featuring many national

The Le Mans MGB driven by Andrew Hedges at Nürburgring during the 1963 Tour de France Automobile

overdone the red 'plonk' at lunchtime and was ticked-off by Stuart when he started to offer silly pit signals to the 'Mini Train'.

A night halt at Cognac was welcome even if the menu card in the hotel bar was tempting with its 100 different cognacs, some costing as much as £1 a tot. In the morning there was one-hour race at the local military airfield, which service crews were forbidden to enter, the competitors being issued with samples of Martell as they arrived at the control.

Paddy was leading on handicap but both Pauline and

dishes and national costumes. There was a go-kart track on which several members of our team had a go, hindered by Dunlop staff who would persist in rolling old tyres across the track. Geoff Mabbs managed to shear the front wheel off one kart and our Brian Moylan even managed to overturn a kart with some damage to his chin, leg and best trousers!

Wheels have always been an important item on a rally car and a new product shown at Earls Court Motor Show was a sandcast alloy wheel. Made by Tech Del Ltd, it was called the Minilite wheel. They were shown fitted to a Mini Radford de

Stuart Turner Incumbent

Ville and were soon to become a most successful rally wheel.

It was now RAC Rally time and we were wondering how we were going to stop the one-man Swedish show from winning the rally after gaining his hat trick.

Stuart entered two Mini Cooper Ss, one Mini Cooper and two Austin Healey 3000 cars, in the rally, which started from Blackpool and finished in Bournemouth. We used full length dural sump shields on the Minis and at the Blackpool overnight halt there was some late-night work repairing and strengthening the guards which were wearing through where strengthening strips had been added. It was a wet, muddy event and at the finish, Paddy was fourth and Timo was fifth, and the Morleys ninth despite their stopping on a stage near the finish with water in the electrics. All our cars finished the 2,200 mile rally and twenty of the 88 finishers were driving BMC cars.

This event was another good result for the 1071S, which had twin 1½ inch SU carburettors, an AEA731 camshaft, 11.0:1 compression ratio and a 4.1:1 final drive. The production rubber driveshaft couplings were fitted and had to be changed during the rally because the rubber collapsed. One new development was the introuction of the single-filament quartz-iodine bulbs which were received very favourably by the drivers. At this stage they were not available in twin filament form and were fitted to the long-range lamps only.

A successful year for the team: but could we maintain the impetus?

The co-drivers go through the map marking ritual. L-to-R: Ross Finlay, Val Domleo, Henry Liddon, Mike Wood, Tony Ambrose and Erle Morley, 1963 RAC Rally

Typical wet conditions for Pauline and Val, 1963 RAC Rally Below: A streaming Oulton Park circuit for Timo Makinen/Mike Wood, 1963 RAC Rally

1963

Donald and Erle Morley

Barbara Johansson drove a Mini Cooper entered by BMC Sweden, 1963 RAC Rally

The Morley brothers stopped with water on the ignition, 1963 RAC Rally

Monte Magic

4

Monte Magic
1964–67

Heated Screens On The Monte

THE ENTRY FOR the Monte Carlo rally was four Mini Cooper S 1071 cars, two Mini Coopers and an MGB for the Morley brothers. The S types were mechanically similar to RAC spec but with the addition of radiator muffs, electrically-heated windscreens and the Mini Moke sump shield replacing the full-length forest type. The windscreens were a new development by Triplex which incorporated a gold film between the laminations through which a current was passed to heat the

Cockpit of the winning 1071cc Mini Cooper S, 1964 Monte Carlo Rally

screen. During testing the drivers showed some dislike for the tinted effect of the gold film, which tended to make the eyes focus on the screen instead of the road ahead. As a result, a crate of standard laminated screens was taken out to Reims before the rally in case any of the drivers wanted them changed.

I was servicing with Den Green and Johnny Lay and our first service point was at a control at a motel near Arnhem. It was very cold and frosty as we waited for the cars and we were dismayed to learn from another non-BMC driver that Pauline Mayman had been involved in an accident near Maastricht and had been taken to hospital. This was confirmed by two Rhodesians, Jack Thompson and Jack Heys, driving one of our two Mini Coopers, when they arrived late, having stopped at the scene of the accident to render assistance.

The girls had been involved in a collision with a farmer in a Chevrolet who had turned across their bows on a straight road, without warning. The car caught fire briefly and was badly damaged, the girls being taken to the nearest accident hospital for treatment.

Engine compartment of the MGB driven by Donald and Erle Morley, 1964 Monte Carlo Rally

We decided that we had time to go to Maastricht to see if we could be of any assistance, before going to our next stop at Frankfurt. In Maastricht, a chap in a car who was alongside us in the traffic leaned over and asked if we were looking for two English rally girls. This stroke of luck found us at the hospital five minutes later. At the hospital we established that Pauline was detained with a broken leg and a gashed forehead which had required twelve stitches, but Val was OK and had gone shopping.

We saw Pauline briefly and there was no doubt that the sight of friendly natives helped her morale. Val returned and insisted on being taken back to the scene on the way to the local BMC dealer who we organised to recover the car. We had to leave, but were happy to know that they were in good hands.

At Frankfurt, the temperature was below minus 10°C and there was sheet ice surrounding the control at a small cafe. When the cars came through, the MGB with a leaking radiator was the only one with any serious trouble, so we phoned Abingdon to ask the crew coming to Boulogne to bring a new radiator. Foolishly we had left our water can on the roof rack where it had frozen solid and so, to thaw it out, we got out the welding equipment. The nozzle was handed over to Ernie McMillen who was at a loose end, who then proceeded to burn a hole in the can in his enthusiasm, much to everyone's ammusement.

Early next morning we proceeded to Paris where we were scheduled to catch a flight to Nice to join the service crews for the Mountain Circuit.

Approaching Paris the fog came down and we had difficulty finding the Austin Agent, AFIVA, where we were to leave the car. Flights were seriously delayed by the fog and, after trying for some hours to get to Nice, Stuart told us to return to Abingdon because we would not be able to get there in time. We stayed at the Hotel Baltimore and we were shattered by the news that Doug Hamblin had been killed in a road accident near Henley-on-Thames while driving to Dover to service the cars at Boulogne. Johnny Lay had phoned his wife to let her know we were coming home early and had learned the sad news.

Doug was a dedicated second in command to Doug Watts and a friend who would be sadly missed. I was concerned that the news should not reach the drivers before the rally finished, but after speaking to Norman Higgins who was of the same opinion, we managed to contact Wilson McComb in Monte and the news was kept under wraps until the action had finished. Den, Johnny and myself drowned our sorrows that night and returned to Abingdon next day in a subdued mood.

Meanwhile at Reims, two of our cars had their heated windscreens changed for the standard type. The rally handicap suited smaller cars but the Ford Falcons were setting the pace with their superior power/weight ratio; for example on the stage after Uriage, the Falcon of Bo Lungfeldt recorded a time of 15m 54s compared with Paddy's time of 16m 13s.

At the end of the last stage it seemed that the Mini Cooper S of Paddy was in a winning position with only the four

119

Monte Magic

Paddy Hopkirk and Henry Liddon speed to a memorable victory, 1964 Monte Carlo Rally

The Morley brothers pass the summit of the Col de Turini, 1964 Monte Carlo Rally

lap race round the Monaco GP circuit remaining. Next morning, although Paddy was not amongst the top ten fastest times, he had done enough and was declared winner, with Timo fourth and Rauno eight to win the Charles Faroux Trophy for the best manufacturers team. To cap the Mini achievements, the Morley brothers won the GT category with the MGB, being placed seventeenth overall.

This was a tremendous result and really put the Mini Cooper S on a pedestal, the smallest car ever to win the Monte. There was a party in Monte to celebrate and Alec Issigonis was flown down to Monte to join the celebrations.

The cars were flown back to England on a chartered BUAF Carvair and the winning car appeared at the London Palladium with Bruce Forsyth.

Right: *First Mini Cooper S Special Tuning leaflet*

Following the Monte win, George Harriman presented Paddy and Henry with new Mini Coopers and Stuart received a bonus cheque for £500. We were entering cars in international events governed by the Appendix J FIA regulations and one important consideration for manufacturers was the cubic capacity of potential competition cars. With BMC, this resulted in two new versions of the Mini Cooper S being introduced in March, the 970cc and 1275cc engined cars, these cubic capacities being designed to fit the 1,000cc and 1,300cc classes.

1964

Power output of the new engines were quoted at 68 and 75 bhp, the bore sizes remaining unchanged, the increase in capacity being achieved by changing the stroke. The 1071 cc engine was to continue in production until August and then in

Right: *Model Carvairs presented to the winning crew at Heathrow, 1964 Monte Carlo Rally*

Left: *Paddy Hopkirk and Henry Liddon at the London Palladium, 1964 Monte Carlo Rally*

September, Hydrolastic suspension and the diaphragm spring clutch were introduced, but more on the suspension later.

In February, the Austin Healey 3000 Mk III was announced (BJ8), its specification including two SU HD8 carburettors and the long awaited rear axle radius rods which we hoped would cure the rear spring breakages which we had suffered on rough events. The body was the two/four configuration with a curved windscreen, and power output was 150 bhp at 5,250 rpm.

After the Monte, Paddy competed in the Austrian Alpine rally and after being pressed hard on some of the stages by a Steyr-Punch (of all things!) he came home winner with his regular co-driver Henry Liddon, driving an Austin Healey 3000.

Austrian Alpine Rally 1964, Henry Liddon offers the passports

Monte Magic

One of my main responsibilities at this time was the preparation of the FIA Homologation Forms and I had been busy getting the new Form ready for the 1275 Mini Cooper S. It was duly forwarded to the RAC and we received confirmation that the model had been recognised to run in international events in time for it to appear in the Tulip Rally.

Austin Healey 3000 driven by the Morley brothers, 1964 Tulip Rally

Timo drove the 1275 S type on the Tulip and we also entered a Mk III 3000, running with bumpers to comply with the FIA regulations, and in my opinion looking less aggressive than the earlier cars. With stages at venues such as Zolder, Nürburgring, Spa Francorchamps and Zandvoort where power was needed, we were pleased that the new cars scored a sweeping success with Timo winning outright and the Morleys in the Healey coming first in the GT Category. BMC cars won five classes on the Tulip, with Paul Easter, Brian Culcheth and Julien Vernaeve also successful, underlining how popular the Mini Cooper and S types were becoming with private competitors.

On to the Acropolis where our fortunes changed with both S types retiring and a further disappointment when the Morley brothers were involved in a road accident during the Scottish, writing-off the MGB 7DBL.

1964 Le Mans

We prepared an MGB for Le Mans for Paddy Hopkirk and Andrew Hedges to drive, once again entered in the drivers' names, the car being similar in spec to the 1963 entry, and retaining the streamlined nose section. Paddy seemed quite pleased that the race car had been allocated the same race number (37) as his winning Monte car. Stuart asked Peter Browning to manage the pits and we sent some mechanics from Abingdon to look after the mechanicals. Peter Browning had just been appointed Assistant Editor of *Safety Fast* magazine, under Stuart Seager who had replaced Wilson McComb.

The old BMC transporter was used to take the car to France and two motor caravans were loaned to supply meals and give the off-duty drivers somewhere to sleep. The total number of personnel involved in the entry was fourteen including timekeepers, pit signallers, refuellers and mechanics etc.

A nine hours practice session was scheduled to allow drivers to qualify in the dark and set up their lamps, the MGB having an identification lamp on the right-hand side of the hardtop. The car qualified for the race within the 99.6 mph minimum for the class and the reserve driver, Patrick Vanson, also got round in under 5 min 2 sec.

In the race, there were one or two incidents, the first when Andrew came in for an unscheduled stop after swiping the bank at Mulsanne and buckling a wheel.

During one of the night pit stops the 'plombeur' sealing the tank managed to break the fuel cap clean off; Nobby and Den had to make a temporary repair before they could scrounge a spare from Marcus Chambers who was looking after the Sunbeam team.

At 04.00 hrs during a routine driver change, Andrew reported sparks coming from the front wheels when braking, a quick inspection revealing that the pads were completely worn out, much earlier than calculated. The mechanics were having a problem getting the welded pads out until Doug Watts put on his spectacles and, pushing everyone aside, soon had the job finished. The pad change took 8 minutes but the car ran on at unabated speed, being timed by radar at 139 mph on the Mulsanne straight. At the 16.00 hrs finish,

Le Mans 24 Hour Race 1964, Paddy Hopkirk sweeps through the esses in the MGB

Rear view of the 1964 Le Mans MGB, note the quick-lift jacking brackets

1964

Paddy was driving, and the car crossed the line having covered 2,392 miles at an average speed of 99.9 mph. The effort won them the *Motor* Trophy for the best placed all-British car/crew.

Wilson McComb was at Le Mans looking after BMC press matters and he was amused to read the conditions printed on his car sticker, which read as follows: 'For to be valid in the garage, this cartboard ought to be entirely glued on the windscreen. It cannot be selled under punishment of immediate shrinkage and judicial pursuits'.

Alpine Rally

Pauline Mayman had been recuperating well from her Monte accident and we were all pleased that she was fit to compete in the Alpine in a Mini Cooper S970, one of four S types entered along with an Austin Healey 3000 for the Morleys.

The main difference between Rauno's 1275 and the other cars, were the aluminium doors, bonnet and boot lid fitted to reduce weight; it was entered in Group III.

The team stayed at the Hotel Residence in the Vieux Port at Marseilles before the start. The mechanics had the habit of having lunch in a small cafe near the BMC garage where the patron looked after them well – too well on one occasion whe he offered round an alcoholic drink from a large bottle containing a fern leaf. This was real fire water and one or two of the mechanics did not do much work for the rest of that afternoon.

The weather was very hot and the service schedule was relentless, although kept within reasonable averages by Stuart for safety reasons. Stuart Turner was always very careful to ensure that his crews had reasonable schedules, although weather, traffic and rally car problems could upset the best laid plans.

One of my stops was near Sigale on a tight section, with very little room to work on a narrow road. When Paddy arrived he required new brake pads and linings and there was some delay getting one of the rear drums back on. The control was just up the road and as Henry Liddon started a count down, Paddy becoming worried that he would be penalised, shouting 'quick boys, my Coupe'. In their excitement, they shot off to the control with the rear wheel nuts finger tight.

Four of the 1964 Alpine Rally entry lined-up in the MG Car Co Ltd compound

Monte Magic

Dunlop R7 racing tyres throw up the dust, Paddy Hopkirk on the 1964 Alpine Rally

1964

My next stop with mechanics Brian and Robin was the night halt in Cannes, and after a drink we packed up the car and set off. Not many kilometres later we came round a corner to find a Mini Cooper rally car stopped beside the road, with the crew standing beside the car throwing stones down the mountain side. David Friswell was the driver and John Davenport co-driver and they gratefully accepted a tow, their car having broken its gearbox. Downhill all the way and coming into Grasse, the Mini driver hooted to indicate they wanted to stop. As we pulled up in the main street, I realised that both the Mini front brakes were on fire, and it took some time to put them out as the red hot discs continually ignited the leaking brake fluid.

taking the car out to Finland. I took the BUAF flight from Southend to Ostend and then drove to Puttgarden in Germany where I took the car ferry to Robyhaven in Denmark. The route was then to Helsingor where another ferry to Helsingborg brought me into Sweden.

At Stockholm the car was loaded on to a Bore Line ship, the rally car hanging rather precariously as it was crane loaded for the overnight voyage to Helsinki. The Mini shared the forecastle with the three-car Trabant team also on their way to the rally.

I was met by Timo

*The Morley brothers
Austin Healey 3000, 1964 Alpine Rally*

We continued towards Cannes with now only the handbrake on the Mini but this was becoming dangerous as the car kept catching us up so we had to abandon it on a garage forecourt.

Paddy retired, but at the finish both Rauno and Donald Morley were penalty free to win Coupes, the Morleys winning a Silver Coupe for three non-consecutive Coupes. Pauline and Val won the Ladies to celebrate their return to the fray, making it quite a good event for the team.

We did not send a full team to the 1000 Lakes, but Stuart arranged to supply a car for Timo and I was given the job of

and the Oy Voimavaunu AB service manager and the Mini was soon delivered safely to their premises. I was scheduled to fly home in the morning but as we left the garage Timo said he was going to practise some of the stages, would I like to go? We called at a friend's house and set off in a VW Variant 1600 estate for a stage, two hours drive from Helsinki. From the start of this stage the two Finns carried out a running commentary between themselves while hurtling through the darkness. My stomach did not like the jumps and I soon asked them to stop. Timo suggested I wait beside the road for a few minutes and they would come back and pick me up. The wait, sitting on a pile of logs in the pitch dark in total silence was a bit eery and it seemed to be ages before they came back. Timo's friend was in fact Hannu Mikkola, an up-and-coming driver who was competing in the

Monte Magic

rally in a Volvo, later also to become a world class driver.

Timo duly competed in the rally and with service asistance from Voimavaunu, came home fourth overall and class winner.

Special Tuning
The success of the Mini Cooper and now the S type was increasing the demand for special parts such as we were using on the works cars, and Stuart was well aware of the extra work that this was giving Neville Challis and his chaps in the stores. A number of discussions had been held concerning the supply of non-standard parts through BMC Service Ltd at Cowley, and agreement was reached for them to be channelled through BMC Service via a new department which would be formed at Abingdon.

In June, a circular was sent out to all overseas distributors headed 'BMC Parts for Special Tuning and Competitions'. This outlined the creation of a new department to be called the BMC Special Tuning Department which would be the supply point for competition parts, the source of technical information and would have a workshop where customers could pay to bring their cars to be prepared for competitions or just given improved road tuning.

The build-up would start in July and at that time Abingdon would become responsible for the stocking of such Formula Junior/Formula Three parts which were currently held at Cowley. Stuart's long term aim for the department was that it should generate sufficient profit to support a competitions programme, and in an ideal world, a self-supporting Competitions Department. (More about the Special Tuning Department in Chapter 8.)

In a way I was glad that the new Department was being formed as it would relieve me of the considerable task of dealing with the ever increasing volume of customer queries and requests for information, which although very interesting was having to take second place to my other duties, one of the most important still, being the preparation of FIA Homologation forms. It was not unusual to have as many as thirty letters waiting to be answered which was not fair to the customers who wanted to get on with their motor sport, and reflected badly on the department.

The preparation of the Homologation Forms took a lot of time if it was done accurately, because one could not rely on the accuracy of drawings, or spec sheets, it often being impossible to tell if the ones supplied were the latest. The only way was to take a new car and to actually strip down some parts and measure the actual metal; this was not popular with Doug and Tommy in the workshop when manpower was required to strip engines or space needed to take photographs, with a heavy car preparation schedule.

The Last Liège
The 1964 Liège was to be the last in the original form. The authorities in Germany and Austria had finally withdrawn their permission to allow the cars to speed through their territories

One of the first competitions parts brochures, 1964

1964

on public roads. I think we had all seen it coming and it was no surprise that this was to turn out to be the last of the great Lièges.

The entry was three Austin Healey 3000s, two MGBs and a lone Mini Cooper S for John Wadsworth and Mike Wood. Several Minis had tried to finish the event, among them David Hiam who this year was driving one of our old MGBs, 8 DBL, as a private entry.

Mk3 refuelling rig for the 1964 Spa-Sofia-Liège Rally

There were 98 starters this year and with a route of 3,000 miles, the average speed had been increased over many sections. For example, on the Perast to Stolac stage the time schedule for 1963 was six hours but this year the same section had to be done in 4¼ hours. This was also one of the roughest sections and Rauno was to lose twenty minutes on it.

I was teamed up with Tommy Eales and our first service point was at Villa Dont just over the border in Italy. It was what Stuart would call an emergency service point, because at this stage the cars had not done much serious motoring. Dunlop had sent one of their trucks from their Depot in Milan with a supply of SP tyres. It was late evening when the cars came through Villa Dont and the only surprising problem we had was with the Healey of Timo and Don Barrow. The rear tyres were down to the canvas. We soon had the wheels off, the Dunlop fitters quickly fitted up new covers, and Timo was away. I don't think Timo ever really liked the Liège and he was driving the car more to wear it out than to win!

Our next service point was in Sofia, Bulgaria, only 900 km away, which we set off for straight away, more or less non-stop to ensure we were there on time. Rooms had been booked at the Grand Balkan hotel, beside the control. We arrived with about five hours in hand, so we checked the bookings and took the opportunity to have a bath and a rest, having taken the precaution of bringing our own bath plugs.

We duly 'set up shop' near the control, in the middle of the dual carriageway which had been closed by the police for the rally, overlooked by thousands of spectators. The spectators were very well behaved and anyone who was foolish enough to put his or her feet off the kerb was likely to get a baton across the head! Only one or two other service cars from rival teams had ventured as far as Sofia but we each had our own policeman keeping his eye on us and our equipment and the crowd at a distance.

When the rally cars arrived at speed with their headlamps blazing it was fairly hectic. The main problem was the Mini Cooper S which had broken front sump shield mountings. This resulted in the leading edge scraping on the ground like a snow plough. We could take it off but knew that without it the car could not survive the next section. After a few minutes deliberation we decided to lash the front of the guard to the front bonnet platform with a towrope, which looked a bit unsightly but might do the job.

Mini Cooper S 1275 finishes the 1964 Spa-Sofia-Liège Rally, John Wadsworth and Mike Wood

After a quick rest in the hotel, with Tommy and me making sure that they did not oversleep, the crews were soon off towards Yugoslavia, each car leaving the control with a police escort in dramatic fashion, lights blazing and sirens wailing. The crowd loved it.

We immediately took off for our next stop which was to be up the Adriatic coast another 1,100 kilometres away. We were now feeling tired and despite stopping regularly to change drivers, we stopped on the Autoput south of Belgrade for a quick shut-eye. The road was new with no markings so we pulled off on to the dirt verge to avoid being run down by long-distance trucks. The next thing I remember was waking out of a deep sleep by a tapping noise. It was Jimmy Simpson of Castrol who had spotted our car and stopped thinking we had broken down. After a brief chat we carried on in convoy to our next stop.

We had not seen the two MGBs or Timo at Sofia because both had retired with clutch/gearbox problems caused by overheating due to the full length sump guards, while Timo had run out of tyres and retired to the nearest bar!

At Novi the remaining crews came through looking very tired and dusty where they were supplied with large quantities of glucose drink. Rauno was in the lead and, after changing tyres, etc, we sent him off with fingers crossed, realising that there was still a long way to go.

Rauno did not take 'wakey-wakey' pills and Tony Ambrose did quite a bit of the driving; on one section with 77 miles to do in 37 minutes, he had arrived at the control with only 15 minutes lateness, an average of 89 mph, not bad for a co-driver!

Rauno won the 1964 Spa-Sofia-Liège rally from Erik Carlsson (Saab) and Eugen Bohringer (Mercedes), a wonderful result. Tommy and I felt that we had done a Marathon as

127

Monte Magic

Paddy Hopkirk and Henry Liddon press on before retiring with gearbox problems, 1964 Spa-Sofia-Liège Rally

well with a total of 2,000 km between our three service points. Our only other finisher was, much to our delight, the Mini Cooper S which arrived home in twentieth position, the tow rope having done its job.

At the Motor Show, in September the Austin 1800 was announced fitted with the five-bearing crankshaft, 1798 cc transverse engine and Hydrolastic suspension. Hydrolastic suspension was also introduced on all Mini Saloons but not Vans and Travellers.

Before the announcement of Hydrolastic suspension on the Mini, Jack Daniels, Project Engineer at Longbridge, had loaned us a car (272 MOX) for assessment of the new suspension in rally conditions. Paddy had tested the car in France and reported that it was a bit bumpy on the northern French roads. Fitted with a 1071 S engine Timo and Donald Morley had tried it on fast pot-holed track but found that it bottomed-out too much.

Timo and Don Moore had then tried the car at Snetterton with no complaints and it was then returned to Longbridge where Jack Daniels had some modified units fitted. John Wadsworth and Rauno tried the car during a Liège recce with similar findings, the ground clearance sagging as the units became tired.

With modified suspension units again fitted, Rauno and Tony tested the car during a recce of the Tour de France and

Early Mini 850 Tuning Leaflet

Above Right: *Emergency service point, 1964 Spa-Sofia-Liège Rally*

Right: *Winners of the last 'Liège': Rauno Aaltonen and Tony Ambrose, Austin Healey 3000*

1964

Monte Magic

subsequently visited Longbridge to discuss the development of the suspension with Jack Daniels.

Further testing was carried out in Bramshill Forest, trying various pressure settings, settling on an optimum pressure of 290 psi. In October, another run at Bramshill with Paul Easter, Barrie Williams and John Wadsworth ended when the driveshaft couplings disintegrated, and John Wadsworth managed to tip 8 EMO on to its roof. These were the latest 'red spot' couplings, which seemed to indicate that the suspension was now working too well for the couplings, and Hardy Spicer units were fitted. Testing continued, with some runs at Andrew Hedges' farm where another fault occurred when the steering arms came loose. This was cured by careful lapping of the arm to the hub and wire-locking the bolts. The driveshafts were strengthened by fitting stronger constant velocity joints incorporating circlips which would need a four ton pull to separate the shaft and joint.

Tour de France

The entry for the Tour de France was four Mini Cooper Ss and a single MGB following the performance of the car in last years event. Rauno would drive a 1275 car, the other three being 970s now that this model was Homologated. One of the mods following our experience the previous year was to increase the size of the twin fuel tank interconnecting pipe to permit easy refuelling. With the small bore interconnecting pipe it was quite easy to leave a car only partly filled.

Timo heads Paddy, 1964 Tour de France Automobile

The start was from Lille where final scrutineering and final preparations were taking place. Just before the Tour, Paul Easter received an unexpected phone call from Diana Kirby, Stuart's secretary, asking if he could go on the Tour de France. Don Barrow was ill and would not be able to accompany Timo. Paul's unhesitating 'yes' was followed by instructions to come to Abingdon straight away, collect some money and some spare driveshafts, and then catch the 15.00 hrs flight to Paris followed by a local flight to Lille. There was no mention of a fee but at Abingdon he was told to account for the money he had been given.

Paul had already gained quite a lot of experience in his own Mini on continental rallies and had won his class on the 1963 Acropolis. Unfortunately Timo and Paul ended their rally prematurely near Grenoble. Paul was driving when a car came out of a side road, the collision sending the Mini into a kilometre stone. Paul felt sure that his first works drive was going to be his last.

The MGB suffered head gasket failure and despite Den Green's effort to patch it with plastic metal, the car was forced to retire. At Reims, John Wadsworth pushed another French competitor off the circuit without damage to either car. Paddy and Rauno also retired with mechanical trouble but Pauline Mayman was first in class with her regular co-driver Val Domleo.

When Paul got home he duly turned up at Abingdon to account for his expenses and was told he better keep the money as none of the other co-drivers ever had any money left over!

October and November were always very busy with Monte recces and preparation for the RAC and Monte Carlo rallies. This did not prevent Stuart from arranging two more driver test sessions, this time at Silverstone on 22 October and 4 November.

Tour de France Automobile 1964, Andrew Hedges/John Sprinzel set off in the Le Mans MGB

A fleet of seven cars was available, with Paddy Hopkirk, Timo Makinen, Donald Morley, Warwick Banks, Clive Baker, John Fitzpatrick, Andrew Hedges and John Moore invited to attend the first session. The track was damp in the morning but after lunch it dried out and virtually all the drivers had a go

1964

in each car. The cars were one race and one rally spec Austin Healey 3000, an MGB, a Sprite, a Midget, and 970 and 1300 Cooper Ss. It was a fairly hectic schedule to get through with each driver doing five flying laps, the results being quite interesting to study afterwards. Donald Morley did not produce any particularly quick times but Paddy was one of the fastest in each of the cars.

Lap times, 1964 Stuart Turner driver test day

The second test day included the Swedish rally driver Harry Kallstrom and one Jackie Stewart, an up-and-coming F3 driver. It is no surprise now to note that Mr Stewart was fastest in the two Healey 3000 cars, the MGB, the Mini with Hydrolastic suspension, and the F3 car which Ken Tyrell had sent along.

Rauno and Tony in Argentina

As a result of winning the Spa–Sofia–Liège rally, Rauno and Tony Ambrose received an invitation to compete in the Gran Premio d'Argentina, a 3000 mile road race from Buenos Aires to Cordoba, north to Salta near the border with Bolivia and then back to BA. The invitation came from Siam di Tella Automotores of Buenos Aires who manufactured under licence the di Tella Magnette, an MG Magnette fitted with a 1500 cc engine, with a 90 per cent local content. The event had been won for the last three years by Mercedes who once again entered with a full works team, including Ewy Roskvist and Eugen Bohringer. Rauno and Tony spent a very hot dusty two weeks covering the route only to miss the event when it had to be postponed because of floods.

The rescheduled event now was to finish only 26 hours before the start of the RAC, so there was no guarantee that they could get back in time and they had reluctantly to say adios and come home.

To attract increased media coverage, the RAC arranged to start the RAC Rally from London. With the co-operation of the Ministry of Defence the Duke of York's Barracks right in the heart of the capital was made available for the start and finish while Rally HQ was situated at the Kensington Palace hotel.

We had a large entry of eight cars, two of them in collaboration with BMC Sweden who had been very active with their own programme, managed by Bo Elmhorn. Their two cars were driven by Harry Kallstrom and Carl Orrenius. We had two Mini Cooper S for Paddy and Rauno, two Austin Healey 3000s for Timo and Donald Morley and an MGB each for racing driver John Fitzpatrick and Pauline Mayman.

The route went first to the West Country where the cars tackled a number of stages including Porlock Hill. The cars left London at 07.00 hrs and Timo went into an early lead with Paddy and Rauno also in the top six. We used a Lansing Bagnall fork lift truck to inspect the underside of our cars near Basingstoke, which attracted some attention. Into Wales, Tom Trana was closing on Timo and Harry Kallstrom was up to third followed closely by Paddy. Timo went off the road which

Monte Magic

The Morley brothers take the Liège winning Austin Healey 3000 through the forests, 1964 RAC Rally

Tony Ambrose testing a loop-aerial radio system at Silverstone

Pauline Mayman on a forest stage in the 1964 RAC Rally

1965

dropped him back and by the time the cars reached Oulton Park in the fog, Harry was in the lead. As the cars moved north to the breakfast halt at Turnberry it was foggy and the lead was now taken by Tom Trana in his Volvo. Pauline was having problems with the MG doors and was having to climb in through the windows until the mechanics could fix them.

When the cars reached Perth 50 had retired; Paddy hit a tree and was out and both Rauno and Pauline retired with mechanical trouble. By Barnby Moor, Harry Kallstrom had also gone out with a broken gearbox which was a pity as he had been disputing the lead at the time. One thing to emerge from Kallstrom's drive was the remarkable state of the underside of his car compared with some of the other Minis. Despite being one of the fastest drivers on the rally, and with the cars low ground clearance, it was difficult to understand how he had kept the car so undamaged. Harry's car incidentally was LHD, green with a white roof and was destined for BMC Sweden as one of their quota of export cars.

We had raised the suspension on the Minis front and rear, with packing washers in the struts not only to gain some ground clearance but to keep the suspension as level as possible to ease the load on the rubber driveshaft couplings.

The Morleys had an accident but managed to finish although only in 21st position while Timo did much better coming second overall behind Tom Trana's Volvo.

Nineteen Sixty-four had been a very good year indeed.

1965

1965 – Snowy Monte

After his experience of Paul Easter as co-driver, Timo told Stuart that he would like Paul again for the Monte. Stuart was not too keen because he had doubts whether Paul could handle the maps, his international experience having been mainly as a driver of his own car. Timo insisted and a fee of £50 was agreed for the Monte to see how things went between them. Timo had had trouble with co-drivers previously, but had quickly gained confidence in Paul, and although Stuart suggested that he ought to do a navigational recce of the main road route from their Stockholm start point, Paul declined. During the recce Timo, Paul and Henry Liddon tested three cars on part of the rally route to establish which spec would be most advantageous.

Modified number plate and number plate lamp on the Morris Mini Cooper S of Timo Makinen, 1965 Monte Carlo Rally

With two Finns in the team, discussions over studded tyres became long and complicated, each driver wanting his ideas to be taken up. Somehow their ideas had to be slotted into what Dunlop could accommodate and what was practicable. The decision was that two types were to be made by Rengas-Ala in Finland by having a special carcass moulded on brand new Dunlop covers to take special studs, named 'chisels' and 'spirals'. These tyres were larger in diameter and this had the effect of increasing the rolling resistance and

ground clearance, important in deep snow, and providing sufficient rubber to retain the studs. The more conventional studs were inserted into Dunlop Weathermaster tyres, with the design of the type of flange(s) causing most heart searching.

Aluminium wing extensions on one of the Group 3 1965 Monte Carlo Rally cars

In all, we carried almost 520 tyres out to France for the rally, including racing tyres for dry conditions. The work load was high, with two of the six Minis entered in Group III for Rauno and Timo. They were subjected to some extra hours work lightening the bodies as much as possible with aluminium doors, bonnet and boot and perspex side and rear windows. The rear seat pan and bulkhead looked like an egg rack with lightening holes, and all sound-deadening material was laboriously removed. The front grille was made out of an

Monte Magic

Austin Westminster grille with hand-rolled alloy wing extensions also fitted. Protection was added to the petrol tanks to prevent studded tyres wearing holes in them, and the two rear-mounting Lucas spot lamps were used as dip headlamps to permit the use of the latest quartz-iodine bulbs in the main headlamps. Power figures were taken on the rolling-road dynamometer at the end of B block, with Timo's car producing 75 bhp at 6,500 rpm at the front wheels.

Triplex had further developed the heated windscreens, the current being passed across the glass by fine vertical filaments instead of the gold film used on the earlier screens.

The team of service personnel totalled sixteen and they travelled in Westminsters and Morris Oxford Traveller service cars, plus the BMC transporter which had first seen service at the 1955 Le Mans.

I was at Gap with Johnny Organ to meet up later with Nobby Hall and the transporter. The first cars through Gap were the Athens starters due at 07.00 hrs but we became worried when Geoff Mabbs arrived in his privately entered Mini Cooper S to tell us that Rauno was runing late having had some electrical trouble, traced to the distributor.

When Rauno's time of arrival passed we decided to drive down the rally route in the faint chance that we might find them still in trouble, but after an hour they had still not passed so we reluctantly returned to Gap. The rally car eventually arrived well OTL much to their and our disappointment, the trouble having been finally traced to a loose

Paddy Hopkirk at speed on one of the dry stages, 1965 Monte Carlo Rally

We had spread the entries with Paddy and Timo starting from Stockholm, Rauno from Athens, the Brothers Morley and Raymond Baxter from Minsk in Russia and Harry Kallstrom from Paris.

Rauno's car for Athens was taken down to Marseilles in company with Geoff Mabbs where the cars were loaded on the ferry. One of the mechanics travelled on the ferry with the cars while Geoff flew to Athens, meeting the ferry with the co-drivers when it eventually arrived.

The two cars for Minsk were shipped to Gdynia with a mechanic, the two Stockholm cars were shipped to Sodertalje unaccompanied and Harry Kallstrom's car was taken to the Paris start by the mechanics.

condensor. They decided to stay in Gap and carry out a recce of the next stage before the cars came through, to advise the crews on tyre choice.

Back at the hotel there was a message from Stuart to collect some 'chisels' (deep snow tyres) from Castellane, and because the only vehicle which could carry them was the transporter, I decided to go myself to collect them, leaving the skilled men in Gap in case I did not get back in time. The roads were dry and frosty and I returned by about 17.00 hrs with the tyres, just as a few snow flakes started to fall.

By 18.00 hrs it was snowing hard and by 22.00 hrs there was 6 inches of level snow in the town. The full rally was due through at 22.40 and Nobby and I were in the back of the transporter trying to keep warm with a Camping Gaz stove. When an hour had passed after the first car was due we feared that there had been a major blockage of the route.

Suddenly out of the quiet night we heard the unmistakable sound of one of our cars, which arrived in a flurry of snow and blazing headlamps. It was Timo in car No 52, which we fitted with new front tyres, refuelled and sent him quickly on his way.

Austin 1800 driven by Courtenay Edwards, Tommy Wisdom and John Sprinzel press on through the snow, 1965 Monte Carlo Rally

Where was the rest of the field? Cars began to trickle through and we were glad when it was time to go inside to thaw out and go to bed. We later learned that only 35 cars arrived in Monte within the scheduled time limit, five of them being Abingdon-prepared cars.

We had borrowed a transporter from the Cooper Car Co Ltd which was scheduled to come through to Gap with Den Green and three of the mechanics, but the snow had given them problems. Between Grenoble and Gap they became stuck on a hill, and as the heavy Albion slid back down the road with the wheels locked, it was only one of the Lancia service vans, also stuck, which saved it from going over the edge. During this manoeuvre, Den suddenly realised that the cab was empty, his 'co-drivers' having jumped out.

After a 200 km detour, they made their way towards Nice, but near Marseilles, the cab filled with steam and shortly afterwards the engine seized. A phone call to Monte brought the Castrol publicity coach out to collect some of the vital studded tyres, while part of the load was collected by a passing Dunlop truck. After the rally we apologised to Ray Simpson for the damage the spiked tyres had caused to the upholstery.

Two of the BMC cars to get through the snow to Monte were the Austin 1800s also prepared at Abingdon, these being the *Sunday Telegraph*-sponsored car and the ITN car which had been prepared in Special Tuning. Of our retirements, Harry Kallstrom had clutch failure, while Raymond Baxter never made the start because his car blew its engine on the way from Gdynia to Minsk. Despite our efforts combined with those of Dan Daley of MAT Transport, we could not get a flight plan authorised through the Russian Embassy to send out a new engine.

With the surviving cars at Monte and only the Mountain Circuit to go, Timo was in the lead (112 m 11 s) followed by a Citroen (120 m 19 s) and a Porsche 904 third (127 m 40 s), a margin of eight minutes, which seemed unassailable, but even with 400 miles and six stages to complete nothing is certain; to win you must cross the finish line!

The overnight halt was very welcome and the next day was occupied sorting out and loading the tyres, checking the service vehicles, refuelling, etc. My schedule took me to Beuil on the Mountain Circuit with Nobby Hall to man an emergency service point after Stages 3 and 5. It was a cold frosty night with the usual horde of spectators, some of whom had found some wood and had a nice fire going beside the road. The only car to stop with us was the ITN Austin 1800 driven by John Fitzpatrick, asking us to check the brakes which had been fading badly. There was no fluid leak, and the front pads were good so he was soon gone. What we did not know was that about 10 kilometers down the gorge, the brakes faded so badly that the car went over the edge into a ravine, the car landing on its side, with happily only slight injuries to the crew.

Timo had to replace the points on his car which he and Paul managed in about four minutes (you try it in four minutes!), but even so he was fastest on five out of the six stages to win comfortably. There was still the trauma of scrutineering to face, but we were confident that the cars would not be found to contravene the regulations. The Morley brothers had broken a driveshaft but were still classified 27th and Paddy won his class. This result was well received at Longbridge and George Harriman sent instructions that a party was to be laid on for the team and the trade support personnel who had assisted with the effort.

Norman Higgins and Les Lambourne were sent out to represent John Thornley, travelling first class to Nice, unaware that Alec Issigonis was on the same flight, travelling tourist! At the airport, there was a mix up over the car for Alec, and somehow Norman and Les ended up going to Monte in the car, having to keep a low profile for the remainder of the weekend.

There was a tremendous party at the Pirate, where two of the highlights were Doug Watts riding a donkey round the tables and the sight of Alec Issigonis and Geoff Mabbs balancing on the floodlit rocks beside the restaurant, swaying to the music, gin and tonic clasped tightly in their hands, looking as though they would fall in the water at any moment.!

Next day we organised the recovery of the 1800, with two mechanics going out with a recovery truck to winch the car up the side of the ravine.

Just before the prize-giving ceremony, attended by Prince Rainier and Princess Grace of Monaco, there was a panic when the winning car would not start. The trouble was traced to the fibre insulating washer missing from the moving point in the distributor, left out when Paul and Timo changed the points during the rally. It is a mystery why the car ran at all with this part missing.

The win created tremendous publicity at home, there being appearances on the London Palladium, the TV Trophy, a road test by Roger Bell of *Motor* magazine at MIRA, and one car going on display at the Racing Car Show at Olympia.

The BBC staged another Mini Monte for television, this

Monte Magic

Timo supervised by Paul and the MG Transport Department, squeeze the winning car into the hotel, 1965 Monte Carlo Rally (A. G. Goodchild)

1965

Timo and Paul honoured by Oy Voimavaunu Ab in Helsinki after winning the 1965 Monte Carlo Rally

year held on a frozen lake in an Estate owned by Saab in Sweden. Brian Moylan and me took two Mini Cooper S rally cars to the event, driving through Belgium, Germany and Denmark in very cold weather conditions. Raymond Baxter was commentator for the programme which I am sure made very good viewing for the enthusiasts at home.

Stuart had a meeting with Paul and asked him if he would do the rest of the year with Timo for a fee of £150, treble the Monte fee, which he agreed to do. Arrangements between drivers and the Company were changing, gone were the days of the 'old boys network and friend of the team manager' situation and, although it was not until Paddy won the 1964 Monte that he was paid a retainer, Norman Higgins shudders today when he recalls that the Flying Finns were being paid retainers in the region of three times Stuart Turner's salary plus a loan car for the year.

Rauno Aaltonen in the snow on the 1965 Swedish Rally before transmission problems

Production of the Mini Cooper S 970 stopped in January, the required number of cars having been manufactured to comply with the Homologation requirements, and also because it was now competing in the showrooms with the 998 cc-engined Mini Cooper which replaced the 997 cc model.

An entry of four cars on the Swedish Rally ended in a disaster with all four cars retiring with differential failure due to a lubrication problem thought to be caused by the intense cold. Before the cars arrived at Gothenburg one of them was suffering from inconsistent clutch operation thought to be failure of the crankshaft thrust washers, so as a precaution, I flew out to Gothenburg with a balanced crank/flywheel assembly under my arm, which did not amuse the Swedish Customs very much.

137

Monte Magic

MG Midget Coupé

One project undertaken by the MG Development Department under Syd Enever which was eventually to be of benefit to the Competitions Department, was the construction in 1962 of three MG Midget Coupés. The shape of the aluminium bodies was developed from wind tunnel tests with the structure based on the steel production Midget floorpan. The aluminium panels were assembled using a combination of epoxy resin and rivets, the final weight being over 300 lb lighter than a production Midget. Two of the cars were loaned to Dick Jacobs who raced them successfully mainly in club events, but at the end of 1964 they were returned to the factory where we took them over and prepared them for the 12 Hour Race at Sebring. We prepared two MGBs in addition to the Midgets and the Donald Healey Motor Co prepared two Sprites and an Austin Healey 3000.

which the locals had not seen before. Within minutes the track and pits were under water, but to everyone's amazement the race was not stopped.

The cars crept round with some drivers having to lean out of the door to see where they were going. Timo found that he had about four inches of water in the car, and as it surged up and down inside, he was obliged to open the door each lap on one particular corner, to allow some to pour out. Our 'rally' drivers went particularly well during this period, one of the Sprites making up two laps on the overall race leaders, while in the pits conditions were chaotic, with spare wheels actually floating about.

Al Pease in one of the MGBs was pushed off the track and later lost some time when the battery cable failed as the result of the first incident. Darkness had fallen by the time the race finished and the BMC cars had between them won three

Loading the 1965 Sebring cars at Abingdon for shipment to Florida

classes and come second in two others; a good result.

At Sebring, Stuart looked after the MGs with Tommy Wellman, and Geoff Healey looked after the Healeys with Roger Menadue while timekeeping was under the control of Peter Browning.

At 10.00 hrs the race got under way, everything going to schedule for the first 4½ hours, with the MGBs changing drivers and refuelling at 2½ hour intervals. The sky then darkened and the heavens opened with a storm the like of

Luckily the Circuit of Ireland did not clash with Sebring so Paddy was available to compete with local co-driver, Terry Harryman. The rally started in Bangor, Co. Down and Paddy soon took the lead from Vic Elford in a works Cortina GT. By the time the cars reached Killarney for the overnight halt, Paddy had lost his lead, but on the Sunday Run, as the run out from Killarney was called, Paddy used racing tyres and was faster by 16 seconds than the next fastest car on Molls Gap stage. Having regained the lead, with the help of Terry's local experience, Paddy held on to gain outright victory to win the

1965

Gallaher Trophy, the *Autosport* Trophy, and the Londonderry Trophy for first in class.

The schedule was very full and we were still on this winning streak. The extreme weather experienced on the Monte continued for some time and entrants on the Tulip Rally had to contend with some unseasonal snow and ice. The two

Paddy Hopkirk almost brushes the rock face on his way to victory, 1965 Circuit of Ireland Rally

car entry was repeated, with Timo in Mini Cooper S and the Morley brothers in a new Austin Healey 3000 Mk III (DRX 257C). The Healey was fitted with auxilliary headlamp pods inboard of the main headlamps, hand made by Billy Wilkins in the MG panel shop. We also were supporting the entry of Julien Vernaeve in a works spec privately-owned Mini Cooper S; Julien had previously competed on the Alpine rally with none other than Jacky Ickx as co-driver.

At the first of the nineteen stages at the Nürburgring, Timo was fastest followed by the Sunbeam Tiger of Peter Harper, then the big Healey. As the rally moved south, the battle for the fastest times was between our two drivers, the bad weather having seen the cancellatioin of the Ballon

The Morley brothers on Zandvoort circuit, 1965 Tulip Rally

d'Alsace stage with two others shortened. Clever distribution of studded tyres by Stuart had given our cars an advantage, and by the time the cars were at Zolder, the two Mini Cooper Ss and the big Healey were occupying the front three places on times. However, with the class improvement system being used again, the final placings gave Timo third and the Morleys eighth position overall. A disappointing result, but once again the cars had demonstrated their speed and reliability.

Monte Magic

Luxembourg Slalom

We had been invited by Charles Saviola, the Morris Dealer, to send a car over to Luxembourg for the International Slalom which took place the weekend that the Tulip finished. Paddy was asked to represent BMC and I took the Mini Cooper S (CRX 89B) over for the event, meeting Paddy off the plane in Luxembourg.

The course was laid out with straw bale markers in a large car park, with practice taking place on the Saturday. On Sunday Timo and Julien Vernaeve arrived with their rally cars, fresh from their Tulip success, and gave demonstration runs in the morning session, in the wet, attended by big crowds.

The event proper started with a parade of the top drivers marching behind their national flags; Timo looking a little lonely, being the only Finn taking part. Safety precautions were a little lacking and would have given the RAC a few grey hairs, and unfortunately there was an accident at the crowded finish line when a Porsche 904 ran into some spectators resulting in at least one broken leg.

Paddy did his stuff with two spectacular runs winning the saloon car category and finishing seventh overall behind such cars as a Brabham F1 machine!

Special Tuning Manager

Shortly after returning to Abingdon, Stuart had a chat with me about the job of Special Tuning manager, the position shortly to become vacant with the departure of Glyn Evans. I was asked to go up to John Thornley's office where John offered me the job. This was a surprise and I was given the weekend to think it over. I came to the conclusion that I really wanted to carry on at the 'sharp end' and not, as I put it to John Thornley on Monday morning, just a parts manager (with due respect to parts managers). I declined the offer and was asked if I could recommend anyone within the company who could do the job. Before Special Tuning was formed, I had developed a good relationship with Basil Wales of Product Problem Liaison at Cowley where he was the sports car specialist dealing with technical problems from the dealers. As a result, Basil was approached by John Thornley and accepted the job of Manager of Special Tuning.

1965 Targa Florio

It is a long journey to take cars to Sicily but the entry on the Targa Florio turned out to be worth the trip. An Austin Healey 3000 Mk III for Timo and Paul Hawkins and an ex-Dick Jacobs MG Midget for Paddy and Andrew Hedges were entered, and the Donald Healey Motor Co sent an open prototype Austin Healey Sprite.

There were 59 starters for the race over the 45 mile lap road circuit. Doug Watts supervised the pit team. During practice, Castrol put a film cameraman in Timo's Healey to get some footage for the film they were making of the race. The race started off for our cars without any major dramas, until the Healey stopped about 2 miles from the pits with a broken rotor arm. Paul was driving and he ran back to the pits to collect a new rotor (unaware that there was a spare in the car). When he found out that there was a spare in the car, I think the pit crew learned a few new Australian words! It was particularly annoying to have this breakage as the car was leading a

Targa Florio 1965, Paddy Hopkirk in the pits with the MG Midget Coupé

1965

Monte Magic

Ferrari GTO in the class at the time, but Paul's athletic efforts brought the car home second in class to a GTO.

Apart from a spin, Paddy and Andrew went well in the Midget but could not get in front of a fast Abarth Simca; they also finished second in their class.

As soon as the Castrol film was finished, the editor wanted to fill in some missing sound track of the section taken with Timo and also Paddy's spin that they had been fortunate (?) enough to catch. I spent a session with Peter Browning watching and timing the gear changes on screen and then I drove one of the Austin Healey 3000s up White Horse Hill and along the Oxford By-Pass with the sound recordist and Peter jammed in the car trying to simulate the correct gear changes. To record the MG spin, I did a number of reverse spins with the MG Midget Coupé in the MG car park, and when the final version of *Mountain Legend* was screened it was difficult to spot the dubbed sound.

Acropolis Fire

Despite some unsuccessful attempts to win the Acropolis, Stuart decided to have another go with a lone entry for Timo and Paul Easter in a Mini Cooper S. Stuart took just one 'barge' with Gerald Wiffen and Pete Bartram, having the misfortune to crash the service car at about half distance.

Dramas began fairly early on with first the exhaust falling off then the carpets catching fire in the front footwell.

Acropolis Rally 1965, Timo's car just before a small fire during welding operations

Later, as the car arrived to catch the ferry at Patras, the driveshaft couplings were rapidly disintegrating, but Paul, who is no mean mechanic, soon had the car on its side on the ferry changing the couplings, while Timo, who thought that their rally was now over, had retired to the bar. The captain of the ferry was very irate when petrol started to drip into the bilges but by now Paul had the car mobile again, although with the sump guard pushed into the back of the car. He dragged a reluctant Timo out of the bar, managing to get the sump guard back on with the help of Castrol's Jimmy Simpson at the next control. With one stage to go Timo was now leading the rally, but then one of the trailing arm brackets broke causing the tyre to wear through on the bodywork.

Stuart was now again mobile and was at the next service point where the car was turned on its side for a welding repair. Unfortunately, in the rush, the dripping petrol ignited and the car went up in flames. As Timo dived in to save his wallet, Paul found himself being dragged without ceremony behind a nearby stall by a shopkeeper. The fire was put out and repairs made to get the car mobile, but unfortunately the heat had caused one carburettor to stop working and, although they were able to set off, the engine petered out before they could reach the next control.

Guards 1000 Race

An interesting event which we became involved with was the cigarette company-sponsored race at Brands Hatch, with £1,000 going to the overall winner. It was run in two parts of 500 miles (189 laps) each, with an overnight rest during which

1965

time competitors could take their cars away and rebuild them if necessary. It had been planned to run the event in the dark but as planning permission was refused this scheme had to be abandoned.

The idea was to attract amateur drivers in near standard sports and GT cars. Two of our cars were entered (an MGB and an Austin Healey 3000) by Don Moore who prepared the MGB engine.

Warwick Banks/John Rhodes were teamed up in the MGB with Paddy Hopkirk/Roger Mac in the Healey. Paddy was initially scheduled to drive the MGB but told Don that he did not think that it could win against Jaguar E-types etc, and managed to persuade Stuart to make a Healey available.

Scrutineering caused a few competitors problems when the officials had a clamp-down on the regulation which stated that the full width of the tyre should be covered by the bodywork over at least one third of its circumference. Many entrants had to fit 'ears' to their wings to make their cars comply. We sent a small team of mechanics down to Brands to look after the cars, which brought the comment in one of the motor magazines after the race that the two cars had 'works' written all over them. I suppose this was a little unfair to the genuine private entrants who were hoping to achieve success without 'works' cars to compete against.

The race began with a rolling start behind a Ford Mustang Pace car driven by Roy Pierpoint with the Morgan of Chris Lawrence going into an early lead. The MGB was going well with the Healey up to second overall when it threw a rear tyre tread; this was quickly changed and the car continued at unabated speed.

At about half distance Paddy was shown the Black Flag when the observers spotted a rear wheel about to collapse. Paddy had already noticed the lack of rear end stability and

The Don Moore prepared MGB driven by Warwick Banks/John Rhodes wins the 1965 Guards 1000 Race at Brands Hatch

was just coming in to the pits anyway. The car had more wheel spoke trouble and later Don called Paddy in for a change of brake pads when it became obvious that he was losing his brakes. As soon as the wheels were off the problem was obvious with the pads completely gone and the caliper pistons punched through the pad backplates. This gave Doug Watts and Nobby a few difficult minutes sorting out the brakes but the car was soon back in the race. At the end of the 189-lap first part, the MGB had come first followed by a private MGB driven by Anita and Trevor Taylor. The 'Don Moore' team retired to the BMC dealer's workshop on the South Circular road where the only major items changed were a new clutch for the 'B' and new shock-absorbers for the Healey. The overnight hotel at Blackheath was a bit of a 'flea-pit' and we were glad to get back to Brands in the morning for the second part of the race.

Paddy fought his way up through the field after the earlier delay while the MGB had a brief stop with a leaking oil filter. The Healey suffered more spoke collapses while the Banks/Rhodes car was now battling with the Taylor family's car, which in turn was suffering from overheating.

At the end of the Guards 1000, the Don Moore MGB was declared overall winner with a race aggregate of seven laps more than the next car, and the Healey coming fourth overall, once again proved the reliability of the cars. It was a great result for Don who had built the winning car and, accordingly, took all the publicity. Don had already had a long, happy association with Abingdon and there is no doubt that he was one of the most meticulous and knowledgeable engine specialists in the country with his expertise going back before the days of Lister Jaguars, for which Don built the engines.

Paul Easter described the 1965 Scottish Rally as a 'Liège with thistles', the dry hot weather and rough stages causing havoc with many cars. Timo and Paddy were entered in Healey and Mini respectively and were front runners from the start. The Healey was soon in trouble with the sump guard

Monte Magic

The privately entered 'works' MG Midget in the pits for the 1965 Nürburgring 1000 Km Race

Timo Makinen on the limit in the 1965 Scottish Rally

1965

ripped off, and despite heroic welding repairs on more than one occasion, a spare had to be sent up from Abingdon. Paul recalls this rally as a battle to keep the sump guard on, interspersed with demon stage driving by Timo. This was one of the most exciting drives he had ever had because time and again Timo regained the lead. By half way all their efforts came to nought when the final drive pinion sheared; Paddy also retired with a broken gearbox.

works entries in a rally in Czechoslovakia where no BMC cars were exported, except the odd one privately, and where there were no dealers. One good 'competition' reason was that the Rallye Vltava was a round of the European Championship in which our cars were doing quite well, and this was an opportunity to gain some points, with the probability of little serious opposition. We had not bargained, however, for an entry of two Lancias for Rene Trautmann and Giorgio Pianta.

Brothers Morley start the 1965 Geneva Rally

The next question was: could we make it three in row at Le Mans with the MGB? The engine was more or less the same spec as before and the streamlined nose again came into use. Tommy Wellman looked after the mechanicals with Gerald Wiffen and the MG garage loaned Mike English to drive the loaned Cooper Car Co transporter. This was the year of the Rover-BRM gas turbine car and despite another reliable run, the MGB was pipped by the Rover for the *Motor* Trophy, finishing second in Class and eleventh overall at an average speed of 98.26 mph.

Our winning ways continued with a convincing win by Rauno on the Geneva Rally with the Morley brothers first in the GT category.

Behind the Curtain

Rallying behind the Iron Curtain? Well as far as BMC was concerned, there was not much of a marketing reason for

The two cars for Timo and Rauno differed in that Timo was using the old rubber cone suspension with Rauno favouring the Hydrolastic system. The engines were running at a compression ratio of 11.2:1 despite the low grade fuel available for the rally, with two 1½ inch carburettors. Both cars used the 4.26:1 final drive ratio and we were using Lucas alternators with a remote external control box. Few production cars were fitting alternators at this time.

The rally start and finish was at the town of Liberec in the north of Czechoslovakia near the border with Poland.

The main party with the rally and service cars crossed the border into Czechoslovakia near Nurnberg in West Germany, experiencing for the first time the Iron Curtain with its visa controls, armed guards and vehicle searches. The sight of the double row of high barbed-wire fences, with the no-mans land strip behind, made one very aware that life for the population beyond was very different to our own.

At Liberec we met up with the crews, Timo/Paul and Rauno/Henry plus Julien Vernaeve who was driving his own car with support from Abingdon. That night we had a session

Monte Magic

in the bar in the basement of the hotel and were a little surprised in the morning how many empty vodka bottles were standing on the table!

In the absence of a garage, the mechanics checked the cars over outside on the verge opposite the hotel, with the drivers giving them a thorough test to iron out any last minute snags.

Bill Price looks under the bonnet of the winning car, 1965 Rallye Vltava

We were just about to pack up for the day when Rauno found that his car would not start. Thinking that the battery lead was not tight he opened the boot lid to be met by flames. There was a moment of panic while someone grabbed an extinguisher, but the flames kept re-igniting from what appeared to be a short circuit. Timo found a screwdriver, and while the flames were doused with a CO_2 extinguisher, he managed to disconnect the battery. We found that the battery cable, routed inside the car, had chafed through where it passed from the boot into the passenger compartment. This was adjacent to the main petrol pipe, and the heat generated by the short had melted the pipe allowing petrol from the two tanks to start filling the boot.

This had happened because we had carried spare wheels/tyres on the back seat from Abingdon, and the weight bouncing on the cable had done the damage. We were very lucky it had occurred where it did; had it happened with only the driver on board the car would probably have been lost. Scrutineering next day was mainly involved with stamping the set number of wheels that each car could use during the rally, a regulation that found little favour, mainly on safety grounds.

Servicing was banned with the exception of the replenishment of oil, water and fuel and cleaning of the windscreen, so we were aware that any mechanical repairs would inevitably result in some cloak-and-dagger operations! I was using a one-off Westminster prototype estate car loaned from Longbridge where it had been built with a view to putting it into production.

The rally started with a race round the streets of Liberec which was a bit hairy with large crowds lining the pavement edges. Map reading was difficult with the local maps (particularly when used to OS or Michelin) and it was as much as we could do to keep to our service schedule, mainly for refuelling and minor adjustments.

The Lancias put up some strong opposition to Rauno who was holding a slender lead while Timo had retired after about 300 km and Julien Vernaeve hit a tree bending his car but not himself.

The rally returned to Liberec for a final five lap race round the street circuit again, which Rauno won comfortably to put himself beyond the reach of the second- and third-placed Lancias. It was a good result in a nice country with, mainly, friendly natives. There was a men-only prize-giving and banquet after the rally where Rauno was presented with, among other things, some very nice locally manufactured cut glass.

Timo had been pestering Stuart for some time to get him a British driving licence and we managed to arrange this in July in Oxford. Stuart had taken the precaution of sending Timo out with Harry Shillabeer of the BMC Advanced Driving School at Abingdon before the test. On the morning of the test, I took Timo into Oxford in an MG 1100 and Timo duly acquired his British licence. He needed the licence to be able to drive British-registered cars in Finland without having to have them re-registered. A number of times Abingdon-built cars had run in the 1000 Lakes with Finnish number plates to comply with local regulations.

Roll Out the Barrel

Our next event was done at the request of the local importer of Austin cars in Germany, A. Bruggemann & Co of Dusseldorf. This was the Nordrhein-Westfalen rally based in Cologne for which we entered an MGB for Andrew Hedges and a Mini Cooper S for Paddy; I was sent over with Tommy Wellman and Robin Vokins in a Westminster to look after service arrangements.

The MGB for the 1965 Nordrhein-Westfalen Rally near Abingdon

There were nine special stages plus five laps of the Nürburgring and ten laps of Zolder in Belgium, Andrew being fastest on the former with Paddy fastest on the remainder of the tests. We found that the organisation was not up to international standard with controls very difficult to find; at times it was more like a treasure hunt.

At a lunch halt in the middle of a forest we had a look at Paddy's engine which seemed down on power; after advancing the ignition, Tommy tried the car down the road which is not really the thing to do in the middle of an international rally. Paddy was by this time a bit fed up, but found that the engine was now back on song. Unhappily this was not enough to overcome the handicap formula which decided the results, with Paddy sixth overall and Andrew eleventh.

The dinner and prize-giving was quite good with Paddy being given a special mention for his performance during the rally (which would have given him victory on scratch!). One of the prizes presented to the team was a barrel of local beer which we proceeded to roll down the steps of the banqueting hall and back to our hotel; it survived the journey back to Abingdon where the lads made short work of it.

Next on the agenda was the Alpine for which were entered three Mini Cooper Ss and an Austin Healey 3000 Mk III plus another S prepared for Pauline Mayman by Special Tuning. Pauline had retired from regular participation in international rallies at the end of 1964 but was determined to have a go at a hat-trick of Ladies wins on the Alpine.

1965

Timo was favouring the rubber cone suspension again whilst the other cars were fitted with Hydrolastic, incorporating the 'red spot' units. To help with the overheating problems, the Minis were also using the six-bladed fan specified for some export markets, and the cars were running on Dunlop R7 racing tyres. When Timo's car was tested on the rolling-road dynamometer, Cliff recorded a maximum power output of 84 bhp at 6,800 rpm, with the other cars giving similar figures.

Pauline Mayman/Val Domleo hotly pursued by Timo Makinen, 1965 Alpine Rally

The team travelled down to the south of France on the wagons-lits car sleeper from Boulogne to Avignon which left a relatively short drive to Marseilles. The rally went quite well with Pauline achieving her ambition to win the Ladies cup, but there was disappointment for Rauno when a brief navigational error lost him the chance of a Gold Cup for three consecutive Coupes, while Timo missed his Coupe by 1.7 seconds.

The Morley brothers had fan belt trouble and some broken spokes which kept them down to second in the GT category, but unusually for an Alpine, we achieved a 100 per cent finishing record to win the Manufacturer's Team prize.

One very impressive performance worth mentioning was by a private entrant, Tony Fall, competing in his first continental rally and winning a Coupe. The rally itself ended in controversy when the leading Sunbeam Tiger was disqualified for having valves of a size (too small) not listed on the Homologation Form, leaving a rather red-faced Marcus Chambers without a well deserved win.

Success at Zakopane

The success of the trip to Czechoslovakia persuaded Stuart to send a single car to Poland for the Polish Rally, a qualifier for the European Championship in which Rauno was now well placed. I think Stuart must have considered that I was the Eastern Bloc 'expert', or perhaps stayed behind, perforce, because he had learned Russian during National Service and was thus considered a security risk?

I travelled out with Den Green and Brian Moylan in company with a Castrol service car on the Transport Ferry Service from Felixstowe to Rotterdam. Our destination was Zakopane, a ski resort close to the border with Czechoslovakia. We crossed the Iron Curtain from Vienna into Czechoslovakia at Bratislava, the border crossing seeming just as daunting as last time, being characterized by long delays

Monte Magic

while our visas were checked, searches and the compulsory exchange of currency. We were stopped for speeding soon after leaving the border by police using radar, the last thing we expected the police to be using, but were let off with a caution.

Zakopane is a very nice town with a spectacular ski-jump, though very green at the time of our visit. We were fortunate to have the assistance of Marek Wachowski, a motoring journalist from Warsaw who had some business connections with Castrol, and who had imported one or two Mini Coopers from England. He really was a Mr Fixit, seeming able to arrange anything from getting hold of an electric welder to arranging for a 'friend' of the police to travel in the Castrol service car during the rally. Brian went in the Castrol car while Den and I used the Westminster, giving us two service cars for the rally. We had trouble with the maps again which were very inaccurate, and after some careful checking, found that the names of some of the towns had been interchanged.

At one test held on the airfield at Krakow, Rauno had the unfortunate experience of scalding his arm when the radiator cap blew off unexpectedly while he was checking the level, leaving him with a painful and bandaged arm for the rest of the rally. Den and I also had a problem when we lost the main part of the exhaust during the first night, having to lash it to the roof rack, the Westminster now sounding like a full blown racing car.

Rauno nurses his scalded arm after winning the 1965 Polish Rally

On the second day our route took us past the site of the infamous Auschwitz concentration camp, now preserved as a museum. With half-an-hour to spare we decided to have a look round – this was partly, I suppose, through morbid curiosity, but I would like to think also to pay homage to the courage of the countless persons who had lost their lives in the camp. There was an unreal atmosphere; it being very quiet with no sign of any form of wildlife. Some of the huts retained the three-tier bunks used by the inmates, and in other buildings behind glass partitions, there were samples of the personal belongings removed from the prisoners when they arrived. I think what really brought home the horror of what had happened was to see the suitcases, many with names and addresses marked on them, and the piles of spectacles, artificial legs, shoes, and so on; an unforgettable experience.

Rauno's main opposition was coming from Erik Carlsson and Pat Moss, both in Saabs, Rene Trautmann in the Lancia and Zasada in the tiny 660 cc Steyr Puch. The results were decided on a handicap system where, for example, the Steyr Puch had an advantage of 6 per cent over the Mini Cooper S and 8 per cent over the Lancia. By 09.00 hrs on the Saturday the last special stage had been completed after a very wet night, but the organisers route took the cars back to Zakopane by such a devious route that they did not arrive at the finish until 16.30 hrs. Despite both the handicap system and his painful arm, Rauno had gone fast enough to win; another good result behind the Curtain.

The black market in foreign currency was fairly widespread in hotels and resturants, but we had been warned by Marek to be careful who we spoke to if approached by persons wanting to change foreign currency. Needless to say, before we left Poland we went shopping in Zakopane to use up some of the Slotys we could not take out of the country, Polish vodka being quite cheap!

Home ground for the Flying Finns and a tremendous result on the 1000 Lakes with the three cars used on the Alpine rally coming first, second and sixth overall (Timo, Rauno and Paddy in that order). A very good result for Paddy and one of the highest positions to be attained by a Brit on the event.

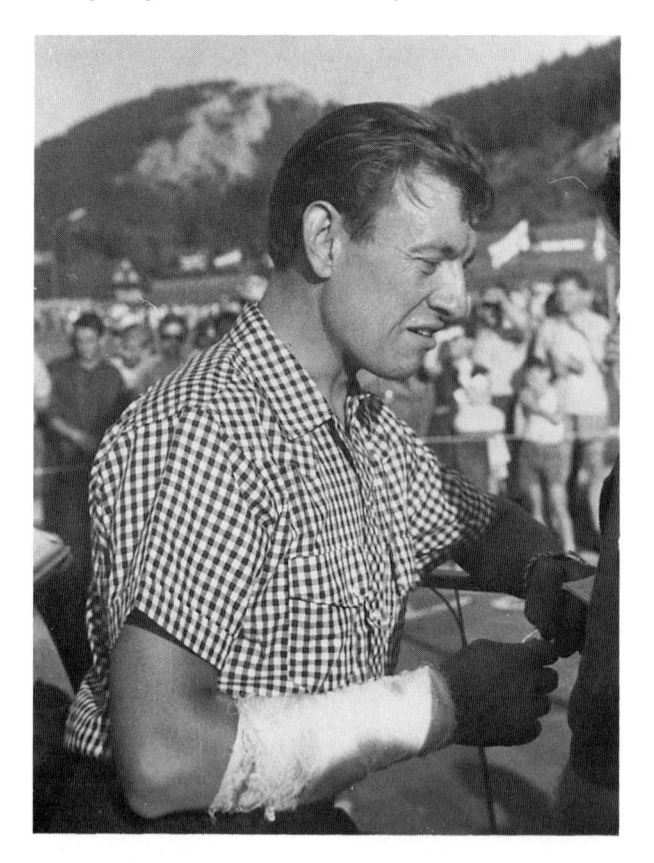

The Three Cities

The prospects of winning the European Championship were looking good and with very few qualifying events left on the calendar, it was almost inevitable that we would enter the Munich–Vienna–Budapest rally (or Three Cities). When the regulations arrived it was seen that the results were to be decided on a controversial class improvement system. To give Rauno every chance, Stuart asked two private owners if they would enter their cars in the same class, acting under BMC team orders. Paul Easter entered his car while the second privateer was Tony Fall, who was already starting to make a name for himself. With Paddy away on a BMC world tour, Henry Liddon partnered Paul and Ron Crellin went with Tony. No official service was permitted so Paul's car became the 'service car' carrying tools, spares and tyres as well as, at times, 20 gallons of fuel. They carried either Weathermasters or racers depending on the stages and resorted to the usual cloak-and-dagger operations such as hiding in field gateways or behind buildings to effect a tyre change or refuel. Despite their weight handicap Paul finished well up and with enough margin to give Rauno a win, finishing as a member of the winning team as well. The points situation now meant that the RAC would definitely decide the Championship.

1965

At about this time we were taking delivery of new cars for the Monte Carlo Rally in January, and with the introduction of a new revised Appendix J, from the regulations it became clear that cars complying with the new Group 1 were going to have an advantage.

Stuart Turner directs Rauno Aaltonen/Tony Ambrose during the 1965 Three Cities Rally

Working in the MG factory one naturally knew when a new MG model was about to be launched. The Earls Court Show was the time to announce the MGB GT, mechanically similar to the Tourer, but with the Salisbury type rear axle replacing the original banjo type.

Although Wilson McComb was frequently having to turn down requests for the loan of cars for road tests, in September he did agree to loan the *Autocar* magazine the Le Mans MGB. It had been on a tour of BMC showrooms and was virtually untouched after finishing the 24 hour race with the exception of having a 4.55:1 final drive fitted instead of the Le Mans 3.04:1 ratio. The road test was successfully featured in one of the *Autocar* series, 'Given the Works'.

RAC Winner

The finale for 1965 was the RAC Rally, the start of which had been moved to the Excelsior Hotel near London Airport. Stuart decided to risk having me as his chauffeur during the rally, and we took Peter Bartram as 'riding' mechanic.

We had a large entry of five Mini Cooper Ss plus two Austin Healey 3000s. The expected Championship battle did not materialise because Rene Trautmann withdrew his entry just before the rally, leaving Rauno to concentrate on winning the event, with the Championship in the bag.

There were 500 miles of stages and as the cars moved into Wales in very wet conditions, Paddy and Timo were already showing on the leader board, with Tony Fall in a loaned works S also in the top five.

Testing in Wales prior to the 1965 RAC Rally

Monte Magic

Stuart was keeping up with the rally and as we headed towards Aberystwyth we passed through an RAC rally secret check. Following Stuart's instructions we were soon hurtling back through the narrow lanes to rejoin the rally route before the secret check. As if any of our crews would exceed the set average speed!

After calling at Oulton Park for a test, the route carried on into Yorkshire, where the forecast suggested that we were in for some snow. Studs were banned but chains could be used, although they were not a practicable proposition particularly on front wheel drive cars. The possibility was discussed as we drove along, of making up some emergency straps to get a car up a snow covered hill in an emergency and so we stopped at several village stores buying up dog leads and chains, while Pete got busy in the back making up some straps. As we got into Yorkshire the forecast snow came down with a vengeance. Near Helmsley there was about six inches of snow on the road with rally cars seemingly coming in all directions.

Timo understeers on the ice, 1965 RAC Rally

Timo, with rally number 2, was first through these stages and Paul was particularly annoyed that the marshals had not sent a course car through Stage 20 to check the conditions, with the result that the first 20 cars became stuck, with four of ours collecting a maximum penalty. Timo also had battery trouble and had to have a push start by spectators and marshals. On the way to Peebles the Morley brothers crashed out of the rally but Timo was driving like a demon, now leading the rally with a gap of no less than five minutes over Rauno who was second.

That last stage! L-to-R: Timo Makinen, Paddy Hopkirk, Bill Price during a brief stop, 1965 RAC Rally

At Perth, Timo and Paul were surprised to learn that they were leading, the weather having brought the rally communications into some chaos. Only 71 cars were still running as they headed south again, and with only twenty stages left Vic Elford was challenging Timo for the lead.

Ice was affecting the stages now and on one stage Paul travelled for several miles clinging on the bumper of the Healey to improve the traction, a rather precarious position with his frozen fingers trying to grip the edge of the vent in the hardtop.

By Devil's Bridge, Elford had retired but now Rauno took up the challenge, and on one particularly icy climb the big Healey almost stopped, giving Rauno a lead of 49 seconds which he held to the finish. We were disappointed for Timo

1965

Monte Magic

1966

after an epic struggle in the icy conditions, but Rauno's win crowned his victory in the European Championship. It's a pity a big Healey did not win the RAC after trying for so long.

Timo, Rauno, and Paul share the champagne, 1965 RAC Rally

The winning car appeared on the BBC TV Trophy programme, 'Sunday Night at The London Palladium' and was then given a full road test by Roger Bell of *Motor* magazine. A few days later, after a quick camshaft change, Rauno used the car to pass the British driving test in Oxford. Fairly late in 1965 the FIA published new Appendix J regulations with significant changes to the specification of cars allowed to run in Groups 1, 2 and 3. For example, Group 1 was for cars built in minimum quantities of 5000 vehicles during twelve consecutive months, with only minor mechanical modifications permitted.

Castrol advertisement, 1965 European Rally Championship

Mk2 exhaust modification on the RAC Rally Austin Healey 3000

1966 Monte Carlo Lights

The first event under the new regulations was to be the Monte Carlo rally, and when the rally regulations were published, the handicap was in favour of the Group 1 cars. There were a number of ambiguous clauses in the Appendix J and as a result, Stuart and Henry Taylor of Ford flew to Paris to sort them out with the Homologation committees. No less than three versions of the Appendix J were issued before the Monte giving Doug and the lads in the workshop many a headache. Our eventual entry was three Group 1 cars, one Group 2 for Raymond Baxter and an MGB for Tony Fall.

The Group 1 cars had to run on standard 3½ × 10 inch wheels and the single 5½ gallon fuel tank. The engine was 'blueprinted' and a 4.1:1 final drive was fitted (one option was allowed). The other modification which was to have a significant effect on the event was the dipping system we fitted for the headlamps. Two additional lamps were permitted in Group 1 and we fitted fog lamps using quartz-iodine bulbs, the main headlamps also having the single filament QI bulbs. To allow dipping, there were two options. By means of a three-way switch the driver could either dip to the foglamps or, in the second position, switch the main beam current through a resistance which would dim the main beam. It was also possible to switch the foglamps separately to use them with the headlamps on the stages.

During the recces with the Group 1 cars, some carburettor icing was experienced, but after some laboratory work, Castrol decided that methylated spirits added to the petrol was the cheapest and simplest solution. They supplied cases of small plastic bottles filled with meths for each service car to carry with strict instructions how much to put in. These had to be kept out of sight, as petrol additives were not strictly permitted.

I took Timo's car to Lisbon for the start, accompanied by mechanic Pete Bartram. We crossed from Southampton to Le Havre and had an uneventful trip down to Spain, having the usual delays at the Customs with the spares documents.

As we came into Lisbon, we were hailed by a BMC van from A. M. Almeida, the Morris Importer, who were to be our hosts. The service manager, Henry Bastos, had sent the van to wait for us and act as a guide to their premises. The hospitality was tremendous, and although we had the run of the enormous workshop, it was quite difficult to do anything on the car, there were so many volunteers. Timo, Paul, Pete and myself were taken out every night on a tour of all the best eating places and night spots.

The Morris workshop made up a 'bed' to our design so that Timo could sleep all the way to Monte. The passenger seat was unbolted and stuffed behind the drivers seat, and then a wooden platform constructed level with the rear seat pan, covered with a thick mattress of foam. This enabled Timo to stretch full length in his sleeping bag, between sampling bottles of port and tins of sardines presented to the crews at the start.

Pete and I set off before the rally started to get to the border at Bayonne in time for our first service point. At

Monte Magic

1966 Monte Carlo Rally cars being prepared in the BMC Competitions Department. The Mini roofs are still black!

L-to-R: Standard Mini Cooper S seat, driver seat cover and co-drivers seat cover with headrest, to comply with the new 1966 Group 1 regulations, 1966 Monte Carlo Rally

Bayonne we picked up another of our mechanics off the train, and Timo and Paul duly arrived. Paul was complaining of lack of sleep, but the car was well, until, that is, we put the prescribed dose of meths in the tank. Unbeknown to us the car was just out of petrol, and on starting, it just conked out again. We had to push it across the road to the petrol station to fill up before it would go. We had a meal in the Bec Rouge that evening, and in conversation with the head waiter, he suggested that if anything other than a French car finished first, it would be thrown out. This comment was to be heard a number of times in Monaco before the rally finished.

All our cars arrived in Monte safely for the start of the Monaco-Chambery-Monaco section with the first special stages. The two works Porsches were making the running on the dry stages but on the icy and downhill sections the Minis were flying. Timo running at No 2 found some delays with marshals not in position, but by the time the cars got back to Monte, Timo was leading.

The French press seemed amazed at the performance of the Minis and there were veiled rumours of cheating. Tony Fall was unlucky to have to retire when the usually reliable MGB burst an oil cooler pipe.

Our lights were not really considered a problem at this stage, but at the end of the Monaco-Chambery-Monaco section a notice was posted at rally HQ asking a crew member from each car to attend the *parc fermé* in the morning for scrutineering, a rather unusual request.

Our service schedule was finalised for the Mountain circuit and in the morning we turned up at *parc fermé*, curious to see what it was all about. It soon became apparent that it was the headlamps that were under scrutiny, each driver being asked to switch them on and then dip the lamps while

1966

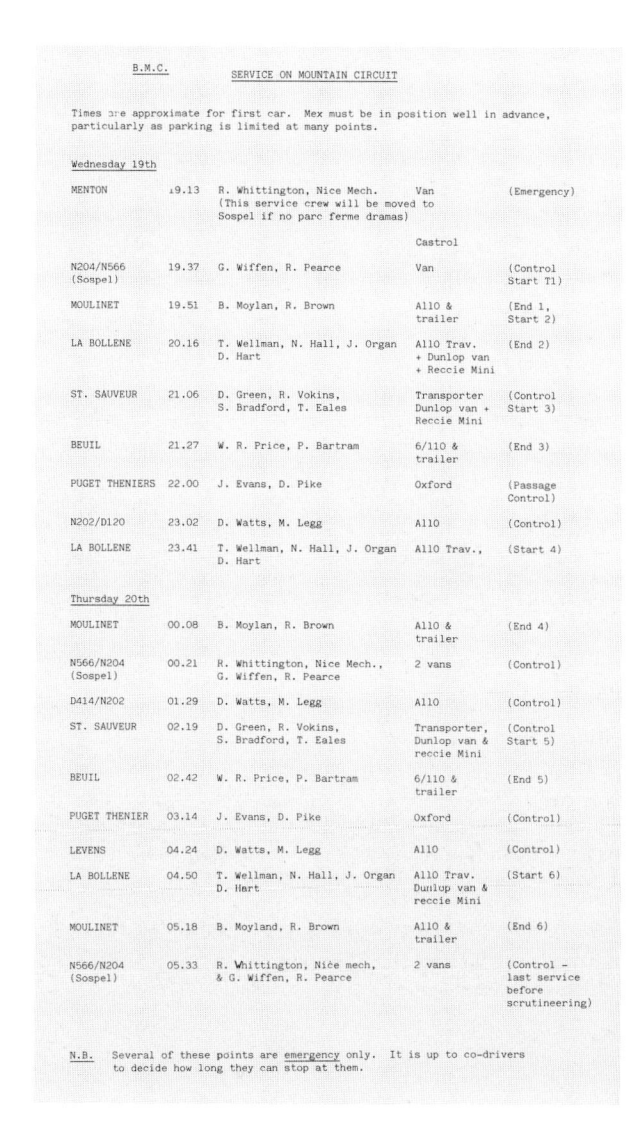

```
                B.M.C.       SERVICE ON MOUNTAIN CIRCUIT

        Times are approximate for first car. Mex must be in position well in advance,
        particularly as parking is limited at many points.

        Wednesday 19th
        MENTON          19.13    R. Whittington, Nice Mech.     Van              (Emergency)
                                 (This service crew will be moved to
                                 Sospel if no parc ferme dramas)
                                                                Castrol
        N204/N566       19.37    G. Wiffen, R. Pearce           Van              (Control
        (Sospel)                                                                 Start T1)
        MOULINET        19.51    B. Moylan, R. Brown            A110 &           (End 1,
                                                                trailer          Start 2)
        LA BOLLENE      20.16    T. Wellman, N. Hall, J. Organ  A110 Trav.       (End 2)
                                 D. Hart                        + Dunlop van
                                                                + Reccie Mini
        ST. SAUVEUR     21.06    D. Green, R. Vokins,           Transporter      (Control
                                 S. Bradford, T. Eales          Dunlop van +     Start 3)
                                                                Reccie Mini
        BEUIL           21.27    W. R. Price, P. Bartram        6/110 &          (End 3)
                                                                trailer
        PUGET THENIERS  22.00    J. Evans, D. Pike              Oxford           (Passage
                                                                                 Control)
        N202/D120       23.02    D. Watts, M. Legg              A110             (Control)
        LA BOLLENE      23.41    T. Wellman, N. Hall, J. Organ  A110 Trav.,      (Start 4)
                                 D. Hart

        Thursday 20th
        MOULINET        00.08    B. Moylan, R. Brown            A110 &           (End 4)
                                                                trailer
        N566/N204       00.21    R. Whittington, Nice Mech.     2 vans           (Control)
        (Sospel)                 G. Wiffen, R. Pearce
        D414/N202       01.29    D. Watts, M. Legg              A110             (Control)
        ST. SAUVEUR     02.19    D. Green, R. Vokins,           Transporter,     (Control
                                 S. Bradford, T. Eales          Dunlop van &     Start 5)
                                                                reccie mini
        BEUIL           02.42    W. R. Price, P. Bartram        6/110 &          (End 5)
                                                                trailer
        PUGET THENIER   03.14    J. Evans, D. Pike              Oxford           (Control)
        LEVENS          04.24    D. Watts, M. Legg              A110             (Control)
        LA BOLLENE      04.50    T. Wellman, N. Hall, J. Organ  A110 Trav.       (Start 6)
                                 D. Hart                        Dunlop van &
                                                                reccie mini
        MOULINET        05.18    B. Moyland, R. Brown           A110 &           (End 6)
                                                                trailer
        N566/N204       05.33    R. Whittington, Nice mech.     2 vans           (Control -
        (Sospel)                 & G. Wiffen, R. Pearce                          last service
                                                                                 before
                                                                                 scrutineering)

        N.B.  Several of these points are emergency only. It is up to co-drivers
              to decide how long they can stop at them.
```

Part of 16-page 1966 Monte Carlo Rally service instructions

Tony Fall slides the MGB in the snow, 1966 Monte Carlo Rally

Bob Whittington straightens the wing as Rauno Aaltonen holds a new studded tyre ready, 1966 Monte Carlo Rally

the beam was shone on a very scientific piece of apparatus, a hat box lid!

Later in the day a list of cars – including ours – was posted 'which may not comply with the highway regulations' stating that a final decision would be made after the rally. Under pressure, a promise was given to clarify the situation before the last night; this was not forthcoming.

Apart from the performance of the Minis, there was not much to report about the Mountain Circuit. The service stops were as usual, hectic, and the main drama was when Paddy swiped the rock face causing one of the vital fog lamps to drop down; this was taped up in roughly the right position.

The Minis were beaten for speed by the Porsches, and Roger Clark in the Lotus Cortina in the dry, although Timo and Rauno recorded times in the top five fastest on the last test. At the end of a frantic night, we drove back into Monte waiting with bated breath for the result to come out over Radio Monte Carlo, and we were not disappointed. Timo was provisionally announced as winner of the 1966 Monte Carlo Rally.

The winner and the next two cars are normally subject to scrutineering, and it was quite usual to have to take the cylinder head off the winner so it could be checked. The entrant is responsible for supplying mechanics to strip whatever parts were to be checked, and in this case Nobby, Tommy Eales and Johnny Evans were detailed to attend scrutineering, virtually locked in a local garage with a gendarme on the door and the press barred.

No one could have foreseen the lengths that the AC de Monaco would go to find something illegal about the cars, the mechanics stripping the engine of the winning car right down to the conrods; in addition to weighing many components, the number of teeth on each gear in the gearbox were counted. This went on for almost two days, and it was obvious that they were determined to find some technical infringement other than the lights with which to disqualify the cars.

The expertise of one or two of the scrutineers left the

Monte Magic

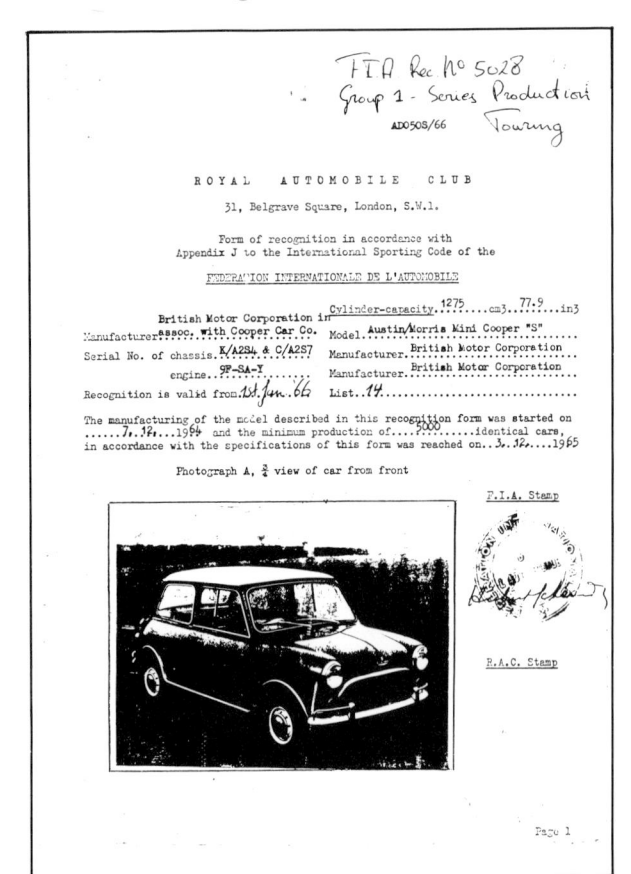

Front cover of Mini Cooper S 1275 1966 FIA Homologation Form

mechanics speechless when for example they had to be shown how to measure the valve lift. One thing that the scrutineers did miss was the Hardy Spicer inner driveshaft couplings. I can picture the official now with his hand on the flange, turning the gears over to check the teeth, quite oblivious to the fact that that type of coupling was not shown on the Homologation Form. They were in production but there had not been time to submit an Amendment Form to the FIA for recognition.

The other thing that caused confusion was the method used to check the front track on Paddy's car. A number of people were asked to sit on the bonnet while the track was measured, naturally increasing the width, which came out 3.5 mm over the stated figure. This infringement was released to the press.

It took some time to get the scrutineers to accept that there was a ground clearance figure quoted on the Homologation Form at which the track should be checked. The figure was eventually rechecked and it seemed that they had now passed the final 'Verification Technique'.

The bombshell dropped when, with the posting of the final results the cars originally listed in the first four places in general classification were not there. An hour later an announcement was made that those cars had been disqual-

Moral victors. Timo Makinen and Paul Easter concentrating hard on the 1966 Monte Carlo Rally

ified because their headlamps did not comply with the Appendix J. Stuart Turner immediately submitted a protest to the organisers, as did Ford and Rootes who also had cars thrown out, driven by Roger Clark and Rosemary Smith.

It seemed that some of the older members of the organising committee just could not accept that the Mini Cooper S could possibly beat much more powerful cars, without cheating in some way. There were all sorts of accusations in the French press, some even suggesting that we had swopped the cars for highly tuned replicas for some of the stages, which of course was utter nonsense.

To counter this suggestion, Stuart arranged to stage a back-to-back test using a standard Mini Cooper S out of Wright Brothers showroom in Monte. To ensure maximum coverage, *L'Equipe*, the famous sporting newspaper, was invited to witness the test, using Paddy's rally car, the two being driven in turn by Timo and Alain Bertaut of *L'Action Automobile*. We used quiet streets at the back of Monte incorporating a number of steep hairpins, and after the runs against a stopwatch, both drivers achieved quicker times in the standard car! This publicity stunt was reported fully in the press next day.

The official protest was thrown out, so the three Minis (1st, 2nd and 3rd), and Roger Clark, were finally disqualified, with the new general classification showing Pauli Toivonen in the Citroen DS21 as winner, followed by two Lancias in second and third position.

The atmosphere in Monte was unbelievable, with the only consolation being the massive publicity – mainly sympathetic – given to the team. In protest, Pauli Toivonen failed to turn up at prize-giving. Despite the troubles, it was decided to fly the cars home again on a Carvair of BUAF.

There was quite a reception committee at London Airport to receive the crews and cars, including the Mayor of Oxford and John Thornley and most of the wives and girlfriends. The 'winning' car appeared at the London Palladium again, this time with Jimmy Tarbuck as compère. I volunteered to help bring the Cooper Car Co transporter home, loaded with more than 450 wheels/tyres, two trailers and numerous spares, travelling with Stan and Robin with an Austin Westminster as back-up car.

This journey was just about the last straw. As we refuelled near the junction with the N44 and N4 near Troyes, a friendly gendarme advised us that the road was closed but suggested an alternative route via Vitry-Le-Francois, an extra 28 km. During this diversion we ran through a radar trap and were let off with a caution, but approaching Laon we were stopped by a motorcycle patrol, who ordered us to follow them to the outskirts of the town where we parked in a lay-by.

It appeared that we were contravening the *Barriere de Degel* signs, limiting vehicles to 6 tonnes weight and below and we were taken to the police station in Laon. We found out

Four of the disqualified drivers interviewed in London. L-to-R: Paddy Hopkirk, Timo Makinen, Rosemary Smith (Rootes) and Roger Clark (Ford)

Monte Magic

Winners of the 1964 and 1965 Monte Carlo Rally and 'almost' third place car in 1966

1966

that the 'Barrier of the Thaw' was in force to prevent damage to the roads when a thaw followed a long period of frost. The inspector told us to go to the Ponts & Chaussees office where we would be issued with a permit to take us through to Boulogne, but when we returned with a ticket showing our gross weight as 14t 190 kg, the clerk refused a permit.

A *Fiche d'Immobilisation* was issued and, despite the intervention of a sympathetic police inspector, the vehicle was now stuck in Laon. As soon as the thaw was finished we could take it to the coast, so after finding the local MG dealer who kindly locked the transporter in his warehouse, we returned to the UK in the Westminster.

Ten days later the MG dealer phoned to say that the roads were now open and we could collect the truck. I took a flight to Paris and then a train to Laon, and after donating a set of studded tyres to the dealer for his MGB, returned to Abingdon.

Monte Magic

This episode eventually came to court, Stuart Turner being charged with sending me on the road in contravention of the *Barrier de Degel*. We were found guilty in our absence and fined 200 francs with 92.35 francs costs. I have often wondered whether the Monte fiasco had anything to do with this episode.

There was a lot of snow for the Swedish rally but the gremlins struck again, with Timo and Harry Kallstrom (BMC Sweden entry), breaking driveshafts, while Rauno hit a snow bank, holed the radiator and then seized the engine.

Paddy and Tony Fall were entered in the Flowers Rally based on San Remo, Tony driving the same Group 1 car used by Paddy on the Monte. Paddy had Ron Crellin with him for the first time as co-driver, having 'divorced' his regular co-driver, Henry Liddon. There was no real friction between Paddy and Henry but Paddy was getting fed up with the same person being in the car and felt it was time for a change.

It was a bit near the Monte to risk any Group 1 infringements, but unfortunately Tony removed the air filter elements to gain extra power and although carrying them in the car, at a spot check he was disqualified. Paddy finished a rather lowly fifteenth overall and sixth in class.

Paddy Hopkirk/Ron Crellin on the 1966 Italian Flowers Rally in a Mini Cooper S 1275

160

1966

MGBs at Sebring

To give two class opportunities, one of the MGBs for Sebring was entered in the Prototype Category fitted with a special cylinder block bored out to 2009 cc, a nitrided crankshaft and Twin Cam conrods. This engine developed 138 bhp making it the most powerful MGB engine we had built so far. The second car was a Group 3 spec car and when both were finished they were taken to Silverstone for a shake-down. Paddy, Andrew Hedges and Roger Mac drove the cars, each doing about 15 laps, finding the prototype car about 2 seconds a lap quicker, at 1m 55s. Fuel consumption was checked with the faster car doing 12.3 mpg and the other car 10.5 mpg, useful information for the forthcoming race.

Nobby Hall working on MGB (8 DBL) at Abingdon before the 1966 Sebring race

Stuart took Doug Watts and Nobby Hall to Sebring to look after the two cars and Peter Browning as official timekeeper. Paddy and Andrew drove the Group 3 car, the prototype being shared by Peter Manton/Roger Mac and the American Emmett Brown.

Soon after the Le Mans type start, the prototype was in trouble with a broken rocker arm, which was replaced, with the car losing about 17 minutes. This car steadily pulled back up through the field and within two hours was leading its class. The Group 3 car also made steady progress, and as other cars retired it was also leading its class.

With only 1½ hours to go Peter noticed that Paddy was missing and it was only when he walked back to the pits that the pit team found out that the engine had suffered a terminal failure; a conrod had ventilated the crankcase. Towards the end of the race Roger Mac did some fast laps to finish in front of the Triumph TR4s, the first British car to finish. The MGB won its class and was seventeenth, a good win for BMC North America.

During the development of the Hydrolastic suspension, various increases in the hardness of the rubber spring in the units had been tried, with assistance from Jack Daniels, the Project Engineer at Longbridge. Jack advised us that he was concerned that, with the increase in rubber hardness, we were reducing the volume of fluid which could be pumped into the system, with the possibility that when the suspension was on full rebound the strut may come out of the top arm.

We had done some testing near Strata Florida, in Wales on a rough track crossed several times by a stream. Because of the distance from Abingdon the mechanics normally stayed at the Vulcan Arms near Rhayader. During March, on one of these test sessions, one of the objectives was to see if we could get the front struts to jump out. Tony Fall was driving the car and after about a dozen runs, he came back to the service area complaining of stiff steering and lack of lock on the offside. The car was turned on its side for a close examination, and we found that the strut had in fact pulled out. This information was fed back to Jack Daniels and he soon had a redesign under way.

In April, a brilliant rallying partnership ended with the retirement of the Morley brothers after a career starting in 1952, with their first International rally win on the Tulip, 1959. Marcus had given them their first BMC drive in the RAC rally but with a busy farm to run their summer harvest commitments prevented them from doing rallies like the Liège. We were all sorry to see the two gentlemen farmers go, but could never forget the highlight of their careers with wins on two Alpine rallies. The Morleys began their rallying in the days when a sports jacket and flannels were the dress of the day.

The Targa Florio always took a small team away from Abingdon for well over a week because it was so far to travel, but this did not deter Stuart from entering two MGBs for Timo Makinen/John Rhodes and Andrew Hedges/John Handley. The cars were taken down by car sleeper to Rome, driven to Naples and then put on the ferry to Palermo, while the drivers flew down.

At scrutineering, there was a bit of hiccup when the scrutineers pointed out that the Group 3 car should have bumpers. A UK-registered MGB had been seen in the car park so a call over the tannoy system was made requesting the owner of the MGB to come to the BMC pits. Two English lads on holiday turned up and were persuaded to loan their bumpers for the race, being wined and dined by the team when they got back to England.

Timo and Andrew took the first driving spells, the cars leving the pits at 20 second intervals, the slowest going first, a feature unique to the Targa. This made timekeeping and maintaining an accurate lap chart quite difficult, but Peter Browning was able to achieve this to such good effect that BMC published a list of results before the organisers had sorted their own out.

The two MGs pulled out a lead on the first lap of about a minute in their class over a Ferrari. This was followed by some heavy rain and when John Handley took over the cars, they had a good class lead. A number of retirements moved the MGs up in the general classification and at the finish, the two cars were 1st and 2nd in class, 9th and 16th overall, with Timo and John Rhodes in the leading car.

Tony Fall had a good win on the Circuit of Ireland in which Paddy had a big accident when he rolled the car three times.

The Tulip was this year run to a new format, being decided on a scratch basis with the fastest aggregate stage times deciding the winner. Stuart decided to enter one Group 1 and one Group 2 car but had a problem with drivers as neither of the two Finns wanted to drive the Group 1 car. This was finally decided by the toss of a coin, which on this occasion, Timo lost.

161

Monte Magic

Stuart Turner, Tony Fall and Henry Liddon relax after Tony had won the 1966 Circuit of Ireland

Timo Makinen in the Group 1 Mini Cooper S, 1966 Tulip Rally

Rauno was able to beat the Lotus Cortinas for the first time to come first overall, while Timo's engine developed a liking for vast quantities of oil. This situation became so bad that they had to carry cans of oil in the car, with Paul frequently changing the oiled-up plugs, pouring in more oil. This did not stop them winning the Group 1 category and their class.

Austrian Alpine Rally

Following Paddy's success in the 1964 Austrian Alpine rally, two cars were entered for Paddy and Tony Fall. We had reluctantly taken delivery of two Vanden Plas 4 litre Rs for use as service cars, which were only available with automatic transmission; this had brought a few complaints from mechanics and staff alike. We took one on the Austrian Alpine and to avoid going over the Grossglockner Pass headed for the tunnel from Bockstein to Mallnitz.

This event was one of the few left where outside service was not allowed, and in addition, the number of wheels carried by the rally car had to remain the same during the length of the rally. Scrutineering took place at the local fire station where the emphasis was on checking each car's ground clearance by making them drive over a 10 cm high block. We were OK but some private entries with older cars and tired suspension failed this test. The drivers had a coloured seal attached to their wrists at scrutineering ready for a 04.00 hrs start next day.

As the cars were collected from the *parc fermé* it was noticed that each road wheel had been marked with paint.

To give us an extra 'service car', I joined forces with Jimmy Simpson of Castrol in his new Austin Westminster with Tommy Eales. We were going to have to keep a low profile but in effect our service arrangements were the same as usual. Leaving the hotel at Velden for our first service stop, we motored down a dual carriageway in the early morning mist and while doing about 50 mph a large deer leapt straight across the road hitting the front of the car with a terrible crash. The deer was killed and the front of the car was quite a mess, but luckily the radiator was intact; Jimmy was most upset to damage his new car.

The main opposition was from two works supported Porsche cars and after two stages they were leading. On the third stage Tony Fall had a puncture and drove 3 km to the end with the steel wheel wrapped round the brake drum.

At the end of the first section there were plenty of officials about to ensure that only the crews worked on the cars, but we had already carried out our unofficial servicing up the road away from prying eyes. Any car wanting to renew tyres had to have them put on the original marked wheels.

Austrian Alpine Rally 1966, Tony Fall and Mike Wood leave a cloud of dust in GRX 310 D

Tony Fall's damaged wheel was beyond further use but the organisers would not let us supply a replacement, and insisted that Tony kept the damaged one in his boot for the remainder of the rally. We did protest but to no avail, and this was made worse when we noticed that one of the Porsche cars was carrying no spare.!

Despite all this, Paddy was leading after the first section and when the rally restarted at 02.00 hrs, it headed over the border into Yugoslavia twice. Paddy was fastest on the last six stages, one of which, on the airfield at Klagenfurt, was five laps with co-driver aboard. Tony hit a pile of logs damaging his steering and retired but at the finish Paddy was confirmed as winner, winning the usual trophies and some gold and silver coins.

After the rally we went with Paddy to have a meal at a restaurant nearby, driven by a lunatic in a VW Microbus who wanted to impress Paddy. At the end of the meal Paddy ordered Irish Coffee; when the poor waiter made an absolute mess of it, Paddy got him to supply another set of ingredients and proceeded to show him how it should be done. A good evening was had by all!

As I mentioned previously, we were now using Vanden Plas 4 litre R service cars fitted with the Rolls-Royce engine. After the first doubts, these were soon accepted by the department, and they turned out to be very reliable and quite fast even when fully loaded.

Acropolis Protest

Peter Browning, in his book *The Works Minis*, described 1966 as protest year, and on the Acropolis we once again had problems. Three Hydrolastic cars were entered incorporating all the latest rough road modification such as full length Dural sump guards, skids under the battery box, skids on the front of the silencers and solidly mounted radiator. Guards were fitted to the front of the brake calipers to stop the flexible hose being snapped off and the latest Hardy Spicer driveshaft couplings were in use; this last development would mean that the cars would not be seen tipped on their sides so often to change the rubber couplings.

Dunlop, as usual, were looking after our tyre requirements in Greece and there were some raised eyebrows when we turned up at scrutineering with the cars fitted with R7 racing tyres.

The route was very rough and caused problems as the battle developed between the Minis and the works Cortinas. Timo was soon in trouble with a broken rear trailing arm outer bracket, which was allowing the tyre to rub on the inner wing.

All seemed lost when they came across Wilson McComb and Roger Bell taking photographs of the rally and, because their transport was one of our Mini Cooper S recce cars (DJB 92B), Paul soon 'borrowed' a bracket from this car, leaving a very worried Wilson stranded beside the road.

The main trouble occurred at a service area where there was little space to park. Brian Moylan, who was in charge of one of our service cars, was obliged to set-up shop inside the control area, albeit with the permission of the control official. Paddy had Ron Crellin with him now as regular co-driver and as they only had one wheel in the control area he did not see a problem.

Later Rauno retired with engine problems leaving Paddy and Timo to fly the flag. Timo made fastest time on the Mount Parnis hill climb but the head gasket was on its way out and Paul was continually topping-up the expansion tank which was fitted inside the car in the passengers footwell. The car finally expired during the traditional race round the Tatoi circuit, leaving Paddy to come home winner.

The results were posted at rally HQ and everything seemed to be in order until a few minutes before the statutory

Monte Magic

Fitting Dunlop R7 racing tyres before the start of the 1966 Acropolis Rally

hour of protest time had expired. A notice was put up stating that Paddy would be penalised for early arrival at a control and for servicing inside a control area. Stuart immediately submitted an official protest, but despite an all-night sitting by the Appeals Committee the protest was thrown out.

In view of the circumstances of the alleged offences Stuart notified the Club that the matter would be refered to the FIA in Paris. The matter did not appear to be totally straightforward to our crews and there were suggestions (unsubstantiated) that one of the teams had done a deal with the organisers. The FIA appeal was also rejected and as a result Paddy was awarded third overall some time later in the year.

Owing to the work load, for the Scottish Rally Special Tuning rebuilt the RAC winning car for Tony Fall and Mike Wood, with Basil Wales and two of his mechanics providing service support. The event was run over 64 stages of very rough Forestry Commission tracks and Tony drove sensibly to score his second win in as many months.

Terry Harryman and Paddy Hopkirk before the 1966 Geneva Rally

On the Geneva Rally Paddy retired but Tony Fall came home second overall and, with two private owners, won the Manufacturer's Team Prize.

As mentioned already we received many requests to loan cars and because the Healey was now not so prominent in the programme, in April we agreed to loan to *Motoring News* the Austin Healey 3000 which Timo had driven on the last RAC. The magazine was thrilled with EJB, recording a 0–60 time of 8 seconds, 0–100 in 19 seconds and a maximum speed of 135 mph. The Healey had been a wonderful car and had achieved five outright wins in International rallies and no less than 38 class wins.

Tony Fall clocked up his third win of the year with a success on the London Rally.

164

1966

Rallye Vltava

The Czech Rally (or Rallye Vltava) started in Prague this year, and we prepared three cars for the event, one being for the Polish Rally Champion, Sobieslaw Zasada who had been doing great things in a Steyr Puch. This car was Group 1 spec running on the standard 3½×10 inch wheels. The two other cars for Timo and Rauno were similar in spec to the Acropolis cars running on either Dunlop SP3 or R7 racing tyres.

We stayed in Motel Stop where we were constantly pressed to change foreign currency by members of the staff.

The rally started with a five lap race round the outside of a large sports stadium in Prague, in which Timo was fastest with Rauno and Zasada close behind. At the first service point, we found that one of Timo's fuel tanks had moved sufficiently for the filler neck to disappear inside the boot. This was soon rectified and the remainder of the rally was fairly uneventful, until Timo suffered a broken rocker arm dropping him from the lead to third position.

However, Rauno was close behind and inherited first place which he held to the finish, Zasada coming in a fine fourth overall, the three cars winning the Team Prize.

The awards presented to the crews included (not for the first time) some very nice cut-glass which was loaded in the service cars, the drivers flying home after the rally. This also caused a problem because every foreign car which comes into Czechoslovakia is registered in the driver's passport. To enable the drivers to get out by air, we had to spend some hours at the Automobile Club having the cars transferred to the mechanics' passports.

Rauno Aaltonen/Henry Liddon in the Group 2 Mini Cooper S during the stadium test in Prague, 1966 Rallye Vltava

No Champagne

The Editor of *Safety Fast* magazine based at the MG factory, was Stuart Seager, with Peter Browning as Assistant Editor. A recent addition to the staff was Richard Shepherd who had been assigned a number of rally reports, to cover what we were up to with our programme, and in the September issue his report was titled 'It's not always Champagne'.

He was referring to our recent outing in the German rally, starting at San Martino de Castrozza and including a number of the most famous motor sport venues such as the Rossfeld Hill Climb, Hockenheim circuit and the infamous Nürburgring. There was tough opposition from a number of Porsche and Alfa Romeo cars but the early performance of the Minis was to no avail. At the Hockenheim circuit, during a ten lap test, both engines expired with blown pistons, caused by seizure of the gudgeon pins. This was a failure which was causing Doug and Cliff some development problems.

Poland and The World Cup

We were having a fairly good summer and I was spending a few days holiday near Bognor Regis with the family. I was a little surprised to receive a telephone call from Stuart asking if I could go out on the Polish Rally, especially as I had not left him my holiday address. My wife was not very pleased that my holiday was cut short, but she had now become accustomed to the peculiar workings of the Competitions Department. Brian Hancock, the MG chauffeur, was sent down for me in the morning and I then had to chase up to the Polish Embassy to obtain a visa.

The convoy of rally and service cars travelled from

Monte Magic

Felixstowe to Rotterdam and then straight down the autobahn, Stuart, unusually, travelling with us. As the World Cup Final between England and Germany was being played that Saturday, he insisted that we found a TV where we could watch the match. In Arnhem, we found a small hotel bar with a TV and watched the whole game, our enthusiasm for the result not being shared by the other people in the room.

Timo Makinen (with beard) and Paul Easter look apprehensive as the scrutineers check the car, 1966 Polish Rally

We had to cross Czechoslovakia to reach Cracow, and had a stopover in Zilma where despite bribing the night porter to keep an eye on the cars, found the Vanden Plas badges missing in the morning.

Preparation in Cracow kept the mechanics busy, especially sorting out one of the recce cars which Stuart was loaning to a local driver after a request from Marek Wachowski, our interpreter and 'Mr Fixit'. In the absence of a garage, the mechanics effected an engine change using an apple tree as a gantry in the Polish driver's garden.

The rally started with a race on an airfield at Cracow, where thousands of spectators braved the torrential rain to see some of the top European drivers in action. I was driving Stuart again with one of the mechanics riding in the back of the Vanden Plas. Our trip behind the Iron Curtain again proved to be successful with Tony Fall's 970S winning outright and Timo coming second, the smaller engine taking advantage of the handicap.

Marathon

After the last Spa–Sofia–Liège ended in 1964, the Royal Motor Union in Liège conceived a new event for 1965 to take its place. This was in the form of a non-stop race round the Nürburgring circuit, lasting 72 hours. The 72 hour event was not a success owing mainly, to the excessive service time allowed the competitors, but the RMU was quick to make

Den Green repairs early damage to the winning MGB, Marathon de la Route 1966

1966

improvements, changing the regulations for 1966 and increasing the length to 84 hours.

The regulations were rather complex with, for example, the average speed achieved during the first 12 hours having to be achieved during the last 12 hours. Each car had a set lap time, and as long as the time was achieved, the competitor was credited with 28 km, the lap distance. One second's lateness attracted a penalty of 200 metres, so it can be seen that one could soon lose all the distance gained. Every ten laps, five minutes extra were allowed for refuelling with twenty minutes for servicing every 50 laps.

After these early dramas the race settled down to a pattern with the two MGs gradually moving up the leader board. By Wednesday, the Enever/Poole car was up to fourth and the other car was tenth, the event being led by a Porsche. Wheel spoke breakages were becoming a worry, occurring at rather too frequent intervals. By Thursday, the MGs were third and fourth having clocked up 2,800 miles by half distance behind the Ford team. The Bianchi/de Keyn Ferrari was now in the lead and seemed uncatchable until it went off the road in heavy rain and retired, leaving the battle to the Ford Cortinas and MGBs. With just 12 hours to go the two MGs

1000 Lakes Rally, Timo winning again

Two MGBs were entered, one being an MG development car, which had already seen service as a 'marathon' car, having averaged 100 mph for 10,000 miles at MIRA during a Shell oils publicity run. The cars were crewed by Andrew Hedges/Julien Vernaeve with Roger Enever/Alec Poole, the latter in the black development car, under team manager Peter Browning.

The race started off in a disastrous fashion with Roger leaving the track on the first lap. He managed to regain the circuit again to return to the pits for a check-up and replacement of the fog lamps. As if this were not enough, Andrew went off at the same spot on lap two, damaging the lamps and splitting the fuel tank. Back at the pits, Den and the mechanics had a hard time getting their charges back into the race, Roger having already lost 1½ laps to the leading car.

were up to first and second, an almost unthinkable situation after such a bad start.

The drama was not yet over, and with only five hours to go, the Enever/Poole car broke a half-shaft as it left the refuelling point, and they were out. The remaining hours were very tense but our luck held and the car driven by Julien and Andrew made it to the finish first, a wonderful result, once again emphasising the reliability of the MGB. Apart from the accident damage and some broken wheels, the only major parts changed were rear hub bearings. The cars averaged about 175 miles to the pint of oil and 16 mpg on fuel.

Tony Fall's luck ran out on the Welsh Rally where he had to retire, but in Finland success was achieved again. The

Monte Magic

previous year we had won the 1000 Lakes and this year an entry of three cars was submitted with a view to repeating the success. The third car was driven by Jorma Lusenius who had been having some success with BMC Sweden. His choice proved to be a wise one because alongside Timo and Rauno, they achieved first, third and sixth place respectively.

I was with the team on the Alpine Rally which once again started in Marseilles, the weather being very hot and sultry particularly in the confines of the Vieux Port where our hotel was situated. Four Mini Cooper Ss were entered, for Timo, Rauno, Paddy and Tony, prepared to the latest spec, the engines giving 85 bhp at the front wheels. Dunlop R7 racing tyres and SP3s were available and, now that double-dipping quartz-halogen bulbs had been developed, this got round the problem of an alternative dipping system. The crews were trying-out some experimental intercomm systems which were being developed with the help of Amplivox Ltd and Lustraphone Ltd in London. The boom microphones were a little heavy and fitting them involved drilling holes in the crash helmets.

Left: *Alpine Rally 1966, hectic service for the Rauno Aaltonen Mini Cooper S*

Stan Bradford, Doug Watts and Bill Price, 1966 Alpine Rally

It was a very tough event with three of the cars retiring, the sole remaining car, driven by Rauno and Henry, coming home in third place behind an Alfa Romeo and Roger Clark in a Lotus Cortina.

The Alpine stages were always very hard on brakes, and made harder by the left-foot braking technique of the 'Flying Finns'. We had been developing the brakes with Lockheed and a number of modifications had improved matters. Asbestos blocks were fitted into the caliper pistons, protruding slightly so that the asbestos was in contact with the pad, which helped to reduce the heat transfer to the calipers. A modification to the rear brakes involved drilling cooling holes in the backplate and bolting the wheel cylinder solidly to the backplate to help heat dissipation.

In September, another chapter in the BMC saga was written when it was announced that BMC and Jaguar Cars were to merge under a controlling organisation of British Motor Holdings Ltd. Sir George Harriman would be Chairman with Sir William Lyons continuing as Chairman of Jaguar which would still operate as a separate company. The MG Car Co was renamed the MG Division of the new Company.

Before the RAC Rally, Timo won the Three Cities Rally bringing his points total in the European Championship to within four points of the title.

Left: *Help arrives for Tony Fall, testing in Wales*

Graham Hill On The RAC

A busy year ended with the RAC Rally, this time sponsored by the *Sun* newspaper, with an entry of no less than eight cars. Sponsorship meant a change in the usual competition numbers on the sides of the cars, the white patch being replaced by a large orange 'Sun' with a much smaller competition number at the bottom. To add to the public interest, two of our top grand prix drivers were to take part, in the persons of Jim Clark and Graham Hill. This was of particular interest to us as Graham was to drive one of our Mini Cooper Ss, partnered by Maxwell Boyd, the car being the official BBC *Wheelbase* and *Sunday Times* entry. The organisers decided to start the 'star' drivers at the front of the field and Graham was seeded No 5.

We now had a civilian permit to test our cars at Bagshot, the military test ground, at a fee of £4 per day, and on 11 November a test session was booked to give Graham the chance to try a rally Mini Cooper S with tuition from Paddy. Also in attendance were Maxwell Boyd, Barry Gill, and a BBC *Wheelbase* film crew.

Before lunch both Paddy and Graham did a number of laps, Graham going off the road a couple of times much to the delight of the photographers. Lunch was taken at the Kings Arms in Bagshot with some filming back at the track to finish off the day. Needless to say, next day Graham was featured in one of the national newspapers pushing the Mini back on to the track with Paddy's help.

Because we no longer had a permanent lady driver in the team, Stuart invited Rauno's sister Marjatta to drive one of our cars in the RAC. A very attractive lady, she had already made an impact in Finland with her rallying performances. Stuart asked Carolyn Tyler to join her as co-driver. In addition to our regular team, Simo Lampinen/Tony Ambrose and Harry Kallstrom/Ragnvald Haakansson made up the numbers.

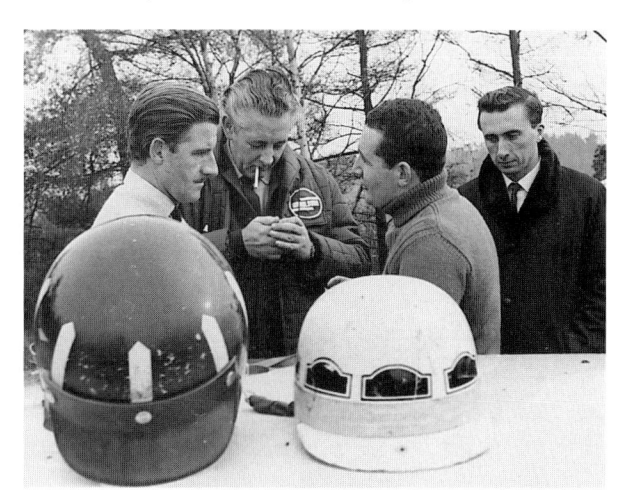

Graham Hill, Maxwell Boyd, Paddy Hopkirk and Paul Easter at Bagshot, 1966 RAC Rally testing

Monte Magic

Marjatta Aaltonen, Rauno Aaltonen, Timo Makinen and Simo Lampinen before the 1966 RAC Rally

One interesting change in spec was the fitting of the standard Cooper S camshaft (AEG 510) following discussions with the drivers and some development work by Cliff. Maximum power went down from 85 to 75 bhp at the wheels but the object was to give the engines more low down torque to cope with the muddy conditions. (Timo opted for the usual race cam.) The new forged, ovalised pistons with special oil scraper rings were used in the engines and grille muffs were made up in the MG Trim Shop for each car, with large front mud flaps mounted on the bumpers.

The rally started in London but it was in the West Country at Porlock Hill that Graham Hill's car showed its first sign of trouble. At the service point at the end of the stage a bad oil leak was spotted from under the car. With the sump guard removed a small hole was located in the differential housing; something had come out from inside! All that could be done was repair the hole with plastic metal and send him on his way.

There was a stage at Lulworth where both Rauno and Tony visited the ditches, but at the end of Stage 4 Timo was leading. The route wound its way into Wales where Simo met disaster when he rolled his car out of the rally. At Oulton Park circuit there was a tremendous crowd but due to planning permission problems they could not be allowed into the circuit.

In the Lake District Timo was still leading but Graham Hill was quite relieved when his transmission finally expired, glad to get back to the comforts of civilisation. It was amazing that the transmission lasted as long as it did, after the original breakage.

By Aviemore, Timo had a lead of six minutes from Bengt Soderstrom in a Ford but there was still a long way to go. When the results were posted at the night halt, it was seen that the times from the Twiglees stage had been cancelled. This was because Rauno had left the start of the stage with the official timing clock caught in the Mini's door handle, the following times having so many discrepancies that the organisers felt it was only fair to scrub the stage.

Above right: *1966 RAC Rally; Rauno and Henry fourth overall*

Right: *1966 RAC Rally; Harry Kallstrom/Ragnvald Haakansson second overall*

Coming out of Scotland, Timo was leading by five minutes as the cars headed for the Yorkshire stages, with Paddy third and Tony fourth. In the dreaded Kielder Forest Paddy broke a driveshaft and was out. Worse was to come, however, when on the Yorkshire moors Timo retired with a blown engine. He had been putting up a whole string of fastest times and with his retirement, went the European Championship.

At Barnby Moor, Soderstrom was in an unassailable lead of fourteen minutes but, another driver who was always sympathetic of his machinery, Harry Kallstrom was lying second. At the finish at London Airport, Soderstrom was declared winner but we were not disgraced with second, fourth and fifth respectively for Harry, Rauno and Tony.

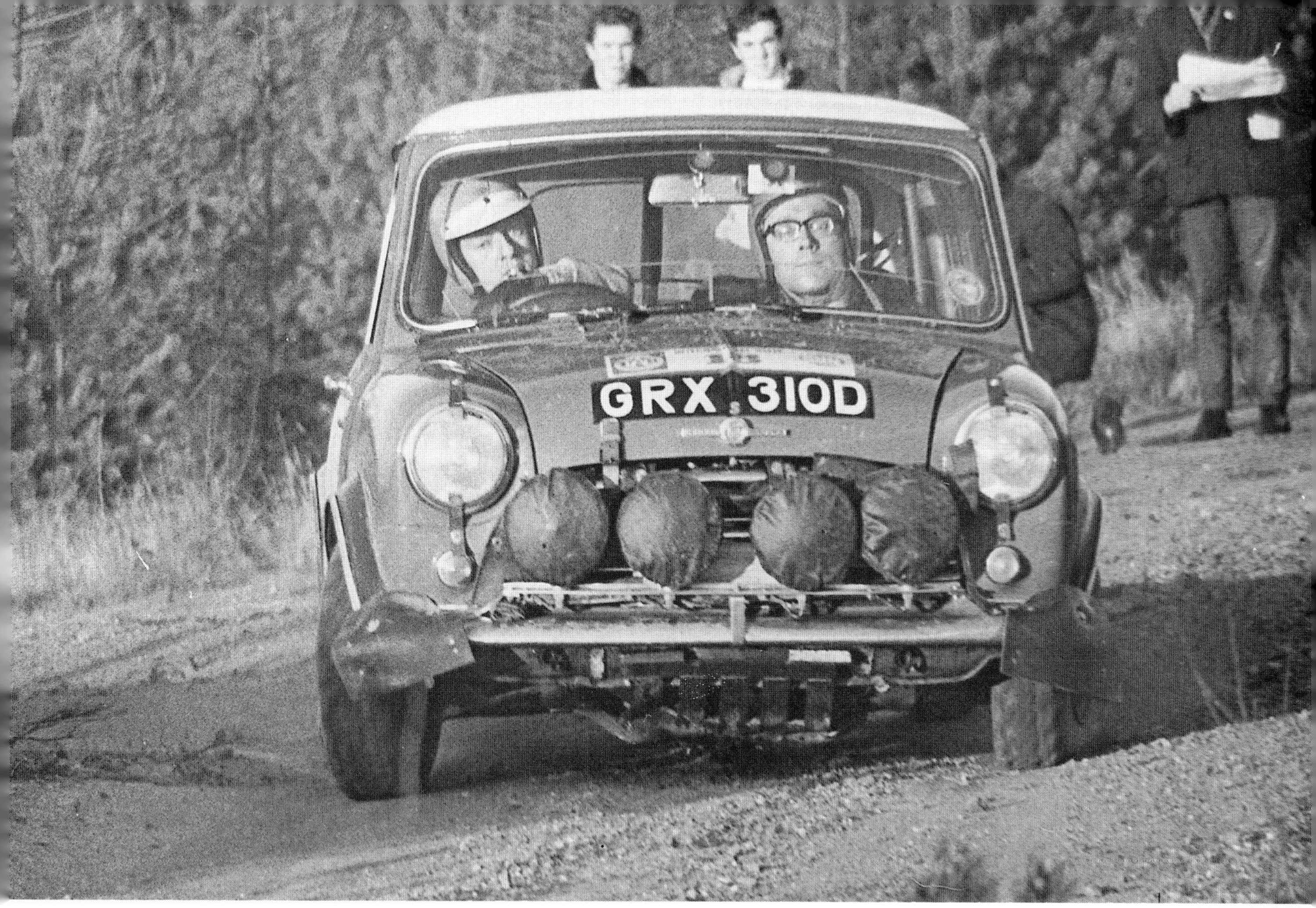
GRX 310D

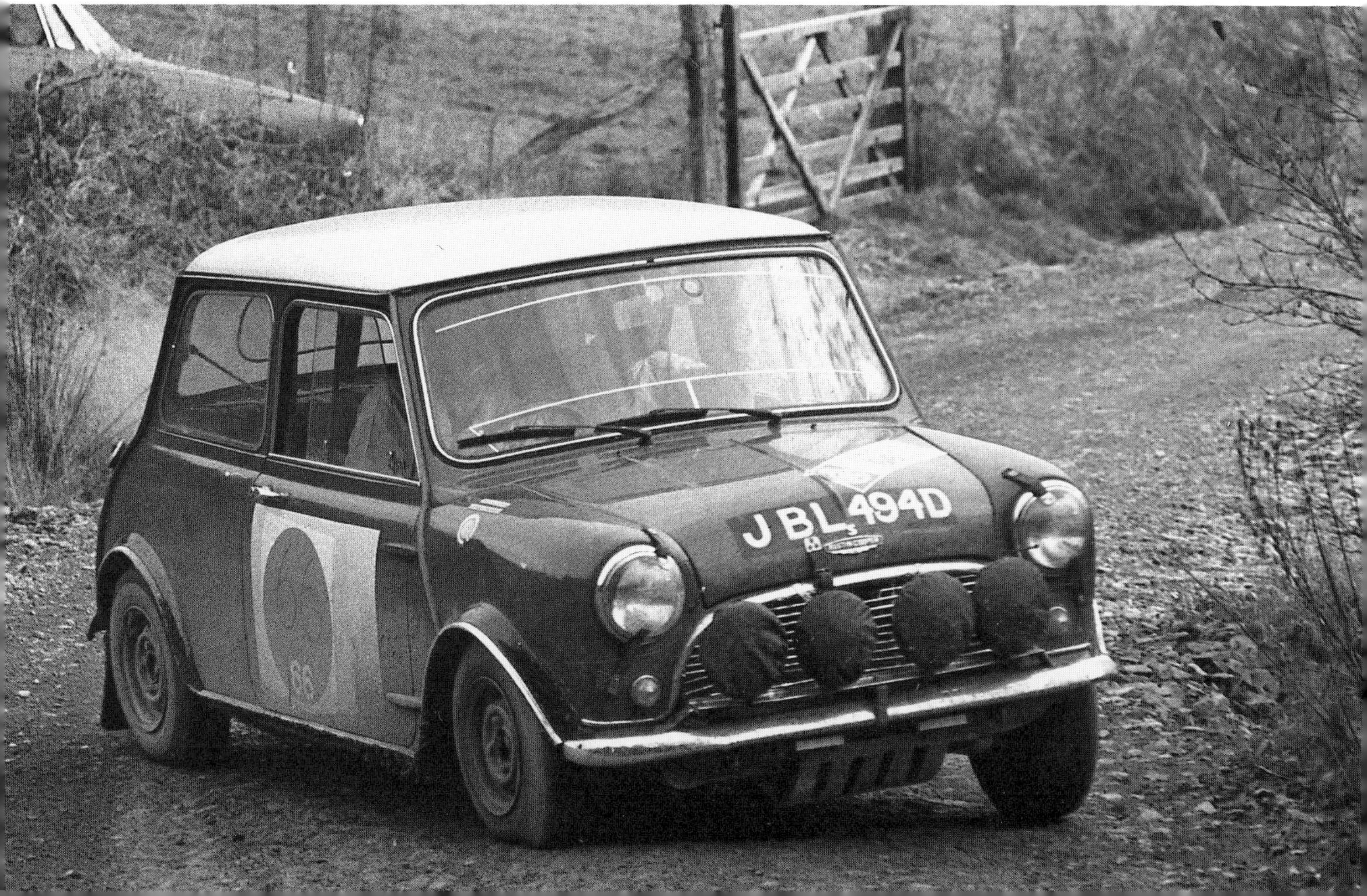
JBL 494D

Monte Magic

Of interest, too, at this time was Stuart Turner's last driver test session, this time at Silverstone. A selection of drivers were invited to try six different cars, under the watchful eyes of John Cooper, Ken Tyrell, Brian Gillibrand, Daniel Richmond, Don Moore, Richard Groves and Geoff Healey. There were three Mini Cooper S cars tuned by Don Moore, Vitafoam and the Cooper Car Co, an MGB (8 DBL) and a Sprite from the Donald Healey Motor Co. The results were most interesting, Tony Fall being consistently fast in the Minis and the two rear wheel drive cars, while Geoff Mabbs and John Rhodes also featured well.

1966 RAC Rally; the engine/transmission for the Timo Makinen/Paul Easter car

Stuart Turner Leaves Abingdon

It was just before Christmas that we learned that Stuart was leaving the Department. As soon as he knew, John Thornley wasted no time in sending for Peter Browning and telling him that he had got a new job for him. He told Peter that Stuart was leaving and that he was to be the new Competitions Manager. John Thornley could be persuasive when the moment required and although the announcement came as a bit of a shock, Peter hardly had time to think about reasons for refusing. He was told firmly that he would go on the Monte with Stuart and would then be on his own.

Peters' qualifications for the job were good with his experience of race organisation, timekeeping, his knowledge of the Department and the personnel and his undoubted organisational skills. I had hoped to learn who was to succeed Stuart before leaving for the Monte, but it was not until reaching Lisbon for the start that I received the news, from Paul Easter, who had read it in the *Daily Express*.

Good results had not come so easily in 1966 with some of our major competitors' cars becoming more competitive. Nevertheless Stuart was leaving at the peak of the Department's success and would join Castrol, allowing him more time at home with his family. Stuart had been an excellent boss, although not a person one could get to know well, with a rather dry sense of humour. He commanded the respect of everyone in the department and there is no doubt that his knowledge of rallying and tremendous organisational skills, together with a knack of getting together the right drivers in the most appropriate cars, had brought the team its success. He had of course inherited a team from Marcus which was already growing in confidence, and one should not underestimate the skill and dedication put in by the two Dougs, Tommy, Den, Cliff and Neville and the lads and lasses in the Department which made the task that much easier.

1967

1967 – Revenge

Following the fiasco of the 1966 Monte there had been much talk of the works teams staying away in 1967 in protest. I think that Stuart considered this almost to be admitting that we had been in the wrong, and was determined to go back, with the blessing of the management at Longbridge whose attitude was 'Let's show them!'

In an effort to reduce the costs, particularly to private owners, the organisers introduced a tyre 'handicap'. There were two categories, one in which competitors could use as many tyres as they could afford but with a 12 per cent handicap, and one in which there was a limit of eight tyres per car over each of the two competitive sections of the rally.

Monte Carlo Rally 1967; one set of test tyres used over 24 kms Col de Turini-La Bollene-Col de Turini

Stuart calculated that the 12 per cent handicap was too much, so after consultations with the drivers and Dunlop, it was decided to enter the cars in the 'tyre limit category'. Dunlop were concerned at the safety aspect of this tyre limit, as were the drivers, because a wrong tyre choice before the start of each competitive section could result in cars running on worn out and dangerous tyres. Dunlop worked hard on new compounds and constructions in the months leading up to the Monte and a number of test sessions were held with a selection of studded tyres.

For one of these tests I was sent down to Monte towing a test/recce Mini on a trailer with a number of special tyres, the bulk of which were being flown to Nice by Dunlop Racing. After losing a trailer wheel near Troyes, in Northern France I arrived in Nice with the recce car on an 'A' bracket. I met up with the Dunlop technicians and Timo and Rauno and over the next two nights the colour-coded tyres were tested at rally speeds. One of the problems with a studded tyre when used on dry roads was the build-up of heat locally in the rubber around the stud which in severe conditions would allow the stud to loosen and come flying out. I took some photos of the various covers after the tests and these were taken back to Dunlop by their technicians to help with the final assessment.

The decision to go for the eight-tyre limit category was not taken lightly because there would be a considerable weight penalty with four extra wheels/tyres to be carried on such a small car. This was overcome to a certain extent by deciding to have magnesium alloy wheels homologated for the Mini Cooper S; these were made by Tech Del Ltd under the trade name Minilite. One hundred and fifty were ordered for the Monte, at about four times the cost of standard steel wheels, but this represented a weight saving of approximately 22 lb with the added bonus of having a stronger wheel and improved brake cooling.

I had to get the wheel homologated in time for the Monte with photos and the appropriate amendment sheet sent off to the FIA, and there were some anxious days waiting for the duly embossed sheet to come back via the RAC Motor Sport Division.

All competitors running in the limited tyre category had to have yellow side patches instead of white for the numbers. This was to allow officials to identify them during the event.

Another problem was where to stow the four extra wheels/tyres. Two normally went in the boot but to put two on a roof rack was out of the question, with the wind resistance and drastic change in centre of gravity. It was decided to carry two on the back seat and, following the problems in 1966, Stuart obtained official permission from the FIA to carry them in that position. The seat cushion was strapped to the back of the seat and to hold the wheels down securely, Doug asked Terry Mitchell in the Design Department at Abingdon if he could design a quick-release catch. In no time at all Terry came up with a strong over-centre clamp which would permit the speedy removal of the wheels. Terry had designed a number of items for the programme, one of them being the famous 'Mitchell' mounting for the rear of the gearbox remote control. This was designed as a fail-safe unit after repeated failure of the production mounting had meant carrying an emergency steel strap to bolt under the remote control if the original mounting broke.

Such was the pressure in the workshop that it was decided that Cliff would be responsible for building all the rally engines, although somehow Brian Moylan and Roy Brown who were preparing Rauno's car had already started building an engine. In the end it was the only one built by the

Monte Magic

mechanics for the car they were preparing, a complete departure from previous build programmes.

With Peter to accompany Stuart on the Monte he found himself in the office one morning helping out with the tyre schedule. This was mapped out on single piece of paper and when Stuart was satisfied, he asked Peter if he understood it. Before Peter could reply he was asked by Stuart to go over into the factory to take a photocopy. Here disaster struck when the machine took a dislike to the tyre schedule which promptly went up in smoke. Peter dare not go back to Stuart without the precious document and spent some time trying to remember its contents and piecing it together from the charred remains.

Five cars were entered with Simo Lampinen again joining our four regulars but Raymond Joss going as co-driver with Tony Fall. Two started from Monte and one each from Lisbon, Athens and Dover. I was sent off to Lisbon again, this time with Timo's car. Crossing from Southampton the roads were dry until, near Bordeaux, there was sheet ice and we were glad of our studded tyres on the service car as we passed many stranded lorries. Snow was falling as we left Biarritz but it did not come to much and we stayed the night at Valladolid where, to their surprise, we bumped into Ray Simpson (Castrol Competitions Manager) and his girl friend, as they stepped out of the lift.

The night was very cold and in the morning snow was lying on the floor where it had been driven through the shutters. After breakfast, the next hours were quite hazardous as we slithered through deep snow and ice until we reached the border with Portugal. The snow was at least six inches deep here with little traffic moving, and we were not much encouraged by an Automobile Club official who told us the road into Portugal was blocked.

After doing a recce of the first mile without the trailer we decide to have a go. The snow had stopped, but progress was slow through having to stop frequently to get the car and trailer unstuck. After about two hours we were joined by two Portuguese in a Morris J4 Minibus, four people in a Vauxhall VX 4/90 fitted with chains and Ray Simpson in his MGB GT running on Dunlop C41 tyres. This little convoy proceeded with the help of shared shovels often charging drifts to get through until conditions got so bad that we had to resort to unloading the rally car. Johnny drove it with the suspension pumped up until we arrived at the next town, Guarda, where we found a hotel at 02.00 hrs the next morning. Not a bad average, 33 km in 8 hours!

Following a good sleep we continued next morning on roads covered with ice, eventually arriving in Lisbon. The Morris Importer was looking after us again with their wonderful hospitality, supervised by Henry Bastos.

Monte Carlo Rally 1967. Timo Makinen, John Evans, Bill Price and Paul Easter at Lisbon

Next day I received a call from Stuart advising us that there had been a problem at scrutineering in Monte where the officials insisted that the rally plates were mounted in a vertical position on the cars; because it looked as though the French were gunning for us again, we were to do the same with our car.

Johnny started to make some brackets to mount the rally plate but the chief mechanic from Almeida took the job out of our hands. This was quite involved as the number plate was painted on the bonnet and as it had to be moved, the bonnet had to be repainted. Within about two hours the job was completed for us!

We had two service points before Monte, one in Spain and the other over the border in France. There was minor panic when two of our other cars arrived without modified rally plate mountings; after some discussiion with the crews we made up some brackets to mount the plate on the roof gutter.

The cars arrived in Monte without problems although Paddy had encountered heavy snow on the run-in from Athens. Tyre choice was going to be very important but with a large element of luck attached to it. We had 'ice note' crews going over the stages as near to the stage start times as possible but unless the weather remained as it was the information would soon be out of date.

Monte Carlo Rally 1967; the eventual winners, Rauno Aaltonen/Henry Liddon on a stage

Apart from Paddy who took plain and studded Weathermasters, the drivers chose SP3 and part-studded Weathermasters to make up their total of eight tyres. Once the choice was made, the officials branded the tyres and the cars set off on the Chambery section. On the first stage the Minis were in the top ten fastest times but on Monte Ventoux, Timo was just beaten by the Porsche of Klass. On the following Gap stage Paddy was third fastest but with the exception of the Col de Granier there had not been much snow to benefit the Minis.

When the rally returned to Monte the interim results showed that the dry conditions had benefited the Porsches, with Vic Elford leading, followed by four of the Minis, these five covered by a span of 58 seconds.

The fastest 60 crews lined up for the Mountain Circuit and with the first stages dry the Minis were going to have problems although they had strength of numbers on their side. Then it started to snow and on the Col de Turini Timo was fastest by 19 seconds with Andersson (Lancia) and Elford (Porsche) both dropping time. On the second time over the Turini, Rauno was fastest but then things started to go wrong.

Mysteriously a boulder crashed down in front of Timo's car smashing the oil cooler and distributor putting him out of the rally.

Right: *This is what happened to Timo Makinen's car on the 1967 Monte Carlo Rally*

1967

Monte Magic

One of the Porches went off the road leaving Rauno with a narrow lead only one second in front of Vic Elford with one stage to go. Luckily the snow kept falling and Rauno finished with a lead of 13 seconds over the next car, a Lancia. The results had to be rechecked and it was not until 14.00 hrs that the official results were published. It was a great win after the 1966 rally with Paddy sixth, Tony tenth and Simo fifteenth overall.

The Company agreed to fly the cars home, and the five rally cars and one recce car were loaded into a Carvair at Nice airport. Team personnel, including myself, who had missed out on the flight last year were given the chance of a seat; it was a pleasant change after the 'Barriere de degel' fiasco in 1966. The year could not have started in a better manner and it was a fitting finale for Stuart running his last Monte. So in effect we had won the Monte four years in a row, if you count 1966, which was quite an achievement; the French do not like being beaten on home ground.

The Swedish Rally had not been a lucky event for Abingdon but the two Finns were off to Scandinavia where two cars were entered using the new Minilite wheels again and with both cars fitted with the Makinen sump guard. The guard had been first built by Timo for use in Finland and when he brought a sample over to Abingdon, we had copied it and used it on rough road events although it was very heavy.

There was a lot of snow in Sweden but in spite of hoping for a change in fortune Timo retired on the second stage with a broken caliper. Simo Lampinen was making the running in a Saab and our luck almost ran out when Rauno hit a snow bank. The car turned over with the loss of his personal documents and belongings when the rear window flew out. They managed to continue and in the circumstances were lucky to finish third overall, our first finish in a Swedish.

Henry Liddon fills up from a 4 gallon Jerribag, 1967 Swedish Rally

The winners return home, 1967 Monte Carlo Rally

1966

Form filling at the Czech/German border en route to the 1966 Rallye Vltava.

Timo leaves the hotel for scrutineering, 1966 Rallye Vltava.

RAC Rally 1966. Paddy Hopkirk/Ron Crellin Mini Cooper S 1275.

1967

The winning Mini Cooper S 1275 driven by Rauno Aaltonen/Henry Liddon approaches Monte on the run-in, Monte Carlo Rally 1967.

Loading the cars on the Carvair at Nice airport, 1967 Monte Carlo rally.

1967

Bob and Dudley Pike attack Timo's car at a service point during the 1967 Tulip Rally.

Team cars lined up at Glyphada Beach, 1967 Acropolis Rally.

Wolseley 6/110 service car waits at level crossing during 1967 Acropolis Rally.

1968

Cockpit of Mini Cooper S 1275, Monte Carlo Rally 1968.

Monte Carlo Rally 1968. Brian Culcheth/Johnstone Syer, Morris 1800 on a stage.

1968

Monte Carlo Rally 1968. Den Green checks the tyres on Rauno's car at a service stop.

Timo Makinen/Paul Easter at a control, 1968 Monte Carlo Rally.

1968

Rauno Aaltonen/Henry Liddon soon after the start of the East African Safari 1968.

Timo and Paul near Zolder, 1968 Tulip Rally.

1968

Henry Liddon (sunglasses) waits while the service crew attend to the Mini Cooper S 1275, 1968 Acropolis Rally.

Acropolis Recce 1968, Austin 1800 at speed (P. Easter)

1968

1967

San Remo Push

Somtimes events clashed, so with Rauno and Timo in Sweden, Paddy and Tony were doing a recce for the San Remo rally. They had had a frustrating time because snow had blocked much of the route preventing serious practising until shortly before the rally. The weather had done a lot of damage to the stage roads which were very rough. On paper it looked like a three-way battle between the Mini Cooper S, the Renaults and the Lancias and it soon became clear that with the road sections being so tight, many cars would collect road penalties.

During the first stages the honours were shared by our cars and the Renaults but by half distance both Renault and Lancia had lost cars and Paddy had taken the lead. The sections around Genoa were particularly rough and Munari in a Lancia retired with a broken sump. Although Piot's Renault was fastest on the last two stages Paddy still held a slight lead. However, it was only when a mile from the end of the last stage that Paddy broke a driveshaft managing to reach the finish with the help of a tractor. Doug Watts was at the end of the stage with Peter Browning and, because it was obvious that to change the shaft would put them right out of the results, Paddy suggested that Doug should push the Mini with the Vanden Plas service car.

With much bumping and banging they moved off, Paddy freewheeling where possible and blipping the throttle and beeping the horn when passing crowds or policemen. There was a time control about half-way to San Remo which luckily was on a steep slope allowing Paddy to creep away from the control by gravity, stimulating severe clutch slip.

The final gamble came when they approached the tunnel leading to the finish control. Doug got up to 60 mph in the tunnel and at the last moment backed-off, Paddy emerging from the tunnel with horn blowing and lamps blazing to do a handbrake turn round the traffic island maintaining just enough momentum to reach the control table. The crowd and officials seemed to be unaware that anything was amiss, and sympathised when he appeared to have clutch failure at that final moment.

When the results were posted, Paddy was placed second overall although the team felt sure that they had been spotted. Apart from John Davenport who tackled the crew unofficially in the hotel, no official protest was lodged and the result stood. It was a very upset John Davenport who had to settle for third place in the Lancia he was co-driving with Ove Andersson.

This was Stuart's last European rally with BMC and it was now time for Peter to take responsibility for the team.

Mini at Sebring

In addition to the two MGBs for the 12 Hour race, a Mini Cooper S was prepared for the supporting 4 Hour saloon car race.

The 1967 Sebring race was the first works entry of an MGB GT in an international event, entered in the Prototype Category because insufficient had been built at this stage for it to be homologated in Group 3 GT Category. It was decided to take advantage of the freedom permitted for prototypes by increasing the cubic capacity of the GT engine to 2004 cc, and

1967 Sebring 3 Hour race, Mini Cooper S ready for shipment

Monte Magic

with a compression ratio of 10.8:1, race camshaft, Weber carburettor and side exhaust, the car was almost as competitive as the tourer despite a slight weight disadvantage. The second car was prepared to comply with Appendix J Group 3.

The Mini Cooper S was driven by Paddy Hopkirk and John Rhodes and this was the first time that an Abingdon Mini had been entered in a North American event. The Mini went well in the race, maintaining a good overall position and leading the 1300 cc class. Despite suffering from fuel starvation due to a faulty refuelling rig in the pits, the Mini was still leading its class when the end of the race approached at 16.00 hrs. Much to the dismay of Peter Browning and his pit crew, the Mini spluttered to a halt in the pit road having just crossed the line before the 16.00 hrs finish time. To qualify as a finisher the car would have to do another lap, so some more fuel was put in and the car finished the race.

Lancia protested that the Mini had contravened the regulations but Peter was able to convince the officials that they had complied and the car was duly awarded the 1300 cc class.

In the 12 Hour Race the MGBs went well and, apart from when Paddy lost about three minutes in the pits after being pushed off the circuit by a spinning Chapparal, the two cars finished eleventh and twelfth overall, the GT being the higher placed with a class win as well. The tourer was third in class driven by Timo and John Rhodes.

In preparation for future racing events, a project was under way to build six sets of special aluminium panels for the new MGC GT, at Pressed Steel. The MGC was not due to be launched until the 1967 Motor Show but of the initial three bodies assembled, the first one was brought in to the workshop to be prepared for the Targa Florio. To avoid any premature publicity of the six-cylinder MG, for the Targa the

Tailgate view of class winning MGB GT driven by Paddy Hopkirk/Andrew Hedges, Sebring 12 Hour Race 1967

Paddy Hopkirk and Terry Harryman start the 1967 Circuit of Ireland

1967

car was prepared with an MGB engine.

For the Circuit of Ireland, Paddy had Terry Harryman as co-driver again. The rally was another success for Paddy who was first, over 50 points ahead of another Irish driver, Adrian Boyd who was driving an ex-works Mini Cooper S.

Safari Mini

One of the prizes for winning the Monte was a free entry in the East African Safari. Rauno persuaded Peter to prepare a car for the Safari, and although this was to be a low key entry supported by the local BMC agents in Nairobi, Benbros Bros, the preparation of the car was carried out with due consideration of the African conditions.

The Mini Cooper S was one of the most unusual Minis ever prepared at Abingdon being fitted with a considerable amount of special equipment. The power unit was more or less to the same spec as the 1966 RAC engines with the standard camshaft to give good low down torque, essential in a wet Safari. Pancake air cleaners were used and extensive waterproofing was carried out on the engine. A modified Hydrolastic pump was mounted on the rear bulkhead to enable the crew to pump up the suspension in an emergency, and with the rear seats removed, the Monte type quick-release clamps were used to retain spare wheels. The petrol pump was mounted at shoulder level to keep it out of flood water, and for the same reason, three large map pockets were attached to the roof lining to keep the documents and maps dry.

Two of the normal spot lamps were moved from the front of the grille to improve cooling, and they were mounted on the front wings close to the windscreen where they could be reached by the crew and cleaned of mud while mobile. Front/rear foot rests and grab handles were added and a hand throttle was fitted which could be used if the car became stuck. A quick release 'fly-screen' was mounted in front of the grille and another one under the front nearside wing helped to keep mud out of the radiator core. Extra jacking points at front and rear and a winch made up the rest of the equipment.

Den Green was sent out to look after the car and he was accompanied by Stuart Turner who had arranged an itinerary taking in the tourist sights of the Middle East. This was to be his last event in his official capacity.

Despite the careful preparation, things did not go well for the Mini on its first Safari. This model had always been dificult to keep cool on hot European events but East Africa was something else. In the opening miles the car ran very hot and on a very rough section, the fan hit the radiator cowling and stopped with the result that the water pump stopped and the fan belt burnt through. The engine suffered severe overheating and despite repairs to the broken parts, as they continued the engine overheated again with symptoms of head gasket failure, finally succumbing with the fine dust also clogging the air filters.

The ill-fated 1967 East African Safari Mini Cooper S

187

Monte Magic

Doug Watts presents Stuart Turner with a set of Corgi Minis as leaving present, March 1967

Corgi Minis and silver tray signed by the staff presented to Stuart Turner

Rauno Aaltonen lifts a wheel during the 1967 Tulip Rally

Den described the best part of the trip as the tourist excursions to see some of the historical wonders of the Middle East.

Following the Safari we had a good Tulip Rally, again run on a scratch basis with victory in the Touring Category going to Timo with Rauno second, and Julien Vernaeve making up the third member of the winning Manufacturer's Team. David Benzimra, son of the BMC importer in Nairobi, was loaned a car for the Tulip with Terry Harryman co-driving, but unfortunately the clutch failed near the end of the rally and they did not finish.

Right: *Timo climbs in as Henry Liddon compares notes with Paul Easter, 1967 Tulip Rally*

188

1967

Acropolis Rally

The next event was the Acropolis Rally with an entry of three cars, the service crews being supervised by Doug Watts. To accomplish the long journey to Greece we took two trailers to Ancona, on the Italian Adriatic coast, to catch the ferry to Patras. The four wheel trailer was left at Ancona to be collected on our return, and because we had some time in hand, a pleasant lunch was taken at a small beach restaurant.

The trip to Patras was quite pleasant and we then had a three hour drive to Athens where we booked into the Glyphada Beach Bungalows hotel. This was a nice place to stay beside the sea but meal service at the scattered bungalows got everyone down a bit with the slow service. There were the usual last minute preparations, car testing, sorting out service schedules and tyres, and getting the cars to scrutineering.

Paddy Hopkirk raises the dust in Greece, 1967 Acropolis Rally

The night before the rally the organisers held a cocktail party for competitors and team personnel and Peter Browning presented Doug, myself and the mechanics with tickets. We had a meal and then after emptying out the seats of one of the service cars went in to Athens to the cocktail party which was held on the roof of the Kings Garden Hotel. It was a very pleasant function where we met many old friends, leaving quite early to return to the hotel. We stopped on the way for a night-cap at one of the many bars on the coast road, then proceeding to a second which was a rather unwise decision. We were involved in a mock race with an English journalist in a hired Fiat and decided it was time to go home.

I returned with Johnny Evans to the hotel and unfortunately tripped over a chair in the dark in my room, which I was sharing with Peter Browning, which was not very popular. The remainder of our group returned about twenty minutes

Monte Magic

later and Johnny Organ who was sharing with Johnny Evans, unfortunately dropped a bottle of lime on the floor as he was preparing for bed. Johnny Evans woke up and jumped out of bed to help clear up the mess but unfortunately trod on a piece of glass cutting his foot badly.

In the morning I was detailed to take the casualty to the nearest hospital for treatment, but I had to leave the room as this large Greek nurse started to probe Johnny's foot with a sharp instrument. The wound was reluctant to heal and Johnny was not able to be much help during the rest of the trip. Back at home his local doctor found a large piece of glass in the wound.

The weather remained hot and sunny for the rally which got under way in the evening from near the Acropolis. I was in a service car with Peter and Robin as the cars headed south. The first stage saw the Mini Cooper S cars take the first three fastest times closely followed by the Lancias and Ford Lotus Cortinas. As the cars headed north again they had to cross the Gulf of Corinth by ferry, and as they ended the first day, Timo and Paddy were at the front as they approached Thessaloniki. It was here that Rauno struck disaster while contesting a 23 km stage. A competitor in a Renault went off the road on this stage and down a 150 ft drop. A doctor spectating a bit further down the stage saw the car go over and decided to offer assistance; he then drove up the stage in his Volkswagen to the scene, only to meet the next rally car on the stage, Rauno and Henry. The resulting head-on collision put Rauno and Henry out of the rally and in hospital, Rauno with suspected concussion. Henry had some nasty cuts on his shins where his legs had smacked the parcel shelf.

The rough conditions were taking their toll and at Volos, Timo arrived with a broken rear sub-frame. The car was turned on its side and the sub-frame welded and Timo was sent on his way. The cars returned to the same sevice point after this next stage but by now Timo's gearbox had had enough, and he was out.

After eleven stages, Paddy was in the lead, with only the driving test remaining, followed by the Parnis Hill Climb and race at Tatoi. On the Hill Climb Paddy was fastest by three seconds, but in the race, which did not affect the results, the oil pressure dropped and Paddy wisely stopped before the line, to complete the final lap slowly to the finish. Paddy had won; revenge after last year's problems.

There was a good prize-giving party where the rally secretary had put on the tables all the guests' place names in Greek; Henry Liddon's name looked like 'Zempy Ninton'!

Peter and some of the crews flew home while the main party, including Paul Easter and his fiancee Liz, and Henry Liddon and his wife Joyce, loaded the cars on the Greek liner *Chania* at Piraeus (the name painted-out on the stern of this vessel was *Warwick Castle*). The crude plank loading ramp caused a bit of drama when one of the Vanden Plas spun the planks away and dropped on to its chassis.

Henry and Joyce had the best cabin and their bath became very useful to keep our flagons of local wine cool for the voyage to Venice. There were many German tourists on board and we had quite a lively trip, the last night dance causing some mirth when I won the Mr and Mrs Chania prize with Liz.

When the ship docked at Venice, I drove with Robin towing a Mini to collect the trailer from Acona. We were stopped at the entrance to the Autostrada because the police would not let us tow a Mini on an A bracket. We eventually met up with the main party at Milan where we boarded the car sleeper train for Boulogne. There was a bit of commotion at Boulogne when the French railway officials realised that the four-wheel trailer was wider than the ramps. One side of the trailer was eventually carried off the train! The trip was rounded off on the sea front at Dover as we regrouped when Henry Liddon received a message from a passing seagull; damn good thing cows don't fly!

Targa MGB 'Prototype'

Three of the MGC lightweight bodies had been assembled by Bodies Branch at Castle Bromwich and Tommy Wellman was supervising the assembly of the first car, MBL 546E, by Gerald Wiffen. As mentioned previously, this was to run as an MGB on the Targa because the MGC six-cylinder car still on the 'secret list'. The overbored 2004 cc engine was similar in spec to the Sebring engine and the suspension was basically MGC with police rear springs and Girling disc brakes front/rear, twin servos and adjustable shock-absorbers. The wheel equipment was supplied by Minilite in the form of $15 \times 6½$ magnesium alloy rims with centre-lock hubs.

The MG GTS (four-cylinder) driven by Paddy Hopkirk during the 1967 Targa Florio

The shell had been painted red, just as all our MGs had been painted, but when we received the regulations for the Targa we realised that prototypes had to run in national colours which was of course British Racing Green. The car was so far advanced in preparation that there was no time to completely strip it out again so the paint job extended only to the externally visible panels.

On 25 April we took the GTS (we had registered it as an MG GTS) together with the other MGB for the Targa, to Castle Combe for a test session, with Andrew Hedges and Geoff Mabbs doing the driving. The Group 3 MGB was all right except for its losing a float chamber when the securing bolt came out.

The GTS was running with a Weber carburettor and completed 22 laps before lunch with Geoff at the wheel, the main complaint being too much front braking. After lunch Andrew tried the car and after lowering the front suspension ½ inch, set consistent times around 1 m 19 s. The Weber was then removed and two inch SU carburettors complete with manifold were fitted resulting in a lap time improvement of ½ second.

The cars were taken to Sicily by Tommy and the mechanics, the drivers and Peter Browning flying down. Peter had a bit of a scare before the race when Timo and Rauno were delayed at Naples airport after an incident concerning some broken Vodka bottles. It had ended with an official being roughed-up and the pair being detained in custody until it had been sorted out.

Official practice was permitted over a closed course on Friday with the drivers taking the two cars out for one steady lap to make sure all was well. A spare MGB had been taken out for practice and Alec Poole recorded fastest time in it

1967

during the practice session.

The race started at 08.00 hrs with the cars starting at twenty second intervals in hot sunny conditions. There was some concern when Paddy brought the GTS into the pits on lap 2 with brake problems, further stops during the race losing a total of twelve minutes. Otherwise the car ran well and Tommy was well pleased, although Paddy was not quite so complimentary.

The Tourer was less lucky when Andrew, normally a very consistent and safe driver, clipped a kilometre stone and went off the road head-on into a tree. He had been leading the GT Category but, although he was unhurt, his race was over. The GTS finished unofficially ninth overall because it did not achieve a distance within 90 per cent of the overall winner, but was awarded third in class behind two Porsches. It is interesting to note that ninth overall was an ex-works Austin Healey 3000 (ARX 91B) owned and driven by Ted Worswick.

Lars Ytterbring from Sweden was loaned an Abingdon car for the first time to drive on the Scottish Rally. With his co-driver Lars Persson, he drove sensibly to achieve a good second overall.

The 1967 Geneva Rally was an organisational cock-up! The rally was eligible for the European Championship Groups 1 and 3, but any cars entered in one of the other Groups were transferred to an event called the Criterium de Crans-sur-Sierre run in parallel with the Geneva Rally. We entered Tony Fall and Julien Vernaeve in two Group 2 Mini Cooper Ss using rear anti-roll bars for the first time.

At scrutineering in the start town, Crans-sur-Sierre, the only hiccup was when the lowered Minis failed to pass over the minimum height blocks, but this was soon rectified by increasing the Hydrolastic pressure.

It was a tough event with only twenty of the 80 starters finishing. Tony damaged his car on a rock face requiring some panel beating while Julien damaged his steering requiring a rack change which was completed in 30 minutes by the mechanics.

At the finish confusion reigned, no one knowing who had won what. Placing all the cars in a single category in the Geneva Rally, the Minis were placed third and fifth but, because they were running in the Criterium, they were placed first and second overall and this was the result they were given.

Austin 1800 Rally Win

The success of the two Austin 1800 cars on the 1965 Monte had prompted Longbridge to look at ways of improving the image of the model. We had done a bit of development work on an old Longbridge development car (LRX 824E) and this had been loaned to Bob Freeborough to do some national rallies to see how it would perform. Much to everyone's surprise he won the Moss Tyres Rally and had come second in another event which inspired some confidence in the car. It was down on power compared with most of the competition, but had the ability to travel very quickly over rough roads thanks to the Hydrolastic suspension.

The Danube Rally was sponsored by Castrol, by whom

Monte Magic

Stuart was now employed, and it was a call to Peter asking if we could enter a car which set the wheels in motion to enter an 1800. A Mini was entered for Rauno and, because there was a class for Group 5 cars which allowed a wide range of modifications, Peter took the opportunity of entering an 1800. Tony was asked to drive the car because he had shown some enthusiasm for it, had owned one and had done the Danube rally in 1966 with Rupert Jones.

Tony Fall/Mike Wood on the 1967 Danube Rally

The engine was full MGB twin carb Stage 6 giving a power output of 135 bhp using a 4.1:1 final drive but the suspension was more or less standard with Aeon bump-rubbers. The car was painted black but, because there was insufficient time to respray it a more photogenic colour, a white roof was added to give it a more sporty look.

With just one service car plus support from Castrol and Dunlop, the BMC cars started from Prague, the alternative starting point being Regensburg in Germany. The route of 2000 miles included nine special stages mainly in the mountains of Rumania and with high average speeds on the road sections of 50–60 mph, the Austin 1800 suspension gave the crew a smooth ride compared with some competitors driving short wheelbase firmly sprung cars.

Before the start there had been some confusion as to whether Rauno would require a visa to enter Hungary, having a Finnish passport. Nevertheless he did start, only to arrive at the border and find he was refused permission to enter, retiring on the spot. The 1800 went very well and apart from a broken rear brake rod, and a fractured radiator mounting bracket, no other problems were encountered. Two of the factory Renaults fell by the wayside with the remaining car coming in second behind the 1800 which surprised everyone to come home first, an unexpected bonus after losing Rauno.

Finnish Hat Trick

There was just one entry for the 1000 Lakes, Timo going for his hat-trick with Pekka Keskitalo. The rally car was taken to Finland on a Russian ship, the *Baltika*, sailing from Tilbury to Helsinki. I took one Vanden Plas service car with Bob Whittington and Roy Brown and we watched nervously as the cars were loaded by crane at Tilbury.

Travelling on a Russian ship was a new experience and after all the horror stories, we found the food and conditions reasonably good. The journey was broken by a call at Copenhagen where we were able to do some sightseeing, arriving at Helsinki after three days to be met by Timo and the Oy Voimavaunu AB service manager, Kauko Ruutsalo, on the quay. The customs clearance was smoothed out and we sighed with relief as the two cars were safely unloaded.

The usual testing and last minute adjustments took place in Helsinki before moving up to Jyvaskala for the start. Timo looked after us well and we even had time for a ride in his Donzi speedboat with its twin six-cylinder Mercruiser engines. He picked us up near the hotel and we had a fantastic ride with the prop coming out of the water at times as we shot across open water to the marina where it was berthed.

At scrutineering there was a problem with the headlamp bulbs not complying with Finnish traffic regulations, but in the end we fitted the quartz-iodine bulbs to the spot lamps only.

1000 Lakes Rally 1967, Timo Makinen and Bill Price watch 'GRX' swing ashore at Helsinki

The rally developed into a struggle between the Saabs of Lampinen, Trana, Orrenius, and Linberg and the Lotus Cortinas of Andersson and Soderstrom (using Tecalemit fuel injection) all pitted against Timo in the lone Mini using rubber cone suspension and his steel, full length sump guard.

Timo was sharing times with the Saabs but the Mini was showing signs of overheating, so we removed the lamp bar. This was done at a very short service halt and in the rush the bonnet safety strap was left undone. On the next stage the bonnet flew open and Timo was forced to complete the stage looking out of his side window. But even so he was only about 19 seconds slower than the fastest car, Soderstrom! The flying bonnet was caught by the photographers and it was rumoured that Alec Issigonis banned publication of the BMC version of this picture!

1967

A slight visibility problem for Timo Makinen on the 1967 1000 Lakes Rally

After half distance Timo started to have gearchange difficulty and we found that the gearbox remote control housing was broken. The car was tipped on its side and copious amounts of plastic metal and locking wire were applied because we were not carrying a spare. It was a continual battle to keep the remote control in one piece, with Timo involved in a tremendous battle with Lampinen over the last stages, ending up winner by a mere eight seconds. A very popular win, to give Timo a hat trick on his home event.

Marathon Minis

When the Marathon de la Route regulations arrived Peter came to the conclusion that 1 litre cars would stand a very good chance of a class win or even win outright. Two Mini Cooper S 970 cc cars were prepared, with full Group 2 engines but with as much lightening as possible including perspex windows and aluminium panels. An auxiliary radiator was fitted beside the oil cooler and an extra oil tank with a pump was carried, controlled from the drivers seat enabling the driver to top up the oil on the circuit if oil consumption became a problem.

The department had acquired from BMC Service for the nominal sum of £1 an old BMC Service Training Unit to convert into a transporter. The vehicle had been extended at the rear

Marathon de la Route 1967, the two 970 cc Mini Cooper S cars being loaded

The A. Poole/R. Enever/C. Baker car at speed, 1967 Marathon de la Route

Monte Magic

by Oswald Tillotson at Burnley (where Mike Wood was employed) and a new spring-loaded tail door/loading ramp was added. The vehicle was painted red/white, and had a cab capable of holding five people with space in the rear for two Minis; it had a two speed axle and was left-hand drive. Its first trip was to take the two 970s to Nürburgring.

The cars were driven by three-man crews, No 39 by Julien Vernaeve/Tony Fall/Andrew Hedges and No 40 by Alec Poole/Roger Enever/Clive Baker, each driver being scheduled to do shifts of three hours on and six off.

Peter's plan went to schedule to start with, the two smallest cars in the race lying eighth and tenth behind the leading Porsche of Vic Elford. At the end of the first day the Minis were up to third and fourth overall – an amazing position – and by next day had covered 2000 miles at an average of 65 mph.

That evening only 26 cars were still running; the Minis were still unpenalised, but trouble lay ahead. Clive Baker, driving in thick fog, suffered a broken throttle cable and in making temporary repairs lost twenty minutes, with a pit stop adding a further six minutes. Later in the night, in thick fog, Alec Poole lost his way, ran off the road with the car ending on its roof. Unable to regain the road after righting the car, he retired.

Various cars were in trouble including the leading Porsche which broke a brake disc allowing the second Mini into a brief lead. At the end of 70 hours a Mini wheel bearing failed and five minutes was lost when the hub refused to come off. However the Mini was still in second place which it held to the end. This was a tremendous result for such a small car which had covered 5,500 miles at an average of 66 mph.

Austrian Teach-In

During the summer I was sent off to Vienna with one of the mechanics, Dudley Pike, to assist Paddy and Rauno who were to be the instructors at a course for Austrian rally drivers. We took a Mini Cooper S with us on a trailer (LBL 590E) while the drivers flew to Vienna, the proceedings being co-ordinated by BMC Austria. The roads used were on a military training area where the accommodation was a bit spartan.

Paddy and Rauno did demonstration runs with each driver in our Mini and then each driver put into practice what he had been taught, using his own car. Rauno is very proficient in German so he handled those drivers whose English was not too good. Viewing some of the driving, I think Paddy and Rauno were quite brave to go out with the local drivers in their own cars. When the drivers were given the opportunity to drive a simulated stage against the clock, one or two were a little too eager and at least two cars were badly damaged, luckily without injury.

One of Tony Fall's complaints regarding the 1800 on the Danube was the bouncing of the rear end under extreme tarmac cornering conditions. A test session was arranged at Castle Combe circuit with Clive Baker doing the driving, the test supervised by Cliff. Clive did eleven laps of the circuit to get used to the car and establish a lap time (1m 26s), the car running on Dunlop R7 184 compound 550 × 13 in tyres, Minilite wheels and having a full tank of fuel. Progressive removal of the spare wheel, the rear Aeon bump-rubbers and the rear anti-roll bar caused a noticeable deterioration in handling with the rear jumping about and the directional stability becoming unpredictable. Refitting the parts and dropping the hydrolastic pressure improved things and after a number of minor modifications the conclusion was that the Danube spec with lowered ride height was the best compromise without some further development.

Group 6 on The Alpine

A new style Alpine had been devised this year with the handicap system scrapped and with minutes chopped off some road sections. Cars from Groups 1 to 6 were allowed to enter and this time we prepared three Group 6 cars for Rauno, Timo and Paddy with a Group 2 car for Tony. Following the success of the 1800 on the Danube, the Alpine was an opportunity to give Brian Culcheth his first works drive, using the Danube car.

Alpine Rally 1967, Brian Culcheth/Johnstone Syer in the Austin 1800

The power was increased by about 10 bhp over previous specs for the Minis, with a Weber 45 DCOE carburettor in use on the Group 6 cars as well as an auxiliary radiator. Weight was reduced by fitting aluminium doors, bonnet and boot lid with perspex side and rear windows. A dual brake system (mechanical and hydraulic) was mandatory on the Group 6 cars, this being achieved by connecting a cable to the brake pedal which in turn was linked to the handbrake lever. Careful adjustment of the cable for scrutineering enabled the driver to demonstrate how the system worked. A little crude, perhaps, but sufficient to get round the regulations.

The first Stage was from Marseilles to Alpe d'Huez a distance of 1,450 km. The furious pace soon brought retirements, including Rauno with broken transmission and Tony who had crashed. At Alpe d'Huez, Timo was third behind the Renaults of Larousse and Vinatier with Paddy in seventh place. Brian Culcheth was going well and was leading his class; the 1800 was a big car to throw around the Alps.

The second Stage was a 700 km loop out from Alpe d'Huez and back; with a further batch of retirements, Timo was third and Paddy fourth. There was frantic work at the next service point with Paddy in a state of excitement shouting, 'Quick boys, my brakes, my brakes'! Stan Bradford, who was a dab hand at brewing up a cup of tea in times of stress, said calmly, 'Have a cup of tea, Paddy' as the rest of the gang attacked the cars. Timo needed new calipers again, whilst Paddy got a replacement servo, with new brakes and tyres all round on all three cars.

The winners: Paddy Hopkirk/Ron Crellin 1967 Alpine Rally

The final Stage to Menton was 1,650 km to be covered in 19 hours. At the start of the Col du Marocaz, Timo suffered a broken throttle cable. With insufficient time to fit a new one he drove for the next two hours on the ignition switch. On the highest sections there was some thick fog which Timo and Paddy used to their advantage by setting some fastest times. By Guillestre Paddy was leading but Timo retired on the final descent of the Col d'Allos when the idler gear bearings failed. At the finish Paddy had held his lead and was declared winner with 'Culch' coming home with a well deserved class

1967

Monte Magic

win in the 1800. This had been one of the hardest Alpines ever with only twenty finishers, five of those being disqualified for being OTL. Well done Paddy, a great result.

The main party with the cars returned on the car sleeper to Paris followed by a drive to Boulogne. I was towing one of the Minis on an 'A' bracket and because we were short of seats, Tommy Eales was sitting in the Mini. Half an hour out of Paris the 'A' bracket suddenly broke free and the Mini veered across the road. Tommy was able to grab the steering wheel and prevent a head-on collision. Phew!

Monza Records

Earlier in the year Peter asked me to do some research into existing International Records with particular reference to Class E for cars of 1,500–2,000 cc. I spent some time at the RAC, Pall Mall going through the record book and came back with the details. The decision to tackle some FIA records was inspired by Castrol who footed about 60 per cent of the budget, but it had the full backing of Longbridge. The record in question was indeed, that for Class E 1,500–2,000 cc. After a test run at Monza to see if the 1800 could cope with the banked track, it was agreed that the run would go ahead. An ex-demonstrator was acquired from Longbridge, a Morris 1800 (LBL 416E) and preparation commenced.

The engine was built to full Stage 6 tune with two inch SU carburettors, bored out to 1857 cc, a compression ratio of 10:1 and a 4.1 final drive. The maximum amount of lightening was carried out with all the trim and sound deadening

1967 Monza Record Run, Morris 1800 during a pit stop

1967 Monza Record Run, Morris 1800 tools and spares

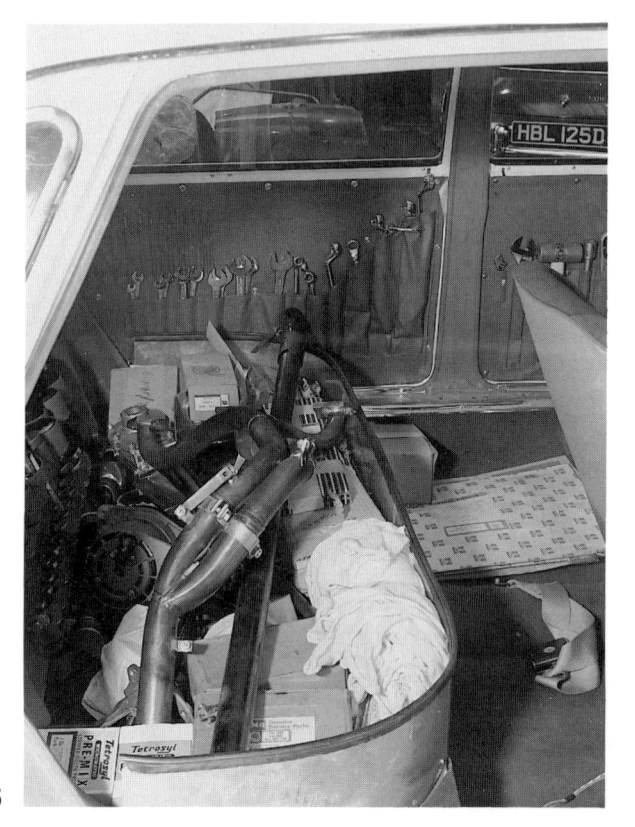

removed and aluminium doors, bonnet and boot fitted plus perspex side and rear windows. A special 20 gallon fuel tank replaced the standard unit with a quick-release filler, and quick-lift jacking points were added at the front and rear of the bumperless body.

The suspension was more or less Alpine spec with adjustable front tie-rods and Minilite wheels fitted with Dunlop 550L racing tyres. A remote control oil reservoir and pump was fitted to enable the driver to top up the oil on the move. As the weather was going to be warm, a bug-deflector was mounted on the bonnet to help keep the screen clear of squashed flies. Pye of Cambridge supplied a two-way radio for communicatiion between the drivers – Rauno, Tony, Clive Baker, Julien Vernaeve, Roger Enever and Alec Poole – and the pits.

The rules for FIA recognised record attempts are fairly strict, and because all spares have to be carried on the car, Tommy devised a special spares box mounted on the rear seat pan with a comprehensive tool roll made up by the MG Trim shop attached to the nearside door.

Tommy was in charge of the three mechanics with Don Hayter from MG Design, and personnel from Castrol, Dunlop, Lucas and SU making up the support team.

The new Transporter was put to good use to take the car to Monza where Peter had Les Needham looking after the timing and lap scoring. The run was blessed with a mixture of weather and with the drivers doing regular spells at the wheel the early enthusiasm soon turned to boredom. Some tyre feathering was experienced at the start but as soon as the suspension settled down this cured itself, and apart from routine servicing and maintenance the records started to fall.

The 4 day then the 5, 6 and 7 day records together with 15,000 miles, and 20,000 and 25,000 km records were taken at averages of 92.64, 93.38 and 92.78 mph respectively. Fuel consumption was 15 mpg and oil was used at a rate of 850 miles/pint.

One or two strange happenings occurred out on the circuit during the seven days which relieved the boredom. These included a ghost seen hanging from one of the observation towers and on another occasion two naked bodies were seen dancing in the long grass. These figures bore some resemblance to persons present! A good effort was made with the team well deserving the champage produced on the circuit to celebrate.

1967

Johnny Evans relaxes during the 1967 Monza Record Run

Just before the Motor Show the long rumoured new MG was announced; this was the MGC with tourer and GT bodies. It was fitted with a new 2.9 litre six-cylinder engine, manual or automatic transmissiion, torsion bar front suspension and 15 inch wheels.

In our efforts to keep in front of the opposition, development of a cast iron eight-port cylinder head was going ahead at Morris Engines at Coventry. One of the first cylinder heads was used to build an injection engine using individual intake trumpets with butterfly type throttle discs, and a Lucas metering unit driven off the front of the camshaft. With the eight-port arrangement, a new camshaft had to be made, similar in profile to the successful AEA 648 cam we had been using successfully in the five-port engines.

Corsican Fan Belts

To give the injection engine a test in rally conditions, the engine was built into a recce car for the Tour of Corsica, an event in which it had been decided to enter two cars. We had been in the event before but not since Pat Moss was snowed-off in 1961 with the Austin Healey 3000.

The cars were prepared to Group 6 specification, very similar to the Alpine spec, with an auxiliary radiator, expansion tank inside the car, and alternators, now standard fitment. Externally the cars were seen to be sporting a 'power' blister on the bonnet but this was in fact a clearance bump to stop the bonnet fouling on the 1100 radiators that had been fitted to help engine cooling. We were also using Minilite knock-on wheels employing a peg-drive system to give us every advantage during tyre changes which would be critical on the rally.

The injection engine development looked promising and, as a result, the plan for the forthcoming RAC Rally was to enter Timo in an injection engined car. Owing to shortage of parts we desperately wanted the recce engine back from Corsica.

Testing one of the Tour of Corsica cars at Silverstone. Note the knock-on front hub

I flew down to Corsica to collect the recce injection car, missing the connection in Paris and arriving at Ajaccio instead of Bastia. The recce car had been taken to Bastia by Norman Higgins, MG Accountant, and Jimmy Simpson of Castrol who then had to do an about-turn and come back to Ajaccio. Norman described this journey over the mountains as the most frightening he had ever made, in the dark in a raging thunderstorm with gale force winds.

I had only been in Ajaccio for about an hour when the car arrived with a breathless Norman, whereupon, Clive Baker guided me to the docks where I scrambled on board the overnight ferry to Marseilles just as the ramp was being raised. I had not seen the Mediterranean so rough and I was glad to have a bunk to lie on, although at times I had a job to stop rolling out. I was ashore at 0800 hrs and after changing some money in the Vieux Port drove to Dunkirk to catch the midnight ferry to Dover.

The ferry was held offshore at Dover because of the rough seas, and when we docked I found that the car, parked on deck in an open garage, had been well and truly soaked with sea spray and would not start. I had to resort to getting a tow off the ferry to Henlys Garage where I dried the car out and was soon on my way home.

Meanwhile, in Corsica the rally got under way with the first of the night time stages. Immediately both cars started to experience dimming of the lights and some overheating. The fan belts were adjusted by the mechanics but they were soon slipping again and within a few kilometres both cars retired with severe overheating and flat batteries. This was unbelievable: the alternator/fan belt spec was unchanged, the cars had been checked and tested before the rally and the fan belts adjusted. What had gone wrong? There was even a suggestion of sabotage. When the team returned to Abingdon, a detailed investigation took place and it was found that we had

197

Monte Magic

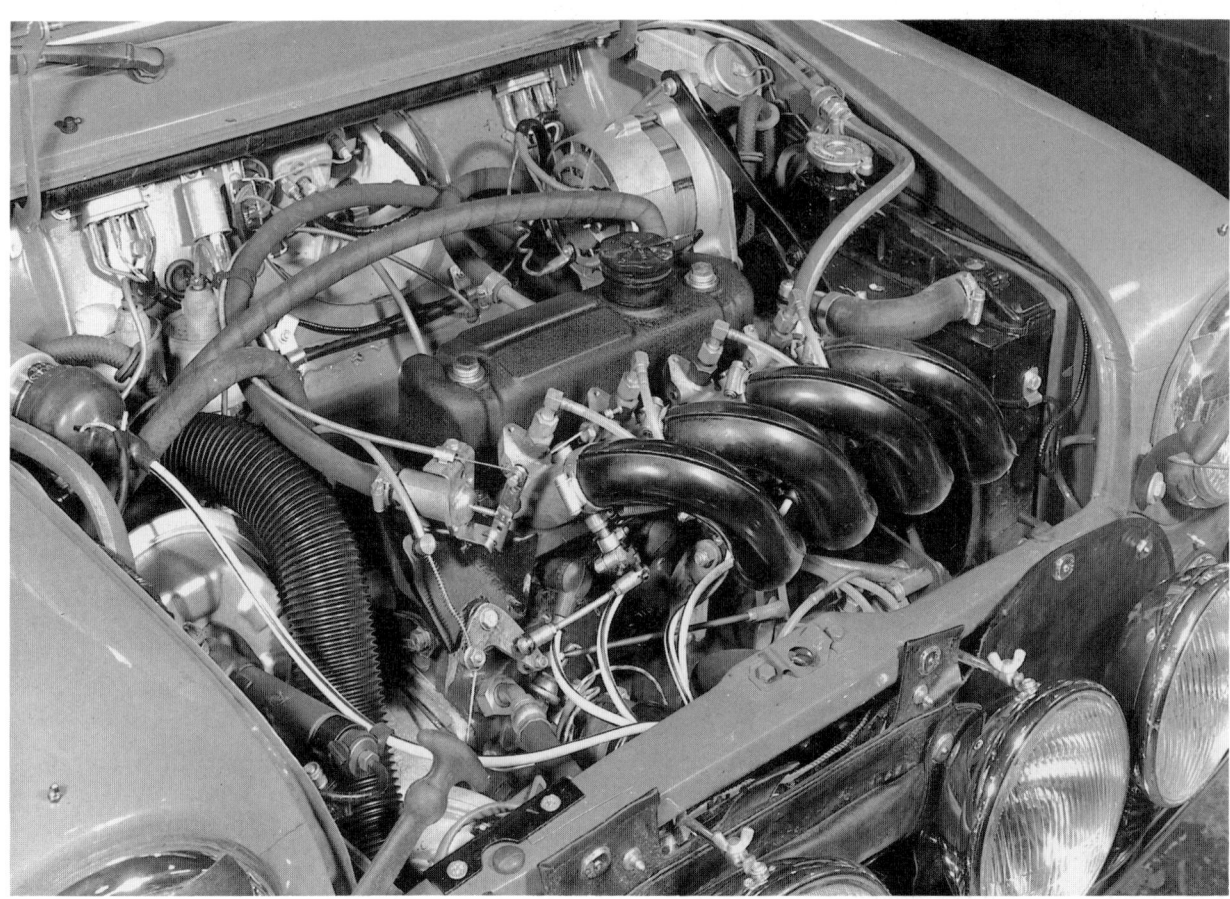

1967

a faulty batch of fan belts. All that work and expense down the drain for the sake of a £1 fan belt. Imagine how Peter felt, having to report to the 'Kremlin' that the cars retired with slipping fan belts!

The RAC Rally, with sponsorship from the *Sun* newspaper again, announced that Group 6 cars would be admitted, which gave Peter one last chance to enter and win with an Austin Healey 3000. Although the eight-port cylinder head was not homologated, the injection Mini was entered in Group 6 for Timo.

Austin 1800 engine compartment, prepared for the cancelled 1967 RAC Rally

Because no other car was available for the rally, Peter decided to loan his own ex-works Austin Healey 3000 (ARX 92B) for the event, which had been reregistered with Peter's personal number PWB 57. Because Timo was in favour of driving the injection Mini, Rauno was nominated as the Healey driver. The car was to be the most powerful Healey we had built, using one of the handful of all-alloy engines, triple Weber carburettors and the exhaust fully enclosed in the body like Timo's 1965 car. A dual braking system was fitted for the first time and – another first – Minilite wheels with knock-on hubs were used. When the car was finished, because it was three years old it had to go for an MOT Test. Imagine the surprise at East St. Helens Garage in Abingdon when Nobby turned up with this gleaming car for an MOT.

Mini Cooper S cars were prepared for Tony and Paddy using the well-tried carburettor engines. As it turned out, all these elaborate preparations came to nought. There had been an outbreak of foot-and-mouth disease during the last few days building up to the rally and it appeared that there would be some route diversions to avoid infected areas. It was not until the night before the rally, at the Excelsior Hotel near London Airport, that a Ministry of Agriculture official arrived for a meeting with the organisers. In view of the serious nature of the outbreak, the difficult desision was made to cancel the RAC Rally. This was naturally a great disappointment, not to mention the financial implications both for the organisers and the competitors.

Fuel injection Mini Cooper S 1275, ready for the cancelled 1967 RAC Rally

As some small compensation, a special stage was televised near Camberley. This gave TV something to broadcast to fill in the gap in their winter schedule, with a number of invited factory teams taking part. Timo drove the injection Mini with Tony Fall as passenger, and was as spectacular as ever. One of the most published photos of a Mini jumping was of this car on the Camberley TV stage. So the 1967 season ended on a low note with no last appearance of the Austin Healey 3000.

Following the appearance of the MG GTS (MGC prototype) on the Targa Florio the specification of the car was revised with the fitting in mind of the six-cylinder engine. Further work on the rear end added turrets to take telescopic shock-absorbers and radius rods on the rear axle. The engine was similar in spec to the Healey engine with an aluminium alloy cylinder head and triple Webers, and close ratio gears in the overdrive gearbox.

With the cancellation of the RAC and a dry spell in

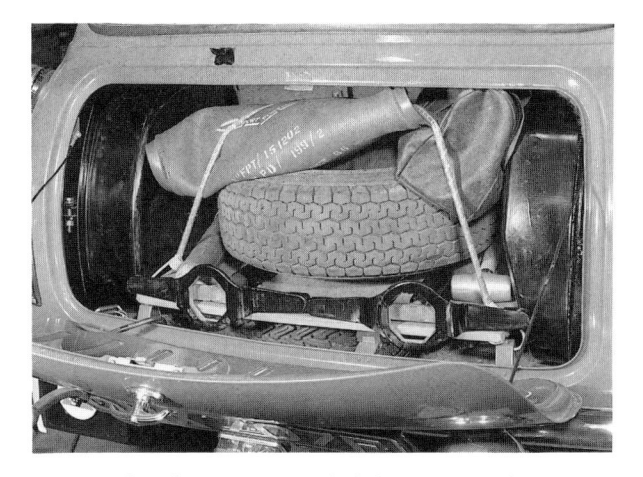

Hexagon knock-on spanners tried during testing for the 1968 Monte Carlo Rally but not used

November the opportunity was taken to test the new spec MGC at Silverstone on the 23rd with Paddy and Clive Baker. A total of 28 laps was completed with no problems other than a broken fan belt and an oil leak from a defective weld on the sump. The main handling complaint was axle patter under heavy braking and too much understeer. The car was lowered, the negative camber increased, and with Aeon bump rubbers fitted to the front there was a substantial improvement with a reduction in the understeer. At the end of the day a best lap of 1m 49.5s was recorded with further attention being needed to low geared steering, spongy brakes, poor lateral support from the seat and the steering column too long. The car was destined to appear at Sebring, Timo having tried the car before flying back to Finland after the RAC cancellation.

In December another chapter in the Abingdon production history came to end with the last Austin Healey 3000 Mk III coming off the line, after enjoying a production run of over 17,000 cars.

Despite predictions that the days of the Mini Cooper S were over, 1967 had been a good year with outright victory in the Monte, Circuit of Ireland, Acropolis, Geneva, 1000 Lakes and Alpine rallies, a record that some other manufacturers, I am sure, would like to have achieved.

Engine compartment of Mini Cooper S with Weber 45 DCOE carburettor

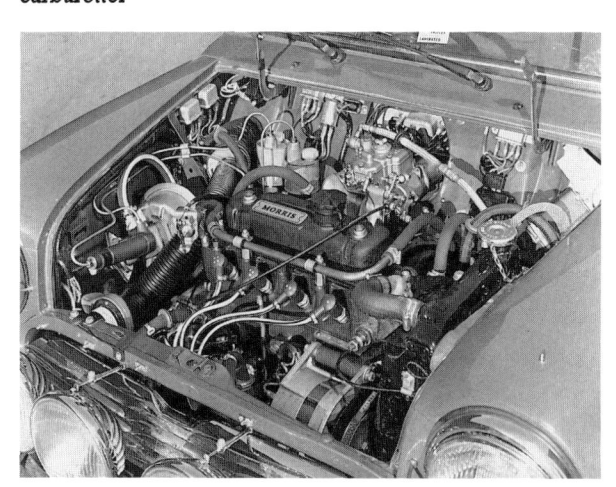

Marathon Year

5

Marathon Year
1968

THE MONTE CARLO RALLY. If there was snow then we surely must have a chance of pulling it off again – that was the general view. As usual the crews were in the south of France before Christmas practising the stages in preparation for our five-car entry of four Mini Cooper Ss and an 1800 for Brian Culcheth.

The starting points were shared out with the two Finns starting from Athens, Paddy from Lisbon, and Tony and Brian from London. The 1800 was prepared by Special Tuning along with two cars for the BMC Publicity Department but the four Minis were, of course, built in the Competitions Department.

Monte Carlo Rally 1968; the controversial 'split' Weber carburettors

Towards the end of 1967 Timo had arrived at Abingdon with some interesting carburettors, based on the Weber 45 DCOE. He had seen a similar set being used by a Mini driver in Finland and had bought a set for evaluation. They were what became known as 'split' Webers, modified so that they could be fitted to the production manifold which had to be retained for Group 2. Briefly, one float chamber was machined off and an SU-type flange was welded on so that they could then be fitted in pairs on the standard Cooper S inlet manifold. Cliff did a considerable amount of work with this new set-up and when he had finalised the spec, an increase in power of about 6 bhp had been achieved. The power figures recorded at the front wheels of the finished Monte cars were:

Paddy 93 bhp @ 6,800 rpm
Rauno 90 bhp @ 6,500 rpm
Timo 91.5 bhp @ 6,500 rpm
Tony 92 bhp @ 7,200 rpm

These figures were obtained with the AEA 648 camshaft, 12.6:1 compression ratio, Downton gas-flowed cylinder head and a 4.26:1 final drive and, of course, the 'split' Webers. Minilite wheels were now used exclusively and Triplex supplied the latest electrically-heated windscreens. The 1800 was not so highly modified but was bored out to 1845 cc with flat top pistons, a compression ratio of 11.5:1 and a 2 inch SU carburettor.

Monte Carlo Rally 1968; cockpit of Mini Cooper S. Note the route card holder for the driver

There had been the usual ritual of discussing and testing the stud options, the Dunlop trucks eventually carrying approximately 750 tyres to Monte for our cars alone. These varied between the Finnish deep snow 'chisels' to CR70 green spot racers for smooth tarmac.

I did my hat-trick of runs to Lisbon, this time taking Paddy's car accompanied by Gerald Wiffen. As we drove through Spain we were dismayed to hear a BBC news bulletin announcing that the BMC team on the way to Athens for the start of the Monte were stranded in deep snow between Naples and Brindisi. Den was taking the two cars for the Athens start down in the transporter with Stan and Robin and had become stuck in a blizzard behind a convoy of Italian lorries. It was so cold that diesel was freezing and it was only after much digging, the use of crude snow 'chains' made at Abingdon, and some luck that they made the ferry at Brindisi in the nick of time. There were no other dramas before the rally, and the 'ice-note' crews, consisting of Donald and Val Morley, Geoff Mabbs and Tony Ambrose, and Bob Freeborough and Julien Vernaeve, were in Monte preparing their schedules.

On the run-in to Monte Carlo, the Athens starters ran into deep snow in Yugoslavia. At one stage our cars were helped by some coach passengers to clear a passage. Paddy was well pleased with his heated screen when he ran into freezing fog in the Massif Centrale. A main service point was set up in a quarry on the approach to Monte for routine servicing and removal of the small roof racks which held two spare studded tyres.

Mary Smith, who had replaced Diana Kirkby as secretary to the Competitions Manager, was already established in the Hotel du Helder where she was manning a telephone and taking/sending messages during the rally.

Peter had taken the trouble of submitting details of our new carburettors to the FIA well in advance of the rally, so we were rather worried to hear a rumour circulating in Monte the evening the cars arrived, that our carburettors were to be subject to a protest. The rumour changed to fact when Peter was summoned to a meeting of the Sporting Commission where he was advised that the Technical Commission were not happy with the carburettors fitted to our four Mini Cooper S. It was considered that the flange welded to the Weber body was an intermediary device, but Peter pointed out that the flange was an integral part of our prototype carburettors; carburettors were free within the bounds of the Group 2 regulations. Eventually the Sporting Commission agreed with this interpretation of the regs but with the proviso that if another competitor protested the situation would have to be reconsidered.

Peter found this unacceptable and decided that he was

Marathon Year

Paddy tries to find some grip with Dunlop R7 racing tyres, Col de Turini, Monte Carlo Rally 1968

not prepared to let the crews risk their necks on the competitive sections not knowing if the carburettors were going to be declared illegal. There seemed no alternative but to withdraw the cars, a point of view which the drivers were not ready to accept unanimously but could understand. Raymond Baxter was now BMC Director of Publicity and was in Monte for the rally. He was involved with the team discussions concerning the carburettors and some felt that he tried to overule Peter's decision to pull-out. The matter was resolved by a telephone call to Longbridge which confirmed that the cars should continue.

The indecision and the belief that we were not restarting delayed the finalising of the service schedule until about five hours before the rally restart. Some of the team were in the town but were rounded up in time for the action to begin.

Unfortunately the delay prevented the Dunlop van getting to the first stage on time. This resulted in our cars doing the dry test on the part-studded tyres that they had arrived on, instead of the required racers. A similar situation arose at the second stage, but the tyres did arrive in time for Paddy and Tony to make a selection.

In the dry conditions the cars were being driven at tentenths and on the descent from Levens, Timo's car started to overheat and lose its lights. The crankshaft pulley had come

Den Green closes Rauno Aaltonen's door during service stop, 1968 Monte Carlo Rally

Brian Culcheth/Johnstone Syer, Morris 1800 during the 1968 Monte Carlo Rally

loose and drive was lost to water pump and alternator. Timo and Paul managed to coax the car to end of the Monte–Vals les Bains–Monte section but when they arrived at the final control, the engine was so hot that it was literally glowing. This was disputed by many people but Paul saw it with his own eyes and still cannot understand why it was still running!

Only 80 cars were classified at the end of this section, with our remaining three Minis lying in fourth, fifth and seventh positions behind the Porsches. There were now just (just ?) six stages of the Mountain Circuit to go and we had no less than 21 service points covering the route with most of the mechanics seeing the cars through three times.

Wheel change for Rauno Aaltonen/Henry Liddon, 1968 San Remo Rally

Timo's car was virtually finished but it was decided that if it would start in the *parc fermé* and get to the start control it would be classified as a finisher even if it could go no further. The car amazingly did start the section but after booking out of the control, Timo and Paul diverted to the Tip Top bar before it seized again.

The drivers did their best in the dry conditions, slithering across the only snow on the top of the Col de Turini on their racing tyres. The dry conditions had favoured the Alpines and Porches, the Minis being just out-powered on this occasion. At the finish we were placed third, fourth and fifth with the 1800 24th and second in class. We won the Touring Category and the Challenge L'Equipe for the best team and although some people were not very complimentary, I think it was another fantastic result. With some snow, we could have been first, second and third again!

There were further questions about the carburettors at final scutineering where the carburettors and manifolds were examined minutely by the Technical Commission but in the end they were accepted and the results stood. One point that Cliff had kept quiet about was a small blanking plug which had been inserted in the inlet manifold balance pipe to aid clean running. Although it had a small bleed hole drilled in it we have often wondered what view the scrutineers would have taken if it had been found.

So another Monte was over, once again surrounded by controversy. It seemed that someone, somewhere did not want us to win, but this year the weather was the winner.

During the Monte, leaflets were circulated publicising an event called the *Daily Express* London to Sydney Marathon, and described as the greatest motoring event of modern times. The total length was to be 10,000 miles and with a first prize of £10,000 this caused much interest although many were sceptical that it would actually take place. However, with such names as John Gott, Jack Kemsley, Tommy Sopwith and Dean Delamont on the organising committee, there had to be some optimism that it was not a hoax.

Back at Abingdon, *Safety Fast* Magazine had a change of staff when Murray Loake resigned to accept the position of editor of the Austin magazine at Longbridge. Clive Richardson was appointed as Assistant Editor of *Safety Fast*.

After the Monte, two cars were entered in the San Remo Rally for Tony and Rauno but both retired with mechanical trouble.

The programme was looking a little thin for the rest of

1968 and there was some disatisfaction with the lack of money and development time being allocated. There was a rumour in the workshop that there was possibly to be a merger of the Competitions and Special Tuning workshops. Peter realised that this was unsettling so sent out a memo to all personnel in both departments explaining his proposal. He pointed out that if we were to continue in motor sport we must keep on winning, and to win we must have a proper development programme in an effort to beat the high performance machinery being pitted against our cars.

The plan was that the staff of the Competitions Department and Special Tuning workshops would merge, to enable a special development section to be formed. Two people under Cliff Humphries would form a permanent development section in the Special Tuning workshop while the rearranged Special Tuning mechanics would remain under the supervision of Bill Burrows. There would still be limited space and personnel to carry out customer tuning. The final decision, however, could not be made until Basil Wales, Manager of Special Tuning returned from a trip to Denmark, at the end of March.

MGC At Sebring

Sebring was the first event for the MGC GT lightweight six-cylinder car, entered in company with an MGB GT (LBL 591E) which was prepared for an all American crew to drive. Peter took over Den Green and two mechanics for the race which was also supported by the Donald Healey Motor Co with an Austin Healey Sprite and an MG Midget.

Scrutineering and practice were fairly uneventful and the mechanics managed to get in some fishing and water skiing before the race.

The race started with a Le Mans type start with our cars getting away safely. Paddy Hopkirk in the MGC was called into the pits when some waste paper was seen to be blocking the air intake. Paddy and Andrew Hedges in the MGC circulated quickly and at the finish achieved the best ever finishing position in this race by a BMC car with tenth overall. The MGB did not do as well as previously, being down at eighteenth and fifth in class.

Marathon Year

1968 Sebring line-up. L-to-R: Austin Healey Sprite, MGB GT, MG Midget and MGC

MGC engine compartment, 1968 Sebring 12 Hour Race

Testing the MGC for Sebring 1968

African Disaster

A comprehensive test programme was underway at Bagshot with an Austin 1800 in preparation for our forthcoming entry in the East African Safari. Apart from the abhortive run with the Mini Cooper S this was our first serious attempt on the Safari, and to compile comprehensive route notes Henry Liddon was sent out to do a recce. We were guaranteed maximum support from Benbros Motors and one of the sons of the Managing Director, David Benzimra, was asked to co-drive Timo, much to Paul Easter's disappointment.

The worry of sending the cars and spares to Kenya was solved by chartering a Britannia aircraft from British United Airways which allowed more time for preparation and would avoid the unreliable Mombassa docking facility. In addition to some of the crews, Peter, Doug Watts, five mechanics, Jeremy Ferguson of Dunlop and some of his staff took up the remaining seats left after the three cars and spares had been loaded; some of the mechanics used the rally car seats to relax during the flight.

Group 2 cars could only use the homologated single carburettor, the engines being similar to the Alpine with a number of other modifications to cope with East African conditions. A large oil cooler, twin ignition coils mounted high under the bonnet and air horns were fitted and the distributor had an elaborate breather system fitted to allow the car to run in deep flood water.

The rear seats were removed and, inside, a Hydrolastic pump was mounted on the rear bulkhead along with triple Tudor washer bottles. The usual hand and foot rests were

1968

East African Safari 1968; the three 1800s and the transporter with the chartered Britannia

One of the 1800s before retirement, 1968 East African Safari

Marathon Year

mounted front and rear with a perspex 'bug deflector' across the bonnet. Two long range lamps were mounted on top of the front wings with anti-glare shields and a special snorkel pipe was carried in the car to go on the exhaust in the event of floods.

The mechanics spent many a long hour on final preparations in Nairobi. To add to the problems, Peter badly damaged his finger when it was accidently shut in a car door while he was engaged in getting a car out of a mudhole. He was rushed to hospital for treatment and was handicapped with a very painful hand for the remainder of the trip. The weather changed and it soon became obvious that mud teams would be required at likely black spots with tractors standing-by to render assistance. The rally was run in two stages: the first of 1,428 miles to Uganda and back; the second of 1,646 miles into Tanzania and back to Nairobi. Within 500 miles of the start ramp in Nairobi, Rauno was up to third position making full use of the Hydrolastic suspension, but unfortunately Timo was out of luck before the cars reached Kampala when his oil cooler broke.

Tony Fall, with his local co-driver Lofty Drews, had trouble with the front suspension when the alloy housing supporting the top arm shattered. This was replaced, but in the muddy conditions they were outside the maximum lateness permitted despite an extension of the time allowance by two hours. Rauno also had a front housing shatter and after repairs was also too late at the Nairobi control. The Benbros Motors privately-entered 1800 crashed, rolled over and also retired, ending a rather disastrous Safari for the 1800s. We had expected them at least to be in at the finish. Much had been learned and it was hoped that this experience could be fully exploited next year. Doug and the mechanics took a ride to Mombassa after the wreckage had been cleared up and were able to visit the Indian Ocean beaches and some of the night spots. The team duly returned in the Britannia for a full debrief at Abingdon.

In April, Ron Crellin decided to hang up his helmet to devote more time to his business and family, having had a successful spell with Paddy since he started with him on the 1966 Flowers rally.

The BMC Bonus Scheme was reviewed annually and further increases were announced for the 1968 season, with the main awards being for outright wins in the Monte, Safari, Acropolis, Alpine and RAC rallies.

The Circuit of Ireland usually clashed with the Safari, and because the other members of the team were in East Africa, Paddy was entered along with Lars Yitterbring, the Swedish driver. The two cars were lightweight Group 6 cars with the usual aluminium panels, etc, and Weber carburettors giving 91.5 bhp at the front wheels. I was looking after the service arrangements, Peter being away on the Safari, but this was not to be a successful trip. Running on Dunlop R7 racing tyres most of the time, Paddy and Lars set a very hot pace

Paddy Hopkirk/Terry Harryman during the 1968 Circuit of Ireland (Esler Crawford)

1968

from the start but could not get in front of the new Ford Escord Twin Cam being driven by Roger Clark.

Although driving a right-hand drive car, Lars recorded a number of faster times than Paddy, and at Killarney was third behind Roger Clark and Paddy. On the second stage after Killarney, Lars hit a bridge parapet and rolled over a couple of times to retire, while Paddy was suffering with overheating of his car. This was not serious and we were hoping that Paddy could pull something out of the bag on the last night. However, it was not to be for he retired with a broken differential on the Lough Eske stage. Roger won the rally, a first-time win with the new Escort. BMC honour was saved, however, with Adrian Boyd coming home second in his ex-works Mini Cooper S.

Tulip Time

The third event in quick succession was the Tulip Rally which, this year, was short of a sponsor and also short of entries. After years of heavy support from British competitors only 77 cars left the start at Noordwijk. This was the lowest number of entries in the history of the rally although there were works entries from BMC, Ford, Renault and Datsun. Following the success of the Twin Cam in Ireland, it looked as though this would be the car to beat.

The two Mini Cooper Ss were using the latest spec engines and, for the first time, the 5½ × 10 inch Minilite wheels to gain an improvement in traction and roadholding. To enable easy identification of the wheels, they were painted gold which blended in quite well with the red bodies. At least one person wanted them red, but after trying two on a car at Abingdon, the feeling was that the cars looked too much like Mini fire-engines!

Julien Vernaeve/Mike Wood Mini Cooper S at Zolder circuit, 1968 Tulip Rally

Timo and Paul were in one car and Julien Vernaeve and Mike Wood crewed the other one. At the first stage at Zolder circuit in Belgium, the Fords and Alpine Renaults were some seconds faster than the Minis in the smooth tarmac conditions, our cars seeming down on power; at the night stop at Annecy attention was given to the timing on both cars which brought about some improvement, both cars being trouble-free mechanically at this stage. The seven hour section from Annecy saw a few retirements but after the rest halt at Rumilly on the next stage on Mount Clergon, Timo had a rear wheel puncture. With only 12 km to the end of the stage Timo pressed-on, ending the test with the remains of the magnesium alloy wheel wrapped round the brake drum.

By lunchtime, Roger Clark was leading Group 3 with Timo still leading Group 2, but on the twelfth stage, on the Col du Brabant, Timo made one of his rare mistakes. A lack of concentration, and the car was off the road, going through a hedge and landing on soft ground without much damage. There were very few spectators at this spot so there was no chance of regaining the road, so Paul and Timo wandered back to the stage start to let the marshalls know they were OK.

When they returned to the car a small crowd had formed, and after they had given their rally plates away as souvenirs, the crowd manhandled the car back on the road. They drove to the end of the stage where Paul calculated that they might be able to get to the next control on time, despite the stage time having been 1 hour 9 minutes. They got the marshalls to stamp their time card to the effect that their rally plates had been stolen, and they shot back into the rally making the next control with seconds to spare.

Timo made some quick times on the remaining stages and Julien, who had been battling with the BMW of Slotemaker, ended up first in Group 2 and third overall behind the two Escorts. For their efforts, Timo and Paul were classified 41st out of 44 finishers. Paul calculated that without the puncture and without going off, they could have won the rally by 1 second!

The Sebring cars arrived back in time from North America for the MGB GT to be rebuilt for Paddy and Andrew Hedges to drive it in the Targa Florio. This was a lone entry, although Tony Fall had negotiated a drive in an MGB tourer owned by J. C. Bamford Excavators Ltd with Peter Brown co-driving. Paddy and Andrew were placed twelfth overall in the GT with the private MGB driven by Tony down in 24th after trouble with the gearbox crossmember coming loose and minor collision with a Lancia.

Last Event for Timo

Two Mini Cooper S cars for the Flying Finns were entered in the Acropolis Rally plus an 1800 for Brian Culcheth, once again up against the new Escort Twin Cam and some quick Porsches.

The rally and service cars were driven down to Ancona to catch the *Heleanna*, described as the largest car ferry in the world, to Patras in Greece. We had no reason to query the claimed size of the vessel when we found out that it was in fact a converted ex-Swedish tanker, access to the car space being through a hole cut in its side. It sported a swimming pool which we eventually persuaded the purser to fill. We did some swimming and managed to throw the Porsche mechanics in, fully clothed, on the second day.

Have you heard that story about the ship sailing across the high seas without a coxswain? Well when I visited the wheelhouse looking for the purser, I found it deserted; I just hoped that there was not too much traffic about between Ancona and Patras!

The rally was about 56 hours long, starting in the shadow of the Acropolis in temperatures up in the 80s. After only two

Marathon Year

stages Timo complained that his car was overheating. Although his fan belt was adjusted it was only a few hours before he retired with a blown head gasket, which was very disappointing on what was to be his last rally with the team.

Henry Liddon reckoned that their car was the best that they had ever had from Abingdon, but even so, Rauno was struggling to keep up with the competition. Brian Culcheth was going like a train in the 1800, the exceptional handling enabling him to keep ahead of much more exotic machinery; for example, his time on the 8.2 km Distomen Hill Climb was eleventh fastest.

I had Tommy Eales with me in a Vanden Plas and we had our share of hot dusty stops including one on the shore of a man-made lake, where the ferry for rally cars was a converted landing craft. We were carrying some experimental freeze-dried chicken and prawns, which needed only water to bring them back to the edible state and although the chicken was rather tasteless, the prawns were quite appetising. We always had our supplies of Chicken Supreme to fall back on! It is my belief that Henry Liddon holds the world record for the amount of Chicken Supreme consumed on rallies, and this was recognised at one of our Christmas parties when he was presented with a giant tin, supplied by Shippams.

Inset: *Timo Makinen's car receives new tyres, 1968 Acropolis*

The rally headed back towards Athens, and at Thivai the sump shield and lamp bar were removed from Rauno's car to improve the cooling now that the rough roads were behind. The usual race at the Tatoi Circuit was a battle between the Fords and the Porsche cars with no heroics from Rauno who consolidated his position at fifth overall. Brian Culcheth had the misfortune to clobber a kerb, bending the rear swing arm, but he continued at unabated speed. We were all glad to get back to the Glyphada Beach hotel for a shower or a dip in the sea. Rauno was placed fifth overall and first in class with Brian second in class and tenth overall. Winning was becoming more difficult.

Lars Ytterbring/Lars Persson on a typically rough stage, 1968 Scottish Rally

While we were away in Greece, Lars Ytterbring drove JMO 969D, prepared by Special Tuning, in the Scottish Rally to achieve a good second overall position. The car was fitted with an auxiliary radiator to help with the overheating (if only the Mini had a front-mounted radiator!).

BMC Canada helped to finance the entry of two cars in the Shell 4000 in Canada, these being a Mini Cooper S and an Austin 1800 for Paddy and Tony respectively. Local co-drivers were called in for this event in view of the precise electronic timing used on Canadian rallies and Tommy Wellman was kept busy making up rear wheel Halda drives for both cars. These drives were first used on the 1961 Monte Minis.

There were only ten stages, quite unlike European stages, consisting of mainly flat-out straights interspersed with 90 degree corners, which favoured the local V8 cars like the Plymouth Barracuda. Paddy went well in the early part of the rally but the overheating bug reared its ugly head, and the mechanics were forced to rig an auxiliary radiator on the front of the car; this resulted in disqualification from the rally.

Tony had a bit more luck, being able to continue after

1968

Marathon Year

Two cowboys and one cowgirl, Shell 4000 Rally 1968

Oh dear! Tony Fall what have you done? Shell 4000 Rally 1968

rolling the car and having the windscreen replaced. A further delay with a faulty fuel pump wire was the only other problem, and Tony eventually finished eighth overall and second in class.

Marathon MGCs

The 'real' MGC had only appeared in one event but a second car was under construction in the workshop at Abingdon using the experience gained so far with MBL. Although lacking race experience, Peter decided to gamble and enter the two MGC cars in the Marathon at Nürburgring, the driver line-up being Tony Fall/Andrew Hedges/Julien Vernaeve and Roger Enever/Alec Poole/Clive Baker. During testing, a problem had occurred with the Minilite wheels coming loose, so that at the last minute Tommy was sent off to Dusseldorf with ten wire-spoke wheels which he took to the circuit in a VW hire car. The hexagonal earless spinners which kept the wheels on were strengthened with steel rings shrunk on the outside and the spinners were tightened with special long-

The second MGC ready for the 1968 Marathon de la Route

1968

shaft spanners. During the event, RMO ran with the Minilite wheels, the other car being on wire.

The cars went well from the start of this gruelling event and after 24 hours were lying second and sixth overall. Unfortunately RMO was showing signs of overheating and was eventually retired with a blown head gasket.

The only problem with the other car, apart from keeping the wheels tight, was when Andrew Hedges lost his brakes. In the pits the pads were found to be welded to the caliper pistons and the mechanics had a struggle to change them. After 17 minutes the car had to return to the fray but with no brakes. Tony managed to keep the car on the road for two laps then returned to the pits where a further 8 minutes was needed to complete the job. Undeterred, the team persevered and at the end of 86 hours the car was classified sixth overall. This was to be the last official MG race entry from Abingdon.

the retirement of Ron Crellin, Peter asked Paul if he would like to do some extra events in 1968 with Paddy. He had already agreed a fee to do five events with Timo but when he found that no extra money was forthcoming he turned down the drive.

Bombay Recce

It was fairly obvious that a recce of the route would be necessary so, using feed-back from the test programme at Bagshot, a special recce car was now in preparation in the workshop. The car was a dark green Morris 1800 Mk2 fitted with the latest spec suspension, a twin-carburettor engine and, on the roof, a special spares container. The most significant change to the suspension was the use of the larger than usual rear Hydrolastic units, which were the same size as those fitted to the front. This would help to take the extra

1968 London–Sydney Marathon recce car

London to Sydney

By May there was an increasing amount of publicity and speculation concerning the London–Sydney Marathon. For example, *Motor* magazine reported several companies 'nibbling but are not yet hooked on the idea'. It was rumoured that BMC were entering the Safari 1800s and Ford, Lotus Cortinas.

The provisional entry list showed Timo as one of our four team drivers but he dropped out before the official entries were confirmed. Timo, along with the other drivers, was now aware of the reduced programme for 1969 and with a full programme less likely to be available to him he opted out of the Marathon, preferring to make himself available for the RAC and possible Monte recces. This gave Paul the chance to go in the crew with Rauno on the Marathon. In addition, with

weight of a three-man crew and also help the rally spares situation.

The two most experienced co-drivers, Paul Easter and Henry Liddon were chosen for the recce of the route to Bombay, with Tony Nash, Paddy's new co-driver, as third man.

The designated route to Bombay was via the following controls: London, Paris, Turin, Belgrade, Istanbul, Sivas, Erzincan, Teheran, Kabul, Sarobi, Delhi & Bombay. One unusual feature was the provision of a choice of routes on two of the sections from Sivas to Erzincan and Teheran to Kabul. In a later bulletin an extra Control was sited in Calais in case ferry delays penalised competitors.

The recce started on 16 July, when the intrepid trio arrived at the Australian High Commission in their best suits for an official send-off by the High Commissioner. After a

Marathon Year

photo session and a change of clothes they eventually set off, travelling through to Trieste where they spent the Wednesday night. In Trieste they each purchased a 0.22 pistol plus some ammunition.

They then travelled through Belgrade and into Bulgaria where near Erdine the oil cooler sprang a leak. They found a hotel for the night, but after seeing the state of the 'dormitory', scattered with personal belongings, they decided that a camp site down the road would be safer and cleaner. In the morning, after a brew-up on the steps of the camp hut, the oil cooler was by-passed and they pressed on into Turkey and Istanbul. A phone call from the Hilton Hotel was made to Abingdon for a new oil cooler. The oil cooler arrived by air, and after fitting it in the Hilton Hotel car park they left Istanbul and spent the next night in Yozgat.

They reconnoitred the southern routes on the Sivas-Erzincan section; the southern route, although several kilometres shorter, involved negotiating a dubious wooden bridge and several very rough kilometres.

The route continued over the mountains to the border with Iran and then the next stop, Tabriz, where they bought some cakes leaving the delighted shopkeeper with a display of BMC stickers for his counter. The road to Teheran was an improvement, with some good concrete stretches, and they spent a comfortable night in the Vanak Hotel.

The southern optional route from Teheran to Kabul across the desert was a diabolical dirt road with many kilometres of 'washboard' surface apparently formed by the six-wheeled trucks which were in common use on these routes.

London–Sydney recce car pauses in Iran. Paul Easter clutches a welcome drink

The southern route was chosen for the first recce run, but near the end of the roughest part, the off-side rear Hydrolastic unit burst, allowing the suspension to collapse onto the bump-stops. 'Chief mechanic' Paul devised a way of supporting the suspension with wood blocks and they were able to limp to Mashad. After some difficulty and haggling with the railway officials, they persuaded the railway company to transport the car back to Teheran, watching with some trepidation as wires were tied through the Minilite wheels to secure the car to the railway truck. They were able to catch a local flight to Teheran where they waited three days for the car to appear, the new Hydrolastic unit ordered from Abingdon being fitted in the Vanak Hotel car park.

To catch up some of their lost time, the crew set off early on their northern route recce stopping the following night at Bodjnoord. Although the rather grotty hotel had its own restaurant upstairs, the recce crew were rather intrigued to see that most of the guests were cooking their own meals in the hotel yard.

Next day the border into Afghanistan was crossed, where followed the luxury of a straight smooth concrete highway, built with American and Russian aid, stretching away for hundreds of miles into the distance. They stopped the night in Herat and then pressed on to Kabul. The heat was intense and with frequent mirages 'melting' the road they were glad that it would be cooler on the rally.

At one spot near a small roadside shack, they had to take avoiding action to miss a table set up in the road, and were dismayed to see that it marked the body of a person who obviously had already been run-over several times.

To pass the time they carried out a survey of the density of traffic on this highway, which was established at 1–1½ vehicles per hour. From Kabul to Sarobi the recce crew took the rally route over the Lataban Pass, although the pass was no longer used by motor vehicles.

The Khyber Pass was next, open only from sunrise to sunset owing to the danger of bandits, and on to Peshawar. Crossing over into Pakistan, where the time difference is BST + 4 hours, brought another change, driving on the left-handside of the road again. The car battery failed here, causing a two-day delay in Lahore while a replacement was located.

On through Delhi and then a night stop in Agra on Thursday 8 August. After leaving Agra, the monsoons started in earnest and they had a frantic 24 hours, crossing flooded rivers, where some bridges were immersed and all but impassable. The Indian lorry drivers just seemed to give up and were open-mouthed when the 1800 ploughed through the floods. Changes of route were frequent and at times the railway tracks were used. Eventually the engine started to

lose power to the accompaniment of pinking and a steadily worsening misfire. Before long the engine expired with a blown head gasket.

They were stranded near Indore in a poor village which produced the most appalling smell. A Sikh lorry driver, recently arrived back in the village to collect a load of onions in his Mercedes truck was asked if he would transport the car to Bombay; after some negotiations a price was agreed.

He had to let various members of his family know about the trip and after getting the whole village to push the car up on a bank to enable it to be loaded, they set off with the recce crew strapped into their safety belts in the recce car on the truck. There were frequent halts while the driver got out his sledge hammer and knocked back in the truck's shackle pins. After a gruelling journey they eventually arrived at the Sun-N-Sand Hotel at Juhu Beach at 0400 hrs much to the consternation of the night porter.

Already installed in the hotel were Den Green and Mike Wood who were scheduled to bring the recce car back overland. Next day Den had a look at the engine at the premises of the local agent, the French Motor Car Co, only to find when he removed the cylinder head that the block was

1968

cracked. The suspension was looking fragile on the off-side rear, scene of the previous failure and all the tyres were – in Den's words – 'shot' or punctured.

Spares had already been sent out by sea but were impounded by the Customs, so with no engine and no tyres the return trip was called off. Den stayed on for a week in an attempt to retrieve the spares but had to leave it to the agent to sort out, hopefully in time for the rally. Mike carried on to do a recce in Australia while the others went back to England via Nairobi.

We had some assistance from the Red Arrows with spares shipments, consignments being flown out by the RAF on a 'take it when you can' basis. One lot went to Teheran on an RAF Comet, while another package went to Ankara on an Argosy, the recce crew checking up on both consignments as they passed through.

Back at Abingdon, Peter had now formed the Development section with Cliff, Nobby Hall and Eddie Burnell, this trio being responsible for the bulk of the 1800 Bagshot Marathon test programme. One of the mods to come out of this testing was a valve arrangement to duct air to the engine from inside the car in the event of deep floods. Brittle driveshafts were also sorted out with the help of Syd Enever, the breakages being cured by using a more flexible material. At the rear, Koni load-adjusters were added to improve the ride and damping but also to assist with the heavy load of a three-man crew.

During the testing three Red Arrows pilots were given a chance to sample the car but on the first run managed to invert it, luckily without too much damage, and after a new screen was fitted it was business as usual.

We had some assistance from the MG Development Department with test-bed time to develop the final spec of the rally engines, the brief spec being as follows:

The standard cylinder block was overbored + 0.040 in to give a cubic capacity of 1846 cc using flat-top four ring pistons with 0.312 in machined off the skirts. The bottom-end used a nitrided crankshaft with lightened flywheel and competition clutch. A useful power band was achieved with a standard MGB camshaft driven by lightened steel sprockets with breathing via two 1.75 in SU carburettors on a standard 1800S inlet manifold. Downton supplied an extractor exhaust manifold and MGB air cleaners were fitted. The gearbox was fitted with the latest production gears, crack-tested, with a 4.1:1 final drive. Clearance between fan and radiator was improved by cutting 0.25 in off the standard 1800 five-blade fan and a large pulley slowed down the alternator. With a compression ratio of 9.6:1, 100 bhp was developed at 5,500 rpm (valve crash 6,700 pm).

Interest in the Marathon was building up considerably and the organisers and the press were busy sorting out aircraft for the first leg. The *Daily Express* hired a Viscount 800 from British United Airways which was kitted out with

1968 London–Sydney Marathon rally cars in early stages of preparation at Abingdon

Marathon Year

Testing Austin 1800 at Bagshot

tables, type-writers, beds (which could double as stretchers), and a dark room, the remaining space being for seats for the press men or women including our own Alan Zafer.

In May, Sandy Lawson had replaced Mary Smith to become Peter's secretary and was rather thrown in at the deep end with the Marathon organisation. Sandy had been working at the BARC but had been lured away by Alan Zafer to join him in the Abingdon Press office. She had then transferred to Competitions but seemed to be taking it all in her stride.

In Australia a very comprehensive service coverage was organised by BMC Australia under the guidance of Peter Browning while on the leg to Bombay, commercial flights would be used to leap-frog the mechanics.

We were getting tremendous support from the trade, amongst which was a special Dunlop SP tyre being produced by Dunlop for the Marathon. Castrol had been working hard organising fuel supplies on the section to Bombay where they had no less than sixteen service points, while in Iran a special high octane brew was supplied by the National Iranian Oil Co.

Castrol-contracted competitors were supplied with fuel on production of special petrol coupons.

Peter had been working on the service plan which was a mammoth task, co-ordinating air and service car movements, with fuel and tyre plans. One part of the plan was to send a 'sweeper' car along the rally route, starting its sweep in Turkey following the Sivas–Erzincan stage. Provisionally the driver was to be Clive Baker but after some discussion Peter changed the crew to include Department pesonnel. I was asked to drive the 'sweeper' with Bob Whittington, the two of us to be joined by a third mechanic at the Iranian–Turkish border for the remainder of the journey to Bombay.

The main reason for sending a service car along the rally route was that the generous time allowance made it quite feasible to get a car to Bombay if parts and mechanics were at hand.

Another reason was that there were such stringent Customs regulations in the countries east of the Bosphorus that it would be essential to recover, or arrange for the recovery of broken or abandoned cars to avoid heavy penalties.

The preparation of the cars was proceeding, based on the unusual decision to start off with bare bodyshells. This gave Neville in the stores a tremendous headache obtaining all the standard parts which would be necessary to assemble them, such as trim, door handles, brackets, locks, etc. If you asked Neville what it was like getting hold of all these parts he would go visibly grey! The other problem building cars from parts was the question of car tax. To avoid this, we persuaded Production Control at Longbridge to issue and supply chassis numbers and plates for the four cars being assembled at Abingdon.

While all these preparations were going on, we had to

1968

change the name of the Department to the British Leyland Motor Corporation Competitions Department with a change of notepaper to go with it. George Turnbull was Managing Director of the new BLMC, and although he was in favour of a motor sport programme, Lord Stokes was not convinced, despite arguments put forward by Keith Hopkins. His attitude was that the Triumph 1300 was a best seller and Triumph were not in motor sport and he also pointed out Volkswagen's worldwide sales without a motor sport programme.

Rumours concerning the fate of the Department had been circulating for some time and, with the reduction of the rally programme, it was left to Peter to tell the drivers that their contracts, with the exception of Paddy who had a two year contract, would not be renewed for 1969. It was obviously going to be impossible to justify keeping them on financially and unreasonable to expect them to stay anyway when their trade was winning rallies.

Evan Green, John Fitzpatrick and Jack Murray pass the Houses of Parliament after the water skiing stunt

I think all the staff employed in the Competitions Department would agree that this period was most unsettling. It helped the situation when Peter put out a memo outlining the 1969 programme. Rallying was going to take a back seat, but there was to be a two-car team of Mini Cooper S cars built and entered by Abingdon in the British Saloon Car Championship, plus one or two races in the European Touring Car Championship. Development of the MGC would continue and official entries would be made in televised rallycross events. The Company was keen to see some Triumph models being used in competitions, but as Peter pointed out, the next successful model would need careful consideration and development.

One last rally was entered before the Marathon got under way and this was a single entry in the TAP Rally in Portugal for Paddy in a Mini Cooper S and the chance to do a major event with his new co-driver, Tony Nash. The outing was reasonably successful with Paddy and Tony coming home second overall behind a Lancia.

The British Leyland reorganisation continued with the axe falling on the car clubs, and the various 'house' magazines, including of course *Safety Fast*, which were replaced by a single publication to be called High Road. Support of the Cooper Car Co Ltd, who had been in effect the works racing team, and Britax was withdrawn although the Britax Cooper Team decided to continue without BL support.

As the start of the journey to Sydney approached, the Australian crew arrived in England. One publicity stunt organised by Alan Zafer involved Jack 'Gelignite' Murray a proficient water skiier. John Fitzpatrick, the racing driver, had a speedboat and Jack was keen to try it out. Alan made a few phone calls to press contacts telling them that at a certain time, there would be an unusual event taking place on the Thames near the Houses of Parliament. John Fitzpatrick launched his boat at Richmond and with Jack Murray on board travelled down the river to Westminster. As the boat approached the Houses of Parliament, 'Gelignite' went into the water with his skis; the surprised spectators witnessed a water skier passing by at speed in a plume of spray. Before the authorities could react, the speedboat came alongside the Westminster pier where the police and the Piermaster were

Shakedown for the 1800s at Thruxton Circuit, 1968 London–Sydney Marathon

waiting. Apart from having to pay a 2 shilling mooring fee, the intrepid party got away with a ticking off, well worth all the subsequent publicity in newspapers next day.

So, with a week to go, the crews assembled at Abingdon finally to check over their respective mounts and Thruxton was booked to allow the drivers to give the cars a shakedown. Alan Zafer arranged for the Cowley photographers to attend at Thruxton because he was anxious to have a good collection of shots of the crews with their cars for distribution later. Scrutineering was held in London where the body and the engine of each car was marked, these being the only parts that could not be changed during the event.

Crystal Palace Start

The start of the London–Sydney Marathon took place at the race circuit of Crystal Palace where entertainment laid on for the spectators included a military band, parades of cars, a hovercraft display and a straight-line dash by Graham Hill in a Formula 1 Lotus. I think that even the organisers were surprised at the size of the crowds that turned up to see the 99 cars start this epic event, estimates varying from between 20,000 and 80,000 people. A briefing was held by Clerk of the Course, Jack Sears, with additional information being supplied

Marathon Year

1968

Some of the team at Thruxton Circuit before the London–Sydney Marathon. L-to-R: T. Nash, H. Liddon, P. Hopkirk, T. Fall, J. Murray, P. Browning, R. Aaltonen, A. Poole and M. Wood

by John Gott and Tommy Sopwith. The briefing was interrupted by a loud explosion caused by 'Geliginite' Jack Murray, who announced that he had let off the biggest banger he could without hurting anyone; it was called the 'super sports'. John Gott thanked Jack for his report!

At 14.000 hrs on Sunday 24 November the first competitor was flagged off the start ramp by Graham Hill, our cars being nicely spread out from a servicing point of view at 4, 31, 51, 61, and the Red Arrows at 64. Once on French soil the first problem was fog, and a reluctance by the French police to allow competitors to use the autoroute. Rauno for example, decided to avoid the police and with some crafty navigation his crew brought the car onto the autoroute out of sight of the waiting police, with the result that they arrived at the Paris control with time to spare.

Some crews got lost in the fog losing time at the control, including the all-woman crew in a Morris 1100 all the way from Aiustralia. This car had been 'tidied up' at Abingdon a day before the rally as it had been rather hastily prepared and did not look like a car that would go far. The works crews generally thought the first sections of the route boring, finding that they had the chance of several hours' sleep at the Turin, Belgrade and Istanbul controls.

My own Marathon had started over a week before the Crystal Palace start when I left with Bob Whittington on the night ferry from Southampton to Le Havre. We were in the company of another service car crewed by Eddie Burnell and Frank Rudman plus a two-wheel baggage trailer; destination Turkey.

Evan Green threads through the crowd at Dover, 1968 London–Sydney Marathon

Sivas to Erzincan

The rally proceeded to Turkey, where the roads became more difficult. Not only was there a dirt surface after Ankara, but the dangerous standard of driving of most of the locals had to be contended with. At Sivas (altitude 7,500 ft) where we had a service point with Dunlop (Jeremy Ferguson) and Castrol also in attendance, the scene was rather chaotic with much mud, and rally cars going in both directions near the control. I had done a recce of both northern and southern routes from Sivas to Erzincan, and with the deep mud found over the last few kilometres of the southern route, had left a recommendation with our mechanics that the northern route was to be used, despite being longer. In fact the organisers had also done a recce and had decided that the whole rally must compulsorily do the northern route.

The stage (normally the public highway) from Sivas to Erzincan was 187 miles at a set average of 68 mph over a reasonable dirt road with many corners and brows. I was at Erzincan with Bob and Frank waiting for the cars just as it started to get dark. Our cars came through in one piece requiring just a check over. The exception was Tony Fall's car which had lost all its spot lamp lenses when baulked by an Australian competitor, Harry Firth in a Ford Falcon.

As soon as the last of our 1800s had gone through, Frank left for Sivas in the BMC Turkey van and Bob and I set off in the direction of Bombay to start our sweeping-up operation along the rally route.

At Erzincan, the overall rally positions saw Roger Clark in the lead in his Lotus Cortina, Gilbert Staepalaere also in a Ford second, with Lucien Bianchi in a Citroen third. We were well-placed with Rauno and Paddy fourth equal followed by Tony Fall.

At the Turkey/Iranian border the Customs formalities were very smooth and Tommy and Brian in a Dodge hire car were waiting for the cars on the Iranian side. One of their responsibilities was to do a recce of part of the route near Teheran. The crews had encountered some snow over the mountains from Erzincan, which we had also run into briefly, but the next section to Teheran was fairly straightforward although crews had to look out for badly marked road works along the way.

Teheran to Kabul

In Teheran, the control was set up at the Philips factory where the facilities were tremendous with opportunity to eat, sleep and work on the cars as necessary. When I arrived with Bob and Tom there were still some rally cars at the control including the three Australian girls' Morris 1100. They were having a leisurely meal and, because we did not want them to get too far behind, we suggested that they got moving, which did not go down too well!

The first 30 km or so were tarmac after leaving Teheran then there was the second choice of routes, south over the desert or north over a smoother, longer more mountainous route. Our crews, along with Citroen's, were amongst the minority opting for the southern route. The total mileage to the next control at Kabul was just under 1600 miles to be covered in a few minutes under 24 hours.

We were a few hours behind the rally now and soon found out just how rough the southern route really was, having to reduce speed to around 30 mph to save the car. Dawn came up and with the exception of stray camels, an occasional organised camel train and a few lorries there was not much company. The car started to break up with, first, the bonnet securing pins snapping off so that we had to strap the bonnet down with rubber straps and then with cracks appearing in the door apertures.

Desert Troubles

At about 09.00 hrs my service car came cross the three Australian girls in the Morris 1100 with the suspension collapsed on the off-side. The steel connecting pipe between the front and rear Hydrolastic units had chafed through on the subframe. A temporary repair with heavy duty neoprene hose only lasted 4 km but after another attempt with an 1800 oil cooler hose they were gratefully on their way.

Meanwhile one of our rally cars was in trouble within an hour of leaving Teheran. Rauno hit some rocks and broke the offside front tie-rod allowing the wheel to move back and jam in the wheel arch. Some quick work with the portable winch connected to the front suspension got them going without much delay. While carrying out the repair, Tony Fall stopped to help but as they were managing OK he was sent on his way.

Marathon Year

Vanden Plas 4-litre R service car used as a 'sweep' car from Turkey to Bombay, 1968 London–Sydney Marathon

About half-way across the desert Tony Fall ran heavily into a drift and broke a front suspension top arm, the wheel folding under the car. With no spare on board, it seemed that they were out, the tired crew dozing in the car.

Before long, the winched-up Rauno car arrived and, seeing the problem, Rauno immediately started to badger the dozing crew to start getting the broken part off. They continued, hoping to send someone back to help. Before long, a Hillman Hunter pulled up with three Iranians on board, and on being shown the broken part, they said 'no problem, we can get it welded'.

Tony and Mike joined the Hunter crew which shot off in the direction of Teheran, to a village about 20 miles away, leaving Brian Culcheth to look after the car. The offending part was electric welded and the Hunter returned to the stranded rally car where the crew fitted the repaired arm. The result of this problem was that they were 5 hours late at the Kabul control, dropping them out of contention. I am still not sure why we did not come across Tony Fall but I think it was because we were too far behind after stopping for the girls.

The long grind across Afghanistan gave the non-driving crew members an opportunity to sleep, because this straight concrete road had very few junctions and little traffic. My Vanden Plas 4 litre was going well and we were cruising at about 75 mph most of the time. We stopped for a quick snack and were amazed to hear a buzzing noise in the distance behind us. Eventually, despite the brilliant sunlight, bright lamps appeared on the horizon and a few minutes later the girls in the 1100 raced past totally ignoring us despite our waving. Only the driver was visible and she appeared to be transfixed by the road ahead!

Kabul to Bombay

At Kabul there was a control and we had a service crew supervised by Peter Browning plus Dunlop and Castrol service. Rauno's car had some further attention after surviving the roads from the desert near Teheran with the winch holding the wheel in position.

From Kabul, there was the stage over the Lataban Pass which the recce crews had found to be terribly rough. There was a surprise in store for the rally, because the local authorities had graded the pass fearing that the roughness would attract bad publicity to the region. An early morning start saw the rally tackling the 48 mile stage with a time allowance of one hour, the fastest time being shared by Roger Clark, Paddy Hopkirk and Lucien Bianchi with a loss of five minutes and Evan Green at eight minutes; overall the lead was still held by Clark.

The Khyber Pass was a bit of an anti-climax after the Lataban but the crews took it all in as they negotiated its historic gradients and corners. The main hazard to Bombay now was the traffic, with literally thousands of people, dozens of bullock carts and many trucks and buses littering the roads making driving very dangerous and tiring.

In Bombay, the service area was situated in the docks in order that the bureaucratic Customs service could maintain their grip on the imported rally spares. The scene was chaotic with spares being issued to the mechanics only on presentation of a similar old part, all carefully logged by the Customs man.

Except for one mechanic, our main party was late arriving after flight delays and the over-enthusiastic local mechanics managed to strip the oil drain plug thread from the Evan Green 1800. The crews started to service their own cars until the service crews arrived. When the main service team arrived, Den Green resorted to refitting the drain plug to Evan Greens car with epoxy resin. The mechanics worked from about 16.00 hrs until 09.00 hrs the next morning tending to the works and private BMC cars.

When the results were posted for the London–Bombay leg, Peter was pleased to see that three of our cars were in the top ten, with Paddy fourth, Rauno fifth and Evan Green eighth. The main fettling was carried out successfully leaving just a few jobs to do in Perth.

I arrived in Bombay with Bob (and Tommy Eales who had joined us at the Iran–Turkey border) just under 24 hours behind the rally, accounted for by our delays in the desert with the Aussies, the rough roads and then several hours' delay at Kabul after being told that the Khyber Pass was closed and we could not go through until sunrise. With hindsight, it was a pity that we were not in an 1800 in rally trim but even so the Vanden Plas with just a sump guard, Minilite wheels and Weathermaster tyres had done very well with its load of spares and, for half the trip, three passengers.

We had a debrief with Peter Browning and Den in the morning after our arrival. On the day of departure of the P & O liner *SS Chusan* we managed to get on board in the guise of porters carrying some of the drivers' luggage. The *Chusan* was a wonderful vessel with panelled cabins and an air of quality despite its age, although I think some of the drivers would probably not agree with that comment after ten days at sea. So, as the rally sailed for Fremantle, Western Australia, Bob, Tommy and myself reluctantly took a flight back to England.

Perth to Sydney

The rally competitors travelled first class on the *Chusan*. Unfortunately a bout of some sort of stomach trouble swept the ship, affecting about forty passengers which did not improve morale. The liner called at Columbo in Ceylon and there was the opportunity of breaking the boredom by a trip to the Mount Lavinia Hotel where a good time was had by all. Certain passengers tried hard to bounce out of the water the launches taking them back to the Chusan. The rally drivers virtually took over the horse racing on board and generally livened the trip up. Paddy commented on his arrival at Perth that the journey was the best advert for flying that he had experienced.

A crowd of about 2,000 people, including Alf ('You silly old moo') Garnett, met the Chusan at Freemantle and it was rumoured that Peter Browning had sent a keg of beer down to the dockers as insurance against any of our cars being dropped from a crane.

All the rally cars had to be steam-cleaned and then were subject to a police check for compliance with Western Australian highway regulations. Over twenty had to carry out repairs to satisfy the police but none of the work could be done until after the start because cars were held in *parc fermé*.

Busy service point in Australia during the London–Sydney Marathon, Peter Browning on the right supervising

The restart was from the Gloucester Park trotting track where local dignitaries and beauties took it in turns to flag off the remaining 72 cars. Peter had taken a small group of mechanics to Australia to cover the section to Sydney, and apart from making a bracket to hold in the sump plug on the Evan Green 1800 and taking off the sirens which were not permitted by the police, there was nothing serious to do at the service point near Guildford. Amongst the floodlights, tents and all the equipment set up by the various teams there was a moment of panic when a deadly snake was spotted and the local Australians made everyone stop work until it had been located and killed. Den had already been introduced to a poisonous red-backed spider when an over-friendly one made a nest on a spare radiator fifteen minutes after it had been laid on the ground.

The first three sections from Perth totalled approximately 700 miles with the leg from Marvel Lock to Lake King being very tough. On this 119 mile section only three cars were penalty-free, Evan Green dropping two minutes over a puncture and Paddy unfortunately losing fourteen minutes when he broke the steering rack on the only section not reconnoitred.

Peter Browning and Den Green had flown to Sydney along part of the rally route in a light aircraft piloted by an experienced local, Ron Tutt. They wanted to see if they could do an aerial survey of the worst sections, but also stopped off so that Den could instruct the BMC Australia crews on the special items fitted to the works 1800s.

Unfortunately at a service point before the Brachina Gorge to Mingary section an over-enthusiastic Australian mechanic checking the Evan Green car over, detected some play in one of the rear wheel bearings. We were using adjustable bearings but, assuming it was the same as the standard unit, he had tightened the nut up really tight. Not long after leaving Brachina the wheel bearing seized and Evan was stranded. Messages to the next service point were not acted upon immediately in the absence of written instructions but eventually a BMC aircraft spotted the car, read their message in the sand and a spare hub was flown in. The delay of 4½ hours dropped them out of the running.

Near Gunbar the Red Arrows crew were treated to a slap-up meal by enthusaistic Australian RAF fans, the team-leader, Flt Lt Terry Kingsley being suitably impressed. At Brookside, Paddy was now lying fifth with Roger Clark still leading overall having been kept in the rally by being given Eric Jackson's cylinder head after he had burnt a valve. On the stage out of Brookside, Roger Clark ran into more trouble when his diff broke, but despite managing to buy a spare from a local he dropped 97 points. With Roger now dropped down the field Paddy moved up to fourth overall at the Murrindal control.

The section from Brookside to Omeo also dropped Rauno down the leader board when they lost 24 minutes due to a navigational error. Paul who was sleeping at the time, woke up, saw a signpost and thinking that they should go left, immediately nodded off again. When he woke again a few minutes later he realised that they had gone right, the error, caused by their tiredness, losing them the time.

Marathon Year

Paddy Hopkirk on a narrow section in Australia, London-Sydney Marathon

Rauno Aaltonen

Brian Culcheth

1968

At Ingebyra there were only about 300 miles to the finish of the Marathon but the battle for the lead was still on. The New South Wales police were making things difficult for the drivers, strictly enforcing speed limits which became very frustrating for tired crews who had been on the road for three days.

The last really tough section was from Numerella to Hindmarsh Station and on this one Paddy had a real go, losing only one minute to take fastest time. Simo Lampinen came to grief when he crashed breaking a track-rod, the overall positions then being Bianchi, Cowan and Hopkirk; with only two easy sections to go that seemed the likely finishing order.

The 97 miles from Hindmarsh Station to Nowra on the coast proved to be a turning point in the rally. Four miles from Nowra with his co-driver at the wheel, Lucien Bianchi's Citroen collided head-on with a Mini being driven very quickly round a corner on the wrong side of the road. Lucien was thrown into the screen and suffered serious leg injuries, being trapped in the wreckage. Next car along was Paddy who stopped at the scene and, while Tony Nash and Alec Poole jumped out with fire extinguisher and bolt cutters, Paddy drove back up the road where he had seen some press men with a two-way radio. As soon as help had been summoned and Lucien cut from the wreckage Paddy continued on his way.

This dramatic accident so close to the finish placed Andrew Cowan in a six minute lead with Paddy second, the stop at the scene of the accident not having caused any more penalties. The final section into Warwick Farm was easy and although Paddy arrived first he sportingly waited for the Cowan Hillman Hunter to come in to receive the applause of the 10,000-strong crowd. When Paddy arrived and was besieged by the press wanting all the gory details of the Bianchi accident, Paddy did not mince his words as he voiced his opinion about the NSW police and how in his opinion they could have prevented the accident with better traffic control.

It was all over: this motoring marathon that some experts had predicted would see only a handful of cars finishing. When the final results were listed, Paddy was confirmed as second overall, Rauno fifth, the Red Arrows 19th, Evan Green 21st and Tony Fall 24th. The 1800s were second and third in the Team prize with the third member of the third place team made up by the Wilsons Caravan Centre private entry which finished 34th.

The prize money amounted to £10,000 to the winner with Paddy receiving £3,000 and Rauno £500. The organisation of the service by Jed Oakley of BMC Australia was first class, receiving a number of complimentary comments from the accompanying press men, although some thought that organised service should have been banned. I think that we would have had a better chance with, perhaps, two of our four cars going with two-man crews, but Peter Browning had left this mainly to the drivers to decide after reccies of the route. As it was, three-man crews were first, second and third overall.

Now that the Marathon was over the regular crews had finished their spell with the Abingdon team and it was sad to think that after all the successes they had achieved, they would not be with us in 1969, with the exception of Paddy.

With the forthcoming race programme, work was started to build race Minis using ex-rally cars. Weslake Engineering were doing some fuel injection development work on our behalf on the 1293 cc engine and had designed and built a throttle slide to take the place of the original separate trumpets. Their initial power figures were looking promising and we felt that the prospects for the 1969 season were looking good, at least on the engine front.

Lord Stokes was keen on good publicity at low cost and cars for the televised rallycross series were also being built, Peter having signed up John Rhodes and John Handley to drive in both the race and rallycross events.

Just before the end of the year two Mini Cooper Ss were entered in the ITV televised rallycross at Croft; we were not disgraced when overall John Rhodes was placed third and John Handley sixth. We had acquired a Sprite Countryman caravan to use as a base at the race and rallycross events with Neville Challis responsible for the cooking arrangements. Many a serving of bacon, egg, sausage and beans was dished up during the series, very welcome to drivers and mechanics alike working in sub-zero or wet and muddy conditions at exposed airfield or rallycross venues.

The year ended with mixed feelings: sadness that the rally programme had been cut so drastically but with renewed enthusiasm and optimism for the new programme for 1969.

Triumphs at Abingdon

6
Triumphs at Abingdon
1969

PETER BROWNING was anxious to ensure that all of the new projects proceeded as smoothly as possible, particularly because we were under close scrutiny from the 'Kremlin', our less-than-affectionate term for Longbridge. On 10 January he told the Department that certain responsibilities would be allocated to the supervisory staff with Doug Watts looking after rally car preparation and new model developments, Tommy Wellman supervising the rallycross cars and sports car preparation, and Den Green taking care of the saloon car racing preparation. He hoped that this would improve communications between himself, the supervisors and the mechanics. It was not intended to establish specialised sections within the workshop and mechanics would be selected for events on the rota system as before.

Right: *Bob Whittington prepares a 1293 cc fuel injection engine with Weslake throttle slide for the 1969 British Saloon Car Championship*

The big surprise for me was that I was appointed Assistant Competitions Manager, taking immediate responsibility for running the race programme.

At this time Alan Zafer was appointed to a new position at the Press office in Berkeley Square and, although continuing as Competitions Press Officer, he was to spend more time in London than at Abingdon. Les Needham would look after the Press Office while Alan was in London and help out with the running of the Department.

Above left: *Abingdon Mini in a snowy BBC TV Rallycross event, February 1969 Lydden Hill*

There was a further rallycross event at Lydden in January in which John Rhodes retired but Paddy finishing sixth overall in a Morris 1300 with a 1275 fuel injection engine.

Triumph Four Wheel Drive

The winter season of televised rallycross events continued in February with a snowy meeting at Lidden Hill where we turned up with a rather unusual car. The powers-that-be felt that the competition emphasis should be on Triumph cars, thus we received from Triumphs at Canley what looked externally to be a Triumph 1300. This particular car had been devised by Harry Webster and built under the supevision of

Left: *Triumph 1300 four-wheel drive car winning the BBC TV Lydden Hill rallycross event driven by Brian Culcheth, February 1969*

Ray Henderson of the old Triumph Competitions Department for the televised TV mudplug between the Army and the London Motor Club at Aldershot. The transmission was based on the 4 x 4 system fitted to the Pony, a military vehicle built for evaluation by Israel with a Triumph 2000 limited slip rear differential and a Spitfire le Mans spec engine fitted. Brian Culcheth won the first heats of the mudplug but then the engine suffered a broken rocker arm.

It was very standard-looking when it arrived at Abingdon but now had the steel removable panels replaced with aluminium, and the inner door mechanisms stripped out along with the rear seats, trim, bumpers, etc. Perspex windows were also fitted to the side and rear to reduce weight, the only obvious exterior change was the blanked-off headlamps.

The February weather produced some heavy snow on the Rallycross weekend and as we drove down to Canterbury there was a blizzard blowing. In the morning it was clear and bright but we had trouble getting into the cars to drive to the

Triumphs at Abingdon

Lydden circuit because the door locks were all frozen up. The narrow road from the A2 to the circuit was blocked by snowdrifts, which caused another delay, but we eventually arrived for scrutineering in a small tent erected in the paddock.

The Triumph was taken off the trailer and driven to be scrutineered, but started to emit clouds of steam almost immediately. Investigation revealed that the engine was frozen solid; we had forgotten to check if the car had arrived from Canley with anti-freeze. The core plugs were sticking out of the block on the end of solid tubes of ice, and we feared the worst. Careful thawing with hot water and the exhaust of one of the Vanden Plas tow cars eventually revived the circulation much to Brian Culcheth's and our relief.

boots, and bonnets plus 1000 sets of perspex side and rear windows. The windows were finished first and these were homologated on 1 January in Group 2, together with longer front suspension arms to increase the negative camber.

Dunlop were anxious to develop a 12 inch tyre to overcome the tyre overheating problems encountered by the 'works' Cooper Car Company cars and to enable us to use this size wheel, it had to be homologated. Theoretically, 1000 cars had to be built with this size wheel but quite by luck the steel wheel that fitted the Hillman Imp would fit the Mini hub. As many thousands of this wheel had been built for Rootes by Rubery Owen and Sankey it was no problem to obtain a wheel production certificate. The wheel was submitted to the FIA, and these items were duly homologated on 1 April 1969 in

John Rhodes in the fuel injection Morris 1300 comes close to another competitor, Croft Rallycross, March 1969

Group 2. We could now use any 12 inch wheel in Group 2 events.

The car was the star of the meeting in the heavy snow, Brian coming home first overall in front of the television audience. Geoff Mabbs was in one of our Mini Cooper S cars but had a spectacular accident to retire rather comprehensively.

Another car prepared for rallycross was a Morris 1300 with, initially, Hydrolastic suspension. To stop the bounce this was changed to Mini-type rubber cone suspension and, with an eight-port cylinder head and fuel injection, John Rhodes made this projectile fly, coming second overall at the next ITV rallycross at Croft, with John Handley fifth overall in a Mini Cooper S.

In our search for more performance from the Mini Cooper S an expensive project was undertaken when the production was set in hand of 1000 sets of aluminium doors,

Peter's revised budget approved for the Saloon Car Racing programme was made up as follows:

Cars, engines & spares	£12,620
Drivers' fees, mechs' expenses etc, travel for testing	820
Drivers' fees, mechs' expenses etc, travel on events	4,005
Expenses for European events incl. Fees, ins. etc	4,410
total	21,855

1969

John Rhodes repeated his success at Croft in the March televised ITV rallycross event, with second overall, John Handley coming fourth in a Mini. As a try-out, Geoff Mabbs drove a Rover V8 which we had borrowed from Solihull but having had no development, it floundered about the track and was not placed. The Triumph 1300 4×4 was driven by Brian Culcheth but did not feature in the results.

The ITV final was held in April at Croft and in this event John Rhodes changed to a fuel-injected Mini coming a very worthy second in the Championship. John Handley had a go with the Morris 1300 and finished seventh overall, but another run with the Rover V8 was not a success. The final rallycross at High Egborough was, unfortunately, the end of the four-wheel drive Triumph. During one of the heats with Brian Culcheth driving, one of the rear suspension trailing arms fractured causing the car to roll, resulting in a comprehensive write-off!

Geoff Mabbs tries the Rover 3500 at Croft, March 1969

Brands Hatch Premier

The first event in our Mini race programme was to be the British Championship race at Brands Hatch in March.

In preparation for this event we took two cars to a very cold and frosty Thruxton on 14 February for John Handley and John Rhodes to drive. One car with more or less standard bodywork, Hydrolastic suspension and the No 1 Weslake development engine completed 22 laps with John Rhodes at the wheel recording a best time of 1 m 34.4 s; then the engine broke (the centre main bearing in the cylinder block had pulled out).

The second car was a stripped rallycross body with rubber cone suspension, a Salisbury limited-slip differential and a 1293 cc fuel injection engine. Both drivers took this car round on a variety of wheels including Cooper 10 and 12 inch and Minilite 10 inch on Dunlop CR 81 Mk2 tyres achieving a best lap time of 1 m 35.3 s. This engine also succumbed after 63 laps, with severe clutch slip caused by idler gear bearing failure. A number of modifications were found to be necessary and these were noted for the next session.

The pace was now picking up, and to give us every chance of a good showing in the first race, the next test session was at Brands Hatch on the Club circuit. Both cars were fitted with the new Weslake throttle slide on the fuel injection intakes, one car using rubber cone and the other Hydrolastic suspension.

The 'dry' car managed a total of 82 laps with anti-roll bar and shock-absorber settings being altered, a change to 12 inch 236 compound racing tyres bringing the comment 'fabulous' from John Rhodes, his best time being 58.3 sec. The other car suffered overheating which eventually resulted in a blown cylinder head gasket, but after this was changed, a lap of 59.0 sec was managed.

For the first race both the Johns requested 'dry' suspension, 10 inch wheels, and the diffs set to 80 lbs ft. Front anti-roll bars were taken off and reverse safety catches fitted to the gear levers.

Despite all our careful preparations, the Brands Hatch trip was rather a disaster. I drove the transporter from Abingdon with the two race cars aboard and on the hill out of Henley-on-Thames the clutch failed, leaving us stranded.

A number of phone calls summoned a long-wheelbase flat-bed lorry, and a van from the MG factory, and a tow truck to collect the transporter. We eventually arrived at the hotel

John Handley flying at Croft. Note the power bulge

rather late after a meal in Henley. Race day was very wet and in the two-part saloon race, John Rhodes was pushed off the track in a start line accident, and then John Handley put his rear wheel on to the grass and spun off ending a disastrous first time out. To finish the day, the flat-bed lorry became stuck in the mud in the paddock – not a very good start for the British Leyland 'works' race team with their smart red and white cars!

The second race in the Championship was the *Daily Express* International Trophy meeting at Silverstone where John Handley and John Rhodes finished, although only fourth and fifth in class respectively. The Broadspeed Escorts were going to be difficult to beat.

With the hectic Mini race programme taking up many hours in the workshop, Tommy Wellman was quietly supervising the preparation of three cars for the Sebring 12 Hour Race in Florida. The two MGCs were going to the Florida race to be entered as usual by the BL MG importer. Paddy and Andrew Hedges shared one MGC with the second car crewed by two Americans, Craig Hill and Bill Brack, while the MGB GT would also have an American crew.

In the race, Paddy/Andrew finished fifteenth overall with the other MGC 24th, while the MGB GT came in eighth in the GT category once again improving the MG reliability record in this event. With no money to develop or race the lightweight MGCs further, it was decided to sell the cars in USA, which was rather sad after only two races and very little development.

225

Triumphs at Abingdon

The end of the Triumph 1300 four-wheel drive car after fracture of a rear trailing arm. Brian Culcheth at High Egborough 1969

The Hopkirk/Hedges MGC during the 1969 Sebring 12 Hour Race

MGB GT on Minilite wheels, Sebring 12 Hour Race 1969

Lightweight Circuit Mini

With his past successes in the Circuit of Ireland, Paddy was entered again in a Mini. The event accepted Group 6 cars this year and with this in mind a lightweight Mini Cooper S was being prepared. The body was deseamed and extensive lightening was undertaken throughout. Virtually everything that could be reduced in weight was examined: aluminium brackets were substituted for steel, the cowls behind the headlamps were made of fibre-glass, the grille was aluminium, as were the doors, bonnet and boot. Perspex windows replaced the glass and a magnesium alloy sump guard (Minilite) was used. Even long bolts which protruded through nuts were cut-off! In the end no-one dared to add up the hours that were expended on this car.

The car (GRX 311D) suffered engine failure with faulty

Paddy Hopkirk/Tony Nash during the 1969 Circuit of Ireland. Note the 12 inch wheels and the Minilite sump shield (Esler and Beatty Crawford)

Paddy Hopkirk and Bill Price discuss a misfire problem during the 1969 Circuit of Ireland (Esler and Beatty Crawford)

cam followers when being run-in and as a result of the subsequent engine rebuild the final preparation of the car was not up to our usual standard.

The Circuit of Ireland was held over the Easter weekend which was also the weekend for two of the rounds of the British Saloon Car Championship. Peter decided that he would look after the race meetings at Snetterton and Thruxton on Good Friday and Easter Monday and I was sent to Ireland to look after the Circuit entry.

The car was eventually finished, and after a running-in period Cliff put the car briefly on the rolling-road dynamometer, recording 92 bhp at the front wheels. We took a choice of 10 × 5½ inch and 12 × 6 inch Minilite wheels with us, the 10 inch being fitted with 500L × 10 R7 race tyres and the 12 inch with 236 compound racers plus low profile 175 × 12 Weathermasters.

Before the start we fitted Sebring-type headlamp units at Paddy's request. After trying the car in rally trim Paddy complained of poor directional stability with the 12 inch racers and a misfire in the 4000/6000 rpm band. All attempts to cure the misfire failed and a new set of carbs and manifold were sent for, but unfortunately, owing to the Easter Holiday, they did not arrive before the start.

I shared a Vanden Plas service car with Tommy Wellman and Robin Vokins, while we also had a Castrol car with one of our mechanics on board, Neville Johnston (manager of one of Paddy's garages) in another car and Arne Poole (Alec Poole's brother) with two assistants in an MG 1100.

Paddy opted to try the 12 inch racers to start with, but the misfire and difficult handling, conspired to ensure his times were slower than the previous year on the first few stages. After stage 7, we changed to the 10 inch R7 race tyres, Paddy now being able to use full power.

At the Breakfast Halt at Bressington, the new carbs and manifold arrived, and were fitted, but the misfire worsened. At Killarney the original set of carbs was refitted and all was well. The cause seemed to have been a clearance problem between the inlet and exhaust manifold, the inlet flange being held away from the cylinder head causing an air leak.

On the Sunday run, Killarney–Killarney, the oil pressure dropped, but after checking the oil relief valve, renewing the gauge and then packing the relief valve spring the situation improved.

The rally became a battle between the Escort Twin Cam of Roger Clark and the Mini Cooper S cars of Paddy Hopkirk and Adrian Boyd, but the Minis were not able to match the speed of the Ford on the faster stages.

Disaster almost struck on the last day when one of the adjustable tie-rods we were using broke just before the end of a stage. This was changed but later in the day another one broke, this time on the road just before a service point. We scrounged some standard tie-rods from a private team, which were used for the rest of the rally. Apart from changing the rear brakes to reduce wheel locking, no other major work was carried out. At the finish, Roger was placed first, with Paddy second and Adrian Boyd third; a reasonable result in spite of the various troubles.

Back in England, Peter had a busy weekend shuttling between Thruxton and Snetterton, where fourth and fifth in class was the best the Rhodes/Handley duo could achieve. We were finding the Britax cars and the Broadspeed Escorts difficult opposition.

Austrian Alpine

Our Triumph involvement began with a test event for a Triumph 2.5 PI Mk1 in the Austrian Alpine Rally. The car was very standard with the exception of brakes and shock-absorbers, the specification being supplied by Ray Henderson at Triumph based on the successful Triumph 2000s which had been run from Coventry previously.

Paddy Hopkirk and Tony Nash drove the car and a strong service crew was taken out by Peter Browning for the event based on Semmering. Unfortunately the car did not last the distance, retiring with clutch failure, and was sent home on the train.

The next saloon car race was the Martini International meeting at Silverstone where the Rhodes/Handley duo did better coming in second and third in class behind the winning Escort. A last minute decision to change to dry tyres proved the right one because the track dried out for the race, allowing a fastest lap time of 1 m 48 s.

Triumphs at Abingdon

Paddy Hopkirk/Tony Nash Triumph 2.5 PI MkI, Austrian Alpine Rally 1969
John Handley on 12 inch magnesium Cooper wheels, Silverstone 1969

1969

John Handley at Silverstone in May 1969. Note the 10 inch wheels

A test session at Silverstone a few days before this race was completed in very wet conditions, the best time being 1 m 51 s. The engines were now giving a consistent 127 bhp on the Abingdon engine test bed and with a modified Salisbury limited-slip differential, Hydrolastic front suspension arms, Mini van rear suspension struts and Minifin aluminium brake drums we were at least settling on some parts of the specification.

The Annerley Trophy meeting at Crystal Palace on 26 May saw both cars breaking the 1968 lap record by over a second in practice, cut short for John Rhodes when the engine lost power and started to oil up spark plugs. A spare engine was fitted for the race which resulted in a third and fourth in class in hot sunny conditions.

John Rhodes showing some body damage at Silverstone 1969; Minilite 12 inch wheels

Scottish Rally

The Triumph 2.5PI (UJB 643G) was entered in the Scottish Rally, this time with Brian Culcheth and Johnstone Syer as the crew. The rough stages found a few weaknesses in the car, mainly of a minor nature until the differential failed. A 4.55 unit was not available as a spare and the high ratio fitted did not suit the rough stages, but nevertheless they finished second in class and 24th overall, our first result with a Triumph. They had used Dunlop SP44 Red Flash Weathermaster tyres and during the event changed three sets of front tyres and six sets of rear.

Brian Culcheth/Johnstone Syer Triumph 2.5 PI Mk1, 1969 Scottish Rally

Triumphs at Abingdon

```
                COMPETITION REPORT

Type of car              - Triumph 2.5 P.I.    Reg. No:   UJB 643G
Event                    - Scottish Rally      Group:     6
Date                     - June 6th - 12th 1969
Driver                   - B. Culcheth
Co-Driver                - J. Syer
Approx. mileage covered  - 3,000
```

When answering this question, if you don't know then put "dont't know" don't guess.

1. ENGINE

Power satisfactory?	Power was good. Car would cope with more
Injection and ignition	Good. Air cleaners came lose. Needs stronger supporting bracket, and some hold on top.
Petrol consumption?	8 - 10 MPG stages. 15 M.P.G. Road
Oil consumption?	1 pint per 1,000 miles
Grade of oil?	XXL
Oil pressure variation?	Road constand 60 lb. Stages 45 - 50 lb. I got the impression that the oil got very hot on stages. Pressure low after stages. Carry out testing with oil temp. gauge.
Any oil surge?	No
Max revs used?	6,000
Any excessive pinking or running - on experienced.	Pinking to start with then wore off.
Any overheating?	Yes to start with. O.K. after removing thermostat. Running Temp - 160 - 170.
Any work carried out?	
Was the sump guard satisfactory?	Yes
Any other comment or suggestion	If standing at start of stage with engine ticking over, immediately stage started, engine would cut dead once or twice.

2. TRANSMISSION

Any noise?	Rough between 5,000 and 6,000 revs.
ANy vibration?	As above. Got worse as rally went on.
Ease of change?	Bit knotchy otherwise good.
Clutch satisfactory?	Yes. Smelt a little when high diff was fitted.
Gearbox and final drive ratios satisfactory?	Excellent with 4.55 diff. Replacement diff far to high geared.
Any other comment or suggestion	The reverse gear relay gave trouble on way to start/O.K. after disconnected. The danger of going into reverse 0/0 and wrecking box.

3. SUSPENSION AND ROADHOLDING

How was the general balance of the car?	Good
How was the steering?	Good. Not enough room between wheel and seats for leg movement. Needs slightly dished wheel.
Type of tyres fitted?	Dunlop SP 44 Weathermaster red flash.
No of tyre changes?	6 front. 12 rear.
What was the tyre wear and what pressures?	Tyre wear varied with stages. Pressure 34 front. 38 rear.
Any road wheel trouble?	No
Any shock absorber trouble?	Yes front struts far to weak. The pair we started with were good, they did about 25 stages before they began to bottom. The second pair of struts supposedly the same as the first did not last more than 12 stages.
Any other comment or suggestion	

4. BRAKING

Brake material used? (to be completed by Comps. Dept.)	Ferodo DS 11 pads. Ferodo VG 95 linings.
Pedal pressure satisfactory?	Fairly high. Better servo?
Did you experience any brake fade and under what conditions?	No

Braking (Contd.)

Did you experience any serious wheel locking?	No
How often were the brakes adjusted?	3 or 4 times.
How often was brake material re-newed?	Fronts once.
Any other comment or suggestion	The brakes were not particularly good. I feel more braking is needed on the front. The brake pedal is slightly too big. My feet occasionally got caught under it when coming off the accelerator pedal. The corner needs cutting off.

5. ELECTRICAL SYSTEM

Was the lighting satisfactory?	Was good. I would like to do some testing, with current set up plus 2 long range.
Did you have any fanbelt trouble?	No
Was the Intercomm satisfactory?	Not used.
Did you make any electrical repairs or replacements?	No
Any other comment or suggestion	

6. BODY

Were there any leaks or draughts?	Rear window began to come out.
Was the seating satisfactory?	Drivers excellent. Passengers could be improved.
Type of seats fitted?	Comps. own drivers. Standard Passengers.
Were the minor controls and switches in easy places?	Yes. Very good (see note 2) further on.
Were the seat belts satisfactory?	No. Kept coming out of adjustment and hard to re-adjust.
Make and type of seat belts fitted?	Britax full harness - both sides.
Did the screen wipers and washers work satisfactorily?	Hardly used. Blind spot on drivers side top RH of screen.

Body (Contd.)

Was the heating, demisting and ventilation effective?	Yes hardly used.
Were the instruments accurate, visible and well lit at nights?	The speedo was hopelessly inaccurate in every way. About 20% out to start with. After new diff. 40% out. Lighting O.K.
Were the rally clocks accurate?	

7. PREPARATION

Was the car handed over to you in good condition?	Yes
Were travel arrangements satisfactory?	Yes
Were the tools, spares and equipment sufficient and satisfactory?	Yes. Boot needs re-organising.
Was Hotel Accommodation satisfactory?	Fair
Were the servicing arrangements during the event adequate?	Excellent
How did your car compare with its rally or commercial competitors?	Very well.
Any other comment or suggestion	

8. GENERAL SUMMARY OF THE CAR'S PERFORMANCE, LIKES, DISLIKES, COMMENTS AND ANY POINTS PECULIAR TO THIS RALLY TO BE NOTED FOR NEXT YEAR'S EVENT?

   1. The hydraulic jack continually broke at the base. I think this type of jack is very dangerous and unless modified should not be used again.
   2. The start button is to far away. Also it is rather dangerous for one of the mechanics went ot open the bonnet and his watch shorted out of starter button.
   3. The fuel pump pressure gauges fluctuates violently all the time is this right?
   4. Navigators map light could be in a better place. Ask J. Syer.
   5. The roll bar with the padding on is to near the drivers head.
   6. The sun visors worked themselves down and had to be removed (same on reccie car).

```
General Summary of performance etc. (Contd.)

  7.  The spare wheel carrier got badly battered underneath.
  8.  Handbrake was useless and would not hold the car on any
      sort of slope.
  9.  The front suspension produced a shake like wheel balance
      towards the end of rally. Despite the wheels being changed
      round this made no difference.
 10.  Exhaust system broke just below manifold join.
 11.  Axle failed.
 12.  The exhaust system was never free of rattling or touching
      the body.
 13.  The starter got dodgy towards the end of the rally.
 14.  One of the rear suspension (protection) plates came unwelded.
 15.  The dipstick got bent one day.
 16.  A lot of heat was transmitted form the gearbox tunnel to inside
      the car.
 17.  The boot lid could be made a lot lighter.
 18.  Sponge required on passengers arm rest only.

ON RECCE CAR GROUP 2

  1.  Battery carrier collapsed.
  2.  Wire came off alternator.
  3.  Passenger glove box came down on rough, needs check strap.
      Same the centre consul in front of gear lever.
```

Drivers test report, 1969 Scottish Rally

Hockenheim Race

To show the flag in the European market, our first continental race with the Minis was at Hockenheim during the second week in June. This event was for Group 2 cars, so the mechanics were kept busy building two new cars with heaters, no auxiliary radiators, bumpers, full interior trim, Hydrolastic suspension plus front shock-absorbers (Homologated 1 May 1968), 5½ × 10 inch Minilite wheels, and with the engines running on the 'split-Webers'.

We had to split the testing between Silverstone and Thruxton owing to pressure of work, but when John Handley tried his car at Silverstone we also took along the first of the short-stroke race engines for a race test. John tried his car and was reasonably happy with it until it succumbed after only six laps to a stiff gearchange thought to be caused by a faulty primary gear bush.

John Rhodes drove the car with the short-stroke engine which had a capacity of 1289 cc (73 × 77 mm) and was producing 131 bhp at 7000 rpm. The brakes had to receive attention after eleven laps when the short race tail pipe was also changed to the long open pipe. The long pipe allowed the engine a pull a further 150 rpm down Hangar Straight but after a further ten laps the car stopped with a broken crankshaft. Back to the drawing board!

John Rhodes' Hockenheim car was ready to test two days later, this time at Thruxton with a Group 1 car taken along as well. The Tour de France Automobile event was on our programme, and the object of the Group 1 test was to establish which tyres would be most suitable on the 3½ × 10 inch steel wheels which had to be used in Group 1. Brian Culcheth did a total of 80 laps on three types of tyre, SP Sport, 500L × 10 184 compound race tyres and 500L × 10 Green Spot race tyres. The Green Spot racers came out best despite not running on their optimum rim size, being over 5 seconds quicker than the SP Sports, and over 2 seconds better than the 184 compound. After the tyre tests Brian continued to lap the circuit at speed to test the wheels which had not been tried on racers for any length of time previously (memories of the 850 Minis).

John Rhodes tried the Hockenheim car and was quite satisfied after adjusting suspension pressures and shock-absorber settings although there was a minor problem with the tyres fouling the rear anti-roll bar.

We took the cars to Hockenheim in the transporter and I managed to get in some more driving of the 33 foot ex-BMC Training Unit. The first problem when we got there, which was a bit annoying, was that the transporter would not go under the tunnel into the paddock, so that timing one's entrance and exit was critical to track closure times.

The weather was very hot and sunny and in the first practice session both drivers complained that the cars were overheating. Running with the bonnets propped open and heaters full on kept things in check, John Rhodes also collecting some body damage when an NSU spun in front of him. By the second practice on Saturday, we had removed the thermostats and fitted blanking inserts and had flattened the grille slats to let in more air. With the heaters full-on the temperature was holding at 95°F, a saving of 15°F. This proved how important the auxiliary radiators were in hot conditions. John Handley's car was not quite as fast as the other car so John Rhodes gave him a 'tow' for about four laps bringing his fastest lap time down by over a second. The grid included 1600 cc cars but the Minis were not disgraced with their third and fourth row grid positions accompanied by the local Mini hero Christian Schmarje.

In the race, the very fast Alfa Romeos were too quick for the Minis but with some heroic slip-streaming, John Rhodes was looking good for a second in class. He had been helped by Christian, but just before the end of the race the German's windscreen shattered; he had had a toughened one fitted! At the end, before an enormous crowd, the two cars managed third and fifth in class, the two drivers having given the spectators some great entertainment.

We were sorry to leave the small hotel on the Monday where we were getting quite a taste for the jugs of ice-cold white wine, not to mention the strawberries served up at lunchtime!

Our next visit to Brands Hatch was on 22 June for the European 6 Hour Touring car race, where our two entries were crewed by John Rhodes/Paddy Hopkirk and John Handley/Roger Enever. The drivers did two-hour spells at the wheel with John Rhodes doing the first and last stints in his car. The front tyres were changed after two hours with fuel being taken every two hours. While Paddy was driving, the offside rear tyre of his car started smoking as if something was fouling, and a pit stop was needed to fit a new tyre and knock the inner wing back with a large hammer. At the scheduled driver stop 20 minutes later, the trailing arm bracket was found to be broken, losing them 6½ minutes in the pits while it was changed. The other car required three pints of oil after four hours and only just made the finish with failing oil pressure caused by the low oil level.

The Minis finished second and third in class, which we were quite pleased with in our first long distance race.

One of our first mechanical failures in the British Championship occured at Mallory Park in the 4000 Guineas meeting when John Handley's car blew a piston, John Rhodes coming fourth overall.

Triumphs at Abingdon

Nurburgring 6 Hour Race

With the need for quick tyre changes we decided to use the knock-on wheel hubs at Nurburgring. This event turned out to be rather eventful with both engines being removed after practice to rectify clutch problems caused by the primary gear bushes moving again. This work was carried out by the mechanics working late into the night in the garages in the paddock. The final drive ratios were also changed from 3.7 to 3.9 to suit the circuit.

Geoff Mabbs had a problem in practice when he lost a wheel on the circuit, luckily without any damage, being rescued by the other car which called at the pits for a new spinner. Investigation indicated that the clearance between the drive pegs and the holes in the wheels was too tight, allowing the wheel to jam before seating fully home on the hub. This problem was rectified before the race.

The long Nürburgring circuit seemed to suit the cars and, despite strong opposition from the 1300 Alfa Romeos, after 28 laps the Handley/Enever car was leading the class. The whole situation changed dramatically when the leading car came in to the pits with the offside rear trailing arm pivot shaft broken. The shaft was changed, Roger Enever took over for the last session but within four miles of the pits, the pivot shaft on the other side broke, stranding the car out on the circuit. The second car also suffered the same fate, a big disappointment after such a good showing in practice. The stress of the bumpy circuit with its numerous corners and steep gradients, and the unforgiving Dunlop D15 sidewalls fitted to the newly Homologated 12 inch Minilite wheels had found a weakness where the drilling for greasing the shaft had been made. The cars were fitted with solid shafts for all future events!

World Cup

There was news now of a special rally connected with the football World Cup which was to take place in Mexico in 1970. When the regulations were published for the *Daily Mirror* World Cup Rally to be run from London to Mexico, a distance of 16,000 miles, plans were soon being formulated by Peter Browning to enter this new marathon. It was going to cost a lot of money but the publicity in worldwide markets that this event could attract looked attractive to the Marketing Division. By the end of July Peter had obtained agreement for his proposed programme for the next 12 months and an official announcement appeared in the National press. Entries would be made in the World Cup Rally with Paddy Hopkirk and Brian Culcheth being joined by Andrew Cowan to head a strong driver line-up. Cars would also be entered in the Tour de France, the RAC Rally and in racing and rallycross.

A few days before this announcement, Peter Browning received a copy of Policy Instruction No. 48 issued by the chairman and managing director, Lord Stokes, to all the companies in the corporation. It stated that the Competitions Department would be entering a number of vehicles in competitions during the 1969/70 financial year under Peter Browning, within approved limits. Mr Browning would keep in close touch with Engineering Departments and would submit details of final specifications of individual vehicles to Chief Engineers for final approval.

This seemed an unrealistic imposition because most Chief Engineers did not have the time anyway, and it looked like a vote of no confidence in the Department. The statement finished off with this sentence: 'Successful performance in competitions can obviously contribute greatly to British Leyland's sales achievements and I will be grateful if the various Chief Engineers would give Mr Browning every cooperation in carrying out his responsibilities'.

So after all the comments made previously, here was the boss giving his official support to the motor sport programme (provided we could achieve some successes).

Spa 24 Hour Race

Our Mini programme continued with an entry in the Spa 24 Hours Touring Car Race, the crew pairings being Rhodes/Mabbs and Handley/Enever.

There was a problem at scrutineering where the Belgian technical committee decided to check the overall width of the cars. The homologation form lists the body dimensions and Appendix J permitted the addition of wing extensions 2 inches wider than the existing body. According to the scrutineers we were 2 cm oversize. The mechanics had to remove some of the fibreglass from the wing extensions to get the cars accepted. The scrutineers also objected to the oil reservoirs and pumps which were operated from the drivers seat for topping up during racing; these were removed.

There were two practice sessions – one in the dark, which was compulsory – which went off without any serious dramas. To cope with the high speeds attainable at Spa, we had fitted 3.3:1 final drives (without LSD) which allowed the cars to record an average lap speed of just under 100 mph (157 kph). Coloured identification lamps were mounted on the roofs and coloured bands painted across the front of the bonnets to help recognition from the pits.

The weather was changeable as start time approached, so we gambled and sent one car off on dry tyres and John Handley on intermediates. Six laps after the start, with a rapidly drying track, John came in for dry tyres and had his tank topped up with fuel.

The race settled down after the first frantic minutes but within a couple of hours the Rhodes car started to sound very rough. At a routine pit stop to change drivers and refuel, the car would not restart despite the efforts of the mechanics. The valve seats had collapsed causing compression loss, and the car was retired.

The other car continued at speed but after about 60 laps was showing signs of oil surge and excessive oil consumption, needing about 2 pints every pit stop. At 150 laps it was lying twelfth overall and second in class behind an Alfa Romeo Junior, but at 170 laps had taken the class lead.

Still with a long way to go we were keeping our fingers crossed for a finish. At a distance of 235 laps, the car was missing badly and in the pits a broken battery lead was quickly repaired. However, after 22½ hours, the engine suddenly expired at the La Source hairpin before the pits with a conrod through the crankcase, a bitter blow after 255 laps of competitive racing.

Weslake continued with some engine development, and for the Oulton Park Gold Cup meeting John Rhodes had a rather special engine in his car. The bore/stroke of 74.0 × 75.5 mm gave a capacity of 1298.8 cc using slipper-type pistons, a steel crankshaft, titanium conrods and an oil baffle plate between the gearbox and engine. The car went well in practice but John could not match the speed of the opposition in the race finishing fourth in class with John Handley just behind.

At the August Thruxton meeting, Geoff Mabbs drove one of the injection Minis for BBC Grandstand with an in-car camera, having to battle up through the field after an early collision with Richard Longman, which was good viewing.

Plans for the Tour de France, RAC and World Cup rallies were taking shape and John Sprinzel had been on a recce of the World Cup European section for the organisers in the Abingdon Triumph 2.5PI (UJB 642G). This car was now being prepared for an intensive test session at Bagshot.

Cliff's development section was handling this part of the testing and between 26 August and 18 September completed 313 laps (610 miles) of the rough road track at the Fighting Vehicle Research & Development Establishment at Bagshot, with Paddy and Brian doing some of the driving. A number of weaknesses were found in the car including the usual shock-absorber failures, some differential mounting breakages, the need to improve the battery clamp and failure of the quill shaft between the diff and propshaft. Bagshot is a real car breaker and everyone was quite impressed by the strength of the car. To complete one day at Bagshot without breaking the vehicle was quite an achievement for any car.

The publication of the World Cup Rally regulations enabled Peter to make provisional plans for the event and sent a note to the crews summarising his thoughts. He confirmed that he expected to enter three Triumph 2.5PI Mk2 cars, model code name Innsbruck, which were to be announced at the Motor Show. The drivers would be Culcheth/Syer, Cowan/Coyle and Hopkirk/Nash. We would also be preparing three new V8 Range Rovers, to be announced to the public in March 1970, with the likely crews to be E. Green/J. Murray, T. Kingsley/P. Evans and Rosemary Smith/Alice Watson. Details of the cars would have to be kept confidential for obvious reasons. Peter also asked that the crews advise him as soon as possible if they were considering taking an extra crew member.

A prototype Range Rover would be made available in October and a 10,000 mile development programme would be commenced immediately. Brief details were also included for two reccies of the South American sections before Christmas.

I went to Bagshot to discuss the Range Rover test with Joe Wood the track controller, the idea being to carry out the tarmac running at the 2 mile circuit at Chobham. In my report to Peter I listed the problems which would prevent our using the track including 70 mph speed limit, no workshop facilities, no fuel supplies and only Monday to Friday working. We decided to make other arrangements but still use Bagshot for the rough road work.

Tour de France Automobile

Our entry for this event was three Mini Cooper S cars for Paddy, John Handley and Brian Culcheth, the latter driving the

Engine compartment of fuel injection Mini Cooper S driven by Paddy Hopkirk/Tony Nash, 1969 Tour de France Automobile

Triumphs at Abingdon

Group 1 car. In addition, Julien Vernaeve was entering his own Group 1 car fitted with a Don Moore engine with full support from us on the event. Paddy's car was fitted with a fuel injection engine while the John Handley car was on a 45 DCOE Weber carburettor.

A test/photographic session was held at Silverstone to bed the cars in and to give the drivers a chance to try them, while Alan Zafer arranged for publicity photographs to be taken. We were using the Minilite knock-on hubs on the two Group 2 cars and the best lap times recorded were 1m 54s for Hopkirk and Handley with Brian Culcheth getting round in 2m 12s on 184 compound tyres. There was a recurrence of the wheel problem when Geoff Mabbs lost a front wheel. In order to get some more miles out of a Triumph 2.5PI, Peter scheduled the ex-Scottish rally car out on the Tour as his service car with myself acting as 'chauffeur' and Dudley Pike the 'riding' mechanic.

to take the tunnel cover off, remove one of the inhibitor switches and top up the oil using a teapot from our canteen. We also had a problem with the side exhaust sending fumes into the car, but this was controlled by keeping the driver's window closed. At Rouen, John Handley found that his clutch was slipping but as the housing had been sealed at scrutineering, we could only keep our fingers crossed and squirt in extinguisher fluid. At Clermont-Ferrand, Paddy suffered from oil surge which brought him into the pits for a top-up.

The two Group 1 cars were going well but Brian was not happy that the Julien Vernaeve car seemed to be much faster than his own car, inferring that, perhaps, Julien's engine was not quite legal!

After the race at Rheims, John and Paddy were fourth and fifth overall in the touring category respectively, John now being 5 minutes in front of Paddy after his problems. Paddy had more trouble at Albi when one of the heater hoses came

Testing at Silverstone for the Tour de France Automobile. L-to-R: Brian Culcheth, John Handley, Paddy Hopkirk

This gruelling event started in Nice and split up into six sections finishing at Nancy, Rheims, Dieppe, Vichy, Albi and then Biarritz. The total distance was 5000 km covered from 18–26 of September, the real test to men and machines coming on the ten circuit races and eleven hillclimbs. These included such famous names as Spa, Nürburgring, Le Mans, Mont Ventoux, Ballon d'Alsace and Col du Minier.

The first section included six hillclimbs and at Nancy, John Handley lead Paddy by almost 2 minutes in their class, while Julien Vernaeve was leading Brian in the Group 1 small capacity class.

On the next section, while on our way to the Nürburgring, the Triumph 2.5PI service car gearbox started to make some very expensive noises and it was with some reluctance that Peter agreed that we should stop to check it. The gearbox was out of oil and in the absence of a syringe we were obliged

John Handley during the 1969 Tour de France Automobile

loose necessitating a pit stop, losing more valuable time. Paddy also lost time on the road when the lower arm pivot came adrift when miles away from a service car.

On Aspin, the last but one hillclimb, John Handley misinterpreted the pace note call from Paul and tried to take a 'fast' left corner 'flat'. The result was that they bounced heavily into the wall doing the car no good at all! The car had been suffering from clutch slip for some time, despite liberal doses of fire extinguisher fluid, which meant that John had really to concentrate on keeping the car in the highest gear possible, particularly up hills.

Paddy found that his car was losing power and with a long road section in prospect and time to investigate, the mechanics discovered a broken valve spring. There was no time to take the cylinder head off, but with some careful juggling with a bent screwdriver to support the valve head, the spring was changed *in situ* in about 15 minutes.

At Nogaro, the Minis gave the crowd something to cheer about. Paddy had to stop to change a plug which had oiled up, (Brian was actually leading the race), but within about six laps was up to third overall behind the Camaro of Marie-Claude Beaumont and Brian's Mini. Paddy then suffered a puncture but from last position he stormed through the field to overtake everyone else before the finish.

When it was all over, Brian's great drive was not good enough to beat Julien Vernaeve, the two Group 1 cars coming first and second in class. Paddy managed fourteenth overall and first in class. So after a fairly quiet season on the rally scene, this was a result despite the mechanical troubles.

The 'Innsbruck' was not going to be homologated in time for the RAC so three new Triumph 2.5PI Mk1 cars were being prepared using all the knowledge accumulated so far from Triumph at Canley and from our own test and limited rally programme.

Salzburgring Minis

Apart from the Guards Trophy race at Brands Hatch in September, where John Rhodes was fourth in class and John Handley retired, the last Mini race outing of the year was to be at the Salzburgring where BL Austria were very keen to see a works presence.

We took the transporter with the two race cars accompanied by one Vanden Plas 4-litre R and, with just one overnight stop, arrived at our small Gasthof not far from the circuit. The tune-shop run by ex-Nuffield Exports Rep, Don Wooding, of Hamburg, had prepared a Mini for Prince Leopold von Bayern so we had at least one other competitive Mini to keep us company. We were blessed with some very nice autumn sunshine and after a reasonably trouble-free practice day the sun came out for the race proper.

There was a tremendous crowd at the track for the meeting and when our cars lined up on the grid, John Rhodes was on the front row with Prince Leopold and an Alfa Romeo 1300, John Handley being in the row behind. The race was very close with the Alfa Romeo's making things very difficult for the Minis but at the finish the two Johns were first and second overall, well clear of the opposition. A very satisfying result in front of the big crowd, much to the delight of the BL Austria.

After supper at our pub, we went into Salzburg to visit one of the night spots for a quiet drink, and we had an amusing time sitting with John Rhodes who was chatting up a tall blond

Congratulations for John Rhodes after winning the Salzburg Saloon Car Race, October 1969

Triumphs at Abingdon

1969

who came to the table, John being unaware that the blond was in fact a bloke! That same night a drunken driver wrote his car off against the Gasthof wall; our party slept through the commotion.

RAC Rally Triumph Team

The RAC Rally had a problem with its sponsorship plans for this year's rally which resulted in the regulations and rally plates having the Sun identity removed. The rally started and finished at the Centre Airport Hotel near Heathrow.

As Alan Zafer's press release pointed out, our entry in the RAC of three Triumph 2.5PIs was the first time that Abingdon had entered a full team of non-BMC cars. It also said that this was to be a development event in preparation for the forthcoming World Cup Rally. The Mk2 model had been announced at the Motor Show and I felt very fortunate to be allocated one as a service car for the rally the first example of the new model we received at Abingdon. The rally cars were running on 7 × 13 inch Minilite wheels so it seemed sensible to fit my car with the same wheels in case of an emergency need for wheels during the event; it went against the grain a bit to have to flare the rear wheel arches on this new car to accommodate the 7 inch rims! Peter Browning was driven on the rally by John Handley accompanied by Les Needham.

Engine compartment of Triumph 2.5PI Mk1, 1969 RAC Rally

Apart from raising the compression ratio to 10.4:1 and a special side exhaust, the rally car engines were fairly standard. The transmission was fitted with overdrive, Koni shock-absorbers fitted front and rear, at 4,55:1 limited slip final drive and the inevitable Ferodo DS11 pads/VG95 linings were included in the spec. Additional jacking points were added to the body on each side designed for use with a hydraulic pillar jack (useful for deditching).

Left: *Cockpit of Triumph 2.5PI Mk1, 1969 RAC Rally*

In honour of his win in the London–Sydney Marathon, Andrew Cowan was allocated start number 1 and led the 153 starters away on a wet and windy morning. The first stage was at Silverstone but the forest stages did not start until after leaving the control at Selby Fork. The Triumphs were not achieving spectacular times but a battle was developing between our cars and the Datsun team for the Manufacturer's Team Prize.

As the cars moved up into Northumberland, Andrew Cowan was complaining of clutch slip but as this improved, we reckoned that the plates were taking some time to bed-in. Snow and ice were now causing problems to the bigger rear-wheel drive cars, and on one or two of the stages the Triumphs and Ford Escorts were running out of traction and required help from spectators.

At the breakfast halt at Dumfries, Waldegaard was leading in a Porsche with the Triumphs not in the top ten, which was hardly surprising for a big car in such icy conditions. As the cars headed for the Blackpool halt, news came through to Rally HQ that heavy snow was blocking some of the stages in North Wales. To check the situation, Peter Harper was despatched by the organisers to try to get through the stages. Alan Zafer had come to their assistance by offering the use of one of the Triumph 2.5PI rally/test cars at Abingdon, which was hastily prepared and sent up into Wales. The conditions had improved by the time Peter went through, so that in the end only one stage had to be cancelled.

At Blackpool the main complaint from the drivers was that the front shock-absorbers were too soft but there were no major repairs necessary. The rally restarted and moved south towards North Wales where the Clocaenog stages were heavy in snow, quite a disadvantage to the wide 7 inch rims of the cars. To help cope with the conditions standard steel wheels were fitted, with snow chains used on more than one occasion.

1969 RAC Rally Triumph Team. L-to-R: B. Coyle, A. Cowan, P. Hopkirk, A. Nash, J. Syer and B. Culcheth

Triumphs at Abingdon

Brian Culcheth and Johnstone Syer flying in the Triumph 2.5 PI during the 1969 RAC Rally

Paddy Hopkirk in the snow – rear chains just visible, 1969 RAC Rally

1969

Andrew Cowan managed to put his car off the road on the third Clocaneog stage in front of the TV cameras, being helped out of trouble by willing spectators. There were many delays to rally cars in this area caused by spectator cars badly parked due the deep snow, and there was a suggestion that extra time would be added to the halt at Machynlleth.

On the last stage before Machynlleth the gearbox broke on Paddy's car leaving him with only one gear. The BMC dealer was open for our use and we hoped that there was going to be time to change the gearbox.

The service area/control was absolute chaos with cars hardly able to move in or out and during this we took the chance of moving the car to the garage where the mechanics started to change the gearbox. The car was supposed to be in *parc fermé* but as the minutes ticked by it became clear that the car could not be at the control for its scheduled restart time. Tony Nash was taken to the control by Peter Browning and in the confusion managed to book out without presenting his rally car, giving the mechanics time to get it finished.

Unfortunately, there was immediately a problem with the clutch not disengaging which gave trouble for the rest of the rally. This was later found to be caused by the release arm fork not being correctly entered in the release bearing holder, inexperience with the model and the pressure of getting it done in less than an hour had obviously contributed but, none the less, it was good experience for the forthcoming World Cup Rally.

The team prize battle between Datsun and Triumph, now separated by only a few seconds, eventually went to Datsun when Brian had a temporary stoppage on his fuel injection pump (cured by a well aimed thump). The Triumphs were first, second and third in the over 2000cc class with Andrew eleventh, Paddy fifteenth and Brian seventeenth overall.

The next few months were occupied mainly with the preparations for the World Cup Rally, including preparing two of the RAC rally cars for a recce of the South American sections.

This route survey started the day after the RAC Rally

Visibility problems during a Lydden Hill rallycross event

One way to cure visibility problems, Lydden Hill rallycross

Triumphs at Abingdon

finished with the departure of Brian Culcheth, Tony Nash and Ulrico Ossio for Rio de Janiero to collect a LHD Triumph 2000. Ulrico was a resident of Lima in Peru, had done some rallying in South America and spoke good English. He had already driven the Lima-registered car all the way from Peru for the recce. This Triumph 2000 had rather weak shock-absorbers so, to give the car some chance of lasting, the recce crew phoned Abingdon for some of the uprated shock-absorbers which we had been testing. After a preliminary look at most of the route from Rio through to Lima, during which time they suffered endless punctures, Brian and Tony returned to England on Christmas eve with copious notes.

Rover Project

Driven by the necessity to find a replacement for the Mini Cooper S, Peter had decided that the Rover 2000 body was about the right size for a race or rally car. At the Gold Cup Meeting at Oulton Park, he discussed his idea of a 'hot' V8 race car with Bill Shaw and asked him if he was interested in actually building the car. Bill decided to take on the project and before long collected a Rover from Abingdon; this was the car which had been driven by Geoff Mabbs in a number of rallycross events.

Because Bill was in the process of changing his workshop premises, he asked JoMoRo Racing in Surrey, run by two experienced race mechanics, to carry out the work. A small batch of aluminium panels was produced by Rover for the car; these were of course only the 'skins' which meant that each door had to be constructed from scratch, while the new wider, flared wings had to be hand made, principally from glass-fibre.

The engine was placed in the hands of Mathwall Engineering who built a 4.3-litre Rover/Buick unit using some Traco parts, with a long-stroke crankshaft to achieve the increased capacity. Power output was in the region of 365 bhp using four Webers.

On the reccomendation of Cliff Humphries, Peter sent two Rover V8 engines to the USA to the Traco tuning firm with instructions to tune the engines to give the best power output available with off-the-shelf parts. These engines were eventually returned with full specification and power curves, one being sent down to Abingdon fitted with four 48 IDA Weber carburettors with a claimed output of 295 bhp. The engine was tried in testing but discarded in favour of the 4.3 long-stroke unit, while the second engine remained at Solihull and was later rumoured to have been purchased by one of Rover's directors.

The gearbox and rear axle were Rover 2000, while the 12 inch front Lockheed disc brakes were housed within Minilite 15 × 10 inch wheels, with rear inboard 10 inch ventilated discs. A number of modifications were made to the suspension, including replacing the rubber bushes with phosphor bronze type, and fitting additional location arms for differential and torque tube. There were obviously going to be many weeks work ahead before the car turned a wheel, but it was hoped to see it on a circuit early in the New Year.

Following the decision to enter a Mini in the World Cup Rally, a Mini Clubman had been purchased and was being built into a rally car. John Handley and Paul Easter were lined up to crew the car and were due to start a recce of the European section before Christmas. This proved to be a frustrating exercise when heavy snow in Yugoslavia held up their progress twice, stranding them in Dubrovnik for three days on the first occasion.

Peter Bartram working on the Mini Clubman recce car for the 1970 World Cup Rally

The RAC Rally Triumph 2.5PI Mk2 service car (WJB 189H) was now pressed into service as a suspension test car. Fitted with prototype Stag front springs, estate car rear springs and Koni shock-absorbers front and rear, the car was taken to the Girling test track at Honiley with Brian Culcheth and Paddy Hopkirk doing the driving. Derek Wootton had produced some 15 × 5½ inch Minilite wheels which were fitted with Dunlop SP44 185 × 15 tyres.

The first runs brought comments from both drivers that the car was suffering from excessive body roll with a tendency for initial understeer to transfer to wild oversteer. An improvement was achieved by increasing front and rear negative camber. After the test, Derek White, Ride & Handling Executive from Triumph Engineering, offered to sort out some stiffer springs and investigate fitting front and rear anti-roll bars.

With the arrival of Christmas, little did we know what would be happening the following year at the same time.

1968

1968 London-Sydney Marathon recce car broken down in Iran – Paul Easter on guard. (P. Easter)

Car 61 ready for the start, 1968 London-Sydney Marathon 1968. (P. Easter)

1968 London-Sydney Marathon recce car on the Lataban Pass near Kabul. (P. Easter)

1968

This was the southern route of the Sivas-Erzincan section the day before the rally, London-Sydney Marathon 1968

Paddy Hopkirk supervises refuelling during London-Sydney Marathon 1968.

The winch holds the front suspension at Kabul. R. Aaltonen/H. Liddon/P. Easter 1800 (P. Easter)

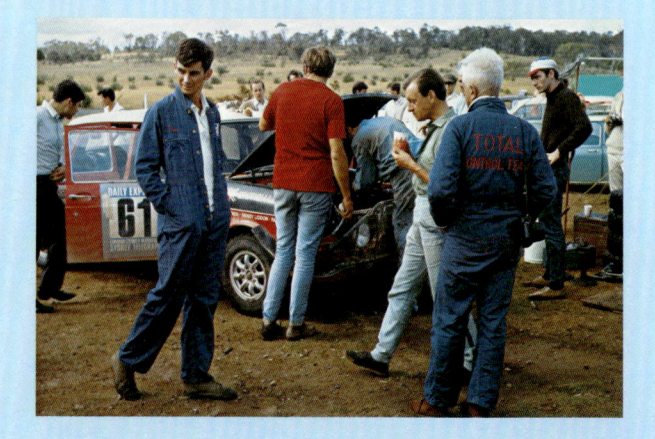

Service point for Rauno Aaltonen (with cup) in Australia, 1968 London-Sydney Marathon.

1969-70

1969 Spa 24 Hour Saloon Car Race. Abingdon Minis in front of the pits.

Typical conditions at Lydden Hill rallycross meeting.

1970

World Cup Rally 1970. J. Handley/P. Easter Mini Clubman 1275 at Wembley. (P. Easter)

Below inset: John Handley examines the expired Mini Clubman 1275 engine, 1970 World Cup Rally. (P. Easter)

1970

Main picture: *Severe weather conditions in Yugoslavia for John Handley/Paul Easter Mini Clubman 1275 recce car, 1970 World Cup Rally. (P. Easter)*

1971

Brian Culcheth/Johnstone Syer starting the 1973 Cyprus Rally in the Morris Marina 1.3 Coupé.

Below: Ron Elkins (BL Special Tuning) discusses progress with Brian Culcheth, Triumph Dolomite, on the 1972 TAP Rally. (G. Birtwistle)

1971–74

The Leyland ST stand at the 1974 Racing Car Show with the Marina fitted with the new aerodynamic aids.

Brian Culcheth/Johnstone Syer in the ex-World Cup Triumph 2.5 PI during the 1971 Scottish Rally. (Foster & Skeffington)

247

16,000 Miles to Mexico

7

16,000 Miles to Mexico
1970

WORLD CUP FEVER now hit the Department. With the Christmas holiday over, the next target was to carry out as much testing as possible and to build seven cars for the event starting at Wembley Stadium on Sunday 19 April 1970.

The secret plan to run three of the new Range Rovers had been dropped, mainly due to production delays at Solihull which prevented us from starting a test programme in time. The situation had not been helped by the Department's unfortunate introduction to the new vehicle which may have had some bearing on the decision. Peter had been invited to see one of the prototypes at Solihull and, at the suggestion of Ralph Nash (Rover ex-Competitions Manager), a small party was taken to the Girling test track at Honiley to try the vehicle. The Abingdon party were awarded their first black mark by parking the V8 in the same pub car park for a quick snack as some of the Rover Directors. At Honiley the grass was very high making it difficult to see round the track, and it was while Geoff Mabbs was driving the Range Rover prototype that disaster struck. The entourage, including Peter Wilks, was standing on a corner at the end of the straight when Geoff arrive at high speed. He locked his brakes in an attempt to get round, but only succeeded in going off the road, launching the vehicle into the air over a low bank. The headlamps flew out, the headlining dropped down and at least one door was damaged. The directors cringed at the spectacle which was not helped by Geoff coming over to the assembled throng and commenting that he had 'experienced a bit of bump steer!'

Second South American Recce

Two of the RAC cars (VBL 195H & VBL 196H) were prepared for a second recce in South America. The cars were shipped to Argentina where the local agent was scheduled to progress them through the formidable customs procedures.

Above left: Brian Culcheth, Cliff Humphries and Paddy Hopkirk in discussion during testing at Bagshot (Colin Taylor Productions)

Left: Brian Culcheth gives Peter Browning a ride in the Bagshot test car

Immediately after Christmas Paddy, Brian Culcheth, Andrew Cowan, Johnstone Syer and Brian Coyle travelled to Rio de Janeiro where they hired three VW Beetle cars from Hertz to do the section from Rio to Montevideo. Ulrico Ossio joined them for an eventful journey, which included having to ford a very deep river at one stage, but eventually they arrived in Montevideo. The cars were so 'tired' that they had to have extensive welding done to the bodies before handing them in.

Meanwhile, the Triumph recce cars were still impounded in customs in Buenos Aires and it was only after the intervention of one Juan Manuel Fangio that the cars were released.

The next eight weeks were spent carrying out a recce of the route to Lima, a distance of 5,000 miles. In Argentina, the 510 mile long Prime (special stage) took them 5 days to complete, with delays from punctures and other minor problems (Brian Culcheth completed this stage in 12 hours on the rally). This stage on the recce finally decided Paddy that he would go with a three-man crew, despite the weight penalty. The discussion concerning the number in each crew continued at Abingdon on their return, but Peter's attitude was that the crews were going to drive the cars, and they were all very keen to win, so why should he interfere. With hindsight, he felt that perhaps two of the Triumphs should have had a two man crew, and not just 'Culch'.

There were some flooded roads to negotiate and while driving through a particularly deep section, the car that Paddy was driving stopped. It had sucked in some water through the air intake hoses which were low down in the grille, the surge of water filling the inlet manifold, resulting in a bent con-rod from the hydraulicking effect. The car would still run so they were able to continue the recce. This problem was communicated to Abingdon with the result that the air intakes on the rally cars were moved from the front grille, and pipes run from the air cleaner to the front heater intake box in front of the windscreen. When the cars arrived in Lima, Brian Culcheth, Paddy and Brian Coyle returned home while Andrew and Johnstone continued through to Panama with the second car.

During this recce, we sent one of our mechanics with a Lucas technician out to the Andes to carry out some tests with the petrol injection metering unit to adjust the units on the high altitude sections. This resulted in specially calibrated units being prepared with a hand control on the fascia to allow the driver to compensate for altitude. The quadrant was marked off in 3000 ft increments and I arranged to borrow aircraft-type altimeters from Smiths Industries which were built into the rally car fascias.

It was becoming increasingly difficult to cope with any work other than the World Cup cars, and during the second week in January, Peter told Jeff Williamson and Brian Chatfield that although we could not undertake further prep-

16,000 Miles to Mexico

Eddie Burnell driving the Triumph 2.5 PI Mk2 test car at Bagshot during testing for the 1970 World Cup Rally

aration of cars for them to drive in the rallycross series, they were welcome to take the cars away and run them themselves. We would supply any parts they needed, and this would leave Tommy Wellman with just two cars to prepare for John Rhodes and John Handley.

To add some variety to the rallycross entries and to further develop the car, the Triumph 2.5 PI Mk1 ex-Scottish car (UJB 643G) was prepared for a rallycross test at Lydden Hill circuit.

I took the car to Lydden with Tommy Wellman and Tommy Eales where we met up with Rod Chapman, who was one of the front runners in recent events. To give us something to compare our car with, he brought along his own Ford Escort Twin Cam, quickly doing a few laps on the snow and ice which covered the circuit, to record a time of 1m 18.8s.

Despite losing the tailpipe and then having the fan belt reverse itself on the pulleys, Rod did thirteen laps in the Triumph before the fan belt came off completely and it was lunch time.

After lunch with a new fan belt and the mixture weakened, Rod reduced his lap time to 1m 7.8s on 195/70 × 13 Dunlop SP44 tyres. A misfire and serious vibration prevented further runs, but Rod did three more laps in his Escort to record 1m 11.2s. He was quite impressed with the car which compared favourably with his Escort, but felt that a lower final drive would be of benefit as he had only used third and top gear. When the car was stripped down at Abingdon we found that the flywheel bolts had sheared; this failure finally decided Cliff and Doug that the World Cup engines should have six bolts fixing flywheels.

Alan Zafer obtained an agreement with the BBC Grandstand programme whereby our Mini in the World Cup Rally would be the official Grandstand entry. This was announced at Lydden Hill on 8 February during the Grandstand rallycross programme where Rosemary Smith also appeared in an Austin Maxi.

Testing the Austin Maxi for the World Cup Rally at Bagshot

Above right: *Fashion show at Lydden Hill rallycross – Rosemary Smith and Alice Watson*

Right: *World Cup Mini Clubman presented on BBC TV at Lydden Hill. L-to-R: Paul Easter, Colin Taylor, Murray Walker, and John Handley*

1970

Rosemary Smith during rallycross at Lydden Hill

Austin Maxis For Mexico

The decision to run Austin Maxis in the World Cup had been taken following the non-availability becoming apparent of the Range Rovers. Rosemary Smith would now drive one car with an all-ladies crew while a second car would be crewed by two of the Red Arrows pilots who had driven an Austin 1800 in the London/Sydney Marathon.

Tommy Wellman took over supervision of the Maxi

16,000 Miles to Mexico

development programme with Cliff sorting out a twin carb engine specification for the car. This didn't leave much time to prepare a test car and carry out an extensive run at Bagshot.

Prototype safety tank in the Austin Maxi test car. Note the modified tailgate. 1970 World Cup Rally

At the end of January the rallycross Triumph 2.5 was ready for another test, this time at Finmere airfield, with a modified camshaft, new Janspeed exhaust manifold and straight-through tail pipe; the power at the wheels was measured at 150 bhp. Cliff drove the car and did about 18 laps, stopping twice to weaken the mixture, before overheating ended the session; once that had been sorted out it would be ready for the 8 February TV event at Lydden Hill.

Tyre selection for World Cup Mini Clubman had to be

Two of the Triumph 2.5PI Mk2 rally cars in early stage of preparation, 1970 World Cup Rally

Left: *Partly finished World Cup Rally Maxi*

Right: *Interior of World Cup Triumph showing wiring preparation*

decided and John Handley was keen to try the MP27 rally/cross tyre on a normal tarmac road. The recce car was fitted with a full 1293 cc rally engine, two Split Webers, Hydrolastic suspension with taps fitted to front/rear interconnecting pipes, rear anti-roll bar, a magnesium alloy Tech Del sump guard and glass-fibre doors. The idea of the taps was to stiffen the suspension on the stages.

On a wet windy night, I took a service car carrying a

1970

selection of tyres with Tommy Eales driving the recce car and we made a rendezvous with John Handley in mid-Wales. We decided on a section of road with several tight corners and a variety of surfaces to carry out timed tests. The 'test' route was about two minutes long and with little traffic about we carried out seven runs using the MP27 rallycross racers, SP68 road tyres, SP44 Weathermasters and R7 500L × 10 racers. The MP27 were over 4 seconds quicker than the R7 over this two minute course and John had no doubt that, tyre wear permitting, he would choose this tyre on the Quatre Chemins Prime (Special Stage); SP 68 would be used on the road sections.

Decompression Chamber

Paddy in particular had expressed interest in the effects of high altitude on people working under stress and with our Red Arrows connections a trip to the Institute of Aviation Medicine at Farnborough was arranged. We were given a lecture on the effects of lack of oxygen at high altitude and then were given the opportunity of sampling the decompression chamber. In the chamber we were given note pads on which to write a simple sentence, the pressure was then gradually dropped, while we continued to write the same sentence. At a simulated 24,000 ft, although we reckoned we were writing normally, the scrawl was unreadable; a very enlightening experience. This confirmed Paddy's fears and as a result it was decided that oxygen equipment would be carried in the cars in the Andes.

BL Entries

On 12 February at the Cafe Royal, Bobby Moore, Captain of the England football team, drew the car start numbers out of the hat. We were relieved to learn that our numbers were spread out with the lowest number, 43, being allocated to Andrew Cowan which would help servicing arrangements. This first entry list did not reflect the decision to be made later concerning the three-man crews but did indicate certain sponsorship deals. The full final BL entry consisted of the following:

43 BL/Football Association	A. Cowan/B. Coyle/ U. Ossio	Triumph 2.5PI Mk2
59 BBC Grandstand	J. Handley/P. Easter	Mini Clubman
74 Evening Standard	R. Smith/A. Watson/ G. Derolland	Austin Maxi
88 BL/Football Association	B. Culcheth/J. Syer	Triumph 2.5PI Mk2
92 BL/Motor	E. Green/J. Murray/ H. Cardno	Triumph 2.5PI Mk2
96 BL/Autocar	T. Kingsley/P. Evans/ M. Scarlett	Austin Maxi
98 BL/Football Association	P. Hopkirk/A. Nash	Triumph 2.5PI Mk2

Alan Zafer had been busy organising sponsorship from the Football Association and agreeing arrangements for Michael Scarlett from Autocar to become a crew member in the Red Arrows Maxi and Hamish Cardno of *Motor* to join Evan Green in his Triumph 2.5.

16,000 Miles to Mexico

Rod Chapman driving the Triumph 2.5 PI at Lydden Hill rallycross, February 1970

Rosemary Smith/Alice Watson winning the Ladies Prize in the Austin Maxi, 1970 Circuit of Ireland Rally

Boot compartment of Triumph 2.5 PI Mk2. Note the twin spare wheels, twin flexible safety tanks and high pressure fuel pumps. World Cup Rally 1970

Rosemary Smith's car was sponsored by the *Evening Standard* which resulted in the white car being painted in broad orange stripes much to Tommy Wellman's horror.

To give Rosemary the chance to get used to the Maxi we entered a car in the Circuit of Ireland with Alice Watson co-driving. The car went very well and the girls managed to win the Ladies Prize, but unfortunately Rosemary strained her arm and started the World Cup with her arm still heavily strapped.

There were also quite a number of visas to obtain for the Abingdon staff and rally crews and I seemed to be making never ending visits to Embassies in London. As the event crept closer, Peter was putting together his separate service plans for the European and South American sections. (The service schedule for the South American section of the rally amounted to 66 pages!) He decided that we would charter an aircraft to carry mechanics to the controls on the easier European sections, and this task was allotted to John Spouse of Southend Air Taxis with a Cessna Skymaster. To fit flying

Engine compartment of Triumph 2.5 PI Mk2 World Cup Rally car. Note the modified air intake pipes.

254

1970

hours in with our service schedule this meant that a second pilot would have to be carried, and John had the difficult task (particularly in the Eastern Bloc) of obtaining clearance to land the aircraft.

There was also the problem of getting the crews, mechanics, wheels/tyres and spares to South America although the entry fee of £600 per car (plus £175 for each additional crew member) included all air fares and sea crossings for car and crew. It was finally decided that we would charter an aircraft, and with the co-operation of British Caledonian Airways, a Bristol Brittania was booked for this task. I had the problem of arranging the documentation for the spares and working out a loading schedule. This was necessary so that the spares could be dropped off in sequence without unloading the aircraft each time, the aircraft being a passenger carrying machine with only small doors.

Behind the scenes, Cliff and his test section were well into the test programme by the end of February, the Triumph 2.5 test car (WRX 902H) having completed almost 3000 miles of tarmac running on the road, at Chobham and Silverstone. Most of the rough road mileage at Bagshot was carried out by 'Fast' Eddie Burnell (ex-MG test driver) with some help from Brian

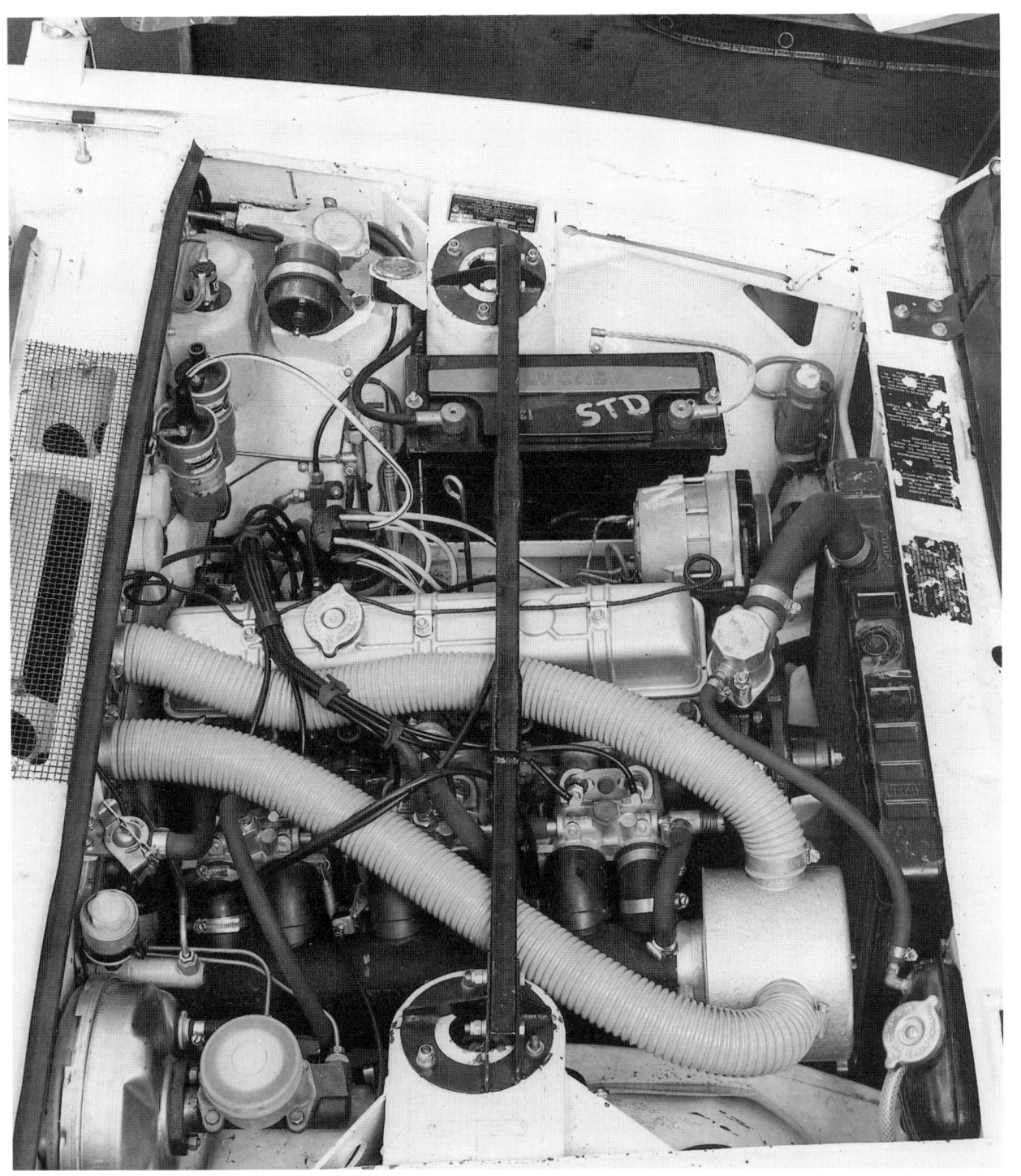

16,000 Miles to Mexico

Culcheth, Andrew Cowan and Paddy Hopkirk, covering a distance of over 700 miles at Bagshot alone. This was an incredible distance on such rough going, but certainly found the weakness in suspension, axle and shock-absorbers.

The eventual spec of the Triumph 2.5PI rally cars included the following modifications:

Bodies specially built by Pressed Steel Fisher incorporating an aluminum roll-over bar, flared wheel arches and vents in the front wings.
Aluminium panels for doors, bonnet and boot. Six special body jacking points.
Perspex side and rear windows.
Air intake in the roof to face level vents.
Co-driver's seat converting to full length bed with special seat cushion. Seats fitted with sheepskin covers.
Special Tudor hinged mud flaps front/rear.
Special cylinder block and crankshaft, TR6 camshaft, Janspeed exhaust manifold, 150 bhp.
Triumph Stag CR gears with overdrive and 3.7:1 final drive with Salisbury Powr-Lok differential.
Koni special shock-absorbers front/rear.
Special stub axles with Stag front disc and rear drum brakes.
Minilite 15 x 5½ inch wheels. Dunlop Special SP Sport tyres.
Fuel tank capacity 32 gallons. Standard 14 gallon tank with 10 gallon LH and 8 gallon RH Marston safety tanks.
Twin HP Lucas pumps and twin Bendix transfer pumps.
Alternating Maserati air horns.
Halda Twin Master, cassette recorder and altimeter in fascia.
Twin spare wheels in centre of boot compartment (lid modified to suit).

The twin side tanks were fitted to give the cars a longer range for the South American Primes. This was a complication with the fuel injection system, but was overcome by using a Bendix lift pump to transfer fuel from the side to the main tank operated by a fascia mounted switch.

The Austin Maxi testing had not been without its problems, the simulated all-up rally weight causing the rear tailgate to continually fly open with the twist of the bodyshell. This was cured by welding the tailgate to the body, leaving a small hinged 'boot' lid at the bottom. The body, at the point where the front wings joined, was also splitting requiring some strengthening plates and, under the floor, the lower front wishbone mounting had to be double skinned.

Rest halt during recce of the route in South America with the ex-RAC Rally Triumph 2.5 PI Mk1 cars, 1970 World Cup Rally

Tommy had been very impressed with the initial testing, as the car had completed about 35 laps without succumbing on its first run. Prince Michael of Kent and his co-driver Gavin Thompson, came down to Bagshot during the testing and drove the test car; they were also driving a Maxi in the World Cup to the same spec, loaned by Abingdon, but prepared by Janspeed Engineering.

Shock-absorbers were added to assist the Hydrolastic

Austin Maxi engine compartment, World Cup Rally 1970

1970

Seven-car team for the 1970 World Cup Rally. L-to-R: B. Culcheth, J. Syer, A. Nash, P. Hopkirk, N. Johnston, Rosemary Smith, Alice Watson, J. Handley, P. Easter, P. Browning (with BL mascot), B. Coyle, U. Ossio, A. Cowan, M. Scarlett, P. Evans, T. Kingsley, J. Murray, H. Cardno, E. Green

16,000 Miles to Mexico

suspension, requiring small turrets at the front with blisters in the bonnet. To compensate for altitude, the Maxis were fitted with a special compensating device on the float chambers of the twin SU carburettors (supplied by SU) also adjustable from the fascia.

Group photographs were taken on the MG sports ground at Abingdon and the final testing of the cars, sorting out the spares and making last minute adjustments, made the last few days at Abingdon a little chaotic.

Just to illustrate the sort of problem that can occur, I will mention the fuel pumps. When the first Triumph 2.5 was ready to take on the road, one of the mechanics went to Oxford with the car he was building. Right in the middle of Carfax the engine stopped and would not restart. There was a strong smell of petrol and the boot was full of petrol. On investigation, it was discovered that all the specially assembled high pressure fuel pumps had had the seals installed incorrectly, so they had to be removed, returned and rebuilt; just another hiccup!

Special Tuning Department had prepared a number of 1800's for the rally and were generally keeping all the private owners driving BL cars informed with bulletins, recommended spares lists, technical help with their car preparation etc. etc.

On Friday 3 April a 'sit-in' was arranged at Abingdon to which all the BL private owners were invited for a talk and slide show by Brian Culcheth and Tony Nash on their South American recce. There was a general discussion on all matters relating to the event, while Dunlop and Lucas representatives were available to discusss tyre and electrical problems. Road books were to be made available to private owners but for security reasons would not be available until Wembley and Rio de Janiero. This meeting was well attended and gave the crews an insight into the conditions to be expected in South America.

I was not expecting to go out on the European leg as I would be sorting out the final details of the spares, etc for South America and supervising the loading of the Britannia at Gatwick. However, at the last minute, Den Green was stricken with a severe chest infection and Peter asked me to step into his place on the Cessna. I must say that flying is not my favourite means of travel and I was not looking forward to the trip.

Austin-Morris 1800 cars prepared for the World Cup Rally by the British Leyland Special Tuning Department. L-to-R: Royal Navy, R. Redgrave, Metropolitan Police, Peter Jopp and Woman Magazine

1970

Only 16,244 Miles to Go

Scrutineering and documentation was held on Saturday 18 April at Wembley Stadium where the engines, gearboxes and axles were marked by the scrutineers, after which the cars were held in *parc fermé* with a security guard mounted throughout the night. The Mini had been showing a tendency to oil up plugs but this was put down to insufficient running-in mileage.

Bobby Moore wishes Rosemary Smith luck watched by Lord Stokes, Alice Watson and Bobby Moore's children at the Wembley Stadium start of the 1970 World Cup Rally

On Sunday morning the final briefing was held by the organisers at 0845 hr. At 1000 hr from a ramp in the stadium under a cloudless sky, Sir Alf Ramsey, Englands Football team manager with Lord Stokes (our boss) beside him, waved off the first car. The remainder followed at one minute intervals until the total entry of 96 cars had departed before a crowd of about 25,000 people. At the end of the Olympic Way the RAC had erected a sign saying 'Only 16,244 to go. Bon Voyage'.

I was at Wembley to see the start with our service crews, witnessing Jack Murray dropping a large thunderflash out of the rear window of his car on the ramp. After lunch, an MG factory Minibus took Robin Vokins, Ron Elkins and myself out to Elstree Airfield where we were collected by the Cessna and flown to Southend airport to clear Customs. John Spouse and Alan his co-pilot were waiting and at about 15.25 hr we left for Munich, arriving at 2000 hr, the view of the runway lights being very spectacular.

After a night in a hotel we were off to the rally control at 06.00 hr where we found Donald Morley was the controller. The rally cars had meanwhile crossed the Channel and

259

16,000 Miles to Mexico

Paddy Hopkirk's Triumph 2.5 PI starts the World Cup Rally, Wembley Stadium April 1970

motored through the night. Our seven cars and crews were in good shape except Rosemary Smith who complained that her Maxi was tending to jump out of fifth gear. The gear cables were adjusted without much hope of an improvement, although in South America it was unlikely that fifth gear would be used much anyway!

My crew then returned to the Airport where we took off at 12.00 hr, one hour behind schedule in driving rain. Our cruising altitude was set at 9000 ft and in low cloud we were flying blind, fully on instruments. When ice formed on the wings, we were relieved when John demonstrated the de-icing device.

At Vienna, our next stop, we were met by the local dealer in an Austin 1800 who drove us at an alarming rate to the control. The rally cars went through with no problems and we were then off to Budapest at 17.20 hr, to test the flight schedule arrangements behind the 'Curtain'.

At Budapest we hired a Moskvitch taxi and, leaving the pilots to refuel and file the next flight plan, we had a fast ride through the city to the control. This was slight anti-climax as there were no problems, and the crews semed rather surprised to see us. Back to the airport and then off to Sofia, Bulgaria.

It was a fine night and we had a good view of the mountains in the moonlight, arriving at 01.00 hr to find the runway marked only by a double line of paraffin flares. We were met at the end of the runway by the security police but with Johnny Evans waiting with a Minibus at the passenger building we eventually got to the Balkan Hotel and bed at 03.00 hr.

The first cars were due at 06.00 hr so we had only two hours sleep before we were up again to meet the crews. They were in good spirits with only minor adjustments and checking to do although the Mini was suffering from a misfire and did not sound too healthy. One of the rear mudflaps on Andrew Cowans car was ripped off on a kerb ouside the hotel which had to be replaced to comply with the regulations. The rally proper was soon to start just up the road with the first Prime in Yugoslavia from Pec to Titograd on one of the old Liège-Rome-Liège sections.

We left our rooms to some of the private owners to use for a 'wash and brush up' leaving Sofia airport at 13.00 hr for Titograd. As we were climbing away to our cruising altitude a MIG jet fighter passed fairly close beneath us. The snow-capped mountains seemed close enough to touch as we flew to Titograd, where the flight controller gave us a lift to the hotel after Customs clearance. The control was near the Hotel and our 'ground' service crew was already seeing to the first arrivals, the biggest job being the private Maxi of Tish Ozanne which required a new driveshaft.

The first Prime was changed to run from Titograd to Kotor owing to the route being blocked by late winter snow. The three Triumphs of Paddy, Andrew and Brian were among the six cars without penalty on this Prime, but the Mini of John Handley was misfiring badly from a fuel feed problem and lost two minutes. The car had been fitted with a foam-filled safety tank in the spare wheel space shortly before the start to supplement the twin steel tanks and there was restriction in the feed pipe to the carburettors. Evans Green's car was also misfiring and oiling up a plug, losing some time to the other team cars.

The cars continued north to the second Prime starting in Glamoc and ending at Bosanska Krupa, 100 miles in 2 hr 50 m. A number of cars, including Paddy's, were delayed on this section by stranded lorries and a wrecked bridge. By now twelve cars had retired from the rally but the remainder headed for Monza and their first night in a bed.

There was a major service point at Monza where shock-absorbers, brake pads, tyres, etc were changed, but the Mini with a plug constantly oiling-up was diagnosed as having piston damage. The Evan Green Triumph suffered quill shaft bearing failure approaching Monza but the mechanics changed it and fitted new injectors to cure the misfire.

Urgent work at Monza on the Mini Clubman of John Handley/Paul Easter, 1970 World Cup Rally

The Cessna completed its first schedule by carrying us from Titograd to Milan where we said goodbye to the pilots and went to Monza to help out with the servicing. There was some confusion with hotel rooms being overbooked but this was sorted out by Peter and we eventually got to bed.

In the morning, an emergency service point was set up to finish one or two small jobs on Evan Green's car, and I then took a flight to Lisbon by DC9 via Madrid.

1970

Brian Culcheth/Johnstone Syer on the San Remo Prime (stage) of the 1970 World Cup Rally

Evan Green's Accident

The rally cars next Prime was San Remo, but here Evan Green's car went on to five cylinders and one front strut collapsed. This was changed and a broken valve guide in the cylinder head was discovered which would require a head change. Hamish Cardno of *Motor* magazine tried to contact the nearest Triumph dealer to arrange a new cylinder head but could not get through.

Just before the next Prime, the LH front wheel came off and the car shot of the stage into the trees stopping dead against a rather large one, 15 ft below the road. The crew was

The Red Arrows crew with their Austin Maxi during the European section, 1970 World Cup Rally

16,000 Miles to Mexico

OK but the car was badly damaged although the radiator was still intact. A marshall located a tow truck and about 2½ hours after crashing they were back on the road. Some French mechanics helped blank off the LH brake pipe, and with only three studs holding the wheel on they set off.

Our mechanics at the next service point were got out of bed and did a marvellous job squaring up the front of the car and realigning the steering. The offending injector was removed and the petrol was vented from it out of the side of the car. They struggled on into Spain feeling very unwell from the exhaust and petrol fumes, having decided to miss two passage controls to keep in the rally.

In Pamplona the combination of petrol fumes and shock made the crew very unwell and when they stopped for Jack Murray to go to the toilet he passed out in the street. They were guided to a Red Cross clinic where they were advised to go to the hospital. An ambulance with lights flashing led them to the hospital where Jack was given an injection and some pills, whereupon he was bundled into the back and off they set again.

By the time the car reached Arganil, the start of the Prime in Portugal, Jack had improved and had done some driving.

I arrived in Lisbon with Robin and Ron and then set off with two service cars for the service point at Arganil, the start of the last European Prime. We were very short of spares as the transporter had been held up by the Customs at the Spanish border and had not arrived. Neville Challis was driving the transporter and he had to phone Norman Higgins, MG Accountant, to ask him to transfer a bank guarantee to Spain to enable the transporter to continue.

We had the use of a small BL garage near the control and for a time there was hectic activity. We were now aware of the problems encountered by Evan Green and intended to wait for his car until it was out of time.

We were at Arganil for over twelve hours, being very glad to see Evan Geen arrive at about 10.00 hr on 25 April. We were able to straighten the front suspension to make the car more driveable and replace the front tyres which were bald. We returned to Lisbon over the now open Prime in case Evan had further trouble, being rather surprised to see below us on the main road near the Lisbon the Rolls-Royce of Bill Bengry on tow behind a Morris J4 van.

Neville Challis had thankfully arrived with the transporter so the service point set up in the workshop of J.J. Goncalves the BL Dealer in Lisbon was fully equipped with spares. The three other Triumphs had already arrived along with the two Maxis, all five had a major service with shock-absorbers, tyres, brakes, etc, being changed in preparation for South America.

Unfortunately the Mini had finally succumbed with a blown piston on the San Remo Prime, so we were now down to six cars.

The Evan Green car arrived in Lisbon last and was attackd by the waiting gang of mechanics, one lot changing

Service for the Triumph 2.5 PI of Brian Culcheth/Johnstone Syer at Lisbon, 1970 World Cup Rally

1970

the cylinder head, others on the suspension while the rest tried to straighten out the front of the body.

The overall positions of our cars at Lisbon were:

6th overall, Brian Culcheth
8th overall, Paddy Hopkirk
11th overall, Andrew Cowan
24th overall, Rosemary Smith
29th overall, Terry Kinsgley
69th overall, Evan Green

The following day most of the BL service team, including Peter and myself, visited a Portuguese bull fight in Lisbon and in the evening dressed up to attemd a cocktail party/buffet held by the rally organisers.

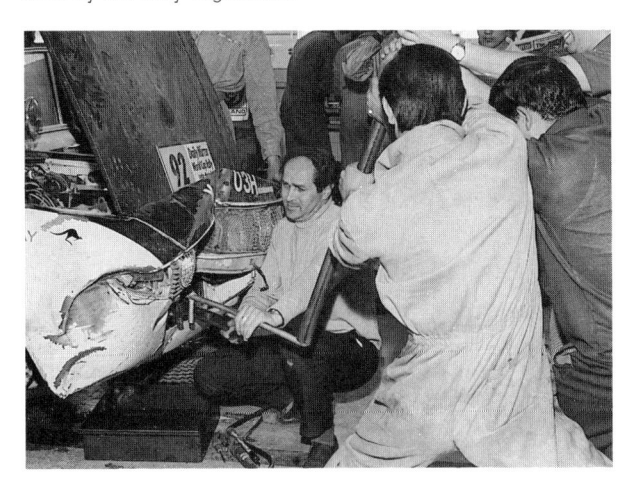

Peter Evans prepares the Red Arrows Austin Maxi for shipment to Rio de Janiero under the shadow of the Tagus bridge, Lisbon, 1970 World Cup Rally

Hectic work to straighten out Evan Green's Triumph 2.5 PI at Lisbon, 1970 World Cup Rally

Back in England, Les Needham supervised the loading of the Britannia and the next morning, the whole BL party were out at Lisbon airport to meet the British Caledonian 'Whispering Giant' for the trip to Rio. Den Green was on board, having recovered from his illness.

South American Section

The flight to Rio de Janiero was uneventful, if slow, calling at Dakar in Senegal and Recife in Brazil for refuelling, arriving at Rio at 02.00 hr on Tuesday 28 April. The interior of the aircraft was an amazing sight with the main bulk of the fuselage stripped of seats and piled with spares and wheels/tyres all held down by large nylon nets. (We took 370 tyres to South America in the Britannia).

Thirty five seats remained at the rear for the rally crews, the BL and Rootes service team, and Dunlop personnel, being fed and watered by two charming B/CAL hostesses. The plan was to drop off the spares and mechanics at Rio and then continue round the route dropping off the spares consignments at Montevideo, Buenos Aires, Santiago and Lima.

After meeting the local agents and ensuring that everything was going to schedule, I returned to the airport with Peter, Alan Zafer and Jeremy Ferguson (Dunlop Rally Manager) for the next stage.

We landed at Montevideo at 01.00 hr next morning, the

'Gelignite' Jack Murray

heavy landing 'disturbing' the rear situated toilets leaving the aircraft with a rather unpleasant smell for the remaining flights. The hostesses made a few disparaging remarks about the Yugoslavian-born pilot after that incident. We had very good assistance from the local agents at each port of call and became acquainted with some more unorthodox entrances at some of the airports.

On the flight from Buenos Aires to Santiago we had to divert to Mendoza until fog cleared at Santiago, but the view over the Andes was clear and spectacular. The coding of the spares had not been executed correctly, so that at Santiago I had to dismantle crates containing windscreens in order to be able to get them off the aircraft.

At Lima we were surprised to see two RAF Vulcan

16,000 Miles to Mexico

bombers parked on the airfield, as we were met by Jerry Stead and Joe Allison of BL Peru. We visited the assembly plant and also met the pilot who would be flying the Peruvian chartered Cessna during the rally.

The Britannia returned to England from Lima and we returned to Rio by scheduled jet flights via La Paz, Asuncion, Buenos Aires and Sao Paulo meeting the local agents and finalising service arrangements on the way.

Rio Restart

On Wednesday 6 May I made arrangements to fly all crew excess baggage from Rio direct to Mexico by Varig Airlines, while Peter and Doug Watts and the crews were finalising route and servicing arrangements. In the evening we dressed in our suits to attend a reception at the British Embassy hosted by Sir David and Lady Hunt for all the British teams.

Next morning I finalised baggage arrangements and in the afternoon, we held a meeting for all BL private owners followed by a reception at the French Embassy for the rally teams.

On Friday 8 May, the morning of the restart, there was a BL final service meeting/briefing for the team at Hotel Gloria, where we heard a rumour that our chartered Cessna was lost over the jungles of Paraguay. I later took all the team baggage for Mexico to the Varig offices in the city.

At about 18.30 hr when I returned to the Gloria, there was a hive of activity in reception with crews trying to pay their bills. As I approached the lift, Andrew came rushing out looking very relieved to see me. 'Have you got my luggage for Mexico?' were his first words, 'I have left my passport in my suitcase!'

After a quick explanation to Peter who had arrived on the scene, I rushed out to find a taxi and sped to the Varig offices, hoping they were still open, only to find them closed. I asked some local lads who were playing cards in an alley if they knew where the manager lived and they took me to a phone and called the airport where I spoke to the manager's brother who also worked for Varig. I went to the airport by taxi and then was taken on a half-hour drive to the manager's apartment.

He was not at home, eventually turning up 23.00 hr. He then took me back to Varig offices in an open Chevrolet Impala, transferring to a taxi when the Impala burst a tyre. Once inside, I opened up Andrew's case, found his passport, returning to the hotel at 02.00 hr next morning, the rally having already restarted.

A service point had been set up soon after the restart where the major job was the fitting of a new overdrive to Andrew Cowan's car with the help of Ernie Garbett from Laycock. Peter had to reassure Andrew that his passport would be taken to the Brazil/Uruguay border to enable him to continue on the rally (fingers crossed). The Cessna had failed to appear so Peter had to spend some time rearranging flight schedules for the mechanics/personnel due to fly in it on the first leg.

With the cars now on the move again, the mechanics started their long schedule of flights round South America. My priority this first day was to reunite Andrew with his passport, and immediately we arrived by Boeing 707 at Montevideo, we located the office of an air taxi firm in the airport who was prepared to fly to the border.

Anthony Shaw, from our agent Frank Surgey, was asked to go with me to the border in a Piper Apache. We arrive at 17.00 hr on a bumpy grass airstrip at the border town with Andrew Cowans' passport plus four shock-absorbers and two front struts, just in case. We has a very good steak at a barbeque restaurant cooked on a charcoal grill and were at the control by 22.00 hr.

The first rally car arrived at 04.15 hr the next morning and as soon as Andrew arrived, one could sense his relief when he saw his passport again. I fitted the front struts to his car as he was complaining his were fading, and then after seeing the others through, left again for Montevideo. The pilot followed the rally route and we passed over another of our service points where Dudly Pike was on duty. We also spotted the Red Arrows Maxi and circled round them as they thrashed along, giving them a wave of encouragment, quite exciting at 150 ft!

The section through Brazil had been one of the toughest but our cars had all survived without major problems. Brian Culcheth had collected two punctures on the Uruguay Prime, averaging 104 mph to the next control. As far as the tyres were concerned, Brian only used the Dunlop Weathermaster tyre on the Yuogoslav Prime with the specially constructed SP Sport for the remainder of the route, incurring only eight punctures to Mexico. Of the 71 who had left Rio only 52 survived the route to Montevideo which had included the Parana, Rio Grande and Uraguay Primes. Brian Culcheth was the fastest of our cars on the first two with Andrew and Brian being first and second fastest overall on the third. When the times were published at Montevideo, Brian had moved up to fourth overall, Paddy seventh, Andrew tenth, Rosemary Smith seventeenth and the Red Arrows 36th. Evan Green was second from last with the serious misfire slowing his progress, undoubtedly cause by the earlier valve guide problem. The crews had a night in bed at Montevideo with the cars in *parc fermé*.

Beechcraft to Saladillo

On Monday morning, Peter, myself and our service team flew from Montevideo to Buenos Aires. From the BA City Airport we took a chartered Beechcraft to Saladillo, a one-hour flight, to set up a service point at the Shell Station near the control, which was also the start of the Pampas Prime.

During the flight, our pilot picked up a radio conversation between another pilot and the airport we had just left, and it turned out to be the long lost Cessna which had just arrived from Lima.

There was insufficient room in the Shell Station for all the teams and one or two ugly situations arose, particularly with the Russian mechanics, as rally cars jockeyed for position; it was chaos! The Red Arrows Maxi required a battery having been involved in a collision with a Ford Popular driven by an old lady which had ended on its roof. A new driveshaft had already been fitted at a previous service point.

When all the work was finished, we went across to the restaurant on the cross-roads for a magnificent Argentinian

1970

steak. We returned to BA in two Valiant cars supplied by our agents, arriving at the City Hotel at 05.30 hr.

At 13.30 hr we were on the Varig Boeing 707 flight to Santiago, where we were met by Eric Blake of BL Chile in a Minibus. Doug, Den and two of the mechanics soon arrived after being delayed by flight troubles and we all went to the service point at Buin. The first rally car arrived at 23.00 hr and we remained at the garage until 09.00 hr waiting for BL stragglers to come through. Our crews took on their oxygen bottles and masks here, as the next hours were to be driven at altitudes up to 15,000 ft.

Local residents investigate the Australian 1800 recce car in Peru, 1970 World Cup Rally

On the Chilean Prime the Ford Escorts made the pace, taking the four fastest times, but Paddy and Brian were next, only eight minutes adrift. The Evan Green car had finally expired after the Pampas Prime when the tired piston ventilated the crankcase; it was a valiant effort to get so far. We had a sleep in the afternoon until 19.00 hr then at 02.00 hr the next morning, six of us left Santiago in two taxies for Los Andes, our taxi driver being armed with a 'cowboy' type ivory-handled revolver under his seat.

BL Chile had arranged a deserted garage to work in and we were there from 11.00–14.00 hr with no major problems on our cars. Before leaving, the BL Chile mechanic took us to the local bar owned by a friend where we were given small glasses of local drink called Chicha. This innocuous looking brew had us reeling after about three small glasses and we slept very soundly on the return trip to Santiago!

The rally route now moved back across the border into Argentina for the 900 km Gran Premio Prime to be covered in eight hours, with Brian and Paddy managing fourth and fifth fastest times.

Andrew Cowan Accident

The biggest blow to our team was when Andrew Cowan went off the road near Salta just before the end of the Prime, when following in the dust of the Austin 1800 (Beauty Box) driven by Jean Denton. They had been preparing to overtake and in the dust and the rising sun mistook the direction that the road was

Evening Standard Austin Maxi in the Andes Mountains, 1970 World Cup Rally

265

16,000 Miles to Mexico

bending. The car landed on its roof about 20 ft below the road completely wrecking it. The crew miraculously survived, though incurring head injuries and a cracked vertebra in the neck sustained by Andrew Cowan. The first car along was the Australian, Ken Tubman who left his crew tending the bloodstained victims while he rushed into La Vina for a doctor and ambulance; before many hours had elapsed they were safely in hospital.

The main service party now flew from Santiago to Lima where we were entertained by Jerry Stead and Joe Allison of BL Lima and visited the assembly plant where we would be servicing. Peter managed to get through to Argentina for the latest word on the Cowan crew and we were all relieved to hear that were now in good hands and making satisfactory progress.

We then left Lima for La Paz (Bolivia) on a Boeing 707, arriving at 01.00 hr. The agent had done a wonderful job shipping the spares from Lima by road and had a covered service point for us near the airport complete with crude wooden ramp, all at 13,000 ft.

Within about half an hour another rally car arrived with a hand-written note from Paddy requesting a new quill shaft. This time we sent Den off with another local mechanic in a Land Rover with the correct parts. Just down the road he came across Bill Bengry with his Rolls-Royce which had earlier retired. His offer to drive Den with the quill shaft back to find Paddy was readily accepted as Den knew which car would be quickest. When they arrived, Paddy and his crew had removed the broken part and in no time Den had them on their way.

Back at the service point, one or two of the mechanics took advantage of some oxygen after some hectic suspension changes, but the worst problem was the windscreen on Brian's Triumph which had been shattered by a rock. After checking that we had a screen, the mechanics took out the old one, only to find that the new screen was too small. Although it had the correct part number it was in fact a Triumph 1300

The Triumph 2.5 PI driven by Brian Culcheth/Johnstone Syer to second overall in the 1970 World Cup Rally, in South America

The Bolivian army had set up a medical centre with doctors, nurses and oxygen equipment, and Bolivian TV also turned up with an outside broadcast unit. The number of spectating Bolivian Indians was absolutely amazing: the crowd was about six deep on both sides of the road as far as one could see, being kept in check by hundreds of troops and police. There was a long wait for the first rally car to arrive. We received word from a local radio station that Paddy Hopkirk had stopped with a broken differential some miles away from us. After a quick consultaton, we despatched a new differential in a Land Rover with one of the local mechanics down the rally route.

screen. Panic! The old screen was now in a thousand pieces. In a very sporting gesture, Stuart Turner of Ford loaned us an Escort screen. It was not the right shape but with the help of the faithful 'tank' tape, he soon had clear glass to see through, going right through to Mexico with this screen!

Paddy arrived with about ten minutes to spare before being penalised and we had a quick check round his car. The mechanics had finished at the service point by 15.00 hr and, as La Paz was a night halt for the tired rally competitiors, we looked forward to some sleep. In the evening we were invited to a reception at the British Embassy.

Thirty-nine cars reached La Paz and next day they set

1970

off on the Incas Prime, 500 miles in 11 hours, passing the famous Lake Titicaca soon after leaving the restart. Those of us servicing at La Paz left by air for Lima arriving at 10.00 hr, having a quiet day for a change with a session at the local bowling alley with Peter Crisp, a visiting BL overseas rep.

The next Cessna flight was from La Paz to Cuzco and on this one the aircraft ran into a spot of technical trouble. First they had to land to change the plugs on the front engine to cure a misfire, then Brian Moylan, who was in the front seat, noticed the oil pressure on the front engine dropping. The pilot found a small grass strip where a check showed that the oil filter bowl was leaking. This meant another delay in the schedule which had already been reduced from 30 to 24 flights.

Next day, Monday 18 May, we finalised our service arrangements at the BL Assembly Plant, and after lunch at a chicken restaurant, were in position to see the first car arrive at 21.00 hr.

We worked through the night as the cars, including several private owners, came in in dribs and drabs which meant that we did not finish until 07.00 hr. The competitors had a nights rest in Lima and although we managed a few hours sleep, we had to set up a service point to see the cars away in the late afternoon, finishing at 21.30 hr.

Thirty-two cars left Lima with the overall lead held by Hannu Mikkola in an Escort with Brian Culcheth third, although 1 hour 13 minutes behind. The run to Buenventura included the Coffee Prime in Ecuador where Paddy set one of his fastest times, but it was soon afterwards that a momentary lack of concentration caused him to crash off the road. The bodywork was badly bent but mechanically the main problem was a broken oil cooler, Neville Johnston by-passed this so that they could continue.

The next halt was Cali in Columbia which I reached by means of a 707 to Bogota and then a Lockheed Electra. The service point was manned for the arrival of the cars at midnight and apart from the usual changing of tyres, shock-absorbers, etc our main shock was the state of Paddy's car. The mechanics worked tirelessly to make the car shipshape, leaving a few jobs to finish in the morning.

We were at the Texaco service station to see the cars away, refitting tyres by hand as we waited for Paddy to arrive from *parc fermé*. Neville Johnston was feeling better, having thumped his head in the accident; we soon had Paddy on his way. The good news was that Brian Culcheth was in second place behind the Escort of Mikkola with only two Primes, but many miles still to go. It was a fairly short run from Cali to Buenventura where the surviving cars were loaded on board the Italian liner *Verdi* for the voyage to Cristobal at the other end of the Panama Canal. (This was necessary as the Pan American Highway did not yet connect Central and South America).

By 11.00 hr I was out at Cali airport with Den and Martin Reade to take our Cessna to Panama City. We met Gonzales the pilot and as we loaded our gear, we asked him what was in the orange waterproof bag. 'That is our jungle survival bag!' was the answer. The dashboard seemed to vibrate rather a lot as we took off and slowly climbed to 10,000 ft to clear the mountains, now being able to see clearly the jungle below! We had a very bad one wheel landing in a storm-force cross-

Remote service point for Doug Watts with the Maxi driven by the girls, 1970 World Cup Rally

16,000 Miles to Mexico

wind at Panama City airport just before a tropical rainstorm arrived.

We stayed at the El Panama hotel with its wonderful Wurlitzer organ, and met the BL dealer, Veco, to finalise service arrangements. Next day was a spare day for us as the rally cars were on a 30 hour boat trip, so next morning we borrowed a Ford Falcon from Castrol to drive over to Cristobal to see the rally cars unloaded. Another tropical storm arrived as we drove into Cristobal, and before long the streets were flooded to such a depth that the kids were swimming in the flood water.

We were at the Veco garage at 19.30 hr and slept on the concrete floor waiting for the rally to arrive, eventually getting to bed at 02.00 hr after a tiring service stop with our four remaining cars still reasonably fit.

I then flew to Mexcico on a TACA flight leaving the others to go on to another service point, arriving at 12.55 hr.

The route now ran north through San Jose up the Inter-American highway to Honduras, Guatemala and Mexico with the Costa Rica Coffee Prime next on the agenda. Paddy, determined to make a real effort on this Prime, beat Mikkola by six minutes, with Brian third fastest.

In Mexico City I had to book a flight to Oaxaca, having been too far behind schedule to arrive in time to join Eddie Burnell with the truck. Next morning, Tuesday 26 May, I caught the 07.15 hr flight to Oaxaca getting a lift with Prince Michael and Gavin Thompson from the airport to the Victoria Hotel, where I met up with Eddie.

The cars arrived from 09.00 hr where things were a little hectic for a while, with only the two of us at this service point. There was now only one relatively short Prime left to do and unless the leading Ford broke down, the result seemed certain. Paddy and Brian really charged through this 100 mile stage, which the local bus did in 11 hours, but could make no impression on the leaders. The rally proper finish at Fortin de las Flores where the whole population seemed to have turned out, to give the crews a tremendous reception.

The run to Mexico took three hours, with two or three tolls to negotiate, before the cars arrived at the Aztec Stadium. I had returned by road from Oaxaca with Eddie in an Opel car, having to refit one of the rocker arms halfway, arriving at the Camino Real hotel at 01.00 hr.

The other mechanics were now converging on the hotel from their last service points and transport was arranged to get them to the Aztec Stadium to see the finish at 16.00 hr. Just before the rally cars arrived, a tremendous thunderstorm broke over the city with much lightning and it was with some relief that the sun came out just as the convoy arrived. There was a good crowd and much camera activity as garlands were offered to the winners and to our ladies crew who had won the Ladies Prize in the Maxi. Twenty three cars finished and our final overall positions were:

2nd B. Culcheth/J. Syer Triumph 2.5PI (£3000)
4th P. Hopkirk/T. Nash/N. Johnston Triumph 2.5PI (£1500)
10th R. Smith/A. Watson/G. Derolland Austin Maxi (£1000)
22nd T. Kingsley/P. Evans/M. Scarlett Austin Maxi

Brian Culcheth and Rosemary Smith also won their respective classes.

So the greatest rally of all time was over, and the tired crews and service teams were able to relax for the first time for several weeks. The mechanics volunteered to drive the rally cars to the local dealer, where next day we prepared them for shipment. In the evening the prize-giving banquet was held to the accompaniment of a Mexican band; the steak was very rare but the music quite good. Next day the team were invited to a party at the residence of the British Military Attaché.

On Saturday we were off to the airport to fly home on the Britannia, but owing to an accident with a bird which broke the windscreen, we had to fly first to Montreal on a Braniff DC8. After a long wait we boarded the 'Whispering Giant' for the long flight to Gatwick, enlivened at breakfast time by Doug Watts pouring brandy on his cornflakes when the milk ran out. At Gatwick, a coach took us into London for a reception attended by Lord Stokes at the Lancaster Hotel.

It was a disappointment not to win, but the world-wide publicity gained for BL products had been enormous. The cost of the event to Abingdon was never really established, as Norman Higgins did no totalling of the various costs, and in the end no one asked. The result was not quite good enough for Lord Stokes, as future events were soon to prove.

As a matter of interest, I kept a record of my own flights during the rally, which were typical of the schedule covered by many of the team personnel, which read like this:

44 separate flights in 11 different aircraft
Cessna Skymaster
Beechcraft Bonanza
Piper Apache
Bristol Britannia
Lockheed Electra
DC8
DC9
BAC 111
Boeing 727
Boeing 707
Caravelle

Scottish Rally

Before we left on the World Cup Rally, Peter had made plans to enter two cars in the Scottish Rally; a Triumph for Brian Culcheth and a Mini for Paddy. Cliff had supervised the rebuilding of the World Cup test car with triple Weber carburettors instead of the normal fuel injection. This was kept quiet as it was not exactly good publicity for the factory team to run a PI car on carburettors. The World Cup Mini had had its central tank taken out and a new engine prepared after the recent failure in Italy.

The other project which had been progressing while we had been away was the preparation of a second Rover V8 by Bill Shaw. Using the experience gained with the first car which had now had several Club races driven by Roy Pierpoint, this second car was destined for the 86 hour Marathon at Nürburgring in August. Bill Shaw was carrying out the work at his North London premises using a Repco 4.3-litre engine.

The return to Abingdon had been a bit of an anti-climax after the hectic schedule of the World Cup and there was time

1970

B. Culcheth/J. Syer driving the Triumph 2.5 PI fitted with triple Weber carburettors, 1970 Scottish Rally

Paddy and Tony in the ex-World Cup Mini Clubman on the 1970 Scottish Rally

16,000 Miles to Mexico

to clear up the workshop and generally sort out all those unfinished administration tasks.

The Scottish in June saw an epic struggle between Brian and Paddy, in a Triumph and Mini respectively, the Triumph 2.5 engine giving 153 bhp against the Mexico engine's 127 bhp. As on the 1969 Circuit, Paddy started off on 12 inch wheels but only got into his stride after changing to 10 inch again, although this was not enough to beat Brian who was outright winner with Paddy second. This was the last rally that Paddy was to do for the Abingdon team after a long and successful association.

Peter Resigns

July saw the end of Peter's struggle to get the hierarchy at Longbridge to agree to a planned long-term programme. In protest Peter offered his resignation to the board, although he agreed to stay on until his successor had been appointed (if not announced).

Rover V8 prepared by Bill Shaw Racing for the Marathon de la Route 1970 at Nürburgring

Preparations for the Marathon at Nürburgring were proceeding and to enable the wiring to be finished off by Lucas Racing Division, Bill Shaw brought the Rover V8 to Abingdon. There were a few jobs to be done mechanically which enabled the mechanics who were going on the trip to familiarise themselves with the car. To give it a test run, we took the car to Goodwood race cicuit where Roy Pierpoint did a total of only 20 laps, the main problem to emerge being a bad propshaft vibration. A phone call to Doug Watts before we returned to Abingdon, was made, requesting a new propshaft, which was ordered from Hardy Spicer.

Engine compartment of the Rover V8 for the Marathon de la Route 1970

The Axe Falls

A few days before team was due to go off to Germany, Peter attended a meeting a Longbridge with George Turnbull to discuss, so he believed, his possible successor. He also had a brief meeting with Lord Stokes. Peter did not return to the MG factory until after normal working hours but I was still in the workshop office nattering with Tommy, Doug and Den. We were just going out into the yard to go home when Peter drove in and being naturally curious at the outcome of his meeting, we asked what had transpired. Can you imagine the shock when Peter told us that the Department was to close on 31 October. He asked us to keep the information confidential for the moment until the 'Kremlin' had decided when to make the news public, when he could then tell the remaining staff. This was an awful blow, but I suppose not altogether unexpected under the current regime.

Before we left for the Marathon de La Route at Nürburgring it was agreed that the staff of the Department would be told the news on the day we travelled. As some of the team were going to be on the ferry, I was asked to get them together on the journey and tell them the bad news so that they would not hear unofficially from elsewhere.

Rover at Nürburgring

We set off for Germany with the two cars, accompanied by Bill Shaw and Doug Watts and in the bar on the ferry we spilled the beans; not the best way to start out on an event where everyone would be under some pressure. This was not the end of the saga; unbeknown to us, the decision to tell the remaining staff at Abingdon was postponed with the result that one of the mechanics phoned home and unwittingly let the cat out of the bag. It just seemed to be typical of the organised chaos which was evident throughout the company, particularly since the Leyland take over.

Back to the Marathon; scrutineering was no particular problem but we were still waiting for the special propshafts which were being supplied by Hardy Spicer. When eventually they were ready the event was about to start, which meant that the only way to get them to Nürburging was by air. A light aircraft was chartered and Den Green arrived at Liège to be whisked out to the 'Ring where we had a service crew waiting in the forest.

Last rally vehicle prepared by the 'old' team, October 1970

The race cars left Liège and had an easy run to the circuit on this neutralised section. Although no service was permitted, we took the liberty of guiding the Rover into our 'secret' service point just near the 'Ring where the propshaft was rapidly changed.

The 86 hour race started at 01.00 hr on Wednesday 19 August in grid order of their start numbers, putting the Rover and Mini at numbers 20 and 21 behind the three works Porsche 914/4 cars which were on the front of the grid.

The full 17.68 mile circuit was used and at the allotted time the cars thundered off into the darkness to complete the

16,000 Miles to Mexico

south loop before coming back past behind the pits. We leaned out of the back of the pits looking for the coloured identification lamps on the roof of our two cars, and were amazed to hear the bellow of the V8 approaching first. The Rover swept past and disappeared out of view and then it was quiet. We thought that there must have been a multiple pile-up on the southern loop until some seconds later the Mini arrived with the pack on its heels. This was a most dramatic start and did wonders for a very demoralised team.

The Rover settled down to a lap time of about 13 minutes, while the Porsches were obeying team orders and were lapping in about 17 minutes. The lap times had previously been calculated by the team which was rumoured to have already done two 86 hour test sessions on the circuit!

John Handley

The Rover seemed to be going too quickly and at the first driver change and refuelling stop, Bill Shaw was quick to discuss the fast lapping. It transpired that the car was doing 13 minute laps without stress, requiring only about one gear change per lap. The Mini was going well but we were less confident about its lasting power.

As dawn broke, the cars were maintaining station with the Mini in second position on a sun drenched circuit. At about 09.00 hr the Mini came into the pits with severe overheating and it was soon clear that the head gasket was blown. The mechanics headed by Doug Watts attempted the impossible; to change the gasket in 15 minutes, unfortunately running out of time but achieving the task in just under 25 minutes. The car was taken round for one more lap just to prove that it still worked before being retired.

The Rover was the source of some amusement in the Porsche pits as they made it clear that they thought we were mad circulating the car at that speed. The propshaft vibration had not been cured by the special propshaft and at each stop the mechanics had a close look at the shaft and the tail end of the gearbox. After about 15 hours the vibration began to become serious and oil was now being lost from the damaged gearbox housing. Regrettably, after 16 hours we decided to withdraw the car before the rear end of the gearbox disintegrated and possibly caused an accident; the lead over the next car was now three LAPS!

This was a tremendous performance which caused quite a stir, suggesting that the car could have had quite a future, with further development. The official announcement to the world that the British Leyland Competitions Department was to close was made on 24 August although by now the facts had leaked out to the motoring press.

Briefly, the statement said that the closure was not due to lack of money but to release key personnel from the design and development departments who were devoting too many man hours to competition development. The Special Tuning Department would continue to operate and expand at Abingdon. Many people questioned how long it could survive without the support of Competitions Department-developed parts.

The Marathon de La Route was not quite the last event that the Department entered as Brian Culcheth and Andrew Cowan were in Australia competing in the Southern Cross and Rally of the Hills. They both retired in the Southern Cross but Culch was fourth overall in the Rally of the Hills in the Abingdon Mini Cooper S.

Although two new Mini Clubman cars with eight-port cylinder heads and twin Weber carburettors were being prepared for the Sherry Rally in Spain for Paddy Hopkirk/Tony Nash and Brian Culcheth/Johnstone Syer, the entry was cancelled on instructions from Lord Stokes.

This was particularly frustrating for the crews who had already completed a full recce and prepared pace notes for the stages. There was bitter disappointment in Spain where the BL dealer had already had the recce crews on local TV. BBC Wheelbase were featuring the rally in one of their programmes, and they even offered to cover some of the teams expenses to get Berkeley Square to change their minds, to no avail.

The next weeks were spent clearing up the department which would be taken over by Special Tuning, the responsibility to dispose of the cars and equipment being handed over to Basil Wales.

Three mechanics, Eddie Burnell, Brian Moylan and Gerald Wiffen, were taken on by Special Tuning while the remainder of the staff were offered positions in the factory. Doug Watts went into rectification/road test, Tommy and Den became Line Foreman and Cliff ended up on the Trim line. One or two people left MG but the rest were offered really rather menial tasks in the factory although no one was made redundant.

I was offered a position in Special Tuning, reporting to Basil Wales but I could not see myself settling to this change and after about two weeks took voluntary redundancy and left the factory at the end of October; the Department officially closed on 31 October 1970.

The Press gave wide coverage to the closure and Lord Stokes received much criticism for breaking up the team. His remark that he would rather have clots testing his cars rather

1970

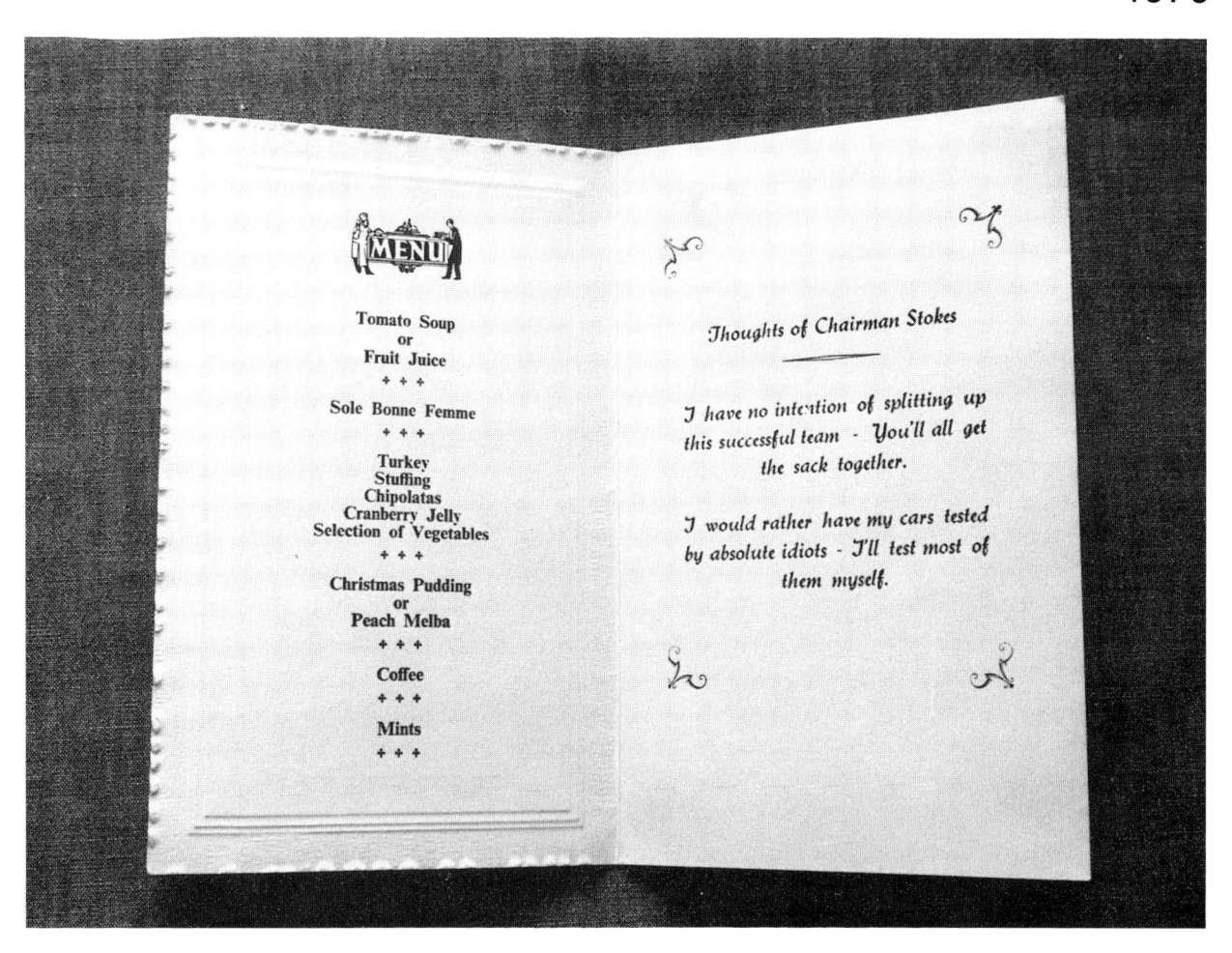

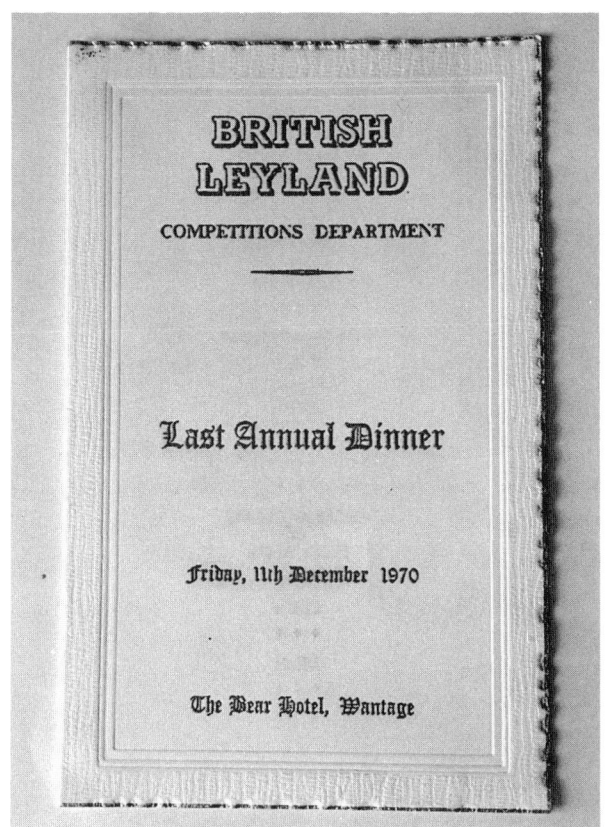

Last Annual Competitions Department Dinner menu, 1970

than professional drivers was widely reported. At Abingdon, many letters were received from drivers and friends of the Department, old and new, including Jack Sears, Tish Ozanne, Marcus Chambers, Tony Fall, Tony Ambrose, John Gott, to name a few, registering their shock and disappointment that the team was being disbanded.

Sandy Lawson organised a last rave-up which was held at Steventon Village Hall near Abingdon but it was a rather subdued affair compared with the usual parties held by the lads. Many of the personnel from the companies who had supported the team over the years attended and it was just as well that Lord Stokes could not see the dart board with his photograph pinned in a prominent position!

Although the Department had closed, arrangements for the annual Christmas dinner went ahead at the Bear Hotel at Wantage. The menu was adorned with The Thoughts of Lord Stokes:

'I have no intention of splitting up this succesful team – You'll all get the sack together.

'I would rather have my cars tested by absolute idiots – I'll test most of them myself.'

It was a good evening in the circumstances although sad that it was to be the last Departmental Christmas dinner.

273

Special Tuning

8
Special Tuning Department
1964–74

THE BMC SPECIAL TUNING Department was formed in 1964 by Stuart Turner to cater for the demand for competition parts for BMC cars, particularly the Mini Cooper models. Glyn Evans, deputy to Gordon Phillips, Manager of the MG Service Department took over the new Department which was formed mainly from personnel in the Service Department.

The Corporation was running down the various service departments and all MG work was being transferred to Cowley. Most of the staff became Special Tuning staff with Bill Lane foreman of the workshop, and Bill Burows chargehand. Some tuning work was now carried out on a few customer cars, but the bulk of the workshop time at this stage involved PDIs on export cars and MGs for other divisions in the Corporation.

Basil Wales (Manager, Special Tuning), HRH The Duke of Kent, and F. R. W. 'Lofty' England (Jaguar Cars) inspect a Special Tuning kit

Early in 1965 when Glyn Evans decided to leave MG, a decision had to be made concerning his replacement. Stuart had a chat with me about the vacancy and then I was asked to go up to see John Thornley where John offered me the job. This was a surprise and I was given the weekend to think it over. I came to the conclusion that I really wanted to carry on at the 'sharp end' and not, as I put it to John Thornley on Monday morning, a glorified parts manager (with due respect to parts managers). I declined the offer and was asked if I could recommend anyone within the company who could do the job. I suggested to John Thornley that Basil Wales of Product Problem Liaison at Cowley might like the job. I had frequent contact with Basil, who was the sports car specialist with PPL, often discussing mutual problems resulting from some of my correspondence.

Rally and rallycross cars prepared by Special Tuning for BL Netherlands with the Special Tuning transporter

Basil had been an apprentice at Morris Engines Branch at Coventry and during this spell had the opportunity to travel on the Liège rally. He had been involved with the development of the supercharged engine used in the MG 'pear-drop' Utah record car but did not go to Utah. Eddie Maher, the Chief Engineer at Morris Engines arranged for him to go on the 1957 Liège instead, travelling with Tommy Wellman and Gerald Wiffen in one service car with Marcus and his wife in the other.

Basil was contacted by John Thornley and came to Abingdon for a chat about the vacancy and was eventually offered the job which he accepted. Basil Wales started in his new job in April 1965 before Glyn had left so that there was a bit of overlap.

It was not long before Basil found that Production had their eyes on the Service Department space. Discussions took place between Stuart, Basil and MG management and it was agreed that Special Tuning would move into the Competitions Department bay (B1) in B Block and Competitions would move next door. A much larger stores area was required together with office accommodation and the structure which became known as the 'Grey Battleship' was constructed in B1.

This incorporated a new stores to house jointly Competitions and Special Tuning parts on the ground floor, with offices on the first floor. There was a large general office, a managers office and also two offices for Stuart Turner and myself, Stuart's secretary and the junior typist, plus a small office for the Competitions Press Officer. Two holes were knocked in the wall between B1 and B2 downstairs to give access into the new Competitions workshop office and from the stores to the workshop.

Basil found that the Department was losing money doing PDIs on new cars and one of the first things that happened was the transfer of this operation to BMC Service in London. It took some months for this steel structure to be built and I think Doug and Tommy were a little sad to leave the overhead crane behind which had been very useful for lifting cars etc. It seemed a shame that with the new stores/office structure in B1 it could not now be used.

Basil established a technical correspondence section with Mike Garton being one of the first technical correspondents. The three main objectives of the Special Tuning Department were to supply competition parts, prepare tuning data sheets and to carry out a limited number of conversions on new and customer cars.

Setting up the parts business was a blessing to Neville Challis in our stores as he was now able to concentrate on procuring prototype parts, the developed and established parts being allocated Special Tuning part numbers and stocked in quantity in the adjoining stores. Basil had been a little concerned when John Thornley had suggested that the Department would probably run at a loss, despite Stuart Turner's hope that eventually the profits could support a competition programme, but sales started to increase.

In 1965 Ron Elkins joined the Special Tuning Department from Cowley to take charge of the technical section and act as second in command to Basil. The preparation of a wider range of tuning kits was under way to complement the MGA,

Special Tuning

Austin Healey Sprite and MGB tuning books (prepared by Syd Enever).

Regular bulletins were published in *Safety Fast* magazine and other motoring periodicals to keep customers up to date with what was on offer. The rally programme maintained a continuing development of new components and as soon as anything new was seen on the works cars, private owners were on to Basil to find out when they could buy the same part.

Within a year an extensive list of parts was on offer, including everything from perspex 'Sebring' lamp covers for the MGB to a variety of camshafts for the 'A' series engine and close ratio gears.

The Department attended many events with the Special Tuning coach carrying tuning parts and display boards, and service was offered to private owners on major international rallies such as the RAC, Scottish and Welsh. Basil made himself a little unpopular when he produced invoices and charged private owners for parts on events; I think it was felt to be penny-pinching by competitors who had been helped by the works mechanics in the days before Special Tuning. In the absence of a private owners support budget, Basil had of course every right to charge for parts supplied.

As our own programme increased, there were a number of occasions that the Special Tuning workshop, now under the supervision of Bill Burrows following the retirement of Bill Lane, built cars for the works programme. One of their best results was the car prepared for Tony Fall and Mike Wood for the Scottish Rally in 1966 which they won outright, followed by the second overall achieved by Lars Ytterbring in 1967, also in the Scottish.

One customer worth a mention is Jean-Louis Marnat, the French race/rally driver. He ordered a 1275 Mini Cooper S engine built to a fairly hot Special Tuning spec. What Special Tuning did not know was that the engine was destined to be put in a Mini Marcos entered in the Le Mans 24 hour race. At the start of the race this engine was still being run-in, but nevertheless, the car went like a rocket finishing fifteenth overall at an average of 89 mph, confirming the meticulous preparation put into this customer engine.

In 1967 Daniel Richmond, of Downton Engineering, sold Longbridge the idea of producing Stage 1 kits for production vehicles, approved by Engineering and covered by the Manufacturer's warranty. The obvious outlet for these kits would be Special Tuning and within months Basil Wales was ordering the parts for these official kits.

A special press day was organised at the Home Sweet Home pub near Benson where the invited motoring journalists were given a press pack detailing the various kits available for BMC cars. Cars fitted with a variety of kits were made available for the press to try round the lanes of Oxfordshire and the day was quite successful.

The kits were priced at £44 for the 850 cc Mini, up to £66 for an Austin 1800. When the press reports were published, Basil noted with interest that the only one which was accurate was printed by the *Daily Mirror*, the *Mirror* motoring correspondent had published the Special Tuning press release more or less word-for-word!

The labour turnover in the Department was small although there had been some changes in the Technical section with Mike Garton leaving and MG ex-apprentices Mike Dickin and Fred Pearce joining Ron Elkins. Sales turnover had reached a level of around £550,000 by 1967 with a profit of 30 per cent which to the accountants at Longbridge seemed to be too good to be true. As a result, George Turnbull sent Jim Backus down to audit the accounts and after careful vetting, there were no more questions from Longbridge concerning the Departments finances.

Wind of Change

The Leyland merger in 1968 brought about some changes at Abingdon with the Special Tuning Department being renamed the British Leyland Special Tuning Department. The Department inherited Triumph tuning parts from Triumph at Canley but sales of most of these items were slowing down.

There was also a change in the reporting structure, which relieved Peter Browning of responsibility of the parts business, with Basil now reporting direct to Les Lambourne, MG Plant Director.

In 1968 the London–Sydney Marathon gave Special Tuning the opportunity to prepare customer cars, among them being an Austin 1800 Royal Navy crew led by Captain J. A. Hans Hamilton.

Competitions was determined to extract the maximum from the Mini Cooper S and in an expensive weight-saving excercise, 1,000 sets of aluminium doors, bonnets and boot lids were ordered together with a similar number of perspex windows; the quantities were required to comply with FIA regulations.

The racing Minis were using the Engines Branch designed eight-port cast iron cylinder head and Special Tuning had the task of supplying demand for this item from customers. Competitions later used the Jim Whitehouse (Arden Engineering) designed aluminium eight-port cylinder head, which was Homologated in July 1970. The aluminium cylinder head sold well and Basil had considerable trouble meeting demand.

With the success of the London–Sydney Marathon, in 1970 the London–Mexico World Cup Rally brought Special Tuning some more preparation work from private owners who had entered the event. Based on the works spec used in the London–Sydney event a very good specification was offered. The customers who had their cars prepared by Special Tuning were the Metropolitan Police team, the Royal Navy team, *Woman* Magazine, Peter Jopp and Reg Redgrave, the cars being built to more or less the same specification with a typical cost for the mechanical modifications of approximately £2000 per car. There were a number of experienced rally competitors in these five cars including Peter Jopp, Jean Denton, Liz Crellin, Pat Wright, Phil Cooper and Willy Cave.

The all-ladies crew named their car 'The Beauty Box' and attracted a considerable amount of publicity through their sponsors, *Woman* magazine.

To help these crews and all the other private competitors, two of the Special Tuning mechanics, John West and Martin Reade, were detailed to accompany the 'works' service crews on the rally to service the private owners as a priority, but to also help with the Abingdon cars. The high standard of preparation paid off as two of the five cars prepared by Special Tuning finished the rally with Reg Redgrave ninth, and 'The Beauty Box' eighteenth overall, out of only 23 finishers.

1964-74

Competitions Axed

The announcement of the closure of the Competitions Department so soon after the World Cup Rally came as a shock to everyone at Abingdon and was obviously going to put some pressure on Special Tuning in the future. Without a race/rally programme and the continuing development of competitions parts from the Department next door, many predicted that Special Tuning could not survive for long.

The closure of Competitions left Basil with the responsibility of disposing of a certain amount of equipment and cars. J. C. Bamford made an offer for all the competition vehicles, but when asked to assess the situation by Les Lambourne, MG Plant Director, Basil advised him that he could get much more money for them by selling them separately. Norman Higgins, MG Chief Accountant, handled the sale of some of the vehicles and eventually all but the ex-Monte winners and a few other show vehicles were sold privately. Basil decided to scrap some of the Competitions stock, mainly special panels which Basil felt would be difficult to replace at a later date, which did not go down too well.

An agreement was reached whereby three of the 'redundant' Competitions Department mechanics were taken on by Special Tuning, but this could hardly be called a nucleus with which to rebuild Competitions, should the Company wish to continue with a competition programme at a later date.

With Competitions closed it was not long before MG started to look at the vacated space in B Block, but for the time being, Special Tuning remained in the B1 hangar.

Team Castrol

With reorganisation taking place, it took some time for the dust to settle and it was into 1971 before any further outside 'unofficial' competition activity was undertaken.

Brian Culcheth/Johnstone Syer in the ex-World Cup Triumph 2.5 PI on the 1971 Scottish Rally

Special Tuning

Brian Culcheth had been retained with a contract by British Leyland International to do promotional and demonstration work for them, and it was Brian with Simon Pearson of Triumph Public Relations Department and Roger Willis of Castrol who worked out a plan to rally the ex-World Cup Triumph 2.5PI under the Team Castrol banner. Bill Davis, a director of Triumph, was in favour of the project and with about £5000 of Castrol money, a number of UK rallies were earmarked, starting with the Welsh Rally.

The car which was prepared for the Welsh was XJB 305H, the actual car with which Brian and Johnstone Syer had come second overall on the World Cup rally, but with some of the World Cup modifications removed. The car was one of the first to be rejected at scrutineering because the roll-cage cross bar was not fitted. A waiver had actually been issued by the RAC for the Welsh and as soon as that arrived, all was well. The car was serviced by a crew from Special Tuning but, unfortunately, fuel feed problems and a time consuming puncture kept them out of the top ten, Brian and Johnstone eventually finished fourteenth overall.

In June the car was entered in the Scottish Rally. With further weight reduction and more power, the car proved to be more competitive. Brian and Johnstone climbed up to fourth overall but left the road on the Minard stage, then went off again later in the event, dropping to tenth overall at the finish.

MG Production wanted the space in B1 hangar and the Special Tuning workshop moved next door into the old 'Comps' workshop in B2. At this time the Advanced Driving School moved into the old 'Comps' office on top of the 'Grey Battleship' to release some more space in A Block.

The next event for Brian Culcheth was the International Cyprus rally, this time in a 1.3 Morris Marina two-door coupé running on twin SU carburettors. The budget for this outing came from the British Leyland International Division based in London. With Johnstone Syer, his regular co-driver, Brian led the rally throughout until penalties caused by a broken throttle cable dropped the car to second overall. The emphasis behind all of these events sponsored by BLI was to support the model marketing programme.

Basil obtained additional finance to do some testing in preparation for the 1971 RAC Rally, where Brian was to drive a 1.3 Marina sponsored by BBC's Wheelbase programme, this time taking BBC man, Willy Cave as co-driver.

A 1.8 engine was fitted in the test car for a number of sessions at Bagshot, the extra weight adding to the stress the car was being subjected to. Basil reckons that the reason that Ford did not ensure a quick 1.3 car was entered in the small capacity class on the RAC was because Ford Competitions had seen the 1.8 Marina testing at Bagshot.

One thing that caused Basil a little embarrassment was the loan of a tuned Mini Cooper S engine to Russell Brookes who was working in the Rover Product Planning Department. On the RAC, the Marina and Russell's car were in the same class and it looked as though Russell was going to beat the Marina when he took advantage of the snowy conditions. Basil began to think up excuses to explain why an engine he had loaned had been responsible for beating the works car, but in the end Brian finished first in class and eighteenth overall thus saving the day! The RAC Marina was shipped off to Denmark for the Danish Motor Show where DOMI, the Morris Importer,

Brian Culcheth/Willy Cave in the Morris Marina 1.3 Coupé prepared by Special Tuning, 1971 RAC Rally

'Scottish Rally' sump shield stocked by Special Tuning

displayed the rally car on the Morris stand. At the Show, Special Tuning obtained an order for 600 Stage 1 tuning kits valued at £35,000, which helped the 1971 sales figures.

On the strength of Brian's results in 1971, Bill Davis agreed more money for 1972, with money to develop the new Triumph Dolomite being made available.

Triumph on the Safari

During 1971 Earls Court Motor Show duty Brian Culcheth met the Triumph dealer from Nairobi. Brian was asked if he would drive a Triumph 2.5PI for them in the forthcoming East African Safari and arrangements were put in hand to dispatch a new car to Abingdon.

When the Triumph 2.5PI for the Safari arrived at Abingdon, there was no time to waste to have the car prepared and then shipped to East Africa. The body was strengthened at Pressed Steel but otherwise the specification was fairly basic with a World Cup spec engine, suspension modifications confined to shock-absorbers and other detail changes learned from earlier events like the RAC and World Cup rallies.

Local co-driver, Lofty Drews, accompanied Brian although Johnstone Syer went to Africa to assist with recce notes

1964-74

Triumph 2.5 PI prepared by Special Tuning for the East African Safari being seen off by Brian Culcheth

East African Safari 1972; Brian Culcheth/Lofty Drews Triumph 2.5 PI enter a flooded section

Special Tuning

and servicing. Simon Pearson was sent by Triumph to look after Public Relations and also to assist the local dealer and his service team. Brian had a bad start to the event, suffering lack of sleep due the late arrival of the car from England. On the scrutineering day, Brian and Lofty drove the car up from Mombassa to get the car scrutineered at the last moment, the remaining few hours being spent finally preparing the car.

During the rally the car suffered a number of mechanical problems. Only 100 miles from the start they hit an antelope and were only able to continue after buying a radiator from a Triumph 2000 owner. Later the gearbox lost most of its gears, and during a service halt the mechanics were lucky not to be covered with boiling oil when checking the level; new oil cured the problem. After Kampala the rear screen fell out, by which time the body had started to crack. Brian decided to attack the last section in a do-or-die effort with a fastest time resulting in his finishing thirteenth overall and first in class; a very good result in his first Safari. The body at the finish was in a sorry state with the boot section noticeably sagging and about to fall off!

East African Safari 1972; body damage to the Triumph 2.5 PI driven by Brian Culcheth/Lofty Drews

Dolomite Rally Car

During this period, Triumph at Canley had been building a Dolomite with a prototype 16-valve engine under the supervision of Ray Henderson (ex-Triumph Competitions Manager) with some of the chassis development being carried out by

1964-74

Gordon Birtwistle also an ex-Triumph Competitions man. The car, with the blessing of Triumph Director Bill Davis, was being developed as a pure competition car and in the summer was taken to the Military Vehicle Experimental Establishment test track at Chobham where Gordon met Brian Culcheth and 'Fast' Eddie for an assessment of the vehicle after some initial testing on MIRAs handling circuit.

This was in preparation for the first outing of the car in the 1972 Scottish Rally in which an entry was made for Brian and Johnstone. The car was entered as a Dolomite and the crew and mechanics from Special Tuning were told not to reveal too many secrets of what was under the bonnet. The engine was the four-cylinder, 2-litre, 16-valve unit which was to appear officially in the new Triumph Dolomite Sprint production car. On the rally, the car was able to put up some competitive stage times but weak shock-absorbers, which needed frequent changing, kept Brian and Johnstone out of the top ten, finishing nineteenth overall and second in class.

The car was returned to Triumph at Canley for a thorough overhaul and investigation by Engineering Division and was rebuilt for an entry in the TAP Rally in Portugal at the end of the year.

BLI had found some more money for an overseas event for Brian, and following the excellent showing of the Marina in Cyprus, a Marina 1.3 was entered again. BLI personnel accompanied the crew with local mechanics doing the servicing and for the second year running, Brian and Johnstone were second overall.

The Triumph for the TAP Rally was only finished at the last moment and it was Simon Pearson from the Triumph Public Relations department who drove it down to Southampton in time to catch the ferry. Servicing was provided by Gordon Birtwistle (taking a week's holiday) in a Range Rover loaded with spares and tyres, assisted by Ron Elkins from Special Tuning. John Lloyd, Chief Engineer at Triumph, had agreed that Gordon could carry out this servicing operation, although unofficially, as it enabled Engineering to keep a close eye on what happened to the car.

Left: The prototype Triumph Dolomite Sprint driven on the 1972 TAP Rally by Brian Culcheth/Johnstone Syer

Brian Culcheth and Johnstone Syer went very well on the event, leading at one stage, until very near the end when losing power, one of the axle top locating links broke and put them out of the rally. When the car was returned to Canley, Gordon was asked to give the car a road test just to see how it had fared and was surprised to find that it was running on three cylinders; a rocker arm was broken. This was all interesting material for the engine development section at Triumph who were finalising the spec for the Sprint production engine which would be launched within about 18 months. This was the first of a number of outings for this particular car (CKV 2K) which was the forerunner of the Dolomite Sprint rally car.

Brian Culcheth testing the Dunlop Total Mobility (Denovo) tyres at Bagshot prior to the 1972 RAC Rally

There was still no official competition programme, but with the 1972 RAC Rally coming up an agreement was reached with Dunlop to run a Marina using Denovo tyres exclusively during the rally. This new concept in run-flat tyre design was being promoted heavily by Dunlop who saw the RAC rally as an ideal proving and publicity ground for the tyre which required a specially designed rim. The entry was made by Dunlop Ltd, and the Morris Marina 1.3 coupé was painted in distinctive Denovo livery.

The weather turned out to be typical RAC with heavy snowfall at one stage causing problems. At a service point in the Kielder Forest, Brian Moylan was in charge of the service car and, because they had some time to wait before the rally came through, they had a sleep in the car. To reserve a space behind their car for the rally car when it arrived, some of the Denovo wheels/tyres were set out on the road, and it was a very embarrassed Brian Moylan who discovered that some of them had been stolen while they were asleep (two were subsequently found thrown down a bank nearby).

As the rally moved towards Scotch Corner, the Marina lost oil pressure and Bill Burrows decided that the only chance of continuing was to change the big-end shells. The alternator bracket was also broken and in the panic to get away in the heavy snow that was falling, Brian Culcheth left without his spare wheel. Basil Wales, who was at the service point, chased after the rally car with a spare but spun on the treacherous surface of the A1 damaging his suspension, which did not please Bill Burrows who had more repair work to do. The Marina did not survive the rally, however, because the big-ends soon failed again, which was disappointing for Dunlop and Special Tuning.

Four Wheel Drive Clubman

Once again, for 1972, there had been a televised series of rallycross events. One new development had been the introduction by the Ford Motor Company of a four wheel drive Capri. The organisers had been taken unawares by this development and in the muddy and sometimes snowy conditions the car proved to be rather competitive.

After the penultimate event of the series, Basil Wales

Special Tuning

received a phone call from Charlie Griffin at Longbridge, asking if Special Tuning could build a four wheel-drive car for rallycross to beat the Ford. There were only ten days before the last event, so it was rather a tall order but Basil agreed to see what he could do. He knew that out in the car park was the chassis of a prototype 'Ant', a 4 × 4 military vehicle built by Longbridge for assessment by the Ministry of Defence. Competitions had acquired this vehicle some years previously but had not had the opportunity to do anything with it.

The transmission mechanicals were built into a Mini Clubman bodyshell using a rally spec engine with eight-port cylinder head. The 1275 crankshaft fouled the gearbox casing so that had to be machined to give sufficient clearance. The front gearbox had a pinion shaft coming out at the rear to which was connected the rear propshaft. The special rear differential assembly had to be mounted on a bracket at the rear, while the rear suspension used Mini type hub carriers, coil springs and Koni shock-absorbers. Driveshafts at front and rear used the Hardy Spicer-type couplings.

Bill Burrows was responsible for building this vehicle with Bill Hine and Eddie Burnell doing most of the assembly and fabrication work. To give the car a shake-down and compare it with a conventional Mini Cooper S, Basil invited Bob Freeborough to bring his own rally car over to some gravel pits near Abingdon where a back-to-back comparison was made. The results were encouraging enough for an entry to be made in the final event of the Wills TV Rallycross series. Brian Chatfield was entrusted with the car which gave Roger Clark a run for his money in the Ford Capri four-wheel drive car to gain a fine win in front of millions of viewers.

In 1973, BL Director John Barber was behind the decision that the Company should become involved in racing. Much of the credit for this decision being due to representations made by Simon Pearson. Although involved in political battles for control of the Corporation, John Barber was a motor sport enthusiast and felt it would improve the image of BL.

The 1970 World Cup Rally resulted in another World Cup event in 1974, taking in the Sahara Desert. Special Tuning built a V8 Marina for this event for Major Helmsley but unfortunately the car retired with a broken axle.

Triumph Dolomite Sprint

In June 1972 the Triumph Dolomite Sprint was introduced with the 2-litre four-cylinder, 16-valve engine; at last a car with some competition potential. Simon Pearson at Triumph had been more or less instrumental in persuading the management compete in the British Saloon Car Championship and with the forecasted production quantities, there seemed to be every possibility that sufficient cars would be built in time to have the model Homologated in Group 1 (5000 cars built in 12 months) on 1 January 1974.

Brian Culcheth was still contracted to BLI as a Promotions Executive and was hoping to do some events in 1973 for BLI. Kevin Best (son of ex-works BMC rally driver Ken Best) had been working for Austin-Morris at Longbridge and joined BLI at the end of 1972 in the Promotions Department working for David Welch. Peter Battam of BLI had been coordinating the BLI events in which Brian had competed and was responsible for sorting out the budget, with Kevin taking over this responsibility in 1973.

BLI moved into Leyland House, Marylebone Road, London in 1973 and it was from there that entries in the 24 Hours of Ypres, Semperit, 1,000 Lakes and Cyprus rallies were organised using the Morris Marina 1.3 (1.8 in the Semperit).

Class wins were the objective, and the first event in Ypres saw the team achieve its first result of the year with first in class and tenth overall. This was disappointing, nevertheless, because Brian had climbed up to an incredible fourth overall until electrical problems dropped them down the field. The car was using the turreted rear shock-absorbers and axle radius rods for the first time.

Third in class on the Austrian Semperit rally followed, and then an exciting battle with Markku Saaristo in his Skoda in the 1000 Lakes in Finland. Despite the local knowledge of the Finn, Brian put up a strong challenge but was unable to take the class, coming in second by the slim margin of 14 seconds. One of the main troubles experienced on this event was the rear shock-absorber turrets which had to be welded after the tops started to split.

Triumph Dolomite Sprint prepared for the 1973 Scottish Rally

BLI were keen to maintain the image of the Marina in Cyprus, following the good result in 1972 and were not disappointed when Brian and regular co-driver, Johnstone Syer duly won the class again in the faithful Marina 1.3, NBL 786L, which had now seen quite a lot of service. They would have been higher in general classification if the car had not fallen off the jack when they were changing a wheel. Two locally-built Marinas were driven by Chris Sclater/Henry Liddon and Phil Cooper/Dave Valance and, although the Sclater car retired with a broken axle, Phil Cooper finished despite a noisy gearbox. Special Tuning had developed a four-Amal carburettor installation for the 1.3 engine and this was used on the Cyprus Rally and was also being successfully used on 1275 Mini Cooper S engines, particularly in rallycross.

Cyprus Rally 1973; Brian Culcheth/Johnstone Syer Morris Marina 1.3 Coupé raising the dust

In addition to the events with the Marina, the Leyland Benelux Team, in conjunction with BLI, competed in the European rallycross series and national rallies in the Benelux countries, with Special Tuning preparing the cars and providing some on-event servicing.

In a small way, participation in these events helped to maintain some sort of contact with motor sport, at the same time encouraging sales of Special Tuning parts which was essential for the survival of the department.

Yet again MG Production was looking for extra space in B Block and it was during 1973 that plans were put in hand to move Special Tuning into part of the newest building on the MG site, C Block, situated in the middle of the car park. It had been used for a number of activities including Rectification and Tuning of new cars, but to house Special Tuning office accommodation had to be built on at one end of the building. At the end of 1973, the move took place with the whole department moving to C Block at the other end of the factory; the last internal move.

1964-74

Special Tuning
1974

1974 – Management Changes

The racing programme continued with BL contracts for Broadspeed, Equipe Arden, Bill Shaw Racing and Aldon Automotive.

I was working for Mann Egerton Ltd at High Wycombe and, although I had kept a close watch on any developments at Special Tuning which might signal a return to motor sport, in my heart I could not really see any chance of going back to Abingdon if it did happen. I kept in touch with Brian Culcheth and it was through him that I learned that a reorganisation at Abingdon now looked probable.

Marina V8 Pick-up prepared by Special Tuning in association with Car & Car Conversions *magazine*

Keith Hopkins, BL Publicity Chief had obtained agreement in 1973 to use Special Tuning profits to support motor sport events and this brought about the relaunch of Special Tuning.

Through Brian Culcheth and Simon Pearson, I was asked to go up to London to have a chat with Keith Hopkins and Simon, where it was explained what was happening and I was asked if I would consider going back to Abingdon as Workshop Supervisor. I could hardly believe this was happening to me and it was several weeks and another interview with the Personnel Department before I received written confirmation of the position at Abingdon with a salary £1000 more than my salary as a Service Manager.

There was some delay in a date for me to start caused by internal personnel problems but in May 1974 I returned to Abingdon as Workshop Supervisor, reporting to Basil Wales. I felt a little uncomfortable at first, as this was a new position which some members of the Department considered should have been filled internally.

The workshop was a little short of work at this time and although BLI were still providing the budget to run a car in a limited number of events for Brian Culcheth, this did not occupy many man-hours.

Before I returned to Abingdon, one event on the BLI programme was an entry in the TAP Rally in Portugal with a newly prepared Triumph Dolomite Sprint (FRW 812L) for Brian Culcheth and Johnstone Syer. Peter Battam from BLI co-ordinated the entry, and Gerald Wiffen and Les Bowman looked after servicing from Special Tuning. Unfortunately, the rally was rather short lived, because the Sprint bent its steering rack on one of the first stages, and although a new unit was fitted by the mechanics, they ran out of time.

MGB V8 engine fitted to the special Marina V8 Pick-up

One of my first problems when I returned was to sort out a problem with the expense accounts submitted by the TAP mechanics. MG had lost the services of Norman Higgins, Chief Accountant, who had taken a position at Cowley and the new man had no concept of the problems which could be encountered by mechanics in foreign lands. When I arrived at his office, he was trying to reconcile the expenses claimed by the mechanics with the number of petrol receipts handed in. This was often a problem and I tried to explain the discrepancy with examples from my own experience. It was a perennial problem for the staff involved with overseas events, trying to make their expenses agree. The mechanics would often quote the Competitions staff from a well known oil company who were given what seemed to be large amounts of money to cover their expenses while attending events, but apparently did not have to submit an expense account or receipts at the end. This was expenses being handled on a day-money basis, something that we tried for years to introduce.

The first week I was back in Special Tuning the Welsh Rally was in progress. Special Tuning had a particular interest in the event as a Triumph Dolomite Sprint had been prepared for the *Birmingham Post*/Colliers sponsored rally team. The car was being driven by John Bloxham and Richard Harper and I went off down to Wales for a few hours just to see how the car was performing. This team was professionally turned out and supervised by Johnny Jones of Colliers. They had a very well equipped Range Rover with, among other things, a workshop vice built into the front bumper. The weather was awful and I did not get much chance to see the car in action.

Development of the Sprint continued as far as finances would permit and at the end of May we took the 'old' CKV car

The new Leyland ST workshop in 'C' Block at the MG Division. A Triumph Dolomite Sprint is in preparation in the foreground

Kit development on an Austin Allegro in the Leyland ST workshop

284

1964-74

Special Tuning

to Bagshot with a representative from Girling. We were testing adjustable Girling shock-absorbers, strengthened trailing arms and a No-spin limited slip differential. The steering rack bent after only about five laps of the Alpine course, which gave us the opportunity to fit a special-material rack which we hoped would improve the problem. The test was terminated when the rear propshaft universal joint broke.

Next day we were back, but after eleven laps, a rear trailing arm fractured and, on examination, the strengthening appeared to be faulty. We returned on the third day, this time with John Bloxham along to see what we were up to. After eight laps, the differential broke, the mechanics changing the axle with the unit out of FRW which was fitted with a Salisbury limited slip diff. A few laps later, another rear trailing arm fractured confirming our fears concerning the design of the trailing arm.

Meanwhile, BLI were anxious to promote the Triumph in Belgium and money was found to make a one-car entry in the 1974 24 Hours of Ypres, a mainly tarmac event. The car which had been used in Portugal, FRW 812L, was used and we took a service crew over from Abingdon. This was my first event looking after a rally entry since 1970.

British Leyland Belgium did a good job with local publicity and the car attracted quite a lot of interest with its wide fibreglass wing extensions covering the 6½ × 13 inch Minlite wheels. Brian Culcheth and Johnstone Syer once again put up a very good performance and were lying second overall on the penultimate lap when they were let down by the self-adjusting rear drum brakes overheating, resulting in the fluid catching fire. This small conflagration was put out at the service point but by the time a new wheel cylinder had been fitted, it was too late to continue. The next modification would have to be the fitting of manual adjusters for the rear brakes. Another problem which showed up was the heat transfer to the front lower ball-joints. On the Sprint, the steering arms incorporate the lower front ball-joint and at rally speed the heat from the discs was melting the nylon thrust pads; new ball-joints with steel cups were developed.

Two months after I returned to Abingdon, John Kerswill was appointed as Sales and Marketing manager with the object of developing a new strategy to improve sales and relaunching the tuning kits.

In July, I was surprised to be told by Basil Wales that he was leaving the Department after ten years. He had been offered the job of reorganising the multi-franchise parts business at Cowley. Despite rumours at the time suggesting that he had been 'eased out', Basil had felt like a change and saw this new job as a chance to move on.

This left a vacancy for Keith Hopkins to fill. This came about almost by accident at a Divisional PR meeting at Cowley, when Richard Seth-Smith arrived about 20 minutes early. There was a discussion taking place between Simon and Keith which Richard unwittingly walked into. Making his excuses he turned to leave but was asked to stay; the discussion concerned reorganisation of the Special Tuning department. The comment that they now had a workshop supervisor and a marketing manager and all that was needed now was someone in overall charge, brought the comment from Richard Seth-Smith, 'I'll run it'. Keith Hopkins asked 'Seth' if he was serious, adding, 'what do you know about motor sport and tuning?' Richard explained that he had been involved in a

Les Bowman preparing the 1974 Avon Tour Dolomite Sprint

company manufacturing rally and race seats and had also done some racing himself. Keith Hopkins said he would think about it if he was serious and after a further discussion a few days later, Richard Seth-Smith was appointed Manager of Special Tuning to replace Basil Wales.

Avon Tour of Britain

In 1973 the BRSCC had organised an event on the lines of the Tour de France Automobile, with sponsorship from the Avon Tyre Company called the Avon Tour of Britain. This consisted of a mixture of circuit races and special stages, with entries confined to Group 1 cars with only one type of over-the-counter tyre permitted (quantity free).

This year, with sponsorship from Castrol, Unipart and *Autocar* we were able to make an entry for Brian Culcheth who took along Ray Hutton from *Autocar* as co-driver. A new Sprint was hurriedly built (RDU 983M) and after a short test session, German Dunlop SP Sport 205/60 VR 13 tyres were chosen. The Sprint proved to be very competitive but ran into trouble on one of the airfield stages in Lincolnshire.

I was with the service crew at the end of the stage and we were dismayed to see the car come to rest about 400 yards from the end. Brian and Ray pushed the car to the finish and we were soon investigating why the engine had stopped. There were signs of a small fire in the vicinity of the rear carburettor and the fuel pipe was burnt through. After the pipe was repaired no sign of a leak was apparent and they were soon on their way.

Avon Tour of Britain 1974; Kevin Best (in Nomex) discusses final points with David Welch (BLI) while Bill Price talks to Brian Culcheth

At Oulton Park, just before the end of Brian's race, the car came past the pits with a misfire. On the last-but-one lap, he failed to come round; the car had cut out and with smoke appearing from under the bonnet, Brian headed for a marshals post where an under-bonnet fire was quickly extinguished. The car was towed in to the paddock but this time the damage was more serious with the clutch hydraulic pipe also gone. Repairs took rather a long time which would mean Brian having to average 80 mph to get to the next control on public roads which was out of the question, so he was out.

1964-74

I was determined to find out why the car had caught fire. Assuming that the carburettors had ejected petrol out of the overflow pipes, we rigged them up to a catch tank. Five laps of the Club Circuit at Silverstone produced a third of a pint of petrol in the catch tank. A different type of float chamber lid was fitted which completely cured the problem; so simple!

The next event for BLI was an entry in the Criterium Antibes–Grasse in the south of France for the Sprint (FRW 812L). In addition, the *Birmingham Post* crew, John Bloxham/Richard Harper, also entered, making a two-car team to service during the event based in Antibes. Brian and Johnstone had done a reasonable recce and Kevin Best and Peter Battam were in attendance for BLI and the French PR manager also made an appearance.

Our luck was out again when at the start of the first stage a short-circuit occurred under the fascia as Brian turned on the headlamps; this resulted in having to do the stage on spotlamps alone. At the stage finish we found also that there was a lot of oil in the engine compartment blowing from the oil catch tank.

Only a few stages later the alternator failed and we found that the position of the long alternator bolt prevented us from changing it without removing the radiator, the car retiring shortly afterwards with a holed radiator. The *Birmingham Post* car did not fare any better, retiring with a bent steering rack.

The run in the 1000 Lakes in 1973 had resulted in a good class second but Brian was determined to gain revenge with a

Brian Culcheth hangs the tail out in the Group 1 Triumph Dolomite Sprint; Avon Tour of Britain 1974

BLI-sponsored entry this year. A new car, NBL 782M was used, fitted with the Amal four-carburettor engine and with two mechanics from Special Tuning to assist with servicing. Brian and Johnstone had a good event defeating the opposition to win their class, an excellent result for a Brit in Finland.

Special Tuning

Brian Culcheth/Johnstone Syer jumps the Morris Marina 1.3 Coupé during the 1974 1000 Lakes (Colin Taylor Productions)

Sprint Development

We discussed the Sprint rear suspension with Triumph design department and Brian Culcheth and decided that an improvement in wheel movement, traction and general handling, could possibly be achieved by modifying the linkage to a four parallel link system with lateral location by a Panhard rod. The old Dolomite test car, CKV 2K, was carved about at the rear end and with design assistance, unofficially, from Triumph at Canley, the modifications were carried out.

Don Moore built us a rally engine and with this unit we went to Bagshot on 8 August for the first try-out. With help from Derek Wootton from Tech Del Ltd we had also purchased some of the new cheaper aluminium Minilite 6 × 13 inch Sport wheels. The wheels had a better inset than the magnesium 6½ × 13 inch wheels Special Tuning had obtained for the Dolomite, and would hopefully reduce the steering rack bending problems.

The car managed eighteen laps of the rough road circuit at Bagshot before the Panhard rod bracket failed but not before Eddie Burnell had assessed a significant improvement in traction and handling. The Girling shock-absorbers seemed unable to cope with the axle movement and, despite sterling work by Girling Competitions department, we came to the conclusion that Bilstein shock-absorbers, now used by most of the top teams, just had to be tried.

Although Bilstein did not have their own rally test track, Hugo Emde suggested that the quickest way to find out what spec was required was to take a car over to the factory at Ennepetal in Germany and have some test units made up. I went over to Germany with 'Fast' Eddie (as Brian was not available) and FRW 812L, where we spent a day with the Bilstein engineers and Hugo, testing the first units on private forest tracks near the factory. We came away with a set fitted to the car and some spares with alternative settings to test. The quality control inspection of the Bilstein shock-absorbers at the small Ennepetal factory was very impressive.

Richard Takes Over

Richard Seth-Smith eventually arrived to take up his new position and his enthusiasm was like a whirlwind coming through the Department which the staff took some time to appreciate. Plans were now being finalised to relaunch the Special Tuning Department with a new name and image, with John Kerswill streamlining the distribution of parts by appointing exclusive Special Tuning distributors. Many of the appointed firms had a competition background or experience and it was envisaged that stockists would also be appointed supplied direct from the appointed distributors.

These plans were all revealed in a press release dated 1 November 1974 headed 'British Leyland launches Leyland ST' the main objective being to generate 'youth appeal' in the Corporation's wide range of cars. A new logo and decals had been designed to promote the new image. A mention was also made that the department was carrying out an assessment of the competition potential of all models produced by the Corporation. The Department was now part of the Austin-Morris Division.

The Austin-badged version of the Marina was now on sale in North America and Kevin Best of BLI was organising a

Engine compartment of the Austin Marina 1.8 rally car

promotional tour incorporating entries in the two international rallies for Brian and Johnstone. The two events were the POR Rally in USA and the Rideau Lakes in Canada in which an Austin Marina 1.8 would be entered. The new Marina Coupé NBL 782M, was converted to look like an Austin by fitting the large USA spec bumpers and the appropriate badges, together with a 1.8 engine. The chassis spec was the same as with the 1.3 engine, including the axle radius rods and turrets to take the telescopic rear shock-absorbers. BLI found the extra finance to send out two mechanics from Leyland ST, with John West and Eddie Burnell being selected for the trip.

The promotional part of the tour was very successful with Brian giving around 28 radio and seven TV interviews as well as dealer appearances and driving test demonstrations. Rallying does not have a very big following in the USA and on one TV press release, 'Culch' was described as a cross between Evel Knievel, the stunt man and Parnelli Jones, the racing driver. At one promotion at a large department store, Brian was among a number of celebrities entertained to lunch, including Elizabeth Taylor, and when interviewed by TV on leaving, he was asked what it was like having lunch with Liz Taylor. The interviewer was rather non-plussed with the answer, 'I hope she pays the bill'!

As far as the rallies were concerned, the two events were a failure for the Marina. The first was the Rideau Lakes in Canada where the gearbox broke. We received a panic phone call from Brian asking if anything could be done for the next event in USA.

There was no possibility of obtaining special gears but we did have some sets X-rayed and carefully inspected for faults so, at least, a good set could be selected and sent over for the rally. However, the power of the 1.8 engine proved too much and the gearbox broke again in the POR Rally.

Richard Seth-Smith had a meeting in August with Unipart and they agreed in principal to support a four event rally programme in conjunction with Castrol, starting with the 1974 RAC Rally. The car would be a Group 2 Sprint on the RAC, Welsh and Scottish rallies and a Group 1 car for the Tour of Britain.

For the RAC an entry was made for Brian Culcheth/ Johnstone Syer in a Sprint with the improved Panhard rod rear suspension. Further testing to establish the best shock-absorber settings was carried out at Bagshot at the end of September and early October, with a modified propshaft and high ratio steering rack also on test. Just before the RAC, David Welch arranged a demonstration for director John Barber, but although the old test car, CKV 2K, was taken to Bagshot, he was unable to attend owing to other commitments.

The 1974 RAC started in York with the Triumph Dolomite Sprint (FWR 812L) looking very smart in its Castrol/ Unipart colours with Dunlop decals indicating the continued support from Dunlop Rally division. The crew started off steadily with Johnstone in his usual cheerful manner, commenting that they would play themselves in for the first two days then attack on the second two!

Unfortunately, while going steadily in a respectable position, the car hit a fallen tree which had been dislodged by the previous car on one of the Clocaenog stages in north

Special Tuning

Wales. The tree penetrated the cockpit behind the nearside front wheel, went through the dash panel and ended up against the gear lever, narrowly missing Johnstone Syer. The crew were miraculously virtually unhurt, but their rally was over; our rallying fortunes were not yet improving.

Right: *Johnstone Syer/Brian Culcheth at scrutineering, 1974 RAC Rally*

'FRW' RAC Rally; countdown at a stage start for the Triumph Dolomite Sprint of Brian Culcheth/Johnstone Syer

Below: *The Triumph Dolomite Sprint of John Bloxham/Richard Harper prepared by Leyland ST, 1974 RAC Rally*

290

1964-74

1974 RAC Rally; Brian Culcheth on a stage with the Triumph Dolomite Sprint

Allegro Development

Another project which we had been working on during the last months of 1974 was the building of an Allegro 1300 two-door rally car. Austin/Morris division were keen for some publicity for the model and the 1300 cc two-door saloon seemed to be a possibility to run instead of the 1.3 Marina, particularly on rough road events with its front wheel drive and Hydragas suspension.

'Fast' Eddie Burnell testing the Austin Allegro 1.3 at Bagshot, 1974

The car was lighter than the Marina and with some special suspension units supplied by Moulton Developments and a Cooper S spec engine the car was ready for its first test run at the end of the year.

The first run in the car was when we were invited to attend a presentation in Wales, given by John Foden and John Davenport, to introduce entrants and competitors to the proposed Tarren stage.

I was driven to the presentation by Brian Culcheth in the Allegro which was also attended by Chrysler, Castrol, Dunlop, Kleber and Goodyear plus a number of journalists. After lunch we went out to the stage, which was hidden from the road and consisted of a stretch of typical forest track, without the trees, but with the disadvantage of not being a complete circuit. The Allegro was driven over the stage by Brian and I had a ride in a 2-litre Avenger driven by Colin Malkin as well. The highlight of the afternoon for the visiting journalists was when the Avenger became stuck in a fast flowing ford with Colin and myself aboard. As a commercial venture, as far as I know the project did not get off the ground.

The first test session proper for the Allegro was held at Bagshot with 'Fast' Eddie doing the driving, the car covering 26 laps with only a broken driveshaft to hold up proceedings.

The old Dolomite test car (CKV 2K) also had a run at the end of November when Russell Brookes and Andy Dawson were invited to try the car and comment on its general handling and performance; Alan Blake of Avon tyres and David Richards were also present. I was driving the car round with one of the mechanics before the drivers arrived when the car suddenly lost its steering and ground to a halt with the

Special Tuning

Austin Allegro 1.3 engine compartment

right-hand front stub axle sheared off. Jerry the track controller soon organised the six-wheel army recovery truck to pick up the car and a new stub axle was fitted for the test session.

Both Russell and Andy did about twelve laps of the top loop of the rough road course changing to Avon Snow Grip Radials for a few laps. Afterwards, both drivers felt that the suspension was firmer than an Escort and had slightly less grip in first and second gear, although Russell did not agree with Andy that the car needed more power (the 200 bhp Don Moore engine was fitted).

On the commercial side, Leyland ST was busy getting ready for the Speedshow at Olympia, at which we had a stand. In conjunction with Jim Oates at Cowley, a spoiler and rear air dam had been developed for the Marina Coupé and a metallic blue press car was prepared with the aerodynamic aids fitted as the star attraction on the stand.

A long-needed assessment of non-moving parts had been undertaken by John Kerswill and this had identified numerous parts which should be disposed of to make space for new lines and to bring in some cash. Among the items which were offered in a public sale at Abingdon on Saturday 14 December were over 1000 sets of Mini perspex windows, 120 1800 and Triumph 2.5PI Minilite wheels, an eight-port Mini race engine, a Weslake Rover V8 4.2-litre engine, and a Leyland P76 4.4-litre V8 engine, It was unusual to let the

Austin Allegro 1.3 fuel tank

public into the factory for a sale, but our arrangements were agreed by the MG Plant management and security and it went ahead as planned. The first customers were waiting at the gate when we arrived at the factory and we were told by the security police that the first was there at 07.15 hr. We took several thousand pounds that day and cleared out many redundant parts. I couldn't help wondering why Basil Wales had not sold off this stock years ago.

1974 Aerodynamic Aids Leaflet

The Special Tuning staff behind the scenes did sterling work during all these changes and without their enthusiasm John Kerswill would have had very much an uphill struggle. Richard Seth-Smith retained Betty Cross as his secretary when he took over from Basil Wales and it was not until I moved into his seat that I realised how lucky we were to have such a reliable friend to back us up.

1972 Dunlop Rally tyre range. Top to bottom: *M&S crossply, M&S 564 snow tyre, M&S M type, SP 44 radial, M&S R type, SP Rally Super*

Leyland Returns

9

Leyland returns to Motorsport
1975

THE NEW AUSTIN 18/22 (not yet called the Princess) was due to be launched in March, but a suspension modification was required on all the new cars built and awaiting delivery to dealers. The production people at Cowley were trying to find the easiest way to accomplish this task. Richard Seth-Smith was brought into the discussions as Special Tuning had a good size workshop and a team of skilled mechanics. Although Special Tuning had just been relaunched, Richard felt that he could not turn down this request for assistance with the new model launch imminent. We had formed a provisional plan for

Mintex Rally 1975; Pat Ryan/John Gittins, Morris Marina 1.3 moving to a class win

a mini-production line in the workshop to modify all these new cars when at the last moment, Cowley decided that the task of ferrying all the vehicles from Cowley to Abingdon and back was too time consuming and costly. What would have happened to the Special Tuning department if this project had been undertaken, I cannot imagine, but I think our willingness to help scored us a few 'Brownie' points!

The tuning business was slowly expanding but we felt it would be to our advantage if we could install a rolling-road dynamometer to enable us to carry out more of our own development work. Richard fully backed this idea and with his work behind the scenes, we obtained financial approval to purchase a Sun chassis dynamometer. The biggest problem was that it had to be housed in a sound proof building and, as there was insufficient money available to erect a separate building close or adjacent to C Block, we regretfully agreed to sacrifice the space of two working bays in the workshop. The MG facilities people were a wonderful help in procuring secondhand materials to build the booth, with most of the galvanised panels and sound isulation coming from a dismantled paint booth at Cowley.

Granite City Rally 1975; Pat Ryan/John Gittins on a forest stage in the Morris Marina 1.3

We also wanted an engine test-bed, and in anticipation, space was allowed for it in the booth. We had learned about a portable American bolt-on engine dynamometer which connected direct to a mains tap. The agents for these Go-Power units was Piper FM Ltd of Ashford, and with their assistance, we purchased a Go-Power unit, the finance being 'fiddled' through the system as piece of non-capital expenditure at approximately £1700. The unit was installed using a homemade cooling system which enabled us to start testing the Sprint engine.

Team Unipart/Castrol

At the start of 1975 Kevin Best, who was working for David Welch at BLI, became responsible for their rally budget, taking over from Peter Battam who had looked after it since 1971. Richard Seth-Smith got together with Castrol, Unipart and BLI, and at the end of the first week in January he was able to confirm to all parties involved that a central rally budget had been agreed covering a programme of ten events to the end of October. A sum of £16,000 was allocated for car preparation with a further sum of £5,200 to cover mechanics' time and expenses in running the programme. Brian Culcheth would drive the Group 2 Sprint and was to be joined by Pat Ryan in a Morris Marina 1300 in six of the events with the object of winning the 1300 Class. The team was to be known as Team Unipart/Castrol and the list of events was as follows:

Mintex Rally	Sprint & Marina	February
Hackle Rally	Sprint	March
Granite City Rally	Sprint & Marina	April
Welsh Rally	Sprint & Marina	May
Scottish Rally	Sprint & Marina	May/June
Jim Clark Rally	Sprint	July
Avon Tour of Britain	Sprint (Group 1)	August
Burmah Rally	Sprint & Marina	August
Manx Rally	Sprint	September
Dukeries Rally	Sprint & Marina	October

Team Unipart/Castrol 1975; L-to-R: B. Culcheth, J. Syer, J. Gittins, P. Ryan

Leyland Returns

Scottish Rally 1975; Morris Marina 1.3 throws up the stones. Note the 11 inch spot lamps

The first event however, the Tour of Dean, was extra to this programme. Financed by Leyland ST it was to see the first outing of the Allegro together with the Sprint with Brian Culcheth and Johnstone Syer. Russell Brookes was to drive the Allegro, bringing along Andy Bodman as co-driver. There was a test session at Chobham, for Russell to try the car resulting in the differential breaking after ten laps but not before we had confirmed that the latest Hydragas units with a 50 per cent increase on the bump setting at the front were a considerable improvement. Brian Culcheth brought David Welch along from BLI to see the Allegro performing.

The Sprint for the Tour of Dean was on show on the Castrol stand at the Speedshow and could not be removed until the show closed on the Saturday night. Richard Seth-Smith made sure that the car was extricated as soon as possible and two of the mechanics drove it down to Newport.

Scrutineering was held at 06.00 hr next morning and with some optimism, the crews set off on the event, supported by Range Rover and Austin Maxi service cars. Our enthusiasm was short lived when on the first stage Brian made a rare mistake, clouting a bridge with the rear wheel, and bending the axle. Russell Brookes in the Allegro did not last long when the transmission broke and he was also out; just as well this was a try out before the first Team Unipart/Castrol event.

One thing that had become apparent was that the Allegro final drive was too high. We decided to fit a 1.087:1 transfer gear set for the next outing which, with the 4.1 final drive, would give an overall ratio of 4.63:1.

The success of the Triumph Dolomite Sprint on the circuits in 1974 was good enough for Simon Pearson to obtain authorisation for Broadspeed to run two cars in 1975, this time sponsored by Castrol and Piranha Ignitions, but entered by Leyland ST, although we would not have any direct involvement in running the cars. They were smartly painted in silver with black flashes and a Leyland ST decal at the top of the windscreen. A third car would be run by Bill Shaw, also in the British Saloon Car Championship.

A Finish at Last

The first event of the official rally programme was the Mintex Dales with the Sprint and the Marina, Pat Ryan taking John Gittins as co-driver in the Marina. The Marina had been fitted with an eight-port cylinder head and two 40DCOE Weber carburettors prior to Pat Ryan giving it a shakedown at Chobham. The Allegro had been rebuilt with the lower final drive, but two test sessions had resulted in differential pin and drive-shaft failure. We decided to lend the Allegro to Phil Cooper, who would make the entry, to continue the development programme.

The Mintex started and finished at the Selby Fork Hotel, with a *parc fermé* in operation after scrutineering. We used our Range Rover for servicing and Kevin Best brought one of

1975

the BLI Range Rovers as a second service vehicle, the mechanics being kitted out in their new red overalls. The rally was the first outing for the 'official' Unipart/Castrol team and we were pleased that Brian was able to bring the car to the finish in seventh place without any major mechanical troubles. Pat Ryan did better by winning the 1300 cc class with the Marina, while Phil Cooper finished with the Allegro after a stirring drive and at least one broken driveshaft.

In conjunction with the programme of rallies, a series of 'Open Evenings' was organised with assistance from Castrol and Unipart, held at Dealer premises. These featured films, a quiz, a question-and-answer session, and a panel of experts including the drivers. A display of competition cars was put on and the new Leyland ST leisurewear, including the orange ST rally jackets, was offered for sale. These evenings were enthusiastically organised by the dealers with large crowds attending at each venue.

Win in Scotland

Johnstone Syer did not have to travel far from his home at Dunfermline for the next rally on the programme, the Hackle Rally, based on Kirkcaldy, Fife and starting at the premises of the Triumph dealer, Rossleigh Ltd. We were offered garage space for the vehicles by Rossleigh, which was very convenient, with an 'Open Evening' being run the night before the event. The Balgeddie House Hotel, recommended by Johnstone, made us very welcome and we had a very comfortable stay. The rally was run on the Saturday from 08.00 hr until 18.00 hr over fifteen stages in more or less constant sunshine. Brian was really on form and with support from our two Range Rover crews, and stage times consistently in the top three, came home winner a mere 21 seconds in front of the next car, a Ford Escort. This was a tremendous morale booster and we were honoured by *Autosport* magazine with a full front cover colour photograph of the Sprint.

The Marina joined the fray for the next event, the Granite City Rally based on Aberdeen. The BLI Range Rover now had a tow bracket which enabled us to trailer both the rally cars to Aberdeen, once again taking two mechanics with Kevin and myself using the BLI vehicle.

There had been heavy snow over much of the route just before the rally which made the stages very muddy, with some snow still causing problems. Brian and Pat Ryan both performed well with Brian being beaten by three Escorts into fourth position and Pat winning the 1300 cc class. The difference in recorded times between Brian and the winning Escort driven by Roger Clark was only just over 40 seconds which in these national rally sprint events against well developed, lighter and more powerful cars, was respectable.

Following the initial runs with the Allegro, it was obvious that to run yet another model was going to stretch resources, not to mention the complications of servicing a third model. To give the Allegro some exposure, an agreement was reached with Howells of Cardiff, the BL Distributors, to lend the car to them for the remainder of the year. The car was to be sponsored by *The Western Mail* with additional assistance from Castrol and Avon tyres and would be entered by *Western Mail*/Team Howells with Pat Ryan driving when not engaged with the Marina. Pat gave the car runs in two small rallies early in the year and it made its first major appearance in the Welsh Rally, with Dennis Cardell driving.

The Welsh Rally in May was our next event and once again the Sprint and the Marina were in action. We based our operations on Howells of Cardiff, with the two Range Rovers crewed by mechanics this time, with one vehicle detailed to look after each of the rally cars. I used an Austin Maxi with Kevin Best to supervise the service operations.

The Marina was using 5 × 13 inch wheels on the front and 6 × 13 inch wheels on the rear fitted with Dunlop M&S tyres. The Sprint was running regularly on the Minilite 6 × 13 inch Sport wheels now and a further development had been the fitting of front ventilated discs, a servo for the rear brakes and manual rear brake adjusters; both cars had race tyres available for the tarmac stages.

The Marina caused much comment when it appeared at scrutineering sprouting Lucas 11 inch long-range lamps, although Andy Dawson had used them on the *Car & Car Conversions* Marina on the RAC Rally; the lamps came originally from a Foden truck.

The rally was not without its dramas. Brian visited the scenery on the Brechfa 1 stage, at a spot where several cars went off owing to a misleading warning arrow, dropping off the leader board. During the second part of the rally, this stage was used in reverse and this time Brian suffered a broken suspension tie-rod, sustaining a maximum penalty for the stage, finishing eleventh overall.

Meanwhile Pat Ryan in the Marina had broken an axle-shaft on stage 36 but with the aid of his limited-slip differential was able to limp off the stage. The service crews managed to rectify the problem and with his large class lead, held it to the finish to claim the third class victory in three events. The result gave Glen Hutchinson, who was handling the PR for the events, the opportunity to prepare an official press release giving the results of the International Welsh rally, including a fourth in class for the Howells Allegro.

MGB Jumping

The Jubilee version of the MGB GT was launched in May 1974 and the *Daily Mail* planned to advertise a new car competition on TV with a dramatic clip of film of an MGB GT bursting through the front page of the newspaper. We were asked to assist with making this film which was shot on the MG Sports field in Abingdon. A wooden ramp was constructed and 'Fast' Eddie volunteered to drive the car. The MG Development department let us have an old tourer to try out the ramp and after two runs decided on an approach speed of 55 mph to prevent the car from digging in to the turf. When a skid plate had been fitted to the front crossmember, the brand new MGB GT was accelerated at the ramp, bursting through the giant Daily Mail front page quite spectacularly. The new car did not survive unscathed, finishing with damaged suspension and a crease in the bodyshell; not surprising after a heavy landing from about 2½ ft up!

Overleaf top: *'Fast' Eddie Burnell jumps a new MGB GT for a* **Daily Mail** *TV advertisement on the MG sports ground 1975*

Mail
GREAT NEW CAR CONTEST
then a warning
Inside today
Onion man's £500,000
a senior Saudi Arabian
London yesterday.
Short's

Castrol
UNIPART
Castrol
TEAM UNIPART
LUCAS
LUCAS
SOE 8M
UNIPART
Castrol
7
TEAM UNIPART

1975

Scottish Gloom

We were encouraged by recent results with the underdeveloped Sprint and the three class wins with the Marina, but the Scottish in June brought further gloom. A new Sprint had been prepared for this rally, or to be more precise, the old car used in 1974 by John Bloxham (SOE 8M) was reshelled. The Marina appeared at scrutineering sprouting the Lucas 11 inch long-range lamps again. The Scottish was to be as tough as ever, with no less than 44 stages, with the start in Glasgow and the overnight halt and finish at Aviemore.

From the start the new Sprint did not seem to be handling as well as the old FRW and Brian was having difficulty in getting into the top ten on stage times. Through Sunday night and into Monday morning the car maintained a steady rate of progress but on the Kindrogan stage, Brian misjudged an open right-hand bend and the car flew off the road landing upside-down in the trees, luckily without serious injury to himself or Johnstone.

Richard Seth-Smith was following the rally and was on hand to take Brian and Johnstone to Aviemore, Brian nursing a bump on the head, but Johnstone more concerned about his broken hip-flask.

The Marina was having a struggle against the two 1300 works Skodas in the class, and in an attempt to catch them, Pat rolled the car heavily and retired soon after the Dumfries halt, ending the team's Scottish appearance. The only consolation came when, Brian captained a team of rally drivers against a rest-of-the-world team driving Minis supplied by the BL dealer, Macrae & Dick, to win a driving test competition on the ice of the Aviemore skating rink.

Richard Seth-Smith Moves On

One of the problems that Richard Seth-Smith had been battling with was the desire of Unipart to take over the Leyland ST competition parts business. John Kerswill was naturally against the move with discussions coming to a head in June when Richard told Keith Hopkins that he was not prepared to run the Department without the parts business. Richard was told that the parts business was to stay at Abingdon but as the Product PR job was more important, he was asked to go to Redditch to run the Leyland Cars Product PR department. Reluctantly he agreed, with the proviso that he retained overall control of Leyland ST.

Below left: Scottish Rally 1975; Triumph Dolomite Sprint of Brian Culcheth/Johnstone Syer in typical dusty conditions

Two 'Open House' rally forums were included in the schedule for our next visit to Scotland for the Jim Clark Memorial rally starting in Duns. The first forum was held in Kilmarnock at Appleyards (Ayrshire) Ltd where the team arrived to put the Sprint rally car on display. Unipart sent their promotional coach and Christine Dwyer, Roy Choules and Ken Williams were in attendance to assist the dealer with the preparations. The forum was well attended and the team then moved on to Kelso for the second forum at Croall Bryson Ltd where a second successful event was held.

We stayed at a hotel in Cornhill-on-Tweed near Coldstream for the rally which brought Brian a welcome result after the disappointment of the Scottish accident. The route included stages on the Otterburn Ranges and the hard-fought rally saw many retirements. The Sprint suffered a bent steering rack making the car difficult to handle, with insufficient service time to change it, but nevertheless, Brian came home in third position overall; a good result.

Our Second Avon Tour

Ray Hutton of *Autocar* once again accompanied Brian on the Avon Tour of Britain, in the Group 1 Triumph Dolomite Sprint (RDU 983M). The tyre chosen for the event, which permitted one make/type of readily available road tyre, was the Dunlop 205/60 HR 13SP Super. We had been developing an improved exhaust system for the Sprint in conjunction with Janspeed, and this single-box big-bore system had been homologated for the car giving an increase in power and mid-range torque. There was now some interest in the Sprint from private owners and Tony Drummond driving a Sprint sponsored by Cox of Keighley and a second car driven by John Handley and John Clegg were included in a manufacturer's team entry.

The Tour started from the Post House Hotel, Great Barr,

Bill Price ponders over the specification of the Avon Tour of Britain Dolomite Sprint; 1975

Birmingham and as we were concentrating on servicing just Brian's car, we had one Range Rover with two mechanics plus another with myself and Kevin Best out on the event. The experience with the Sprint since the last Tour had ironed out several problems and with Bilstein shock-absorbers now normal fitment, the car went extremely well only to be beaten into second place by Tony Pond driving an Escort.

At the awards presentation in a marquee at the Post House, Brian nearly brought the house down when he planted a chocolate cake in Ray Hutton's face, moments after being presented with it to celebrate his birthday; the cake was inscribed 'Give it plenty'.

The last journey to Scotland was for the Burmah Rally, starting and finishing in Dunoon, with sixteen stages to be covered between midnight and midday. Servicing was banned around the first five stages. On the fourth stage – the Rest and Be Thankful hill climb, this time run from top to bottom – Brian suffered a broken front suspension ball joint and was stranded in the middle of the stage.

Leyland Returns

Avon Tour of Britain 1975; Brian Culcheth Group 1 Dolomite Sprint

Brian Culcheth looks happy with his birthday cake; Avon Tour of Britain 1975

Ray Hutton looks unhappy having just received Brian Culcheth's birthday cake, Avon Tour of Britain 1975

We had seen Brian enter the stage and were driving down the main road to see him come out. When he did not appear, we returned up the hill and looking down could see a car stopped on the stage. With no two-way radio, Kevin and I climbed down the hillside to find it was Brian with broken suspension. There was no time to repair the car which was in a dangerous position with competitors passing every minute, and the car was reluctantly retired. Oh for a two-way radio!

The last Team Unipart/Castrol appearance was on the Manx International Rally in the Isle of Man, but despite our optimism for the car on tarmac, it all went wrong when the car expired at a stage start with a stripped crown wheel. It was not much consolation when talking to Ray Henderson at Triumph later, to hear him say that that was a weak ratio and they always changed the cwp after each rally. With limited finance, we had not changed the differential before the Manx.

TR7 Plans

At the end of 1974 the various existing and proposed car models had been considered for use in a future motor sport programme. The usual considerations were chewed over comparing the ways of promoting the company's products. One new model which did feature strongly was the Triumph TR7, due to be launched in USA in 1975 with a proposed release date in Europe in May 1976. The two-seater 2-litre sports car had the right image and we were told that during its evolution a V8 engine would be fitted.

As early as September 1974 Richard Seth-Smith arranged for a viewing of the new car which was in its early production phase at Speke near Liverpool. I accompanied Richard, Brian and Simon Pearson to the factory and we were shown the car in its various stages of manufacture by the enthusiastic production staff. The car seemed far from ideal in many areas with similar rear axle location to the Sprint, a short wheelbase, single OHC engine and was rather heavy. The wedge shape with the possibility of homologating the right parts, plus the knowledge that a V8 engine was coming, made this model about the only one which had a chance of being developed for rallying.

We had seen prototypes of the SD2, a hatchback replacement for the Dolomite, fitted with a fuel-injected 16-valve Sprint engine and Macpherson strut front suspension, but unfortunately this model was cancelled in the rationalisation programme.

Early in 1975 we managed to obtain an old LHD development TR7 from Triumph engineering with the news that plans for an official programme in 1976 were being formed. It was not going to be easy to develop the car but first it had to be homologated. Careful consideration was given to the existing specification with the result that we decided to list the 16-valve Sprint cylinder head, to enable us virtually to transplant the Sprint rally engine into the car. The Sprint gearbox was homologated as an option, as the 77 mm five-speed gearbox was not yet available and it would take time to produce close-ratio gears for it. The heavy duty axle which would be standard with the five-speed gearbox was also listed as an option.

RAC Rally 1975; B. Culcheth/J. Syer on the way to winning the Group 1 Category in the Triumph Dolomite Sprint

The certificate certifying that 1,000 cars had been manufactured in twelve months was based on LHD cars built for the USA. Ron Elkins prepared the FIA homologation forms which were submitted to the RAC and we were advised that the FIA had approved the model for use in international competitions, from 1 October 1975.

A bodyshell was obtained and work started on the preparation of the first car, entrusted to Martin Reade, one of the most experienced mechanics in the Department. Safety Devices made a prototype roll-cage and with some unofficial assistance from Triumph engineering, the specification of a rally axle was drawn up. The plan was to use a Salisbury 4HA differential assembly, as used on Jaguar models, with new heavy-duty axle tubes but retaining the original hub bearings.

1976

Drivers for 1976

To run two Triumph TR7s in 1976 would mean finding another driver to team up with Brian Culcheth. From the Company's point of view there was a desire to use British drivers as anyone signing up to drive with Leyland Cars would have to agree to make himself available for promotions and dealer activities and it was felt that a Brit would be most suitable.

The proposed programme was discussed with three drivers, Will Sparrow, Russell Brookes and Tony Pond. Russell Brookes was already a British Leyland employee at Rover, and although I had a brief chat with him at the Hilton Hotel in Stratford-on-Avon apparently he was not prepared to leave his job with BL, which would be necessary to meet all the promotional commitments as well as the rallies. I visited Will Sparrow at his house near Alcester and also Tony Pond at his home at Uxbridge. Will was not too sure about the suitability of the TR7 or whether he wanted a full time works drive, Tony's questions were more to do with the car. We had fitted the old LHD car with some Koni front and rear shock-absorbers to stiffen the suspension, and it was a short drive in this standard USA specification car, and our straight forward approach which, I believe, made up Tony's mind.

The third team member, Pat Ryan, was invited to drive either a Marina or Allegro in support of the TR7 programme in 1976 with the objective being to win the 1300 cc class again.

The news became public knowledge on 22 October 1976 when a glossy press folder was sent out labelled 'Leyland Cars in Motor Sport 1976 – Race & Rally programme'. This detailed the rally programme, the Dolomite race programme, the new Jaguar race programme and the Leyland Cars Mini Challenge. The Abingdon team was at last back into rallying officially, after a break of five years.

Although the TR7 was taking up many man hours there was still the continuing 1975 programme to maintain. The last rally for the Group 2 Sprint and the Marina was the Lindisfarne, and not the Dukeries as scheduled, with Brian finishing third overall and Pat Ryan winning the 1300 class again, a total of four wins out of six events for the Marina.

RAC Group 1 Sprint

The decision was taken to enter Brian in a Group 1 car in the RAC Rally because it would have a good chance of winning the category. In contrast a Group 2 car would be unlikely to gain an advertisable result against the strong international competition. The Tour of Britain car was prepared for the RAC being painted in the newly designed Leyland Cars livery of

Leyland Returns

red/white/blue. The new livery was largely the work of Alan Zafer with asistance from BLI who also produced a manual in colour, of designs to suit all Leyland Cars' vehicles, including commercials.

The Allegro was also entered in the RAC, having been returned from Howells, with Pat Ryan being accompanied by Mike Nicholson. The engine now sported an eight-port cylinder head with twin 40 DCOE carburettors and with some further small modifications to the transmission and gearbox we hoped for better reliability. The Marina 1.3 (NBL 782M) was loaned to Phil Cooper who had Andy Marriott as co-driver. Andy was also on a reporting assignment for BBC Radio and planned to give regular interviews during the rally.

TR7 Progress

To build a new rally car from scratch is quite a task, although at this stage we had a good 16-valve Sprint engine to go in the car which meant that the chassis and suspension could take priority. Weight would be a problem and some of this was reduced by removing the lateral crash bars in the doors (15 lb each) and modifying the bumpers which weighed in at about 48 lb each; nearly 130 lb already. The roll cage was quite a problem as it encroached into the passenger space close to the driver and co-drivers heads. The fascia had to be rebuilt

Right: First Triumph TR7 rally car being prepared in Leyland ST workshop; 1976

Phil Cooper/Andy Marriott in the Abingdon Marina 1.3, RAC Rally 1975

I suppose it was wishful thinking to expect the Allegro to last an RAC and, sure enough, on the Olivers Mount stage at Scarborough the transmission broke. The Sprint went extremely well and Brian brought it home first in the Group 1 Category (the objective), first in Class and sixteenth overall.

because the standard unit was based on a printed circuit, this being necessary so we could select the instruments we wanted. The tachometer used on the first cars was a small diameter Smiths Formula 1 unit, rubber mounted.

The standard subframe was modified to take the Sprint engine and in the absence of the five speed gearbox, a Sprint overdrive gearbox was prepared with a special propshaft to suit.

1976

Triumph TR7 2-litre rally car engine compartment

Martin Reade fits ventilated disc brakes to the first TR7 rally car

The brakes were Lockheed ventilated discs at the front, with drums at the rear while we waited for a supply of rear discs. Twin servos were employed, while twin master cylinders, operated via a balance bar with a hand adjustment on the fascia, were mounted on a special pedal box. A selection of Bilstein struts and rear shock-absorbers were ordered, while Girling gas pressurised units were also to be evaluated. To improve weight distribution a lightweight Varley battery was moved to the boot.

The main component delays were with the axle and the close ratio gears for the five-speed gearbox. The Engineering procurement manager at Canley, an extremely prickly character to deal with, was processing the order with a request for part of the order to be completed during the first two months of 1976. Although we intended to compete in all the RAC Rally Championship rallies with the TR7 it was soon obvious that we would miss at least the first two events.

Service Vehicles

With a full programme ahead, I was determined that we should have better service vehicles. The Range Rover was fast, had the advantage of four wheel drive, and could tow a trailer, but with its relatively small carrying capacity and high floor height, it was not suitable for carrying a comprehensive spares kit plus a range of wheels/tyres.

Leyland Returns

Unfortunately there was nothing available in the Leyland range similar in size to the Ford Transit so we decided to use the new Sherpa. We ordered two to start with, one with a side loading door, and kitted them out with an extensive set of Linvar plastic bins. The vehicle with the side door was fitted with a rear bulkhead allowing access to the oil, water, petrol, jacks, axle stands, tools, etc through the rear doors.

Wheel changing is always a time-consuming business so a source of compressed air was located in the form of a modifed air conditioning compressor. Kits of brackets were available to bolt the compressor straight on to the 1798 cc petrol engine, and the compressor fed into two Leyland truck brake tanks, driven through an electric clutch. Air hose connections were provided at the rear of the vehicle. All the mechanics had to do when they arrived at a service point was plug in the air guns, run the engine at a fast tick-over and turn the switch on the dash to energise the electric clutch; this system would run two guns flat out. Initially the compressors had a tendency to throw conrods, but this was solved by fitting a no-loss oil separator to retain the oil.

A full length roof rack with ladder and high power flood lamps were also fitted and finally the vehicles were painted in the new Leyland Cars colours.

New Manager for Leyland ST

Richard Seth-Smith had moved to Redditch as the Product Affairs Manager for Leyland Cars while we waited for a replacement to be announced. It came as rather a surprise when I was offered the position of Manager of Leyland ST, reporting to Richard Seth-Smith who retained responsibility for the department and control of all motor sport activities. I was concerned that I might not have the time to devote to the rally programme and hoped that John Kerswill would continue looking after the commercial business as thoroughly and successfully as he had done so far.

This left me with a vacancy to fill within the Department, a new Workshop Supervisor. There were a number of people working in the factory who had been in the old Competitions Department and I also had experienced personnel within the workshop to consider, although the next in line, Bill Burrows, was retiring shortly. After a number of interviews, Den Green was selected as the new Workshop Supervisor. The announcement that I had been appointed Manager was made on 19 January 1976 with Den Green receiving his offer letter on 19 February.

We had already increased the workshop strength by recruiting Bob Whittington and Dudley Pike from within the factory, both ex-competitions department mechanics. A further increase in mechanics would have to be made when headcount approval had been obtained, which was not without its difficulties.

Shellsport Tour of Dean

As predicted the TR7s were not ready for the first Championship rally, the Shellsport Tour of Dean. The work load was such that we decided to enter only two cars, the Allegro 1.3 and a Dolomite Sprint for new boy Tony Pond and co-driver David Richards. The Sprint was the Group 1 car driven by Brian in the RAC so successfully, retained in this form for the Dean.

The Allegro managed a finish this time and a class win, while Tony, despite some minor mechanical problems, in-

Service stop on the 1976 Snowman Rally for Brian Culcheth/ Johnstone Syer

1976

The new TR7 rally car emerges from the workshop for the first time

cluding an alternator change, had a hectic drive to get into the finish control with less than a minute to spare. The effort was rewarded by a Group 1 category win in his first drive for Leyland Cars.

The Sprints were brought out again for the Snowman Rally in Scotland, with FRW looking resplendent in her new Leyland Cars livery. There was quite a lot of snow about for the rally and we were glad to have some narrow Dunlop snow tyres to put on for some of the stages. Tony Pond on his second drive with the team was out of luck when the engine lost oil pressure with main bearing failure. The Allegro was entered again but retired with a trifling electrical fault, when the battery master switch cut out the ignition. By the time the crew had discovered the problem they were out of time. Brian and Johnstone finished fifth overall in the wintry conditions. On the way home, Brian, Kevin Best and I visited Brian's house on the Ardmurchan peninsula to see how the building work was progressing.

The TR7 build programme was progressing slowly and although we had told the press that we were aiming for the Mintex for the new cars first outing, it was becoming obvious that the Welsh would be a more realistic target. The two Dolomites and the Allegro were entered in the Mintex Rally with Tony driving the Group 1 car. The Allegro again broke the transmission but Tony won the Group 1 category with Brian coming home seventh in the faithful FRW.

TR7 Testing

The first car (KDU 497N) had its first test run on 4 March 1976. We took the car to Finmere airfield near Bicester to sort out the specification of the brakes. Tony drove the car because Brian was on another assignment, and Ian Bentley from AP Racing attended. Although a rear disc brake set-up was on the drawing board we were running with rear drums until the parts were available. Most of the day was spent changing servos, master cylinders and rear wheel cylinders to arrive at a spec which Tony felt would be satisfactory to start the testing proper.

At this stage the rear suspension was the standard layout with parallel lower links and the two angled top links. On 9 March the test car was taken to Bagshot for it's first run in anger on a rough dirt road with both Brian and Tony present. Although we only did about thirteen laps changing shock-absorbers, adjusting the ride height, both drivers were fairly happy with the feel of the car. Visibility from the cockpit came in for some criticism with Tony favouring the headlamps in their raised position to enable him to 'point' the car accurately. The electrically operated headlamps mechanism had been removed to save weight and a simple strut fitted to give the headlamps two positions: up or down.

It was then back to Scotland for the Granite City Rally based on Aberdeen. The poor Allegro failed again with broken transmission and Brian had a brake caliper ripped off by a cracked disc causing his retirement. Tony demonstrated his talent with an excellent fourth overall in the group 1 Sprint, comfortably winning the Group 1 category.

Leyland Returns

1976

Austin Allegro retires on the Granite City Rally. L-to-R: Mike Nicholson, Bill Price and Pat Ryan

No, not the three stooges. Bill Price, Mike Nicholson and Pat Ryan on the Granite City Rally 1976

Left: *2-litre 16-valve engine of TR7 rally car*

The pressure was really on now for us to be ready for the Welsh Rally which was to be held only a few days before the European launch of the TR7. To keep the press happy a combined test session and press day was arranged at the MVEE track at Chobham. *Autocar, Motor, Autosport* and *Motoring News* attended, with various changes to suspension spec being made in between giving the journalists rides in the

First rough road test for TR7 at Bagshot

Leyland Returns

car. The five-speed 77mm gearbox was fitted but still without the close-ratio gears which still seemed to be light years away. The car was received with enthusiasm and the following week glowing reports appeared in the magazines, with comments like 'TR7 – Stratos beater' and 'Fantastic' taking the headlines. This all seemed a bit premature with the car only on its *third* test session!

two cars in time for the Welsh Rally.

The Allegro had been handed over to Howells and Pat Ryan was now to drive the Group 1 Dolomite Sprint on future events with Mike Nicholson.

Welsh Rally 1976; Bill Price talks to Brian Culcheth just before the start in Cardiff

Welsh Début

As the close ratio gears were not going to be available, for the next test session the Sprint gearbox with overdrive was fitted, using a gear lever knob similar to the type used on the Austin Healey 3000 rally cars. On 7 April we went off to Dinas Mill in Wales with the TR7 to test the car in rally conditions and spent all day sorting out shock-absorber and spring specifications. We also tried the latest Dunlop A2 'forest racer' tyres which were proving to be very quick on the smoother stages. Although we intended to use Bilstein shock-absorbers on events, we also tried some Girling gas-pressurised units to assess the specification for customer sales. One problem which did become evident was a certain amount of axle tramp dependent on the tyres fitted.

On this test session, we were accompanied by a BBC Midlands TV film crew under the direction of Derek Smith, who were making a documentary around the development and early competition life of the Triumph TR7. This was intended to be a no-holds-barred film, although the cameraman was warned not to get in the way on events.

We returned to Finmere for a brief session to try alternative axle link bushes and then it was a race to finish the

We duly turned up for the Welsh Rally at Cardiff and the cars in their patriotic livery were the major talking point. The mechanics were now getting the Sherpa service vehicles as they wanted them and we were all set to go. My service vehicle was a Marina Estate with Den Green accompanying me. I never like starting rallies in the dark but at 21.00hr on Thursday 6 May 1976, the TR7's set off on their first event.

TR7 cockpit; note flexible mounting for the tachometer and overdrive switch on the gear lever knob

The excitement of the appearance of the cars was soon forgotten when on the first stage Brian's car was overheating severely and was obviously in serious trouble. Although the mechanics did what they could the head gasket had failed and Brian was out. What a start!

Tony was getting used to the car, never having driven a stage in the dark, but after eight stages as the cars approached Devil's Bridge, the oil pressure started to flag. On stage nine the engine lost its oil pressure and there was a heavy rumble from the main bearings. To prevent a major engine blow-up we reluctantly decided to withdraw the car at Devil's Bridge. The service crew looking after the Sprint

1976

remained on the event and after some problems, Pat brought the car home third in class.

This was naturally a very disappointing start to the TR7 programme but the head gasket problem was not altogether surprising. Broadspeed had already identified a problem with the Dolomite Sprint race cars and had produced some special cylinder head studs. It was a source of great annoyance and frustration that only one set could be made available for the Welsh engines and they were fitted to the engine in Tony Pond's car, built by Broadspeed (Culch had a Don Moore engine).

BLI asked us to prepare a car for the Lucien Bianchi rally in Belgium and a new Dolomite Sprint was entered for Brian Culcheth and Johnstone Syer. Further developments had been taking place with head gaskets but unfortunately a new, untried, latex-coated gasket was fitted for this event. This was a costly mistake resulting in the car's retiring with a blown head gasket early in the rally.

both cars and with further detailed suspension work it was off to Ayr for the Scottish. The BBC film crew were following us all the time now and included in their footage the team service briefing in the hotel before the rally.

The weather was quite good for the rally which was due to return to Ayr for the overnight halt before continuing to Aviemore for the finish. The engine gremlins struck again when after ten stages Tony Pond lost a piston, and with oil being forced out of the water pump aperture the car was retired. Meanwhile, Brian's car went on to three cylinders and limped into the overnight halt at Ayr. We had a quick conference and Richard Seth-Smith decided to take an unprecedented step to enable one car to continue in the rally and gain a bit more exposure. A phone call to Abingdon soon had the stores van on its way with the spare test engine. A plan was formed to change the engine immediately after the restart, using the premises of the local Leyland Cars dealer. Next morning the team of mechanics was assembled, and as

Scottish Rally

Investigation of the Tony Pond engine revealed that the cylinder block had fractured in the area of the centre main bearings. Because this had occurred on a number of engines, a Broadspeed modification was introduced in the form of a 'ladder' to brace the bottom of the cylinder block.

Modified head gaskets and studs were now available for

soon as Brian arrived, the doors of the workshop were shut tight and the race against time began. In just over 1 hour 20 minutes the lads changed the engine and Brian and Johnstone were away.

The average speed required to keep in the rally would have given the local law officers grey hairs but they made the next stage at the Loch Lomond Wild Life Park still in the event.

Leyland Returns

Den and I had followed in our Rover 3500 and caught up with the rally car in a layby alongside Loch Lomond where the engine had lost power. Advancing the ignition and tigtening the distributor cured the problem and the car continued. It went extremely well over the Rest & Be Thankful hill climb but on the Glen Kinglass military road, with the car airborne over a jump, the engine exploded, depositing pieces of conrod, etc on the tarmac. So ended another disastrous outing; our attempt to give the car some extra exposure had failed, despite our 'illegal' engine swop. Pat Ryan did not have a very good rally either only managing fifth in class with the Sprint.

The Jim Clark rally was next on the programme but we decided that we would miss this event to concentrate on sorting out our engine problems. We were already committed to a two-car entry in the Texaco Tour of Britain with Brian and Tony in Dolomite Sprints, and in addition, the drivers were anxious to improve the traction of the TR7.

With advice from Triumph Engineering we fabricated the first Panhard link set-up on KDU, similar to the arrangement on the Dolomite Sprint. Two test sessions at Donington at the end of July and the beginning of August proved that the Panhard link suspension had made a significant improvement to traction and reduced the axle tramp. Tony came away from this last session with renewed confidence and looking forward to the Burmah Rally.

Brian Culcheth waits for the next race while co-driver Ray Hutton talks to Bill Price, Texaco Tour of Britain 1976

To improve communications, I hired some Pye two-way radios from a company in Wales and these were fitted to the rally cars and service vehicles. The range was not very good and reliability was poor but it was a start.

The result achieved by Brian in 1975 gave us some confidence for a good result in the Tour of Britain with Tony, last year's winner, now on our side! The engine gremlins were still with us when at the Cadwell Park test Tony's engine broke again having felt very rough since the start of the event. Brian had better luck; in the first race the accelerator pedal jammed down under the throttle stop forcing Brian to use the ignition key to slow the engine. Brian beat Ari Vatanen on all the stages but lost out on the race circuits where he was shunted off by Ari on one occasion. Despite nursing a bent steering rack, Brian came home second overall for the second year running behind Ari Vatanen. Poor Tony was becoming very disenchanted with Broadspeed engines.

Burmah Finish

The 1976 Burmah Rally saw our first result with the TR7. On the first stage Tony made a mistake and went off the road and, although undamaged, just could not get going; very frustrating, particularly as Richard Seth-Smith was able to talk to the crew on the radio. Brian had an early spin and there was also a shortage of the Dunlop A2 tyres which reduced the axle tramp and were quicker. There was no doubt that we were the poor relation as far as Dunlop was concerned at this stage, without a winning car. Richard was so worried with the poor showing of the cars so far, that he had a word with Brian and said to him, 'Get to the finish whatever you do!' Brian drove steadily and in the dusty conditions, came home sixteenth overall to save the day. We still had the logistical problems of running two models on rallies but this did not prevent Pat Ryan from giving us a very good result in Group 1 with a win in RDU.

Much badgering of Neville Key, manager of the prototype procurement department at Canley, had eventually produced a handful of close ratio gears for the 77mm five speed gearbox. Ken Tomlinson, with the blessing of his boss, Laurie Knight, built some gearboxes with the new gears and these were fitted to the cars for the Manx International Rally. The drivers had looked forward to the all-tarmac Manx ever since sampling the car on the tarmac at Chobham test track, but with no tyre experience with the car we went to Cadwell Park with Dunlop to sort out tyres and suspension. We ordered 8 inch rear Minilite wheels to use with the latest Dunlop slicks.

The Isle of Man has a very faithful, long serving BMC/Leyland Cars dealer, Mylchreest Motors, who were looking forward to 'works' participation on their home territory. On the crossing from Liverpool, BBC TV filmed an interview on deck for the documentary, discussing the prospects for the event; glad the sea was smooth!

Pat Ryan changed his co-driver for the Manx, which permitted reconnaissance of the stages, taking Fred Gallagher who had some experience of pace notes, in the Group 1 Dolomite. The team was invited to a party at the home of Brian Mylchreest before the event, which was very generous and very enjoyable.

From the start, Tony was on the pace closely followed by Brian behind the Escort of Vatanen and the Porsche of Curley. The cars seemed at last to be competitive and apart from a broken engine mouting on Brian's car, which was fixed in the front drive of Brian Mylchreest's house, no major mechanical problems were experienced. Tony hit a bank bending the front of the car, and then spent some time with one headlamp up and the other down. Brian was a little annoyed at the finish when he realised that he had missed out on fourth overall by only 1 second from the Porsche of Brian Nelson. He actually lost 24 seconds to Nelson when he had to drive on the ignition switch for eight miles when the broken engine mounting jammed the throttle open.

With Tony third and Pat Ryan ninth the three cars also won the manufacturer's team prize. The Mylchreest family were delighted and arranged full page advertising in the local paper to celebrate.

During the summer we were asked what we could do

The service team at the start of the 1976 season. L-to-R: M. Reade, J. West, L. Bowman, W. Burrows (Foreman), W. Price, B. Moylan, G. Wiffen, E. Burnell

Leyland Returns

with a Triumph 2500 which Tony Pond was to drive on the International Caravan Rally. In the parts bins I had seen the original manifolds that were used on the Triumph 2.5 on the 1970 Scottish Rally, complete with carburettors and after some discussion with Den, Bill Burrows and Tony we decided to fit them, retaining the engine in otherwise standard form. Some uprated shock-absorbers and rear springs were also fitted with competition brake material front/rear. The car was driven with considerable enthusiasm by Tony with his regular co-driver, Dave Richards beside him, and it was only caravan damage at the finish that denied Tony and Dave first place.

puncture, and Pat Ryan was second in Group 1.

Broadspeed was contracted to run the Jaguar coupé racing programme and with the news that Richard Seth-Smith was moving to work for Fiat, there were rumours that Leyland Cars was to appoint an overall supremo to supervise all aspects of the Leyland Cars motor sport programme.

Right: *Tony Pond/David Richards making waves on the Castrol 76 Rally in the TR7*

Below right: *Pat Ryan/Mike Nicholson Group 1 Dolomite Sprint on the Castrol 76 Rally*

Brian Culcheth and Johnstone Syer (in hats) look dejected after retiring from the 1976 Lindisfarne Rally

All three cars were out on the Lindisfarne, although the TR7's were still using the race camshafts partially due to pressure from Redditch to use the Broadspeed spec but also due to shortage of the Don Moore Group 2 cam. Both Brian and Tony were complaining of lack of torque in the forests, but this did not worry Brian because on the third stage he slid off and then the ignition failed with a small wire in the distributor broken. Tony finished ninth overall with Pat Ryan first in Group 1 to salvage a result.

Our long term trade sponsors, Castrol, were looking for a good result on the Castrol Rally held in Wales and both cars were now fitted with the Don Moore camshaft. Although losing about 4 bhp at the top end, the torque band dropped by about 1500 rpm with pleasing results. Tony used some fabricated short steering arms, and both drivers were achieving top three stage times with this new spec. Tony obliged with third overall, Brian eighth, after losing time with an eight-mile

1976 RAC Rally

Two new cars were prepared for the RAC Rally incorporating the latest modifications, with the parallel link/Panhard rod rear suspension, incorporating the latest fabricated top link section. The two RAC engines were built by Don Moore with our own limited staff only able to cope with the Dolomite engine build programme. Don Moore had designed a modification to strengthen the bottom end of the cylinder block. This involved making special steel main bearing caps with extra bolts which tied the cylinder block together.

With the RAC coming up, we entered Tony in the Raylor Rally to test the new high-geared steering rack (which we had been able to get, at last, from Alford & Alder), and to finalise the RAC suspension spec, this time with Mike Nicholson co-driving. The conditions were typical RAC and it was with some satisfaction that Tony achieved our first win with the TR7.

The RAC started in Bath and there was tremendous interest in our cars. Many schools and hospitals had been

1976

Leyland Returns

Loading the Leyland Sherpa service vans at Abingdon

Tony Pond/Mike Nicholson winning the 1976 Raylor Rally in the 2-litre TR7

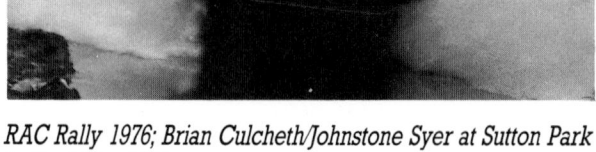

RAC Rally 1976; Brian Culcheth/Johnstone Syer at Sutton Park in the 2-litre TR7

encouraged to adopt a rally driver; for example Brian visited the Bath & Wessex Hospital School and had a enthusiastic welcome; pictures and photos of the cars adorned the wards.

On the rally, Tony started brilliantly to hold second place for most of the first day and night until a front wheel puncture lost him 6 minutes off the road. Brian ran into a gate post on stage 5 in the Forest of Dean, losing 40 seconds and later spun on the Blidworth stage dropping to 41st overall. Kielder forest was very rough and Brian found the axle tramp problem returning, unaware that the locating tubes for the top axle links were starting to split.

The tubes were repaired twice, once at Carlisle and once with tyre levers welded in place for added strength. At the half-way halt at Bath, plans were made to fit new locating tubes. On the run-in to Bath the gearbox lost all but fourth gear but Brian made the halt with Den and me in close attendance in a Rover 3500.

Next morning at the local dealer the mechanics managed a gearbox change and fitted new suspension support tubes in 52 minutes, a magnificent effort. Tony retired in Wales with the same suspension problem which had afflicted Brian, but Brian, despite the new gearbox, was forced to complete the rally with only three gears working in the new box. They had restarted from Bath in seventeenth place but pulled up to ninth at the finish. The Dolomite blew its engine in Kielder early in the rally.

Change At The Top
Towards the end of the year rumours mounted concerning the appointment of a Leyland Cars motor sport supremo; the rumours included the name Mike Parkes. It was known within Leyland Cars that Alan Edis was keen to take over control of motor sport activities and he was in fact responsible for recruiting the new man. Simon Pearson was responsible for liaison between race specialists and Leyland Cars and it was as he arrived for a meeting with Alan Edis that he walked in on a discussion between Alan and John Davenport. John was running the Press Office at the RAC Motor Sport Division and had, of course, considerable experience as an international co-driver.

The rumours had, of course, caused all sorts of speculation as to who would be appointed, and the concensus of opinion in the department was that they hoped it was a rally man and not someone race orientated. So when the news was announced that John Davenport was to be the Director of Motor Sport for Leyland Cars, most people breathed a sigh of relief.

Although John Davenport was not due to start officially until 1 January, he attended a motor sport meeting at Abingdon in the Board room in December. My responsibilities were to remain unchanged, with the administration of the rally programme and overall responsibility for Leyland ST, with John Kerswill looking after sales and marketing. The year ended with a note of optimism for an improved showing in 1977.

—1977—

1977 – John Davenport Takes Over
So with the New Year, John Davenport arrived at Abingdon. At Leyland ST we had a small showroom, really too small for even one car but which had been used to display some of the leisurewear and tuning kits right at the corner of C block. With the arrival of John Davenport, an office had to be provided which was a bit grander than anything available, so the showroom got the chop.

When the press release was sent out outlining the 1977 programmes, there was a change in title, the glossy brochure being labelled 'Leyland Motorsport 1977'. The subsections within the folder were headed:

TR7 Rallying
Dolomite Sprint Rallying
Jaguar XJ5.3C Racing
Mini Racing
Unipart F3 Racing

We had no direct involvement at Abingdon in the Jaguar or F3 Racing, although John Davenport was in overall control. The Mini Racing section detailed the Mini Challenge in which private competitors could compete in a series of races throughout the year for cash prizes with a new Mini 1275 GT going to the championship winner.

The Jaguar programme was to be continued by Broadspeed and the F3 racing, sponsored by Unipart, was using the Dolomite Sprint 16-vlave engine.

Our interest was the twelve-event rally programme for the TR7, including six continental events including the Tour of Elba rally, 24 Hours of Ypres and Tour of Corsica. In addition the Dolomite Sprint would compete in the RAC Rally Championship including the RAC Rally. The only thing that was missing from the press release, which was picked up by the motoring press, was the names of the co-drivers to accompany Brian Culcheth, Tony Pond and Pat Ryan.

BLI had paid into the 1976 rally budget and this continued for 1977, although Kevin Best of BLI had a bit of a battle when the question of the continental events was being considered. Although John Davenport wanted to dictate what events he could do, BLI put their foot down, making it clear that as long as they were footing the overseas bill, they would have a say in choice of events. The department was now under the control of Product Planning with John Davenport reporting to director, Alan Edis.

The first event for the Sprint, the Tour of Dean, was a disaster, with Pat Ryan retiring following an accident. Although the co-driver situation had not been resolved officially, Mike Nicholson was with Pat on the Dean and looked like continuing for the rest of the year.

Boucles of Spa
The rear discs were now ready for the TR7 and the installation was tested at Finmere just after Christmas. The latest Don Moore spec engine was now fitted with 48DCOE Weber carburettors instead of the 45s used last year.

Before the official programme started, arrangements were made to enter Tony Pond in the Boucles of Spa Rally in Belgium. Agreement had been reached, just for this event, for Fred Gallagher to accompany Tony and with two Sherpas and a Range Rover we travelled over to Spa for the event. On the motorway the other side of Brussels, the engine on one of the Sherpas lost compression, with the result that Den and I had to motor back to Brussels where we bought a set of pistons from the local Leyland dealer. These were fitted by the mechanics at a roadside filling station.

The weather was not very pleasant for the rally, but despite the ice and on one stage, very muddy conditions, Tony was up with the leaders. Stig Blomqvist led initially in a Saab but when his gearbox broke, Tony took the lead which he held to the finish. This was the first international win for the TR7 and also a good try out for the Tony Pond/Fred Gallagher partnership.

The car was still suffering from bad axle tramp and it was clear that we would have to concentrate on sorting it out before the next rally. Shortly after returning from Spa, we took the Boucles car to Bagshot with new links for the rear suspension, fitted with a variety of types of bushes. Some

Leyland Returns

TRIUMPH TR7 RALLY CAR

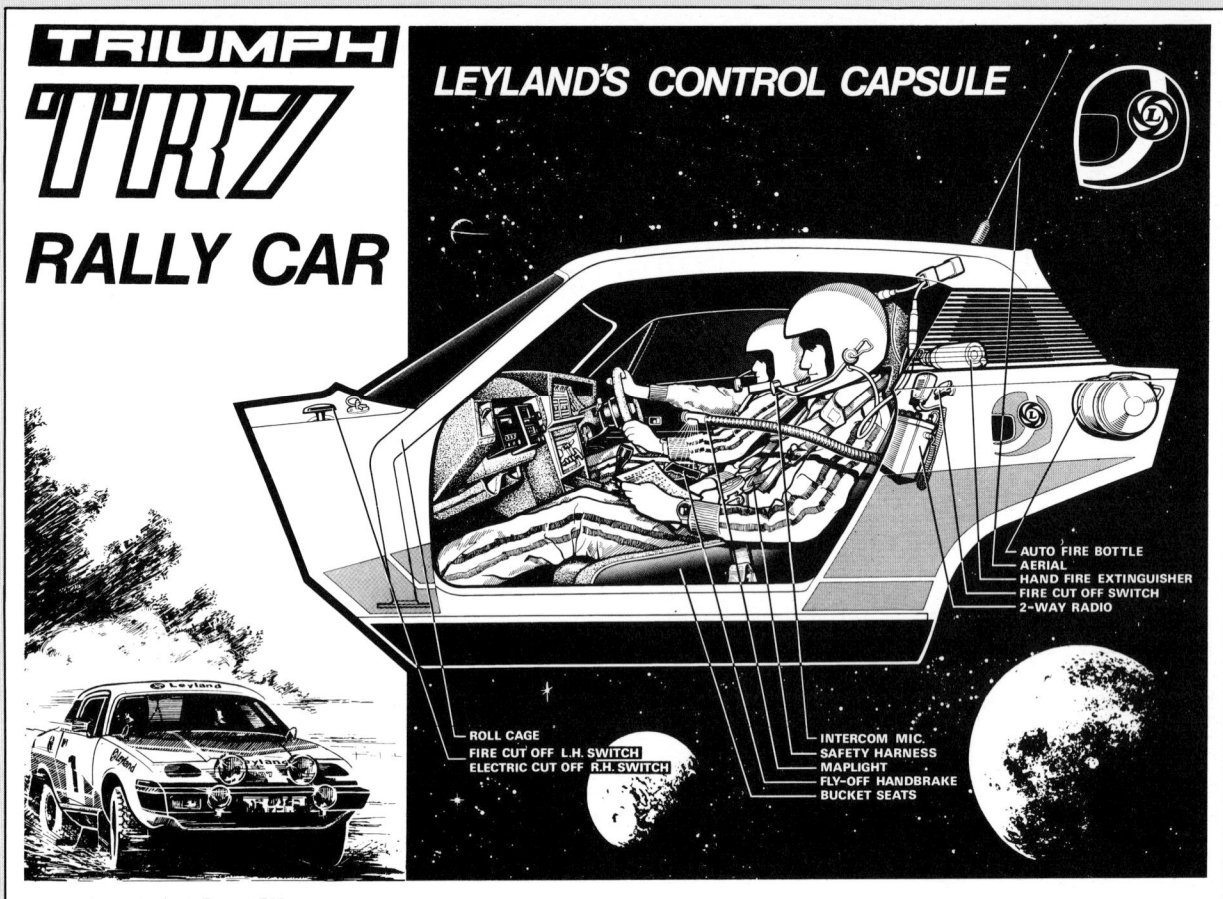

LEYLAND'S CONTROL CAPSULE

- ROLL CAGE
- FIRE CUT OFF L.H. SWITCH
- ELECTRIC CUT OFF R.H. SWITCH
- AUTO FIRE BOTTLE
- AERIAL
- HAND FIRE EXTINGUISHER
- FIRE CUT OFF SWITCH
- 2-WAY RADIO
- INTERCOM MIC.
- SAFETY HARNESS
- MAPLIGHT
- FLY-OFF HANDBRAKE
- BUCKET SEATS

From inside a Leyland rally Triumph TR7 speeding down a special stage—in the forest or on a tarmac track—the world appears to fly past. Sometimes the car takes off in a big way on brows and bumps. And there is always the frightening prospect in motorsport that the car could collide, overturn and, maybe, catch fire.

Leyland has given its rally TR7 crews the best kind of protection to guard against these possibilities. Driver and co-driver are cocooned in a snug capsule, separated from the rest of the car.

A four-point fixing safety harness (with webbing over the shoulders) clamps each crew member firmly into his bucket seat to contain violent movement in every direction. Even if the car overturns, the occupants will stay in their seats, like peas in a pod.

The crew's TR7 capsule is encased in a roll-cage of strong, inter-linked steel tubes to prevent the roof and pillars caving in if the car overturns. The TR7 already has an extra tough shell, ideal for competitions. A laminated windscreen (standard on the TR7) reduces the chance of stone-damage and flying glass. As additional insurance, the crew wear helmets while competing on high speed tests.

In case of a collision, all electrical systems can be cut off with one switch to reduce fire risks. If a fire should break out, another switch will set off an automatic fire extinguisher to cover all compartments of the car. Clearly marked fire and electrical cut-out master switches are positioned inside the car (for the crew) and on each side of the bonnet in front of the windscreen (for outside helpers) and a sharp pull on either does the trick.

Other advanced rallying aids are provided for Leyland's rally TR7 drivers. A two-way radio connects the car to its service vehicle miles away; an intercom built into the helmets allows the crew to talk to each other over the powerful roar of the engine; a Halda distance recorder gives the navigator, equipped with an electronic clock, a precise read-out of his position.

While rally cars remain just about earth-bound, Leyland makes sure that its Triumph TR7 crews work in acceptable conditions of efficiency, safety and comfort. Over and out!

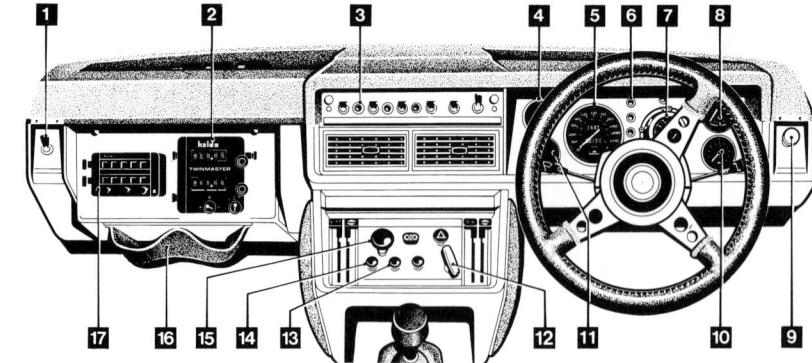

1 Two way radio switch	6 Warning light cluster	10 Oil pressure gauge	14 Map light
2 Distance recorder	7 Rev. counter	11 Temp gauge	15 Co-drivers horn
3 Auxiliary lights and controls	8 Battery condition gauge	12 Electrical cut off switch	16 Map pocket
4 Fuel gauge	9 Brake balance control	13 Halda light	17 Electronic clock
5 Speedometer			

Artwork by Technical Publications Dept., Leyland Cars-Service

Boucles de Spa 1977; Tony Pond/Fred Gallagher at the finish after winning the rally in a TR7

Left: *Unusual promotional leaflet featuring the TR7 'capsule'*

progress was made and a repeat visit next day resulted in a top link 2 inches shorter than before, being settled on for the Mintex Rally.

Mintex Rally

One of the problems of fitting disc brakes to the rear of the TR7 was the provision of a legal handbrake. The calipers we were using were Jaguar, incorporating a handbrake linkage with two small pads, but because of the small clearances we decided to disconnect the cables after scrutineering to avoid any danger of ripping the mechanism off. Although Fred Gallagher had accompanied Tony Pond in Belgium, the decision that he would become Tony's regular partner was not made until just over a week before the Mintex. The decision to turn down David Richards in favour of Fred caused some ill feeling in the Russell Brookes team as Fred had agreed in principal to go with Russell for 1977. Fred had already done the Shellsport Tour of Dean with Russell and it seemed that the first that Russell knew about Fred joining Leyland was a phone call from John Davenport. One of the reasons given for dropping David Richards was that he had not much experience of foreign events. I don't think David Richards was too surprised; before Christmas, when John Davenport's appointment was announced, he had been heard to comment that that would be the end of his spell with BL.

The entry on the Mintex consisted of two TR7s and the Dolomite, with a service line-up of two Sherpa vans and a Range Rover plus a Triumph 2500 as a supervision (chase) car. John Davenport was on this event with Glen Hutchinson the *Motorsport* Press Officer.

Mintex Rally 1977; Pat Ryan/Mike Nicholson Triumph Dolomite Sprint go through the water splash

The rally was based on Harrogate and we were fortunate to have the premises of Appleyards of Harrogate to garage the team. On the second stage, Tony Pond swiped a gate post with the rear wing which pushed the panel in and set off the fire-extinguisher system. The escaping vapour filled the cockpit and it was only with difficulty that Tony and Fred

Leyland Returns

Tony Pond/Fred Gallagher show some battle scars on the 1977 Mintex Rally

managed to finish the stage, requiring several minutes in the fresh air to recover.

Tony drove brilliantly, pressing Ari Vatanen for the lead until punctures dropped him down to third. The weather was very wintery with a mixture of snow, mud and ice and Brian Culcheth dropped down to seventeenth after going off the road on a particularly bad section. The Dolomite had various troubles and came home a lowly 35th overall.

Right: 1977 Mintex Rally; Brian Culcheth finds some snow with the TR7

Tour of Elba

Before our first overseas rally, the Dolomite was entered in the Circuit of Ireland with Drexel Gillespie co-driving for Pat. Den Green took over one service crew but the rally ended in disaster when Pat had a heavy acident with a stone wall on stage 21 when lying sixth overall.

Elba is about 1000 miles from the Channel, a trip which needed a bit of planning with a convoy of two Range Rovers/trailers carrying the two TR7s, and two Sherpa vans. ATA Carnets for the spares and 86 wheels/tyres had to be obtained to get us through the border customs posts, and bookings for the Channel ferries and the ferry from Piombino (in Italy) to Portoferraio in Elba had to be confirmed.

The convoy broke its journey at Mâcon with an overnight stop followed by the long drive along the coast road into Italy. Tony and Fred had taken a standard Dolomite Sprint out to do a recce while Brian and Johnstone flew out and used a hire car.

Inset: Tony Pond/Fred Gallagher display the Dunlop A2 tyre during the 1977 Tour of Elba

The mixed surface event was mainly tarmac and there was strong continental opposition. Both cars went well with Tony battling with the Lancia Stratos of Darniche and the Fiat 131 of Verini for first place. Brian was also well placed but retired when a 10p lever on the twin throttle linkage broke. The supplier of this item knew all about it when we got home. John Davenport flew out to oversee the team and witness his first result; Tony third overall.

The next event for the Dolomite clashed with the Tour of Elba but we sent two mechanics off to the Granite City in

1977

Leyland Returns

Scotland where Pat and Mike achieved a very good Group 1 win with eighth overall in the bargain. The Dolomite was beginning to reproduce the form that we had expected after the 1976 programme.

Welsh Rally

John Kerswill operated the promotional caravan programme in conjunction with our rally entries with the Leyland Motorsport caravans becoming a regular sight on home events, selling the range of rally jackets, hats, umbrellas, decals etc.

The three-car team was back in action for the Welsh Rally, but early on in the event, Tony had an accident, rolling down a bank, while Brian Culcheth retired on the Eppynt tarmac stage when the oil pressure switch sheared off releasing all the oil. Tony was impressed with the strength of the TR7 but the oil loss on Brian's car was a bit of a mystery. The switch was well protected and it was difficult to see how it could have failed.

1977 Welsh Rally; Brian Culcheth discussing points with John Davenport during the Aberystwyth service halt

Triumph Dolomite Sprint and Triumph TR7 in the service park, 1977 Welsh Rally

Once again, Pat Ryan survived to gain second in class and ninth overall. Don Moore was building a large proportion of our engines and with the stronger cylinder blocks which Triumph were producing for us and the racing Dolomites, plus Don's special main cap modification we were achieving very good reliability, although we could do with some more power.

Lucas Racing were doing the wiring on the rally cars with Ray Wood keen for us to use the Lucas injection system. I asked Don Moore to develop two kits, using Lucas injection parts, for the 16-valve TR7 engine and we were looking forward to seeing the first engine on the test bed.

1975

Team Unipart Rally, Service & Promotional team at Abingdon in 1975 with, L-to-R with cars, B. Culcheth, P. Ryan, J. Syer, J. Gittins.

Brian Culcheth/Johnstone Syer rush through the wonderful forest scenery in the Triumph Dolomite Sprint, 1975 Scottish Rally.

1976

The first Triumph TR7 rally car, 1976.

Pat Ryan/Mike Nicholson jumping their Triumph Dolomite Sprint on the 1976 Scottish Rally.

1976

This amazing photograph captures the moment the engine of the Brian Culcheth/Johnstone Syer TR7 expired on the Glen Kinglas stage, 1976 Scottish Rally. (D. J. Berry)

1976

Tony Pond/David Richards towing a Monza caravan with Triumph 2500 TC on the 1976 International Caravan Rally.

1976 RAC Rally press day at Bagshot combined with testing, Tony Pond in Nomex overalls.

1977-78

Mintex Rally 1977. B. Culcheth/J. Syer splashing through a stage with the TR7.

Service stop on the Border Counties Rally 1978, L-to-R: Tony Pond, Den Green, Fred Gallagher.

Derek Boyd/Fred Gallagher with 'KDU' in new colours, 1978 Ulster Rally.

1978

RAC Rally 1978. Tony Pond/Fred Gallagher in Triumph TR7 V8.

1979-80

Per Eklund at a service stop during the 1979 1000 Lakes Rally.

Scrutineering on the sea front, 1979 San Remo Rally.

Investigating the engine problem, 1980 Circuit of Ireland.

1980-81

1980 Scottish Rally lunch halt. Seated L-to-R: Tony Pond, Jim Porter, Roger Clark

Steering repairs to the Project Metro at Lydden Hill rallycross 1981. T. Reeves on left.

Scottish Rally

John Davenport had been coming under pressure from the motoring press concerning the Jaguar race programme which had been having grave difficulties, and if you could believe half that they were saying, he had been rather less than helpful with requests for information.

John Davenport was also coming in for some flak from the press who had apparently been made aware that any information about the programme should be channelled through the press office; in other words don't ring the drivers.

The Scottish Rally was based entirely on Aviemore and with further developments by Dunlop to cure the puncture problems with the A2 tyre, we were trying the tyre without tubes this time. Testing had proved that on hard acceleration on firm gravel surfaces the tyre was turning on the wheel, with the result that a number of the tyre failures could be attributed to the valve's being sheared off.

On the Scottish, John Davenport finalised the service schedule with the co-drivers, which was a relief; but when the event was only a few hours old, we nearly lost Tony when he arrived at a tyre service point with two punctures and no wheels/tyres available. A press car was on hand and with the help of some washers to pack out the steel wheel, Tony was forced to continue with one wheel robbed from the press car. Den and I were amazed to meet Tony coming up the road with this weird wheel/tyre set-up and were able to supply a wheel to keep him going.

Tony was achieving some of the best forest stage times yet with the TR7 and was pressing for the lead when a number of punctures again dropped him off the leader board. Brian Culcheth required an axle change near Dumfries and, despite suffering no less than eleven punctures, finished a very creditable ninth overall. Tony overcame his puncture problems and finished 2nd overall with Pat Ryan in the Dolomite Sprint 12th and 3rd in class. These overall positions gained the Manufacturers Team prize as well; a better forest result.

Ypres Retirements

During the second week in June we took Tony's Scottish car (OOE 938R) to Chobham to test the tarmac suspension specification for the 24 Hours of Ypres Rally in Belgium. The car was fitted with one of the new Borg & Beck three-spoke 'paddle' clutches utilising cerametallic material on the friction pads. We had decided that as the scrutineers were unlikely to look at the handbrake mechanism, we would use rear disc brake pad calipers with no handbrake mechanism and also the softer Ferodo brake material which gave a better feel to the brakes. We also tried new track control arms which were longer to give an increase in the negative camber and after a day of testing with Tony and Brian doing the driving, we went home feeling happy with results.

Tony took a standard TR7 over to practice the stages with Brian using a standard Dolomite Sprint, ten days before the rally.

The team stayed in the friendly Hotel Sultan in the square in Ypres and were well looked after by the family Vandermeersch at the local Leyland dealer's. Despite all our preparations, our luck took another dive when Tony arrived at the service area in the square during the night running on three cylinders. We found that a sparking plug had lost its complete centre electrode but had also burnt a valve, resulting in the loss of compression on that cylinder. The engine was so down on power that, reluctantly, the car was retired.

Meanwhile, Brian was going well, until a lapse of concentration by Johnstone reading the pace notes put Brian off the road to retirement, with little damage to the car. So both cars were out of an event on which they should have obtained a good result.

It was during July that David Wood received a call from John Davenport asking him if he was interested in the job of Engineering Manager with Leyland Motorsport. David had been a Ford Competitions mechanic at Boreham and had run his own engine building business. When he received the call, David was lecturing in Motor Vehicle Technology at the Bury St Edmunds Technical College.

Following an interview with John Davenport and the personnel manager, where the Jaguar racing and Rover SD1 involvement was outlined in addition to the TR7 rallying, David accepted the job, starting at Abingdon as Engineering Liaison Manager in August 1977. We were surprised at the appointment of David, mainly from the point of view that we felt our priority was a chassis development man, and this was not David's speciality.

Before David arrived at Abingdon, I was surprised to learn from Don Moore that the work on the 16-valve Sprint fuel injection engine had been cancelled. Apparently David had turned up at the premises of Don Moore in Cambridge to introduce himself as the new engineering manager at Abingdon. After being brought up to date with developments, David told Don to stop work on the Lucas injection set-up and scrap the parts as he wanted to develop the Kugelfischer system. Don explained the difficulty he had had obtaining data from Kugelfischer when carrying out a project for Ford but despite the parts being ready to try on the testbed, he could not change David's mind. Don was not amused.

Our Dolomite entry in the Jim Clark rally ended with another engine failure which was most annoying as the stronger cylinder blocks were supposed to be the answer to the earlier problems.

Visit to Canjuers

In conjunction with Leyland International, the next event on the calendar was a two-car entry in the 2nd Rallye International Des 1,000 Pistes, held on the French military training area of Canjuers, north of Draguignan. This was the second year that this event had held international status and was notable for being very rough and one of the few loose-surface rallies in France.

The usual convoy motored down to Draguignan where we based ourselves on the Hotel Col de l'Ange. The day before the rally, the team received a request from the organising club for the loan of a Range Rover to use as a course car. The only suitable Leyland vehicle was our tow vehicle which had been showing signs of gearbox trouble on the way down, so we decided to lend this vehicle on the

Leyland Returns

condition that someone from the team drove it; for some reason I was nominated.

No practice was allowed at rally speed, but the competitors had the chance of one circuit of the route in convoy behind an official vehicle. I had the task of taking two officials round on one of these official recces, finding the route was very rough in places, including a river crossing; when I reached the end of the recce, some of the rally cars had already dropped behind.

It was very hot for the rally and it was soon obvious that few cars would finish. Tony Pond retired with a broken axle, and then Brian suffered a broken rear shock-absorber which punctured the petrol tank. Luckily this happened near the end of the last lap, the car running out of petrol 50 yards after the finish. Brian was rewarded by a fine fourth overall placing which pleased Leyland France, and Kevin Best who had flown down from the Nürburgring with John Davenport.

Enter the V8

We had not lost touch with the fact that, before long, the TR7 with the Rover V8 engine would be going into production. With this in mind I had ordered from Borg Warner in Australia, Weber carburettor adaptors to use with an Offenhauser inlet manifold. As these were off-the-shelf, they would be useful in building a test engine for chassis testing.

We had a sister car to the first rally car, KDU 496N, which was now prepared to take the V8 engine. Initially, a stripped V8 engine was fitted so that we could send the car to Janspeed for exhaust manifold jigs and an exhaust system to be made. Once these parts were ready the car could be assembled using the Offenhauser/Warneford manifolds and twin Weber carburettors.

While these developments were taking place the programme continued with two TR7's in the Hunsruck Rally based on Idar Obertsein, West Germany, with most of stages being run on an army training area. This rally had a number of unusual features, including one spectator stage where crews could do a recce during a three-hour period and another stage at the Bilstein factory which could also be reccied. The other point was that service points would not be revealed until the start of each section, which meant that no service pre-planning was possible.

Scrutineering was held at the Bilstein Factory at Schillengen Bahnhof where we had the opportunity to do some more development work before the rally with the Bilstein Competitions Department who had come from Ennepetal with their racing workshop. There was a small Leyland dealer but he was situated some way from Idar Oberstein so most of the pre-event checking and final preparation was carried out in the car park near the hotel.

The rally was a disaster for the TR7s with Brian losing a rear wheel and then Tony hitting a large rock dislodged by another competitor and breaking a rear disc. The car reached the service area and as the rear disc design was such that the disc could not be changed quickly, the axle was changed. This was not a quick job at the best of times and, unfortunately, the car was forced out of the rally when one of the trailing arm locating bolts would not go in.

First V8 Test

The 9 August was another day to remember. The TR7 (KDU 496N) with a V8 Weslake engine was taken to the MVEE test track at Chobham for a shake-down by Tony and Brian, accompanied by John Davenport, and David Wood on one of his first test sessions since joining the Department. The rear suspension was fully rose-jointed and the car completed about 23 laps; a set of 15 inch Speedline wheels were also tried on the car.

Just over a week later, the V8 test car and OOE 938R were taken to Cadwell Park circuit for a test session with Dunlop and Bilstein lasting two days. There the latest spec racing slicks were tried with alternative side wall construction, and the rare opportunity taken to do some sorting out with the Bilstein technicians. The resulting suspension specification was agreed upon by the drivers for the forthcoming Manx International Rally.

A fine result for Brian Culcheth/Johnstone Syer – second overall on the International Manx Rally 1977

The Manx was held during the second weekend in September and we had the full team out with Tony driving his Hunsruck car while Brian had a new car (OOM 512R) and Pat Ryan was in his Dolomite as usual.

Mylchreest Motors were sponsoring the rally and were most helpful in making space for our service crews and vehicles, as well as supplying a Sherpa with two mechanics to bolster our service team. It was a real pleasure to come to the Isle of Man with the family Mylchreest looking after our every need. Once again they invited the team to a super party which put everyone in a good frame of mind.

Unfortunately there was some friction between John Davenport and Brian Culcheth concerning the specification of his rally car. It seemed that John Davenport and David Wood had decided that the rear anti-roll bar was superfluous and had given instructions to leave it off the rally car, despite the fact that Brian had tested this spec at Cadwell and found the car to respond to his style of driving with the bar fitted. Brian was rather annoyed at this and asked for it to be refitted; JD was adamant that the roll bar remain off and Brian was given the ultimatum, drive the car as it is or take the next plane home! Hardly the way to instill confidence in your drivers and maintain team morale. To add to this unfortunate incident, Brian Mylchreest was a little upset when the BL Director of Motor Sport virtually took over his office in the dealership.

First in Group 1 for the Triumph Dolomite Sprint of Pat Ryan/ Mike Nicholson, 1977 International Manx Rally

The cars started really well on this event, with Tony and Brian making fast stage times from the start. To our dismay, however, the engine on Tony's car let go on the ninth stage and he was out. At the bottom of the Tholt-y-Will hillclimb, the Panhard rod on Brian's car broke but the service crew were able to replace it without loss of time.

At about half distance, I was servicing in a Rover 3500, when on the two-way radio Brian requested assistance, as he could smell petrol. We made a rendezvous at a road junction and on lifting the bonnet found that a pin-prick hole had developed in the main petrol pipe sending a needle-fine jet of petrol over the engine. Some quick repair work solved the problem and they were soon on their way; luck was with Brian

5
TONS
Leyland
Leyland
TR7
OOM 51 2R

Leyland
19
19
Leyland
MYX 175P

Leyland Returns

so far. Brian and Johnstone maintained a brisk pace and eventually finished an excellent second overall with Pat Ryan coming home eighth and first in the Group 1 Category. This was one of Brian's best drives in the TR7.

Leyland Cars was in serious trouble financially at this time with poor sales and appalling labour relations. There were threats of heavy manpower cuts throughout the Company which was spreading doubts about a full programme for 1978. Brian had already had an inkling that maybe he would not get a drive next year but John Davenport was not yet able to confirm the programme.

Tour de Corse

Leyland International had an interest in the entry for Corsica, and Kevin Best was present to keep an eye on the local promotions. These included a special wedge-shaped trailer

Tony Pond flies just before retiring on the 1977 International Manx Rally

Brian Culcheth giving members of the public demonstration rides in a rally TR7 during an MG Open Day, Sept 1977

Engine compartment of the Group 1 Dolomite Sprint showing the 48 DCOE Weber carburettors

which had been towed out from England behind a standard TR7 in rally livery. When the trailer was opened up and erected, it formed a display stand for the TR7; it created considerable interest in Ajaccio where the rally was based this year.

Tour de Corse 1977; dramatic night picture of Brian Culcheth/ Johnstone Syer in their TR7

Brian Culcheth had another difference of opinion with John Davenport concerning the car he was to drive in Corsica, expecting to drive the new car which had been used in the Isle of Man. John insisted that the car was destined for the RAC Rally for which, as the RAC was a long rough rally, on the face of it a new car was desirable; Culcheth resigned himself to drive the old original KDU 497N.

We were lucky to have two cars for the rally. On the journey down, the tow bar on my Rover 3500 (with a rally car on the trailer) partly broke away on the autoroute near Lyons. The motoring journalist Jeremy Walton was with me in the car, and we had quite an exciting few moments with the car and trailer snaking about the road until we could slow down. We had the bar welded at a small French garage off the autoroute.

The cars were fitted with the cerametallic clutch after satisfactory test results and the only last minute change was when Tony decided that the gearbox did not feel very good, so a new one was fitted. With only a few hours before the cars would have to be in *parc fermé*, I took the car out for about an hour to give the gearbox some running-in time. This proved to be a complete waste, as on the approach to the first stage, the gearbox seized and Tony's rally was over; what a disaster, and so frustrating after all the work and hours spent practising.

Brian had only slightly better luck and was soon experiencing quite bad clutch slip. Service time on this event is very tight, and there was no chance to even attempt a clutch change until the official hour service halt at half distance. The car was going quite well otherwise and as we approached half distance I discussed with Den and Brian the problem of the clutch. We were carrying the original clutches as spares, and although the mechanics had not had many opportunities to change a gearbox, they felt that it could be accomplished in the hour. With the mechanics all set up with the tools and spares laid out ready, we were slightly unhappy when John Davenport arrived with David Wood and gave instructions that the clutch was not to be changed. Brian soldiered on in a lowly eleventh place which is where he eventually finished.

RAC Rally

John Davenport decided to run four TR7s on the RAC, giving one car to Pat Ryan instead of the Dolomite. This would make servicing very much simpler with only one model of car to cater for. The fourth car was to be driven by Markku Saaristo with English co-driver Ian Grindrod but the car was prepared by Safety Devices of Newmarket with parts supplied by Abingdon. Brian had been up against Maarku in the Marina back in 1973 and 1974 but now they were in the same team.

Triumph TR7 cockpit; note five-speed gear lever and brake balance knob on the right

1977

We had three Sherpa vans, a Rover 3500, a Range Rover and a Leyland Terrier truck in the service fleet. The Terrier had caused some heartache during the service planning as it was subject to the regulations governing driving hours, which meant having a change of drivers during the rally.

We dispensed with the hired radios and through the manager of the Communications Department of Leyland Cars we were put in touch with Dymar Electronics of Watford. They supplied us with VHF radios operating on a mid-band frequency, the frequency also being acceptable to the Home Office, and meant we had our own private frequency on the RAC, after the chaos of sharing the year before. Phil Blenkhorn of Dymar was most helpful and we had no less than twelve radios on the RAC, including one in the 'results' Dolomite driven by Gordon Birtwistle and Eric Silberman.

I am afraid this was not a very happy event for the team. For one thing, there was certainly going to be a reduction in the 1978 programme and Brian Culcheth now knew that he would be without a drive after over ten years with BL/Leyland. The other problem lay with the organisation of the on-event service. There had already been a problem with too many bosses at some service points and where Den or I had made ourselves responsible for being in charge at particular points, we now had David Wood and John Davenport also taking a hand. A number of service points had been nothing short of chaotic, with counter instructions being given to the mechanics so that they did not know what to do next; not very good for driver or team morale.

333

Leyland Returns

The rally was not a great success, with Pat Ryan retiring with gearbox failure coming down the M6 and then Brian Culcheth retiring with broken wheel studs on a stage in Wales. Saaristo put his car on its roof but was able to continue. Tony Pond finished eighth overall, but none of the drivers was very happy with the handling of the cars. For a spell during the rally, John Davenport was accompanied by his boss, Alan Edis, Product Planning Director, who was keen to see how the team was operating; I don't think he was too impressed.

On the plus side, we had probably won the promotional race with three caravans manned by Leyland Motorsport personnel being organised by John Kerswill to cover as many spectator stages and other busy control/service areas as possible.

That was the end of the first year of rule by 'JD'. One could only hope that the next year would be an improvement.

Tony Pond/Fred Gallagher on an early spectator stage, 1977 RAC Rally

1977

Markku Saaristo/Ian Grindrod press on in the snow despite ending on the roof earlier in the rally, 1977 RAC

Pat Ryan gets a chance to drive the TR7 on the 1977 RAC Rally

V8 Power

First outing for the Triumph TR7 V8. Tony Pond at Esgair Daffyd in the Texaco Rallysprint 1978

10

V8 Power
1978–80

BRIAN CULCHETH had not had his contract renewed for 1978 mainly because the reduction in the programme to one car/driver in selected events had been forced on the Department because of the financial state of the Company. It was very sad to see Brian leave after almost eleven years of valued service to British Leyland, which included in particular his valiant efforts to maintain a motor sport presence through his contact with BLI after the fall of the Stokes axe in 1970. Brian had not seen eye to eye with John Davenport on a number of matters during 1977, but his professional attitude did not prevent him from giving 100 per cent service on behalf of the Company.

After a year at Abingdon, one aspect of servicing that John Davenport discussed with Den Green was the idea of having fixed crew pairings in the service vehicles. He thought that the same pair of mechanics sharing a service vehicle on a permanent basis would make for a smoother operation. Den could see that there would be a problem with only a few selected, mechanics doing all the rallies. For one thing overtime was financially very important to the mechanics; and at the beginning of every season, the mechanics' rota for doing rallies was designed to spread the days evenly between them. Anyway, neither Den nor I could really see that there was a problem with the way the mechanics were performing and we felt that, for one thing, the better mechanics tended to raise the standard of the less experienced ones.

Testing of the V8 continued with KDU being used to test the mid range axle. Up to now we had used a 'bastard' axle consisting of a Salisbury 4HA differential assembly fitted with special heavy-duty tubes, but still using the amazing Timken unit hub bearing. The mid-range axle was the standard unit used on TR7 and Rover 3500 which was much lighter than our 4HA axle, and now that limited slip differentials were available for it, we wanted to develop this axle for the V8 but axle shaft flexing was causing some rear brake problems.

1978 Press Release

It was not until 3 February that the press release announcing the 1978 programme was sent out. The announced programme was for a single car entry in the British Open Rally Championship, now sponsored by Sedan Products, a total of seven events including the RAC Rally.

Tony Pond was retained to drive the car with his regular co-driver Fred Gallagher, but there was no place for Pat Ryan who had had a successful season with the Group 1 Dolomite Sprint.

There was also to be a single entry of a Dolomite Sprint in all rounds of the British Saloon Car Championship, driven by Tony Dron and prepared again by Broadspeed. The Leyland Cars Mini Challenge would continue along with the Bonus Scheme.

The first event for 1978 was the Mintex Rally based this year on Harrogate where again Appleyards of Harrogate looked after us with workshop and parking facilities. The car retained the original livery, with the helmet logo now firmly established as a permanent part of the Leyland Motorsport identity.

The weather was not very kind on the Mintex and after a number of body-damaging incidents, Tony and Fred were placed a lowly seventeenth at the finish.

We were pleased with the Dymar radios which were proving to be a great improvement over the older sets. During the RAC rally I had been able to communicate over 40 miles to one of the service crews, although from the top of some high ground. To improve communications in difficult locations, I had obtained a 30 foot telescopic mast which was mounted on the roof rack of a Rover 3500 and erected when required.

The time had now come for a change of livery. A change to basic red was agreed upon with a white-outlined blue wedge on the side of the car. This was a very striking colour scheme, but the suggestion that the roof should be painted white, as in BMC days, fell on deaf ears! Testing continued with the V8 fitted with the mid-range axle, but this came to an abrupt halt on 6 March at Bagshot when the car rolled heavily, ending upside-down without serious injury to Tony Pond. The cause of the accident was found to be fracture of the steering column. The column was designed to collapse in the event of a head-on collision and it was at the sliding joint that it broke. When some of the other rally cars were examined another column was found which, although it had done only four rallies, had visible cracks in the same area.

In consultation with David Wood, I sent the two offending columns to the Executive Engineer, Sports Cars at Canley for examination. The Director of Vehicle Engineering became involved with the investigation as well as Alan Edis (responsible for motor sport). Colums were removed from high mileage development cars but nothing was found, and in the end nothing was done. We took the precaution of changing the columns between events, and the machine marks in the tubes were polished out to reduce the chance of cracks starting.

V8 Power

The first rally using the new red colour scheme was the Circuit of Ireland, with a new car (SJW 533S) for Tony and Fred. The car had always been at its best on tarmac and we were holding out hopes of a good result.

The rally proved to be very short due to one of those annoying problems which can happen to the best prepared cars. On one of the early stages, Tony radioed that the car was overheating and required assistance. Although servicing was not allowed on this section between stages, Den and I were nearby and located Tony to find that the main top radiator hose had blown off releasing all the coolant. We refixed the hose and topped up the coolant but in the next stage the engine temperature gauge went off the clock when the head gasket cried enough; a most disappointing end to the career of the 2-litre, four cylinder TR7.

The V8

TR8 production had started at Speke near Liverpool, and although the planned USA launch of this model was due in 1978, a serious strike at Liverpool delayed the launch for some time. The existence of a V8 engined version of the TR7 was now an open secret but the motoring public had been made aware that this model would not be availabe on the European market for some time.

Homologation of new models was handled by Ron Elkins who had inherited the job from me when Competitions was closed in 1970; he was welcome to it! The content of the homologation form was carefully considered including the various options as we expected the required number of 500 cars to be completed in time for homolgation to be approved by 1 April.

There was a new form of televised motor sport called a rallysprint, and the first outing of the V8 TR7 was in the Texaco-sponsored event at Esgair Dafydd near Llanwrtyd Wells in Wales.

For some reason, neither Den nor myself were required on this event, which seemed strange as my responsibility was the co-ordination of the rally programme, with Den in charge of car build and overall supervision of the mechanics. Sixteen of the top drivers were entered including Brian Culcheth who had signed a contract to drive for Opel in 1978. The event was a success for Tony Pond in the V8, who drove very well to achieve second overall behind Hannu Mikkola after three timed runs and a final, only just over 2 seconds adrift.

The first rally for the V8 was the Granite City Rally in Scotland. The car used by Brian Culcheth on the RAC Rally was converted into a V8 and with the new red colour scheme, and the two-carburettor set-up, this was a test run in preparation for the Welsh Rally.

Unfortunately the rally was spoilt by some poor arrowing on the stages and a number of stage target times which were cleanable by the front runners. Tony held a slender lead till the end of a sunny day, to win by 12 seconds; not a convincing win but a win on the first time out was a good morale booster.

TR8 Homologated

Amidst some controversy, the TR8 was homologated on 1 April 1978 (an appropriate day, some would say). In the

Tony Pond/Fred Gallagher during the 1978 Scottish Rally in the TR7 V8

1978

absence of a showroom-available TR8, the marketing people agreed that the car would be known as the TR7 V8, being visually the same as the TR7 except for a slight power bulge on the bonnet. All new bodyshells now had built-in roll cages with the front and side members built into the windscreen pillars and roof side channels by Safety Devices who were now sole supplier.

The V8 was now eligible for international events and with the Welsh Rally second on the official programme, we entered SJW 533S converted from the circuit four-cylinder specification.

The Motorsport leisurewear caravans continued to attend all the official events from Abingdon, and John Howlett was looking after motor sport press matters based at Redditch, having taken over from Glen Hutchinson at the beginning of the year.

The Welsh Rally started in good weather but during the first morning the car stopped on a stage with an electrical problem in the ignition. John Davenport was near this stage with David Wood in his car and they carried out some diagnostic work by radio until the car mysteriously restarted. Later the car lost its fan belt; a new one was fitted but this, too came off. It was not until the car had run out of electrics and time that a broken bolt head floating loose in the alternator was discovered to be causing intermittent seizure. It was frustrating to go out before the chance to pit the car against the opposition had been realised.

The Scottish Rally was another disaster when Tony rolled the car, though without serious injury to himself or Fred.

First at Ypres

In preparation for an entry in the 24 Hours of Ypres Rally, a test session was held at the old wartime airfield at Bovingdon, with both Dunlop and Automotive Products representatives in attendance. The car was fitted with a Racing Services engine with the dry sump system which had been designed by David Wood and fitted from the start on the V8 cars. A quality control problem was found with some of the 8 inch Minilite wheels which were fouling the front steering arms, but at the end of the day a tyre and brake specification was settled. The engine ran very hot all day which suggested some improved cooling was going to be necessary.

Tony had a new car for Ypres (SJW 540S) and it was with renewed confidence that the team arrived in Belgium. Leyland International were again involved, with the Leyland Belgium merchandising caravan also in attendance. There was some strong continental opposition including Gilbert Stapelaere, the Belgium Champion, and Tony Carello driving a 'works' spec Alitalia Lancia Stratos. Tony Pond led from the start and despite some problems when the servos seemed to be causing the brakes to stay on, Tony won the rally convincingly by over three minutes; a Ford Escort came second and Lancia Stratos third.

Sadly, after all the years of our association with Dunlop Racing Division, we were becoming increasingly disillusioned with the service given and the tyres supplied. This

Tony and Fred winning the 24 Hours of Ypres Rally 1978 in the TR7 V8

V8 Power

Engine compartment of the TR7 V8 fitted with the Weber carburettors and Offenhauser inlet manifold

resulted in a test session in Wales with Goodyear to make a back-to-back tyre comparison during the second week in July. The car (OOM512R) was fitted with an engine using a Crane camshaft, solid valve lifters and adjustable pushrods and the latest spec exhaust manifolds. Cyril Bolton, longtime competitor in BL cars was also present with his co-driver Ian Grindrod, plus Morva Fordham from Chelsea College. Morva was doing research on the effects on the heart caused by stress and wanted to see how hard rally drivers worked. Tony and Fred had volunteered to wear electrodes attached to their bodies during an event which could be recorded by a small tape machine.

The tyre tests were quite interesting with the Goodyear steel M&S being equally good in terms of stage times as the Dunlop M&S but with improved steering and traction. The Goodyear Ultragrip and Special tyres were at least a second a mile faster than the Dunlop A2. This test was probably the first time that a comparison had been made. Previously we had had a 100 per cent commitment to Dunlop, but with BL adopting a policy on the production lines of dual sourcing, the pressure was not so great now to stay with one make.

To try the tyres on an event, without the glare of international publicity, an entry was made in the Border Counties rally with the emphasis on tyre testing.

The Border Rally went off according to plan with Tony finishing fourth after a useful days testing. The tyre situation was now getting a little political but John Davenport was adamant that on the Burmah Rally we would use the best tyres available.

The atmosphere within the Department was not good, and the new management seemed to be able to undermine morale without trying, with an apparent lack of understanding of man-management. John Davenport seemed unwilling to delegate responsibility and would interfere with engineering matters which were supposed to be under the control of David Wood. The situation had deteriorated so much that one could detect the relief felt by the mechanics when JD and David Wood were not on events.

Burmah Rally

John Buffum, the top USA rally driver, had been campaigning the TR7 successfully in the States. As he hoped to do the RAC Rally in December, John Davenport offered him a drive on the Burmah Rally, to gain some forest experience.

Tony was entered in the reshelled Scottish car (SJW533S), this particular bodyshell being prepared by Broadspeed Engineering at Southam. The medical research being carried out by Chelsea College was being taken a step further with Morva Fordham attending the rally, and with Tony and Fred being wired up with electrodes and carrying a recording device on their persons.

The rally started and finished at Glasgow Airport and we used the premises of Appleyards (Glasgow) Ltd to garage the rally cars before the event. On the first day, both cars were performing reasonably well with Miss Fordham accompanying me in my service car and checking on the heart machines at regular intervals.

During the Friday night, Tony retired when the rear anchorage ponts in the 'redesigned' bodyshell fractured,

1978

allowing the propshaft to thrash into a fuel line causing the car to run out of fuel on a stage. This was a serious failure on a new bodyshell and there was some muttering from the mechanics concerning the 'race'-prepared Broadspeed body. I must say it was a little surprising that John Davenport agreed to use this untried shell, especially after all the problems we had had in this area in the past. Safety Devices had done virtually all the development work on the bodyshells, so why try something new without first testing it?

John Buffum had a number of problems including driving some miles on a stage with a flat tyre. With the assistance of his experienced co-driver, Neil Wilson, John came home in eighth position. There had been a number of punctures with the Goodyear tyres which were being tried again, but no obvious conclusions could be reached for the RAC Rally.

testing on the island, we sent over a mechanic with a Sherpa van loaded with tyres, staying there for four days to carry out the testing with a Dunlop racing technician.

David Wood travelled over with me on the ferry for the rally and was scheduled to accompany me in a Rover 3500 service car, with Mylchreest Motors kindly offering their facilities. On the journey to Heysham to catch the ferry, one of the mechanics drove the Tony Pond car to give it a 'loosening-up' and make sure the gearbox was OK. As we turned off the M6 motorway to refuel near Liverpool, Tony's car stalled. It would not start and would not even turn over. On removing the spark plugs and spinning over the engine, we were a bit surprised to see neat petrol come out of the rear spark plug holes. It seemed that the steady throttle running on the motorway had caused a quantity of fuel to collect in the cast Offenhauser inlet manifold, and as the car was switched off,

With the opportunity to add an extra event to the programme and give another driver a try-out, a single-car entry was made in the Ulster Rally, an all-tarmac event starting in Antrim and finishing in Larne, Northern Ireland.

The driver was local man, Derek Boyd, and with Tony not competing, Fred Gallagher was co-driving. Derek took to the car very well and within a short space of time was leading the rally. Three-quarters of the way through, with a now unassailable lead, the rocker shaft snapped putting the car out of the event. The result of the shaft breaking allowed a cam follower to jump out with subsequent loss of oil pressure; another weakness to sort out.

Manx Win

Derek Boyd was entered in the 1978 Manx International, to partner Tony Pond in a two-car entry. To carry out some tyre

Tony Pond/Fred Gallagher flying to victory in the TR7 V8 on the 1978 International Manx Rally

this quantity of fuel was sucked straight into the engine. Instructions were given that any future steady speed motorway running would be interspersed with occasional bursts of full throttle to prevent this happening again.

The Manx started off badly when Derek Boyd's car lost oil pressure when the oil pump drive belt came off on a stage. Although we had service at the end of the stage and replaced the belt, the damage had already been done, so that was one gone.

Tony drove brilliantly to gain an early lead which he held to the end in front of a number of Escorts and Porsche cars. This was a very satisfying result which attracted wide publicity for the TR7 at a time when TR7 sales and Leyland Cars fortunes were in the doldrums.

V8 Power

Another extra event was the Lindisfarne Rally to do some more forest testing before the RAC Rally, but this ended in disaster when the engine ran its bearings; this was part of a problem which would be with us for some time when the engine filled with oil.

Poor Derek Boyd was having no luck at all. As some compensation for his recent mechanical failures, John Davenport agreed to loan a car for the Cork Rally, with a service crew supplied from Abingdon. Den went across with one Sherpa and two mechanics but their rally did not last long when the gearbox seized and, despite being changed the car ran out of time. We were having quite a lot of trouble with the 77 mm gearbox despite a considerable amount of help from the gearbox development section at Triumph who were supplying and continually updating the gearboxes for the programme.

A second TV Rallysprint was held, this time at Donington Park Circuit with sponsorship from Texaco, a competition between a team of race and rally drivers. We loaned a TR7 V8 rally car which was allocated to John Watson and he proved to be fastest race driver, finishing third overall on aggregate.

Corsican Gearboxes

Tony Pond was very anxious to be able to carry out a full recce of the stages following John Davenport's announcement that we would be entering the Tour of Corsica. On a one-off drive, Jean-Luc Therier was brought in to drive a second car, a new LDH car (SJW 548S), with his regular French co-driver, Michel Vial.

It was decided to send a mechanic out on the recce, to service the recce cars, and the first one on the rota, Brian Moylan, set off with a Leyland Terrier truck on 1 October, 1978 to be replaced by another mechanic two weeks later by air.

It was no surprise to me when the press were told that Tony Pond would be leaving the team at the end of the year. Tony had been increasingly unhappy with the way the engineering development of the V8 was being handled and was becoming increasingly isolated from John Davenport. This was a great disappointment to those members of the team who had been with Tony since he joined in 1976, having developed a good working relationship with the one driver who seemed to be able to handle the car.

There was a problem with the ferries from France to Corsica, owing to a French seaman's strike and the main party with the Sherpas and rally cars left Abingdon not knowing whether the Marseille ferries were running. When we arrived at Marseilles, we found that the strike was still preventing any movement, so we had to resort to plan B; this meant driving all the way round the coast to Livorno in Italy to catch a ferry there. The convoy arrived early in the morning after a long delay at the Italian Customs and a night drive, and we spent a couple of hours sleeping in the vehicles until the ferry booking office opened, eventually arriving in Corsica only about six hours behind schedule.

The rally was based in Bastia and Jean-Luc Therier seemed to be pleased with the handling of the LHD TR7 V8 after only a few miles of testing. Additional sponsorship had been arranged with Air Inter who had arranged concessionary fares for the crews, and the Air Inter decal took pride of place on the front spoiler.

Scrutineering was fairly straight forward and with an overnight *parc fermé*, we left the cars lined up in the official *parc* with most of the other rally cars. I say most, because the works Fiats were conspicuous by their absence and enquiries revealed that they had obtained special dispensation from the organisers to work on the cars, fitting some parts which were being flown in late from Italy.

An attractive display of Leyland Motorsport leisurewear

Den volunteered to drive the Terrier truck, which was included in the service plan, and at 13.00 hr on the Saturday, the rally started. There was one particularly long section in the middle of the island which was going to cause a problem with the fuel range of the V8, which was still running on the rather inefficient twin-carburettor set-up. An auxiliary fuel tank had been fitted in the spare wheel well but even so, a refuelling stop in mid-section was planned with a service car standing-by to top up the tank.

The first section followed the east coast from Bastia down through Calvi, with no service point possible for some kilometres. Within the first few hours Tony Pond found his gearbox tightening and when fumes started to come up from the gearbox it was soon obvious that something was amiss. The gearbox seized and shortly afterwards the gearbox on Therier's car suffered the same fate. It was discovered that the gearbox drain plugs on both cars were loose, resulting in loss of oil. This seemed unbelievable and there were suggestions that the cars were sabotaged. We could accept that maybe human error had been responsible for one loose drain plug but not two. It brought back memories of the fanbelt saga on the 1967 Tour of Corsica when sabotage had been blamed by some, but not proven.

RAC Rally

There was some speculation about who would drive for the team in 1979, assuming that a budget was approved, with the Company this winter experiencing more than their share of industrial trouble.

John Davenport loaned a car to Graham Elsmore for the Focol Wyedean Stages two weeks before the RAC Rally and we sent two mechanics with a Sherpa service van to look after the car. Graham had a good first run to finish second overall with Stuart Harrold co-driving.

Graham Elsmore/Stuart Harrold on the way to second overall in the Wyedean Rally 1978

Sponsorship from British Airways was obtained for the RAC, with a slight change of livery including a side stripe behind the rear wheel arch to simulate the British Airways tail fin. To make up a three-car team, John Davenport brought in the experienced Finn, Simo Lampinen, an old team mate and driver of JD, plus the Norwegian, John Haugland. These two were allocated English co-drivers in the form of Mike Broad and Ian Grindrod respectively.

The rally started and finished in Birmingham which was not altogether popular with its difficult one-way system, scrutineering being held at the British Car Auctions premises at Erdington. At scrutineering, the V8s failed the noise test, which was a little surprising, because to the ear, the V8

1978

V8 Power

Simo Lampinen/Mike Broad during the 1978 RAC Rally in the LHD TR7 V8

exhaust was comparatively quiet. The cars were taken away and we 'doctored' the exhausts which did the trick. We had resorted to the rear brake calipers incorporating the handbrake mechanism again, to comply with the regulations, and these passed the scrutineers.

There was some controversy concerning whether we should disconnect the handbrake cables after scrutineering, but JD and David Wood had their way and the cars went into the first stages with them still connected. At the Trentham Gardens stage, Tony Pond came to a halt when the handbrake mechanism became jammed inside the rear wheel, locking the wheel. Fred had to get out and help push the car backwards to free the wheel, losing several vital minutes. The mechanics sorted out the damage which was slight, but Tony was hopping mad and no time was lost in getting the mechanics to disconnect the mechanism on the other two cars.

British Airways sponsorhip for the 1978 RAC Rally. Tony and Fred spray the champagne

In Wales, Simo Lampinen lost his clutch, and despite frantic efforts by the mechanics to change it in time, he was

344 *Later cockpit of the TR7 with large diameter tachometer*

Tony Pond and Fred Gallagher on the 1978 RAC Rally

forced to retire. John Haughland had a steady run to finish twelfth overall but Tony Pond drove brilliantly to come back from his early delay to finish fourth overall behind three Ford Escorts; a good result for Tony in his last drive. He would be missed in 1979.

Before the end of the year, Cliff Humphries rejoined the Department as workshop foreman to replace Bill Burrows who was due to retire in April. We were fortunate in being able to gain approval for a period of overlap to allow Cliff to pick-up as much information from Bill before he left. Cliff had been responsible for much of the engine development in the years up to 1970 and had been employed on MG production ever since. There were a number of other personnel who could have replaced Bill but none with the development experience of Cliff.

1979

1979 Season Starts

When the programme was announced for 1979 the only regular crew was Graham Elsmore partnered by Stuart Harrold. They were to be joined on various events by either Simo Lampinen, Jean-Luc Therier or Derek Boyd; in other words John Davenport was keeping his options open and would choose drivers to suit events. The Department was now to be known as BL Motorsport, but with the livery of the cars remaining unchanged.

The first rally was the Boucles of Spa with a single car entry for Jean-Luc Therier and Michel Vial using the LHD car, SJW 548S. JD asked Fred Gallagher to come over to Belgium to help with servicing and give any assistance he could to the French pair who had not done the rally before. The rally was held in very cold conditions with quite a lot of snow still on the ground. We took four types of Dunlop tyre including 500 × 13 snow tyres and the narrow 564 M&S which were due to have studs fitted by a tyre dealer in Liège.

At the half-way stage, there was some discussion between Jean-Luc and JD concerning studs resulting in a panic visit to the tyre dealer in Liège with a request to fit some studs to the A2 'forest racers'. The car was obviously a handful in the icy conditions and during the last hours of the rally, Jean-Luc retired with a broken rotor in the distributor; well that was the official reason, but I suspect that he didn't want to be beaten by less well-known drivers.

The first official rally for the team was the Galway Rally in Ireland, Derek Boyd being brought in to drive a second car with Fred Gallagher. This was the Chequered Flag car painted in their distinctive black and white livery. The car had been prepared by Abingdon but Chequered Flag were due to take it over after the Galway to do some further events.

V8 Power

They sent over their own service vehicle to assist with servicing and to give their mechanics a chance to familiarise themselves with the car. BL Eire handled local publicity with JD lending one of their cars after flying over.

Derek Boyd set the pace from the start but on an early stage suffered a high-speed accident putting the car sideways into a stone wall. The impact was on the passengers side and Fred Gallagher suffered serious injuries including a broken pelvis. JD was able to obtain the services of a helicopter which had been filming, to get Fred quickly to hospital; a very unfortunate start to the event.

Graham Elsmore was going well and had moved into the lead when they ran onto some diesel oil at a farm entrance, spun into a tree stump with the car cartwheeling and landing upside down in the road. The crew got out with some bruises and manhandled the car off the road into the ditch to allow the rally to go through. So it was out with the tow rope as soon as the stage was open and home with the wreckage.

Back at Abingdon, we found that the Chequered Flag car had been reduced in width by about 6 inches, and it was the general opinion that in any car other than the TR7, Fred could well have suffered much more serious injury. As it was, he was going to be out of commission for some months.

V8 Injection

David Wood was working on a fuel injection system for the V8 but despite being offered assistance by Ray Wood, Lucas Competitions Manager, it was decided to approach Pierburg in Germany. A V8 engine was sent over to the DVG works for testbed work to be completed on the installation, and the Rover works at Springfield had a cast injection inlet manifold made to David Wood's design. David made a visit to DVG and reported that within a few weeks we would have a set of equipment to try on a car.

I had been trying to get David Wood and JD to agree to having a new carburettor inlet manifold made but it seemed that they both had tunnel vision and all that could be seen at the end of the tunnel was the injection system; most frustrating. I felt that we could and should try a four carburettor manifold; it would be no great expense, would prove the point – and it could hardly be worse than the two-carburettor set-up!

JD wanted a driver with forest experience for the Mintex Rally and was fortunate to obtain the services of Per Eklund, the experienced and likeable Swede. With Fred in hospital, Mike Broad joined Per for the Mintex. There was a lot of snow and ice on many of the stages and as a result the rally had been shortened by a day. I was driving John Davenport and John Howlett in a Rover 3500 and when we arrived at Cadwell Park circuit which was a stage, there was deep snow; we radioed the approaching service vans advising them where to park.

Per Eklund/Mike Broad jump in the snow on the 1979 Mintex Rally on the way to second overall

JD instructed me to drive to the entrance of the track, where he bluffed his way past the marshals, and then out on to the actual stage. I then drove round in deep snow, giving the SD1 some stick up the slope of the circuit hoping we would not get stuck. At the stage finish, which used the same gate, we sailed past the marshals, having done an unofficial recce of the stage; this information was passed on to the crews who fitted the appropriate tyres.

We had recently acquired some 15 inch Minilite wheels in order to increase the 'footprint' of the tyre (a favourite JD expression) and Per was using these to some effect. When the rally approached Olivers Mount, my car arrived well before the rally cars. Once again JD bluffed his way past the marshals and I was instructed to drive the stage, which we managed to

1979

complete despite being waved down a number of times by marshals, making our escape the same way as we came in. There were still several patches of ice on the slushy tarmac surface, this information being passed on to the crews. I have often wondered what would have happened if the Director of Motor Sport had been recognised doing a recce of those stages!

Per maintained his pace to finish a fine second overall, but Graham retired on the last airfield stage, when the engine lost its oil pressure. We were worried about this problem of the oil tank being emptied, and when Graham's car was towed out of the stage we had a look in the tank; sure enough it was virtually empty.

Circuit Testing

A week after the Mintex a tarmac tyre testing session in Northern Ireland was supervised by David Wood with Graham Elsmore and Derek Boyd doing the driving, followed

V8 Power

by a second test in southern Ireland based on Killarney two weeks later; this was in preparation for the Circuit of Ireland Rally at Easter.

The Sherpa service vehicles had given very good service but there was a need for something bigger and more powerful which could tow a trailer. Unfortunately there was nothing in the BL range available at this time. At the last Motor Show at the NEC I had a look at the Leyland EA van which was made in short or long wheelbase versions. I had taken the dimensions of the V8 engine with me and after climbing about the vehicle with a tape measure I had come to the conclusion that it would not be a major problem to remove the diesel engine and replace it with a standard SD1 V8 engine.

JD authorised the purchase of a vehicle and Bill Burrows started work doing the modification. The transmission used on this first vehicle was the Borg Warner automatic unit used in the SD1, but uprated to the latest Jaguar specification. Tyre racks were built inside, as we wanted if possible to keep the wheels/tyres off the roof; they made the vehicle top heavy and on a long rally when mechanics were tired, the physical effort required to constantly load and unload units weighing at least 40 lb each was considerable. This first EA was ready for use on the Circuit of Ireland Rally.

New Sales Manager

John Kerswill decided to leave the Department as he felt he was in a rut and wanted a new challenge. John had done a good job of building up and rejuvenating the commercial sales and we were sorry to see him leave. His replacement, Mike Kyle, joined the Department on 19 March 1979 from Unipart. Mike was a motor sport enthusiast and was well aware of the demands that could be made by competitors and customers alike.

Following his performance on the Mintex, Per Eklund had accepted a contract from John Davenport to compete in the remaining rounds of the Sedan Products Open Championship, to be partnered by fellow Swede, Hans Sylvan. The entry for the Circuit was now to be three cars, the third being the Chequered Flag entry driven by Derek Boyd in the reshelled SJW 533S with Roy Kernaghan; Fred was still recovering from the Galway accident. Graham Warner came over for the rally and also sent a service crew to assist with servicing.

Once again luck deserted Derek Boyd when on the first day he clouted a rock, broke a brake disc and was out. Graham had an accident and retired but Per Eklund, not a renowned tarmac expert, was going extremely well and lying in a leading position. On the penultimate stage, a very fast stage with long straights, the engine blew up, a repeat of the oil scavenge problem starving the engine of oil.

The new EA service van was used for the first time on an event, basically as a tyre van this time, without major problems. The performance with the V8 made it as quick as some of the Ford and Bedford service van equivalents.

This month also saw the retirement of Bill Burrows who had spent many years of dedicated service at MG. We were going to miss Bill with his ever cheerful presence and wealth of knowledge; as a farewell, a social event was held in the MG Social Club in Abingdon where a presentation was made by John Davenport. Cliff Humphries now took over officially in the workshop.

Soon after the Circuit, John Howlett organised a test day at Donington Circuit with guests invited from *Autocar, Motor, Autosport, Car & Car Conversions, Motoring News* and *Rallysport* magazines, plus a number of national press people. Two V8 rally cars were available with Per Eklund and Graham Elsmore to act as chauffeurs and an interesting day was had by all.

Welsh Rally

Three cars again were entered in the Welsh Rally, with Simo Lampinen joining Graham and Per. The rally started and finished in Cardiff with an overnight halt at Aberystwyth. Three Sherpas, one as a tyre van, and the EA van as full service vehicle were in use while John Davenport had Fred Gallagher co-driving him in his Rover 3500. It was good to see Fred out and about again although still using his crutches.

Scottish Rally 1979; Per Eklund/Hans Sylvan on a rough section in the TR7 V8. Note the repositioning of the front number plate (Colin Taylor Productions)

The team again had mixed fortunes. On the approach to Aberstwyth, Graham had gearbox trouble and by the last stage of the day, he had only one gear working but managed to get to a garage with a ramp. The service crews were set up in the car park in Aberstwyth but a radio call for assistance was rejected by JD, who presumably wanted to maintain the full team in the town. Den and I caught up with Graham in our Rover and we started to prepare the gearbox, which was almost red-hot, for removal. A service van eventually did arrive but it was too late to keep Graham in the rally; by only two minutes!

Per Eklund retired with engine trouble but Simo Lampinen, despite extensive damage to the rear of the car caused by another competitor at the end of a stage, finished twelfth overall.

Per Wins Rallysprint

The TV Rallysprint was held again at Esgair Dafydd, this year sponsored by BP VF7 oil. We entered Per Eklund and Chequered Flag entered the Circuit car, SJW 533S for Graham Elsmore. It was a good day for BL Motorsport with Per coming first and Graham eighth on aggregrate times taken on one downhill and one uphill run.

John Davenport and David Wood wanted an engineer in the Department solely responsible for suspension development and after advertising in *Autosport* magazine, recruited Richard Hurdwell who had been working at MIRA; Richard started at Abingdon in April.

Graham Elsmore jumping to success on the 1979 Peter Russek Manuals Rally

On the days running up to the Scottish Rally, Simo Lampinen and Fred Gallagher attended two Dealer Open House evenings, at Kilmarnock and Stirling which was handy with the rally starting in Glasgow. Once again we had a strong service team supporting the three cars. Per Eklund went particularly well on this rally, keeping in touch with the

Lombard ESSO
TUD 682T
DUNLOP
Lombard
ESSO
7

7
DUNLOP
OOM 514R

V8 Power

leaders and lying in third position. Before the overnight halt, Graham lost his fan belt and after driving five miles on a stage without it, one of the head gaskets let go. Although this was changed by the mechanics at Aviemore, he was forced to retire next day with severe overheating.

Next day, Martin Reade, one of the mechanics, cut the end off his finger while unloading a trolley jack from his van and I sent him off to hospital in my Rover with John Smith of Lucas who had been travelling with me. I took over his position in the van for the next few miles, but his space was filled by Graham Elsmore next day after he had retired. Graham had a bit of a surprise when he put Martin's overalls on and found the tip of Martin's finger in his pocket.

Fred Gallagher made a welcome return to the team with Simo but with various troubles only managed to gain thirteenth overall; there was some compensation with Per coming home a fine third.

In order to gain more experience with the car, JD loaned a car to Graham to be looked after by Graham's own mechanic and in August, on the Peter Russek Rally with Fred co-driving, they finished first overall.

1000 Lakes Rally

David Wood was progressing with the Pierburg fuel injection specification and despite the fact that virtually no testing had been done with this engine, JD insisted that it was fitted to one of the 1000 Lakes cars. An engineer had come over from Germany and finalised the installation and on the road it seemed to be satisfactory.

The 1000 Lakes is a rather special rally with smooth dirt undulating stages with many jumps, and as the TR7 had not been used on the rally before, it was decided to take a car to Finland to sort out the spring/damper combination and to establish which type of tyre to use.

Per Eklund knew a good forest stage in Sweden, so the car was taken first to Grasmark near Karlstad. I travelled out with one of the mechanics with the EA van and the LHD test car from Harwich to Esbjerg then Frederikshaven to Goteborg by ferry.

Accommodation was provided by Per at his home and we were joined by Simo Lampinen, David Wood and Richard Hurdwell on his first test session with the team. The car was fitted with a Don Moore twin carburettor engine using new Felpro head gaskets and the gearbox had been modified at Per Eklunds request with no synchromesh or fifth speed. After a day of testing in the forest doing about 40 runs, the car was moved to Finland.

I flew to Helsinki with Simo, where we went to the Saab factory to collect his new Saab Turbo car. We then drove up to Jamsa where we met up with the rest of the test crew and continued testing on the public roads there. This was brought to an abrupt halt when steam appeared from the exhaust, due to an area of porous casting in the RH cylinder head. Simo used his car telephone to call Abingdon for a new head to be

Triumph TR7 V8 Pierburg fuel injection engine

flown out and one and a half days later we were able to continue.

Leaving the hotel at 04.00 hr was rather uncanny as it was broad daylight, something we had not experienced before. Using two-way radios to 'police' the main road, we spent another useful day testing to finalise the 1000 Lakes specification. The EA was left in Finland for the rally and we then flew home.

in to the radio transmission, told us not to spend any time bothering with this failure, but we were now at the middle of the stage, guided by Simo on his radio. I ran down the stage for what seemed to be miles (approx 1½ kilometers), jumping into the side every minute in the dark to avoid being run down by rally cars, found Simo, fitted the rotor and he was away.

Meanwhile, David Wood was trying to find a solution to the underbonnet temperature problem but whatever we did

Per Eklund during the Eaton Yale Rallysprint at Donington 1979

The rally cars were shipped out to Kotka from Felixstowe in a 40 foot transporter hired from Austin Rover transport department at Cowley complete with driver, plus a Sherpa service van. SISU, the Leyland truck people in Finland, helped with service vans and crews and we were fortunate to have experienced personnel like Raimo Hartto among them.

We used the premises of the dealer in Jyvaskala and arranged for the local tyre dealer to change tyres at half-distance. I used a local Range Rover with Den Green to supervise the service while JD used Simo's own Rover 3500.

From the start, Per Eklund was up with the front runners but was hampered by the injection system losing power as soon as the underbonnet temperature rose. Simo with local co-driver, Juhani Markkanen, was also going well with the carburettor car until the car stopped on a stage with a broken rotor. Den and I were within radio range and immediately left the service point to see if we could locate the car. JD listening

seemed to make no improvement. At the first service after the halfway halt, Simo decided to have the distributor cap replaced. The SISU service crew, unfamiliar with the V8, managed to get the plug leads crossed up and by the time it was running again, Simo had run out of road time. This was a stupid mistake when the car was running perfectly. Per suffered the loss of the rear window on a jump (remedied by having the aperture covered by plastic) and then found some slight relief to the fuel vaporisation when the rain came down. At the finish, Per was placed eighth overall, a reasonable result in the circumstances finding that on the firmer stages the new 195/60 x 15 M&S tyres suited the conditions. Our first visit to Finland with the TR was not exactly a huge success.

Manx International

With the main team away in Finland, Graham Elsmore competed in the Lindisfarne Rally with his loan car, OOM 514R, but could only manage eighth overall.

Fred Gallagher joined Graham for the Manx with a

V8 Power

three-car team made up with Derek Boyd in the Chequered Flag car and Terry Kaby. Terry had been using a loan car (OOM 512R) during the year but on the Manx was loaned a newer car, SJW 540S. The tyre situation was slightly complicated with two of the cars on Dunlop and Terry on Goodyear with whom he had a contract for the year. For some reason my presence was not required on the Manx, despite my having completed all the arrangements; I must say I was most unhappy.

Graham drove a good rally with the assistance of Fred's pace note experience and finished third overall with Terry Kaby close behind fourth.

San Remo Rally

The San Remo rally was another new event for the team and a major challenge. Per Eklund and Simo Lampinen were entered, with Simo taking Fred Gallagher as co-driver. Both drivers were anxious to complete a thorough recce of the route which comprised both gravel and tarmac stages. Two recce cars and the EA service van were taken out to Italy by two mechanics who stayed in San Remo to maintain and service the cars. An added complication on this event, was having to change from tarmac to gravel suspension and back again.

Once again the Cowley transport department articulated transporter was used to take out the rally cars plus a TR8 car which JD lent to the organisers as a course car, and JD's own Rover 3500. The artic would also bring back the recce cars. Apart from the personnel already in Italy and those mechanics required to drive service vehicles from Abingdon, the remainder went out to Nice by air.

The first tarmac stages suited the cars but Per Eklund was soon in trouble with a jammed brake balance bar which nearly put him off the road, losing him some valuable time.

At a major service point after the tarmac stages, the suspension was changed to the rough road spec. It was on the gravel stages that Simo suffered rear suspension problems when one of the rear trailing arm suspension bolts sheared. Fred managed to get a lift to a nearby service crew and returned with a mechanic and a new bolt but by the time it was fixed they were out of time.

On the return run, we had arranged to replace the tarmac suspension at a service area on the autostrada. A number of the rougher stages had been cancelled giving a much longer period of service time. The V8 of Per Eklund was virtually rebuilt with complete new suspension and a new gearbox while JD had taken the crew to a nearby hotel for some sleep. At the arranged hour they were brought back to the car to resume the rally and set off on the last tarmac section, involving a long autostrada run to Genoa. Unfortunately, they made a navigational error and in their effort to get to the next main control on time, blew the engine. It seemed that the oil scavenge problem could have had some bearing on the failure.

Graham competed in the Castrol 79 rally in Wales with his loan car but retired when a rock damaged the axle drain plug and the differential seized after losing the oil.

The second Rallysprint of the year, sponsored by Eaton Yale, was held at Donington Park circuit with Per Eklund sharing one of our TR7 V8 cars with Alan Jones the Grand Prix driver. In the final race between the rally drivers and Grand Prix stars, standard TR7s were used, supplied by BL and prepared by the Triumph press garage at Canley. The event turned out to be one that Abingdon preferred to forget. The organisers built a water-splash in the rally stage and the TR7 V8 drowned in the water on its first run. JD and David Wood were supervising service and while the mechanics were attending to tyres etc, they attended to 'waterproofing the electrics' by wrapping the ignition in grey tape. On the second run the car again drowned; most embarrassing for BL in front of the TV cameras.

The Scarborough Stages Rally was an opportunity to give Hans Sylvan some experience in the forests when he went as Graham Elsmore's co-driver in the loan car. The rally used some of the traditional Yorkshire stages and they managed to finish third overall.

RAC Rally

Morale in the department had not improved, with relations between JD and most of the staff rather strained. Engineering development lacked the progress we had hoped for and the fuel injection system overheating problem and oil scavenge problems remained unsolved. David Wood wanted to build in a petrol cooler on the injection car but JD, for reasons best known to himself, refused.

Richard Hurdwell was quiet and industrious but had not inspired me with much confidence when he started at Abingdon, making it clear that he wanted to learn about the suspension his way; in other words we just put the clock back. Management meetings seemed to take up more and more time, and there were frequent rows revolving round engineering decisions. There was a reluctance to accept there was something basically wrong with the oil pressure/scavenge system despite the fact that Don Moore had been telling us for months that the scavenge pump was inadequate.

With the injection system making no preogress, in frustration I asked Den to put the wheels in motion to get a four-carb manifold made by Janspeed, hoping that we could get one made without intervention from David Wood or JD. On the RAC rally we would still have to use the original two carb set-up.

British Airways sponsorship was obtained again for the RAC with a four-car entry comprising Graham Elsmore, Simo Lampinen, Per Eklund and Terry Kaby plus a fifth car prepared for and privately entered by USA champion, John Buffum. This gave David Wood another chance to give the fuel injection system an airing, this time in cooler conditions.

The rally was based on Chester and it was the largest BL team so far assembled that arrived in the City. Five service vans, plus four Rover 3500s, a Rover 2600 and a TR8. A rearranged service plan positioned a supervision car at each scheduled service point with that person responsible for seeing the work on the cars was completed as necessary. In theory this was to prevent the chaotic situations which had occurred on some previous events where there were too many 'chiefs' at service points. Meals were provided at main controls at the appropriate times by the 'meals-on-wheels' caravan towed by a Range Rover with David Wood's wife and

1979

Graham Elsmore waits to start a stage in the early morning mist, 1979 RAC Rally

Fred's girl friend doing the cooking.

The selection of tyres included the 622 compound racing tyres with three grooves for the tarmac stages, 175 and 195 × 13 M&S and 15 inch M&S for the forest plus 13 inch Hakka and 15 inch Hellenius snow tyres, just in case.

John Buffum embarrassed the regular team members by heading them all on stage times until putting the car off the road. Although little damage was done, he had to wait until the stage was reopened and a tow from a marshal's Land-Rover pulled him out.

Terry Kaby had engine failure but the other three cars

Simo Lampinen/Fred Gallagher using 15 inch wheels on the 1979 RAC Rally

kept going despite various troubles but were never really on the pace of the leaders. Per finished highest overall at thirteenth with Graham sixteenth and Simo seventeenth. This was a disappointing result which showed that the car still needed some sorting in the forest; where was Tony Pond?

The programme for next year was looking most uncertain but would almost certainly be a reduction on 1979. There were rumours that Tony Pond was leaving Chrysler and speculation that he would return to the Abingdon team.

Per Eklund spins his racing tyres during the 1979 RAC Rally

353

V8 Power

Service point in the Lake District during the 1979 RAC Rally. Per Eklund departs

1980

1980 – Tony Returns
The rumours proved to be correct when JD announced that Tony Pond would return to the team and Fred Gallagher would be retained as his co-driver. Per Eklund was also retained but no news of the programme was forthcoming except that the two drivers would compete in the Rally of Portugal.

Roger Clark and Jim Porter

In addition, the surprise news was that Roger Clark would drive a TR7 V8 with his long time co-driver Jim Porter. Roger had announced his retirement in 1979 but with a newly appointed BL agency this was the opportunity to continue with a product which would help promote his new franchise. Roger had additional sponsorship from Sparkrite and Esso and would compete in the Sedan Products Open Championship. We were now also to be sponsored by Esso, ending our long association with Castrol.

Although David Wood turned a blind eye to the four carburettor inlet manifold initially, as soon as Cliff had run it on the test bed with very good results, he soon took notice and JD was informed. Janspeed made this first one FOC for Cliff.

With the first event of the year being an entry in the Galway Rally for Roger Clark, the opportunity was taken to use the four carburettor manifold for the first time. The service vehicles crossed from Liverpool to Dublin and then drove to Galway. John Howlett accompanied me in my Rover 3500, and we had two mechanics with a Sherpa to look after the rally car.

Roger started off well with the V8 and was lying in fifth position when the gear lever broke off and the engine was inadvertently overrevved causing instant retirement. Not a good start for the Sparkrite/Esso car.

Roger Clark at Olivers Mount, 1980 Mintex Rally

Second event for Roger was the Mintex Rally, this year starting in Newcastle, but disaster struck again when the engine failed. This was very unfortunate after all the publicity that surrounded Roger with his change of make, after so many years with Ford.

Rally Of Portugal
The fuel range with the standard tank had been proving inadequate, but now a new FIA-approved safety tank had been fitted to the cars which involved considerable modification in the rear bulkhead area. The tanks were made by a new

1980

company which had obtained FIA approval but unfortunately, a problem with the inlet and outlet pipes caused much heartache before the start.

Per Eklund and his co-driver went out to Portugal first, to have a look at the route using a car supplied by BL Portugal; the main recce/test party arrived on 7 February. Two recce cars were provided with two Abingdon mechanics while a Dunlop racing technician and Richard Hurdwell flew out as well. A lengthy test session took place to confirm tyre and suspension requirements, although Eklund had an oil problem with his car. His car was emptying the oil tank in a distance of about two kilometres and Per was so angry that he decided that after the rally he would try to do something about the problem. The cars were now using 11 inch rear wheels on tarmac events with 8 inch fronts, the rear tyres being 260/500 × 13 with D50 sidewalls and 760 compound with the same construction on the front.

The crowds of spectators were a problem and at one stage, the road became completely blocked with spectator traffic, the occupants of cars just getting out, locking the cars in the middle of the road and walking off to the nearby stage. We saw quite a number of cars manhandled off the road into the ditch to enable the traffic to move.

The rally ended for us during the second leg when Per stopped on a special stage. The twin SU fuel pump had failed and despite frantic efforts by Per to get going using a washer pump to pump petrol, they were forced to retire.

Upon his return from Portugal, Per called at Abingdon and spoke with David Wood and John Davenport. Supervised by Cliff and David, Per spent the day driving the recce car along the Abingdon by-pass trying to empty the oil tank. Some time was spent experimenting with the engine until fitting a windage tray suddenly effected a cure. It seemed the problem was being caused by the throw of the crankshaft

The main party of mechanics with the rally and service vehicles travelled from Plymouth to Santander in Spain leaving them a drive of about 580 miles to Lisbon. The drivers tried out the cars as soon as they arrived, using the garages at the rear of the hotel at Estoril for the last minute preparations. The injection engine on the car which Tony Pond was driving was suffering with fuel feed problems and this was not cured 100 per cent before the start.

The first stages were tarmac and on the second, Tony suffered a blown engine. Per continued and at the main service at Povoa de Varzim, on the sea front, the car had a new gearbox and axle fitted. Per was using a 'crash' gearbox again but Tony had been worried that this would place too much strain on the unit and had opted for the full synchromesh gearbox.

preventing oil from getting into the scavenge-well in the sump casting, particularly at high sustained rpm. So after all this time, during which steel scavenge pipes had been fitted between sump and pump, larger bore pipes between engine and oil tank (in the boot), and a larger capacity scavenge pump tried, a cure was found.

The next event for the Sparkrite/Esso car was the Circuit of Ireland, the engine being fitted with a newly fabricated windage tray.

The rally started from the Ormeau Embankment in Belfast returning after a few stages for a rest halt then restarting at 04.00 hr next mornng from the City Hall. The car appeared to be OK and Roger and Jim went well to Killarney, continuing with fine weather on the Killarney–Killarney loop.

Heading north from Killarney on the third section, the

The HANLEY-HENLEY Championship
Sparkrite
CIRCUIT OF IRELAND 80
9
SEDAN
BILSTEIN
Lucas
CHAMPION
ESSO
ROGER CLARK
Sparkrite
DUNLOP
ESSO

Mirror
12
Rally Sprint
TONY POND
DUNLOP
UYH 863S
ESSO

Roger Clark/Jim Porter during the 1980 Circuit fo Ireland

engine threw the oil pump belt, but the engine suffered no apparent damage and the belt was replaced. Later, the engine lost oil pressure and Roger was forced to retire. Without a trailer, we towed the rally car back to Dublin to catch the ferry, a long tow. Back at Abingdon we found that the engine failure was caused by a fatigue fracture of the windage tray; you win some, you lose some!

Daily Mirror Rallysprint

The rallysprint event at Esgair Dafydd was sponsored by the *Daily Mirror* for 1979. We entered two cars with the added complication that both our drivers were on a recce of the route of the Criterium Alpin in the south of France and so had to fly back from Nice to take part. Tony was allocated John Bellis of the *Daily Mirror* as passenger with Per taking Malcolm Folley of the *Daily Express*. Unfortunately, Tony managed to put his car over the edge, without serious injury but Per was second overall to uphold BL honours. Immediately after the event was over, John Davenport and Den Green with the drivers, had a bit of a rush to get to Heathrow to catch the flight to Nice for the Criterium.

Tony Pond during the 1980 Daily Mirror Rallysprint *– TR7 V8*

Criterium Alpin

Full-blown rally cars were now the order of the day for recces, with mechanics and service vehicles sent out to look after them. The first mechanic went out on 4 April with a recce car towed behind a Rover, followed a week later by another mechanic with a Sherpa service van. John Davenport had asked BL France to organise hotels and to brief the local BL dealer, but to co-ordinate the final details I went out on 11 April with the second recce car. I travelled on the Car Sleeper Express from Calais to Nice, bringing back memories of the Mini days.

I met up with the drivers and co-drivers and spent two days sorting out alternative hotels, meeting the local dealer (with an English managing director) who was most helpful, and delivering the rally entry forms to the AC de Cannes. The Sherpa arrived before I returned to Abingdon having suffered head gasket failure on the way down.

The recce was not without its drama when Tony and Fred had a tyre burst which turned the TR7 V8 upside down, luckily without injury, but giving our mechanic a lot of work.

To get the rally cars plus a Rover 3500 service car to Cannes, we again used a Leyland artic. I travelled out by air arriving at Cannes the day before the other mechanics and Richard Hurdwell. There were the usual last minute preparations which were delayed until the drivers finally arrived from the rallysprint.

The next problem was the tyres; I was horrified when the new Dunlop slicks for front of the cars were unloaded. The cross-section of the inflated tyres showed that they were crown shaped. Hasty contact with the Michelin competition manager produced a few Michelin radials which were tested during the evening on the first stage. The Michelins were a revelation being at least 1 second a kilometre quicker than the Dunlops.

Tony was using the Pierburg fuel injection again but the mechanics had been having trouble with the fuel feed on both cars. Eventually this was traced to the inlet and outlet pipes being incorrectly marked, which on the injection engine was critical. The engine fired-up when more petrol was put in the tank.

The first part of the rally went well with Tony Pond holding third place. In the early hours of the morning, his engine developed an ominous rattle from the valve gear and he was forced to retire. It was impossible to get at the rocker gear with the injection manifolds in position. A little later, on the main road approaching the Turini, I waited for Per Eklund to arrive, having received a radio message that the gearbox was seizing. When we arrived John West, who was in my car, started to remove the gearbox while I contacted the approaching Sherpa. The gearbox was changed in record time but Per had to leave without his sumpshield and some of the exhaust bolts, this being rectified after the Turini test.

Per was now in third position but at the start of the penultimate stage a rear spring broke and the fan belt came off. They got to the end but the alternator bracket was broken. I was in radio contact, despite the mountains, but we were prevented from going down the narrow road to the stage finish by a gendarme. John and I ran about two kilometres with an alternator but by the time we had fitted it and got the car going they were out of time. The ride back to our service car on the TR7 door sills was rather frightening!

Metro Developments

The manager of the BL Motorsport parts business, Mike Kyle, had been beavering away since his arrival in 1979 with plans to relaunch the parts business around the new Austin Metro. This car was to be revealed to the public at the 1980 Motor Show in October. The plan was that a package of special parts would be made available from Abingdon at the same time as the car was launched, a first for the Motorsport department. The kit included cosmetic parts such as an aerodynamically developed front spoiler, wheel arch trims and stripe kit with mechanical 'Pluspacs' to include an engine kit with Weber carburettor and manifold, exhaust system, rocker cover and oil cooler. This was progressing well and was on target for the details to be sent out to the appointed dealers and stockists before the Show. The parts side had not been making a profit and with this new range it was hoped to stimulate sales.

MG to Close

Few people in the country could have failed to hear the continuing saga of the MG factory's messy end. Despite the pressure of the rally programme, we were more than aware of the implications of the closure of the plant. It looked as if MG production would cease sometime in October with the completion of the last limited edition MGB Roadster and GT models. No decision had yet been made concerning the site but rumours were rife, and it was becoming obvious that the Motorsport Department would have to move, perhaps, even, close.

V8 Power

Rothmans Manx Stages

Immediately after the Criterium Alpin, the next event for Roger Clark was the Atcost International Rally (Welsh) with XJO 414V, the car which he had driven in Ireland. The standard production Rover 3500 windage tray was now being fitted to all the V8 rally engines, bringing a cure to the oil distribution problem after about ten failures which could be attributed to the scavenge system. The Welsh brought no more luck to Roger when he retired with fuel pump failure on the last stage when lying seventh overall.

The Michelin tarmac radial tyres first tried in anger on the V8 in France had provided startling results, and with the Ypres 24 Hours Rally and the Manx International looming up, John Davenport obtained sanction to enter Tony in the national event also run on the Isle of Man, the Rothmans Stages. Michelin UK supplied tyres for the rally, which was unusual in having scrutineering on the quay at Heysham with crew documentation held on board the ferry to Douglas. There were no night stages so we could dispense with spot lamps and the car really looked and went superbly with Tony winning the rally with ease, on the Michelin radials.

to use the vehicles. The resulting spec included a rear bulkhead similar to the later Sherpa with a side entry door to a central wheel/tyre storage compartment. The larger items such as axle, struts, anti-roll bar etc were also to be housed centrally with the smaller spares in drawers at the rear.

Fuel can storage was in external lockers both for ease of loading and safety, and an electric welder was also carried. To provide 240 volt power for flood lighting and other small tools, we obtained a motor generator from Honeywell in the USA driven off the 12 volt vehicle system. Because of the necessity to run the engines in service areas, a vertical exhaust pipe was mounted on the side of the body which could be hooked up when parked. Reclining seats were fitted along with usual map reading lights, two-way radio, radio/cassette and storage box for food and brewing-up equipment.

It was soon realised that the workshop would not have labour available to prepare the vans so we decided to sub-contract the work to Del Lines of Atlantic Garage in Weston-Super-Mare who confirmed that he would be able to fit manual transmissions. He had already established a fine reputation for his conversion and rally preparation work and

Tony Pond/Fred Gallagher – Triumph TR7 V8 winners of the 1980 Rothmans Stages rally on the Isle of Man

More EAs

Following the success of the first EA service van, John Davenport agreed to increase the EA fleet. Before we carried out the conversions, a discussion was held with the mechanics to decide on the exact specification. After all, they were going we had no regrets when the vehicles were delivered to Abingdon. The first event for the new EA vans was the Scottish Rally.

Three cars on the Scottish, with Roger joining Tony and Per, brought out a strong service team with no less than three EA vans and three Sherpas to enable us to cover our own tyre requirements.

Tony was fastest TR7 V8 performer finishing fourth overall, with Roger at last gaining a finish after his previous

1980

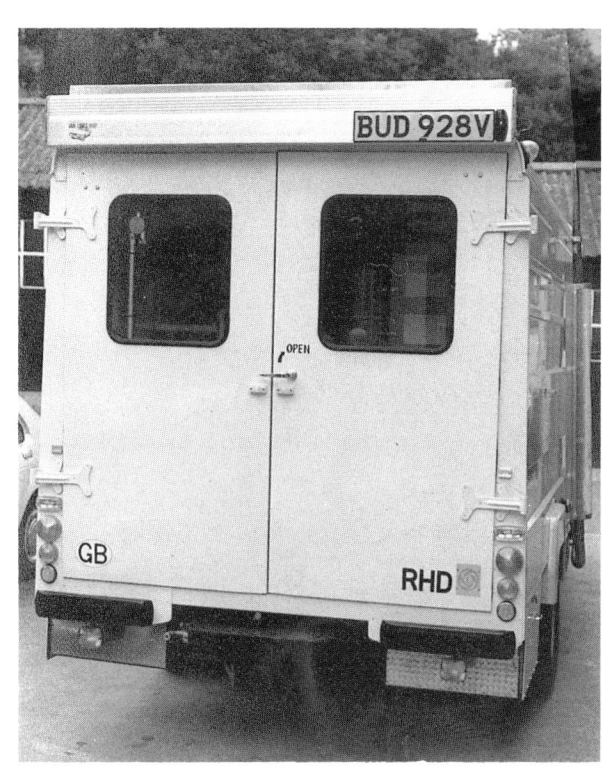

One of the new Leyland EA V8 service vans. The top box houses the canopy (I. Lines)

Interior of Leyland EA service van showing the tyre racks and components mountings

V8 Power

mechanical problems with ninth overall; Per retired with a blown engine.

We had been experiencing marginal cooling on the V8 installation and after testing spoilers, removing bumpers etc, the greatest improvement was found to be achieved by cutting a number plate-size hole in the bumper. On International events this was not strictly legal but we took a calculated risk by covering the hole with the number plate but on stages, the number plate was moved to a position on the front apron between the headlamps.

Four carburettor installation on TR7 V8 (Colin Taylor Productions)

Testing the TR7 V8 on the 'snake' course at Chobham

Roger Clark finding some traction during the 1980 Scottish Rally

1980

24 Hours of Ypres

Both drivers carried out comprehensive recces of the route which had the advantage of being confined to a relatively small area around the town of Ypres. The local dealer owned by family Vandermeersch was very helpful and provided garage facilities. We took a strong team of mechanics to Belgium with the three EA vans and two Rover 3500 service vehicles and stayed at the Hotel Sultan again. The Michelin radials were again used with sufficient quantity of dry, intermediate and wet compounds to cover our requirements at last.

24 Hours of Ypres 1980; the winning TR7 V8 of Tony Pond/ Fred Gallagher on the finish ramp (Colin Taylor Productions)

The first leg of the rally, two laps of a 220 km circuit, was a battle between the TR7 V8s, the Porsches of Beguin, Vincent and Zanini, the two Alfa Romeo Alfetta Turbos of Pregliasco and Verini and the Saab Turbo of Blomqvist. The Porches had various problems but were a continuing threat to Tony Pond when running. Tony had a gearbox change and there were several panic service points with the changing weather conditions. Stuart Turner would have had a smile to himself if he had witnessed John Davenport literally throwing wheels out of a service van in his excitement at one service point.

On the second night Per Eklund ran into a lamp post badly damaging the front of the car but, after some emergency repairs from one of the roving Rover service cars, he made the next service point. Tony maintained an increasing lead and apart from some problems with brakes staying on, was all set for a win. Per managed to take a wrong turn and arrived at a control from the wrong direction but was given a time by the marshals. He kept up a typical aggressive performance until tragically the gearbox failed on the last stage and he retired.

Tony won by a margin of 8 m 14 s, a very good result against some strong opposition, a repeat of his win in 1978.

1000 Lakes Rally

The interesting news for the 1000 Lakes was that Timo Makinen would drive one of our cars. Through his co-driver, Erkki Salonen, sponsorship was obtained from the Pohjola Insurance Co and the popular Finnish magazine, Seura. This was going to be a nice reunion for some of us who had been at Abingdon when Timo drove for BMC, because not only had Timo been a wonderful driver, but he was great character to be with.

Timo Makinen renewing his association with Abingdon for the 1980 1000 Lakes Rally

To choose tyres and to enable Timo to get used to the car, a test session was arranged in Finland during the first week in August. Two mechanics took the test car to Turku and I travelled by air to Helsinki with Richard Hurdwell. With our less than satisfactory relationship with Dunlop in recent months, John Davenport was anxious to test alternative makes of tyre, so that in addition to Dunlop and Michelin, we took with us some 15 inch Pirelli tyres.

We carried out three days of testing with suspension changes as well as tyre assessment taking place. The Pirelli tyres were virtually as quick as the Michelin, but heavier, so eventually we decided on mostly 15 inch Michelins for the rally. Testing took place on public roads again with help from some local enthusiasts with two-way radios. Before our return from the testing, Timo took us for a run in his fantastic powerboat; we stopped for a meal at an island restaurant before returning to the marina in the dark at 50 mph plus!

The rally cars were sent out with the EAs direct to Helsinki from Felixstowe with one mechanic, while the rest of the party flew to Helsinki. Timo seemed to take to the V8 quickly and, as was expected, attracted considerable publicity. Both cars were on the four carburettor set-up, the injection having been put aside for the moment. The rally started off without problems, with Per Eklund setting a fast pace with times in the top three. Timo, lacking much rally practice, was slower but nevertheless making respectable times. We had a few dramas but Timo, for some reason, kept running his fuel

V8 Power

Fred Gallagher – Leyland co-driver 1977–80

Per Eklund – BL driver 1979–80

tank dangerously low, and we were not too impressed with the rather laid-back manner of his co-driver. Unfortunately, Timo let his car get low once too often, ran out on a stage and ran out of time. Per continued at unabated speed to finish an excellent third overall, our best World Championship result.

Rothmans Manx International

We entered two cars in the 1980 Manx for Tony and Roger, once again using the Michelin radial tyres. The organisers had tightened up the number of places where service could be taken which meant that two EAs and a Rover 3500 'chase' car were able to cope with our service requirements. The rally was once again successful for Tony who finished first overall after some brake problems but disappointing for Roger who retired with a broken axle shaft. The traction which we were now finding with the Michelin tyres had found the weak link in the axle which was still using the incredible Timken unit hub bearing.

When labour permitted, Richard Hurdwell had a mechanic working on a special chassis incorporating many of the modifications which had been found necessary to get the most out of the car. This included increasing the rear wheel movement, increasing the wheelbase and moving the engine back. At the same time, a new glass-fibre front body section had been built with the assistance of Jim Oates' special body section at Cowley, incorporating Vauxhall type rectangular headlamps. This was designed to reduce weight and drag and improve air flow to the radiator, and had been instigated by JD. Nobody else seemed to know much about it and as far as I could see we could not use it on an international event until it was homologated, which seemed rather unlikely at this stage.

Left: *Tony Pond/Fred Gallagher winners of the Rothmans Manx International Rally 1980, TR7 V8*

Right: *Per Eklund's damaged TR7 on the ramp at Abingdon, Ypres 1980*

Pirelli Tour of Cumbria

With the RAC looming near, a low-key entry was made in this national rally to finalise the suspension and tyre requirements for the major event of the year. The rally was based on Carlisle and although this was a testing rally for us, the new 'square' headlamp front-end fitted to the car caused much interest. Tony and Fred drove a good event to finish second overall.

Tony Pond/Fred Gallagher TR7 V8 on the Castrol 80 Rally

Two weeks later, we entered Tony in the Castrol 80 in Wales but more trouble with punctures caused his retirement despite my intervention in the middle of one forest stage with spare tyres. It is amazing what you can do with radio communications!

Eaton Yale Rallysprint

The annual rallysprint at Donington was held on Saturday 25 October with Tony Pond sharing his TR7 V8 with Alan Jones, the Grand Prix driver. This was the first rallysprint that I had attended and it was very pleasing to witness Tony Pond finish first overall with Alan Jones second equal with John Watson. Tony was fastest on the rally stages, with his seventh overall in the circuit race in identical Mazda RX7s being good enough to give him victory.

The last event in which we were involved before the RAC Rally was to supply a car and service crew to the winner of the Austin/Morris Mini Challenge. The winner, Harry Hockley, found the V8 a bit of a handful after a Mini and did not figure in the results of the Crest Hotels Forest Stages rally.

The Metro Sagas

As mentioned previously, Mike Kyle and Ron Elkins had been flat out finishing off the specification of the Metroplus, a kit of performance parts for the new Metro hatchback to be announced at the Motor Show. On 14 October, with some relief, Mike sent out a circular to all our appointed stockists enclosing leaflets detailing what would be available, together with the new Motorsport Leisurewear order form. This was received with enthusiasm by our stockists and orders immediately started to come in.

The other thing that was happening concerning the Metro was Project Metro. Some months earlier, Trevor Reeves had approached Safety Devices at Newmarket asking

V8 Power

Project Metro built by Safety Devices for the 1980 Motor Show

Engine compartment of Project Metro

if anything could be done with the new Metro for rallycross. An idea was developed and with only three months to go before the Motor Show, JD agreed to finance the building of a one-off space frame rally-cross car. Two standard Metro bodyshells were supplied to Newmarket from which to build the car and take the GRP mouldings but when the decision was made to show the car at the Motor Show, Brian Wilkinson of Safety Devices could see that he had a time problem.

Working night and day, he and his technicians, using only the front bulkhead from the standard car, built a space frame clothed in GRP panels built by Barry Shepherd of Rawlson at Dover, and fitted with an engine supplied by Trevor Reeves.

The engine was basically a 1275 A type unit with a Motospeed designed 16-valve twin overhead camshaft cylinder head and twin Weber 48 DCOE carburettors. Power was quoted at 197 bhp at 8500 rpm from the 1480 cc dry sump unit! Brakes were Austin Maxi, with double wishbone front suspension, a four-link beam axle at the rear, and 9 × 13 inch Minilite wheels. Brian Wilkinson designed a very attractive red/white/blue livery for the car but this was rejected by JD in favour of an Austin-Morris design. The beautifully prepared car, weighing 560 kg, was finished at the eleventh hour and shipped to the Motor Show at the NEC.

Rumours again; it had been suggested that there was likely to be a severe cut in rallying in 1981 but JD was unable (or unwilling) to give the department any concrete news. With the RAC Rally just round the corner, this was most unsettling for the staff at Abingdon particularly as we still did not know to where or if the Department was going to move.

RAC FINALE

The 1980 RAC Rally started and finished in Bath and I think there were very few people in the department who really thought that this would be the swansong of the Triumph TR7. In addition to the three regulars, Tony, Per and Roger the fourth entry was John Buffum from USA, who had been the SCCA Champion in 1977, 1978 and 1979. JD decided to let him run the Pierburg fuel injection engine under the eye of David Wood to gain some more experience with the system. John had a contract with BF Goodrich tyres in USA and elected to run them on the RAC along with a service crew of his own,

working in conjunction with our team. Our cars were on Michelin tyres following recent events and testing had proved their apparent superiority.

We had a large service team out on the rally with three EAs, two Sherpas, two Rover 3500s plus a Range Rover with a 'flying' emergency crew under Den Green backing-up wherever necessary. I was in a Rover 2600 with Tony Mason co-driving which proved to be a most entertaining experience.

The rally got off to a bad start when on the first stage at Longleat, Tony Pond went off the track and collided with a wooden structure in the lion's den. The roof was crushed and the windscreen smashed, among other things, which gave the lads some hectic moments at the first service point. A new windscreen was taped in place after the roof was pushed back into shape and I then followed Tony up to Blenheim Palace with some motorcycle visors to give to Tony and Fred to protect their eyes from slivers of glass. At the entrance, Brian Moylan (for many years a Competitions Department mechanic) was marshalling and we talked our way past him to get to the stage start to offer Tony the visors.

The rally moved north and on the M1 motorway I had a lucky escape when my car touched the bumper of a crashed Cortina embedded in the centre reservation Armco, while doing about 60 mph. All the traffic swerved and it was a miracle that there was not a major accident.

In Kielder forest Per Eklunds car broke an oil pipe and retired and John Buffum slid off losing a lot of time. Tony had dropped to about 140th after Longleat but was now clawing his way back up the field only to go off again, dropping over 20 minutes.

At Windermere there was a night halt where Roger Clark was in need of a new gearbox. The brothers running the local dealership of R. Smith (Windermere) Ltd arranged an escort through the back streets after the restart and the car was soon on its way after a civilised gearbox change by our mechanics on the garage ramp.

Tony continued to gain time and was up to seventh overall after one of his best drives in a TR7. On stage 58, Roger had his oil pump belt fail and on the very last stage, the unlucky John Buffum also retired with a broken axle shaft. Tony held seventh position to the end to save the day for Abingdon. The rally had been tough and not without administration problems at some service points.

Now all there was to do was pick up the pieces and

1980

hope for a limited TR7 programme next year. One of the problems seemed to be that as the Department was under the wing of the Service Division we were likely to receive headcount cuts similar to other departments in the Division.

Special Tuning & TR7 Chopped

The announcement was made that the 42 acre MG site had been sold. With production ending at the end of October and MG now closed, Motorsport remained as the last working Department, but still without a home. The commercial business looked all set to improve its profits with the Metroplus kits, the Project Metro rallycross car having been the centre of attention at the Motor Show.

Imagine the horror that greeted the news from John Davenport that the commercial operation was to be closed, with the loss of seventeen jobs (out of a total of 47). This came as a severe shock to the staff; it was hardly a fitting Christmas present. In addition, came the not altogether unexpected news that the TR7 had competed in its last rally. There had been signs the previous year that, perhaps, production of the controversial sports car was to be stopped, when the 30 cars prepared to launch the 16-valve engine version were disposed of. Only a week after the RAC Rally a press release was sent out headed 'BL Motorsport – New Horizons' spelling out the sad news. The reason for closing the commercial operation was given as financial, with difficulty being found in generating enough profit to warrant its continuance. The motor sport programme would be replaced by a series of other activities based on Metro and Rover 3500.

A copy of the press release was enclosed with a letter to our stockists explaining the U-turn. This was, particularly, a sad decision for Mike Kyle and his staff who had worked so hard to create the Metroplus package. It was also such a waste of money. With the MG facilities all but closed we had to change the MG phone number, Abingdon 25251 (previously the famous Abingdon 251), to the new anonymous number 23951, from 1 December.

I think most of us in the Department were a little mystified at the proposed Metro competition programme. JD was very secretive and not even David Wood knew what was being planned, more or less until it happened. What we did know was that Stuart in our parts department had sent a standard Metro bodyshell over to Williams Engineering at Didcot. Later it was learned that Williams had been contracted to carry out a design exercise with a view to using a mid-engine layout in a Metro-shaped body. It was disappointing not to be involved in this new project but by now much of our enthusiasm had been eroded simply by the way that JD had run the department; as someone commented: many things had been achieved in spite of JD!

Goodbye Abingdon

Despite the closure of the commercial operation, a large quantity of Metroplus parts were supplied to the ST stockists to satisfy early orders. With the restructuring of the Department, I was given the responsibility of disposing of the bulk of the Special Tuning parts, amounting to approximately £700,000 in value.

David Wood took over the workshop and appointed two of the mechanics as technicians to assist him with special projects. David also had the task of identifying which competition parts he wanted to retain for future projects.

John Davenport was in the throes of sorting out with the Service Division management where the Department would be housed and, although it was to be Cowley, no space or building had been identified. At first, the old Product Training Centre was selected but this was not suitable and then, eventually, the old CKD warehouse in Hardings Yard was earmarked for Motorsport. It was to be shared with the Service Centre and a number of modifications had to be made to the building, in particular to provide office accommodation and a stores and make provision for installing the engine test-bed and rolling-road dynamometer.

We were now well into 1981 with a date to move fixed at 12/13 June, allowing a few days to make good the fixtures in C Block.

The Project Metro was brought into the workshop and Richard Hurdwell supervised the preparation of the car for its first outing, the car never having turned a wheel under its own power previously.

Tom Walkinshaw Racing at Kidlington were preparing two Range Rovers for BL France for the Paris–Dakar Rally (for Metge and Zanirolli) and we sent two mechanics over to help with final preparation. These two, John West and Paul Drake, went on the event to service the vehicles travelling between service points in a Piper aircraft. Of their 21 service points they reckon the gearboxes were rebuilt at 15!

At Easter, the rallycross Metro was taken to the rallycross meeting at Lydden Hill driven by Trevor Reeves, but the steering failed in the first race which was rather unfortunate; our resident chassis engineer looked a bit sheepish! Power was lacking and on the return it was discovered that the timing had slipped.

The MG factory rallied from its death throes for a few days commencing 18 March, with the first of the auction sales of the remaining plant and equipment. I took the opportunity to have a quick look in on the auction and saw the board room table go for £650 with the chairs fetching £1600; a small notice from the gents toilet in B Block, asking people not to throw cigarette ends in to the urinal, went for £28! All very sad.

To add to our sadness, John Howlett, our Competitions Press Officer now with an office at Abingdon, was killed in a car accident on the Oxford–Faringdon road.

The final fling was to hold a public sale on Saturday 16 May which attracted a large number of customers, some just for a nostalgic last look I think, with the remaining parts at the end of the day being sold in bulk to an Australian motor trader.

During the last week in May, the rest of the equipment and parts were taken to the new building at Cowley, now rapidly being completed. The remaining office staff agreed to come in on Saturday 13 June to load the office furniture; the plan was that we would go to work at Cowley on Monday 15 June.

It seemed that a further headcount cut was imminent. John Davenport arrived back from a meeting on the Friday before the Department moved from Cowley and I stuck my head round the office door to say goodnight and asked if it had been decided how many more staff would be made redun-

365

V8 Power

dant. The answer was ten; I asked John what my own position would be and he replied that I would be one of the ten to go. I was not really surprised; with no competition programme for 1981 and with the job title of Competitions Manager, there was no job.

I started work at Cowley on the Monday morning and left the Company at 16.30 hr on the same day along with nine other members of the staff. At last JD had got rid of all the old BMC faces and retained his group of yes men!

Footnote

Finally, I am not sure whether the top management over the years fully appreciated all the hard work put in behind the scenes in the Department, by the supervisory staff, the mechanics, the office staff and the parts people, but without their enthusiastic dedication this period of motor sport history could not have been written.

The trade support the Department received was tremendous, particularly from the staff of Castrol, Dunlop, Champion, SU, Lucas, Ferodo and Automotive Products who spent many a day 'in the field' both testing and with on-event service.

A word of thanks should also go to all the various personnel throughout BMC/BL in Plants as far apart as Cardiff, Llanelli, Coventry, Longbridge and Oxford for all their technical assistance, supply of components and moral support which was given to Abingdon, often unofficially, to keep the programmes going.

So after 25 years and a few months, the Competitions Department at Abingdon was no more, the end of an era. The department did of course continue and it is a source of disappointment to those associated with it both during the Abingdon years and after that the Metro 6R4 programme was such a disaster.

A

Competitions Department Letter Headings

B

Works Drivers' Significant Results

This is a driver by driver summary of the 1st, 2nd & 3rd positions achieved overall in International rallies during the 25 years from 1955–1980.

Rauno Aaltonen

1963	Monte Carlo	3rd
1963	Alpine Rally	1st
1964	Liège Rally	1st
1965	Geneva Rally	1st
1965	Czech Rally	1st
1965	1000 Lakes Rally	2nd
1965	Polish Rally	1st
1965	Three Cities	1st
1965	RAC Rally	1st
1966	Tulip Rally	1st
1966	Czech Rally	1st
1966	1000 Lakes	3rd
1967	Monte Carlo	1st
1967	Swedish	3rd
1967	Tulip Rally	3rd
1968	Monte Carlo	3rd

Paddy Hopkirk

1962	RAC Rally	2nd
1963	Tulip Rally	2nd
1963	Tour de France	3rd
1964	Monte Carlo	1st
1964	Austrian Alpine	1st
1965	Circuit of Ireland	1st
1966	Austrian Alpine	1st
1966	Acropolis Rally	3rd
1967	Flowers Rally	2nd
1967	Circuit of Ireland	1st
1967	Acropolis Rally	1st
1967	Alpine Rally	1st
1968	TAP Rally	2nd
1968	L-S Marathon	2nd
1969	Circuit of Ireland	2nd
1970	Scottish Rally	2nd

Donald Morley

1960	RAC Rally	3rd
1961	Alpine Rally	1st
1962	Alpine Rally	1st

Brian Culcheth

1970	World Cup Rally	2nd
1970	Scottish Rally	1st
1971	Cyprus Rally	2nd
1972	Cyprus Rally	2nd
1977	Manx Rally	2nd

Per Eklund

1979	Mintex Rally	2nd
1979	Scottish Rally	3rd
1980	1000 Lakes	3rd

Tony Fall

1966	Circuit of Ireland	1st
1966	Polish Rally	1st
1966	Geneva Rally	2nd
1966	Scottish Rally	1st
1967	Danube Rally	1st
1967	Geneva Rally	1st
1967	Marathon de la Route	2nd

Harry Kallstrom

1966	RAC Rally	2nd

Timo Makinen

1964	Tulip Rally	1st
1964	RAC Rally	2nd
1965	Monte Carlo	1st
1965	1000 Lakes	1st
1965	RAC Rally	2nd
1966	Czech Rally	3rd
1966	Polish Rally	2nd
1966	1000 Lakes	1st
1966	Three Cities	1st
1967	Tulip Rally	2nd
1967	1000 Lakes	1st

Pat Moss

1959	German Rally	2nd
1960	Alpine Rally	2nd
1960	Liège Rally	1st
1961	RAC Rally	2nd
1962	Tulip Rally	1st
1962	German Rally	1st
1962	Alpine Rally	3rd
1962	Geneva Rally	3rd
1962	Polish Rally	2nd
1962	RAC Rally	3rd

Julien Vernaeve

1967	Geneva Rally	2nd
1967	Marathon de la Route	2nd
1968	Tulip Rally	3rd

Tony Pond

1976	Manx Rally	3rd
1977	Boucles de Spa	1st
1977	Mintex Rally	3rd
1977	Elba Rally	3rd
1977	Scottish Rally	2nd
1978	24 Hrs of Ypres	1st
1978	Manx Rally	1st
1980	24 Hrs of Ypres	1st
1980	Manx Rally	1st

Peter Riley

1959	Liège Rally	3rd
1961	Acropolis Rally	3rd

Lars Ytterbring

1967	Scottish Rally	2nd
1968	Scottish Rally	2nd

C

Event Results
1955–80

1955

Month	Event	Car	Crew	Reg	No	Result
Jan	Monte Carlo Rally	MG Magnette (Aramis)	G. Holt/S. Asbury/J. Brookes	KJB910	49	178 o/all
		MG Magnette (Athos)	R. Holt/A. Collinson/W. Cave	KJB908	58	237 o/all
		MG Magnette (Porthos)	J. Shaw/B. Brown/F. Finnemore	KJB909	36	202 o/all
		Austin Westminster	Mrs. W. Wisdom/Joan Johns		369	68 o/all, 5th Ladies
		Austin Westminster	M. Morris-Goodall/S. Moore	POM753	8	232nd o/all
		Austin Westminster	J. Gott/R. Brookes			
Mar	RAC Rally	Austin Westminster	J. Flynn/Mrs. Flynn			
		Austin Westminster	P. Fotheringham-Parker/Mrs Fotheringham-Parker			
		Austin Westminster	D. Johns/Mrs J. Johns			
		MG TF1500	Pat Moss/Pat Faichney	KRX90	193	3rd Ladies
		MG Magnette	R. Holt/B. Brown		200	
		MG Magnette	G. Holt/J. Brookes	KJB910	198	1st Class 3
		MG Magnette	L. Shaw/A. Collinson		199	
April	Circuit of Ireland	MG TF1500	I. Appleyard/Mrs. I. Appleyard	KMO836	192	4th o/all
		MG TF1500	J. Flynn/Mrs. Flynn	KMO837	193	Finisher
		MG TF1500	C. Vard/L. Young			
May	Tulip Rally	MG Magnette	Pat Moss/Mrs Sheila Cooper	KJB908	139	Ret – engine
		MG Magnette	L. Shaw/F. D. Lawton			
		MG Magnette	G. Holt/J. Brookes			
		Austin Westminster	G. Burgess/I. Walker			Ret – engine
		Austin Westminster	D. Johns/Mrs Joan Johns	POM754	25	
		Austin Westminster	F. Leavens/Mrs J. Leavens			
May	Daily Express Mtg. Silverstone	Morris Minor (BMC entry)	M. Christie			Class G
		MG Magnette (MG entry)	R.W. Jacobs			Class F
June	Scottish Rally	MG TF500	R. Kay/D. Mickel	KMO837	61	3rd class 8
		MG TF1500	N. Paterson/A. Craig	KMO835	63	1st class 8
		MG TF1500	E. Herrald/P. Chisholm	KMO836	62	2nd class 8
			Manufacturers Team Prize			
		Austin Westminster	F. Grounds/		89	6th class 4
		Austin Westminster	Joan Johns/		90	1st Ladies, 7th class 4
		Austin Westminster	Mrs J. Leavens/	POM755	91	4th class 4
June	Le Mans 24 Hr Race	MGA Prototype Ex182	R. Jacobs/J. Flynn	LBL301	42	Ret – accident
		MGA Prototype Ex182	K. Miles/J. Lockett	LBL302	41	12 o/all, 5th class
		MGA Prototype Ex182	E. Lund/H. Waeffler	LBL303	64	17 o/all, 6th class
		MGA Prototype Ex182	Spare car	LBL304	40	
Aug	Liège–Rome–Liège	Austin Healey 100S	P. Reece/D. Scott			Ret – accident
		Austin Westminster	G. Burgess/S. Croft-Pearson	POM754	69	31 o/all, 13th class
		Austin A50	J. Gott/W. Shepherd	LJB371	34	36 o/all, 11th class
			Inter-Club Team			
Sept	Golden Jubilee Ulster TT	MGA Twin Cam	R. Flockhart/J. Lockett	LBL301	34	Ret – manifold
		MGA Le Mans 1500	J. Fairman/P. Wilson	LBL303	35	4th class
		MGA Le Mans 1500	E. Lund/R. Stoop		36	Ret – fuel tank
Oct	Montlhèry Record Run	Riley Pathfinder	R. Porter	KRX820		Production Car
		Austin Healey 100	R. Flockhart	ROB423		Records – Each car covered
		MGA 1500	K. Wharton	KMO3--		100 miles in one hour
		Austin Westminster	J. Gott	ROH744		
		Wolseley 6/90	J. Gott	XFC213		

Appendix C

1956

Jan	Monte Carlo Rally	Austin Westminster	J. Gott/W. Shepherd/J. Williamson	ROH902	114	55 o/all
		Austin Westminster	G. Burgess/S. Croft-Pearson/ I. Walker	POM754	105	82 o/all (ret – accident)
		Austin Westminster	Joan Johns/Pat Moss/ Doreen Rich	POM755	139	85 o/all (ret – accident)
		Austin Westminster	K. Wharton/G. Shanley	ROC616	299	56 o/all, 4th class
		Austin Westminster	R. Baxter/R. Phillips	POM753	334	Ret-electrical
		Austin Westminster	M. Couper/P. Fillingham/N. Lloyd	SOL125	184	1st Concours de Confort
		Austin A50	J. Sears/A. Scott-Brown/K. Best	LJB687	99	76 o/all (ret – accident)
		Riley Pathfinder	J. Bremner/A. Oldworth	KJB13	42	69 o/all (ret – accident)
		Riley Pathfinder	L. Sims/R. Stokes/T. Bounds		166	65 o/all
		MG Magnette	G. Grant/N. Davis/C. Davis	JRX251	34	Ret – dynamo
		MG Magnette	Nancy Mitchell/Doreen Reece/ Susan Hindermarsh	KJB910	327	59 o/all, 3rd Ladies
		Riley Pathfinder	A. Warren/P. Wilson		142	69 o/all?
Mar	RAC Rally	Austin Westminster	Joan Johns/D. Johns	ROH744	12	6 o/all, 2nd class } Team prize
		Austin Westminster	G. Burgess/S. Croft-Pearson	ROH902	14	
		Austin A50	J. Sears/K. Best/P. Garnier	LJB371	16	3rd class
		MGA 1500	Pat Moss/Ann Wisdom	MJB167	79	3rd Ladies, 5th class
		MG Magnette	Nancy Mitchell/Doreen Reece			
		Riley Pathfinder	K. Wharton/G. Shanley	KJB280	45	
Mar	Lyons Charbonnières Rally	MG Magnette	Nancy Mitchell/Doreen Reece	JRX251	132	47 o/all, 1st Ladies
April	Mille Miglia	MGA 1500	Nancy Mitchell/Pat Faichney	MBL867	228	72 o/all, 1st Ladies, 5th class
		MGA 1500	P. Scott-Russell/T. Haig	MJB167	229	70, o/all, 4th class
May	Tulip Rally	MG Magnette	Nancy Mitchell/Doreen Reece	KJB910	147	Excluded-alloy panels
		Austin Westminster	S. Henson/J. Sears/ R. Bentsted-Smith	POM754	84	2nd class
		Austin Westminster	Joan Johns/D. Johns	POM755	86	4th class
		Austin Westminster	G. Burgess/S. Croft-Pearson	ROH744	85	
		Riley Pathfinder	D. Morley/E. Morley/J. Shand	XYK111	88	4th class
May	Daily Express Mtg. Silverstone	Austin Westminster (Austin entry)	K. Wharton			Class D
		MG Magnette (MG entry)	A.T. Foster			Class F
May	Dieppe Rally	MG Magnette	Pat Moss/Ann Wisdom	MBL417		2nd Ladies
May	Geneva Rally	Austin A90	J. Gott/W Shepherd	ROH902		2nd class
		Austin A90	P. Wilson/M. Chambers			3rd class
		Austin A50	J. Sears/K. Best			19 o/all, 1st class
		MG Magnette	Nancy Mitchell/Patsy Burt			2nd Ladies
June	Midnight Sun Rally	MG Magnette	Nancy Mitchell/Doreen Reece			4th Ladies
July	Alpine Rally	MGA 1500	J. Gott/R. Brookes	MJB191	324	Ret – axle shaft
		MGA 1500	J. Milne/D. Johns	MJB314	314	4th class
		MGA 1500	W. Shepherd/J. Williamson	MJB167	308	5th class
		MGA 1500	J. Sears/K. Best	MRX42	330	Ret – accident
		MGA 1500	Nancy Mitchell/Pat Faichney	MBL867	326	15 o/all, 1st Ladies, 3rd class
	Liège–Rome–Liège	MGA 1500	J. Gott/C. Tooley	MJB191	75	13 o/all, 6th class
		MGA 1500	G. Burgess/S. Croft-Pearson	MRX42	24	Ret – sump
		MGA 1500	J. Milne/R. Bensted-Smith	MRX43	15	14 o/all, 7th class
		MGA 1500	Nacny Mitchell/Anne Hall	MBL867	38	26 o/all, 2nd Ladies
Sept	Viking Rally	Austin A105	J. Sears/K. Best	TOL564	47	36 o/all
		Austin A105	Joan Johns/D. Johns	TOL565	49	
		Austin A105	T. Frantzen/V. Steen	TOL563	48	
		MG Magnette	Nancy Mitchell/Doreen Reece	KJB909	45	64 o/all

1955 to 1980

1957

Jan	Monte Carlo Rally	Austin A105	J. Gott			Rally cancelled
		Austin A105	J. Sears			Suez Crisis
		Austin A105	Joan Johns			
		MG Magnette	Nancy Mitchell			
		Morris Minor	Pat Moss			
Feb	Sestrières Rally	MG Magnette	Nancy Mitchell/Anne Hall	NJB365		60 o/all, 2nd Ladies
		Austin A105	J. Sears/K. Best	TOL564	138	42 o/all, 6th class
		Morris Minor 1000	R. Brookes/E. Brookes	NJB277		3rd class
Mar	Lyons–Charbonnières Rally	MGA 1500	Nancy Mitchell/Doreen Reece	MBL867	98	32 o/all, 1st Ladies
May	Tulip Rally	Morris Minor 1000	J. Gott/C. Tooley	NMO933	161	108 o/all, 12th class
		Morris Minor 1000	Pat Moss/Ann Wisdom	NJB277		90 o/all, 16th class
		Austin A35	R. Brookes/E. Brookes			75 o/all, 10th class
		Austin A35	Joan Johns/S. Moore			94 o/all, 10th class
		Austin A105	J. Sears/K. Best	TOL564		41 o/all, 4th class
		MG Magnette	Nancy Mitchell/Patsy Burt			76 o/all, 3rd Ladies, 9th class
	Alpine Rally	MGA 1500	J. Gott/C. Tooley			Rally cancelled
		MGA 1500	J. Williamson/W. Shepherd			Suez Crisis
		MGA 1500	J. Milne/D. Johns			
		MGA 1500	Nancy Mitchell/Pat Faichney			
		Austin A105	J. Sears/K. Best			
		Morris Minor 1000	Pat Moss/Ann Wisdom			
July	Int Class G Records	Austin A35	G. Horrocks/T. Threlfall/P. Rivière/ R. Simpson/J. Taylor/M. Chambers			4 days – 11,572.965 km – 74.91 mph
						5 days – 14,475.451 km – 74.95 mph
						15,000 km – 74.82 mph
						10,000 miles – 74.79 mph
						6 days – 17,341.537 km – 74.79 mph
						20,000 km – 74.89 mph
						7 days – 20,250.512 km – 74.90 mph
Aug	Liège–Rome–Liège	MGA 1500	J. Gott/C. Tooley	MJB167	48	14 o/all, 8th class
		MGA 1500	Nancy Mitchell/Joan Johns	OBL311	5	16 o/all, 1st Ladies, 9th class
		MGA 1500	J. Milne/W. Shepherd	MRX43	24	Ret – accident
		MGA 1500	G. Harris/G. Hacquin			Ret – suspension
		Morris Minor 1000	Pat Moss/Ann Wisdom	NMO933	39	23 o/all, 2nd Ladies, 4th class

1958

Jan	Monte Carlo Rally	Austin A105	J. Sears/K Best/S. Croft-Pearson			Ret
		Austin A105	W. Shepherd/J. Williamson			Ret
		Austin A105	W. M. Couper/P. Fillingham/ P. Tabor	VOH466	318	Ret
		Wolseley 1500	J. Gott/C. Tooley	OJB412	290	Ret – accident
		MG Magnette	Nancy Mitchell/Joan Johns		341	Ret
		Morris Minor 1000	Pat Moss/Ann Wisdom	NMO933	313	Ret – accident
		Riley 1.5	R. Brookes/E. Brookes			Ret
		Riley 1.5	J. Bremner/T. Oldworth	OMO602		Ret
		Austin A35	J Sprinzel/W. Cave		314	Ret
		Austin Healey 100/6	T. Wisdom/J. Hay	UOC741		Ret
Mar	RAC Rally	Riley 1.5	Nancy Mitchell/Joan Johns	OMO600	169	Ret – accident
		Riley 1.5	K. Lee/A. Sinclair		167	3rd class
		Morris Minor 1000	Pat Moss/Ann Wisdom	NMO933	201	4 o/all, 1st Ladies, 1st class
		Austin A35	J. Sprinzel/R. Bensted-Smith	119KMH	129	Ret – accident
		Austin Healey 100/6	J. Sears/P. Garnier	UOC711	90	52 o/all, 5th class
April	Circuit of Ireland	Riley 1.5	Pat Moss/Ann Wisdom	PBL737	41	20 o/all, 1st Ladies, 3rd class
		Riley 1.5	W. Chambers/D. Mcwhir			
		Riley 1.5	F. Biggar/J. Moore			
April	Tulip Rally	Riley 1.5	Pat Moss/Ann Wisdom	OMO601	129	19 o/all, 2nd Ladies, 5th class
		Austin Healey 100/6	J. Sears/P. Garnier	UOC741	13	Ret – distributor drive
		MGA 1500	Nancy Mitchell/G. Wilton-Clarke		49	34 o/all, 4th Ladies, 4th class
		MG Magnette	D. Seigle-Morris/J. Sprinzel	D20		Ret – w/pump
		Riley 1.5	J. Gott/D. Johns	OMO602	101	Ret – engine
		Riley 1.5	J. Brookes/M. Sutcliffe		128	24 o/all, 7th class
		Riley 1.5	R. Brookes/E. Brookes		130	

371

Appendix C

Month	Event	Car	Crew	Reg	No	Result
June	Midnight Sun Rally	MGA 1500	Pat Moss/Ann Wisdom	OBL311	25	9th Ladies, 5th class
		Austin A35	J. Sprinzel/L. Arnstein		78	14th class
July	Alpine Rally	Austin Healey 100/6	Pat Moss/Ann Wisdom	PMO201	423	10 o/all, 1st Ladies, 4th class
		Austin Healey 100/6	Nancy Mitchell/G. Wilton-Clarke	TON792	426	12 o/all, 2nd Ladies, 6th class
		Austin Healey 100/6	J. Gott/C. Tooley	UOC741	416	Ret – NSR hub
		Austin Healey 100/6	J. Sears/S. Moore	PMO203	404	11 o/all, 5th class
		Austin Healey 100/6	W. Shepherd/J. Williamson	PMO202	428	7 o/all, 2nd class
Aug	Liège–Rome–Liège Rally	Austin Healey 100/6	Pat Moss/Ann Wisdom	PMO201	104	4 o/all, 1st Ladies, 1st class
		Austin Healey 100/6	Nancy Mitchell/Anne Hall	TON792	102	15 o/all, 2nd Ladies, 6th class
		Austin Healey 100/6	Joan Johns/S. Moore	PMO203		Ret – accident
		Austin Healey 100/6	G. Burgess/S. Croft-Pearson	PMO202	105	10 o/all, 4th class
		MGA Twin Cam	J. Gott/R. Brookes	PRX707	78	9 o/all
		Austin Healey Sprite	J. Sprinzel/R. Bensted-Smith	PMO200	25	Ret – stub axle
	Man. Team Prize Nos 104, 102 & 105					
Sept	Viking Rally	Morris Minor 1000	Pat Moss/Ann Wisdom	NMO933		2nd Ladies, 4th class 2
Sept	Int Class D Records	Austin Healey 100/6	G Horrocks/J. Clarke/R. Jones R. Simpson/W. Summers/J. Taylor/ T. Threlfall/M. Chambers	VOK490		5,000 miles – 98.50 mph 10,000 km – 97.31 mph 2 days – 98.73 mph 3 days – 97.33 mph 4 days – 97.04 mph 15,000 km – 97.04 mph 10,000 miles – 97.13 mph

1958 European Ladies Touring Car Championship 1st Pat Moss/Ann Wisdom
1958 European Touring Car Championship 6th Pat Moss/Ann Wisdom

1959

Month	Event	Car	Crew	Reg	No	Result
Jan	Monte Carlo Rally	Austin A40 Farina	Pat Moss/Ann Wisdom	XOE778	208	10 o/all, 1st Ladies, 2nd class
		Austin Healey Sprite	J. Sprinzel/W. Cave	PMO200	201	14 o/all, 3rd class
		MGA Twin Cam	J. Gott/R. Brookes	RMO101	106	Ret – accident
		Austin A105	W. Shepherd/J. Milne/ J. Williamson		109	53 o/all, 14th class
		Austin Healey Sprite	T. Wisdom/J. Hay,	XOH277	185	63 o/all. 5th class
		Austin Healey Sprite	R. Baxter/J. Reece		2	Ret – accident
Feb	Canadian Winter Rally	Austin A40 Farina	Pat Moss/Ann Wisdom	246–383	59	1st Ladies
Feb	Sestrières Rally	Austin A35	J. Sprinzel/S. Turner	MRX342	704	3rd class
		Riley 1.5	Pat Moss/Ann Wisdom	OMO602	646	20 o/all, 1st Ladies
		Austin Healey Sprite	T. Wisdom/J. Lucas	XOH277	310	39 o/all, 5th class
Mar	Lyons–Charbonnières Rally	Austin A40 Farina	Pat Moss/Ann Wisdom	XOE778	108	17 o/all, 1st Ladies, 4th class
		Austin Healey Sprite	J. Sprinzel/S. Turner			
Mar	Circuit of Ireland Rally	Morris Minor 1000	Pat Moss/Ann Wisdom	NMO933	1	14 o/all, 1st Ladies, 2nd class
April	Sebring 12 Hour Race	MGA Twin Cam	G. Ehrman/R. Saidel		28	2nd class 6
		MGA Twin Cam	J. Parkinson/J. Dalton		29	29 class 6
		MGA Twin Cam	J. Flaherty/R. Pickering/ S. Decker		30	30 Finisher
April	Tulip Rally	Austin Healey 100/6	Pat Moss/Ann Wisdom	PMO202	6	Ret – accident
		Austin Healey 100/6	J. Sears/P. Garnier	PMO203	5	8 o/all, 1st class
		MGA Twin Cam	J. Gott/C. Tooley	SBL707	28	Finisher
		MGA Twin Cam Coupè	J. Sprinzel/S. Turner	RMO101	29	Finisher
May	Acropolis Rally	Austin Healey 100/6	Pat Moss/Ann Wisdom	PMO201	2	Ret – accident
		MGA Twin Cam	J. Sprinzel/R. Bensted-Smith	RMO101	12	Ret – accident
June	Alpine Rally	Austin A40 Farina	Pat Moss/Ann Wisdom	XOK195	99	Ret-gearbox
		Austin Healey 3000	J. Gott/C. Tooley	SMO745	6	5th GT Cat, 2nd class
		Austin Healey 3000	W. Shepherd/J. Williamson	SMO744	2	Ret – accident
		Austin Healey 3000	J. Sears/S. Moore	SMO746	3	Ret – radiator
		MGA Twin Cam	J. Milne/S. Turner			Ret – accident

1955 to 1980

Sept	Liège–Rome–Liège Rally (Marathon de La Route)	Austin A40 Farina	Pat Moss/Ann Wisdom	XOK195	76	Ret – engine
		Austin Healey 3000	J. Gott/K. James	SMO745	48	Ret – OTL
		Austin Healey 3000	J. Sears/P. Garnier	SMO746	81	Ret – OTL
		Austin Healey 3000	P. Riley/R. Jones	SMO744	84	3 o/all, 7th GT Cat, 1st class
		Austin Healey 3000	G. Burgess/S. Croft-Pearson	PMO203	75	Ret – accident
Sept	Viking Rally	Austin A40 Farina	Pat Moss/Ann Wisdom	XOE778		2nd Ladies, 4th class
		Austin Seven	M. Chambers/P. Wilson	YOP663		51 o/all
Oct	German Rally	Austin Healey 3000	Pat Moss/Ann Wisdom	SMO746		2nd o/all, 1st Ladies
		Morris Mini Minor	Pat Ozanne/Ann Shepherd			
	Mini Miglia National Rally	Morris Mini Minor	Pat Moss/S. Turner	TJB199		1st o/all
Nov	RAC Rally	Morris Mini Minor	Pat Ozanne/N. Gilmour	TMO559	129	Ret
		Morris Mini Minor	K. James/I. Hall	TMO561	126	Ret
		Morris Mini Minor	A. Pitts/A. Marston	TMO560	135	Ret
		Morris Minor 1000	Pat Moss/Ann Wisdom	NMO933	121	26 o/all, 3rd Ladies
		Wolseley 1500	D. Johns/Joan Johns	OJB412	22	46 o/all, 1st class
		Austin Healey 3000	D. Morley/E. Morley	SMO745	9	4 o/all, 1st class
		Austin Healey 3000	J. Sears/W. Cave	SMO746	6	17 o/all, 2nd class
		Austin Healey 3000	J. Williamson/J. Milne		1	Ret
Dec	Portuguese Rally	Austin Healey 3000	Pat Moss/Ann Wisdom	PMO203		53 o/all, 1st Ladies, 4th class
		Morris Mini Minor	Nancy Mitchell/Pat Allison	TJB199	57	2nd Ladies, 54 o/all
		Austin Seven	P. Riley/A. Ambrose	618AOG		64 o/all
		Wolseley 6/99	M. Chambers/D. Green	TBL698	64	58 o/all
1960						
Jan	Monte Carlo Rally	Austin Seven	P. Riley/R. Jones	618AOG	110	23 o/all
		Austin Seven	T. Wisdom/J. Hay	619AOG	229	55 o/all
		Austin Seven	Nancy Mitchell/Pat Allison	617AOG	18	Ret
		Morris Mini Minor	D. Morley/E. Morley	TMO561	263	33 o/all
		Morris Mini Minor	A. Pitts/A. Ambrose	TMO560	284	73 o/all
		Morris Mini Minor	Pat Ozanne/Mrs N. Gilmour	TMO559	307	Ret
		Austin A40 Farina	Pat Moss/Ann Wisdom	947AOF	26	17 o/all, 1st Ladies, 4th class
	Sebring 12 Hour Race	MGA Twin Cam	E. Lund/C. Escott	Ch. Nos 2571-75		Ret – engine
		MGA Twin Cam	F. Hayes/E. Leavens			24 o/all, 3rd class
		MGA Twin Cam	J. Parkinson/J. Flaherty			4th class
	DHMCo	Austin Healey 3000	P. Riley/J. Sears	UJB143	18	3rd class
		Austin Healey 3000		UJB141		
		Austin Healey 3000	G. Gietner/J. L. Spencer	UJB142		5th class, 15th o/all
Mar	Lyons–Charbonnières Rally	Austin Healey 3000	Pat Moss/Ann Wisdom	SMO746	134	Ret – accident
April	Geneva Rally (Crit. de Divonne–Les Bains & Rallye des Allobrogues)	Austin Seven	Pat Ozanne/Pat Allison	617AOG	47	27 o/all, 3rd Ladies, 2nd class
		Austin Seven	D. Morley/E. Morley	618AOG	44	14 o/all, 1st class
		Austin Seven	A. Pitts/A. Ambrose	619AOG	45	Ret – accident
		Austin Healey 3000	Pat Moss/Ann Wisdom	SMO745	112	7 o/all, 1st Ladies, 1st class
April	Circuit of Ireland Rally	Austin Healey 3000	Pat Moss/Ann Wisdom	SMO744		Ret – gearbox
		Morris Mini Minor	D. Hiam/A. Ambrose			Ret
		Riley 1.5	Pat Ozanne/Pat Allison			Ret – sump
May	Tulip Rally	Austin Healey 3000	Pat Moss/Ann Wisdom	URX727	10	8 o/all, 1st Ladies, 1st class
		Austin Healey 3000	D. Morley/E. Morley	SJB471	9	21 o/all, 2nd class
		Austin A105	P. Riley/A. Ambrose	XOJ579	33	2nd class
		Morris Mini Minor	T. Christie/N. Paterson	TMO560	161	36 o/all, 3rd class
		Morris Mini Minor	P. Ozanne/Pat Allison	TMO561	159	72 o/all, 6th class
		Morris Mini Minor	J. Sprinzel/M. Hughes	TJB199	99	43 o/all, 2nd class
		Wolseley 6/99	J. Gott/W. Shepherd		34	
May	Acropolis Rally	Austin Seven	Pat Ozanne/Pat Allison	617AOG	120	Ret – ball joint
		Austin Seven	M. Sutcliffe/D. Astle	618AOG	122	31 o/all, 5th class
		Austin Seven	J. Milne/W. Bradley	619AOG	124	16 o/all, 4th class
		Austin Healey 3000	Pat Moss/Ann Wisdom	SMO745	4	Ret – steering
		Austin Healey 3000	P. Riley/A. Ambrose	SMO744	2	Ret – accident
June	Le Mans 24 Hr Race	Austin Healey 3000	P. Riley/J. Sears	UJB143	23	Ret–engine

Appendix C

June	Midnight Sun Rally	Wolseley 6/99	P. Riley/R. Jones	TBL698	9	9th class
		Austin A40 Farina	Pat Moss/Ann Wisdom	947AOF	22	3rd Ladies, 7th class
June	Alpine Rally	Morris Mini Minor	R. Jones/K. James	TMO559	5	Ret – accident
		Morris Mini Minor	A. Pitts/A. Ambrose	TMO560	1	4th class
		Morris Mini Minor	T. Gold/M. Hughes	TMO561	19	14 GT Cat, 1st class
		Austin Healey 3000	Pat Moss/Ann Wisdom	URX727	76	2 o/all, 1st Ladies, 1st class
		Austin Healey 3000	D. Morley/E. Morley	SJB471	73	14 o/all, 9th GT, 3rd class
		Austin Healey 3000	J. Gott/W. Shepherd	SMO746	74	8 o/all, 4th GT, 2nd class
		Austin Healey 3000	J. Williamson/R. Adams	SMO745	7	Ret – gearbox
Sept	Liège-Rome-Liège Rally	Austin Healey 3000	Pat Moss/Ann Wisdom	URX727	76	1st o/all, 1st Ladies
		Austin Healey 3000	J. Gott/R. Jones	SMO746	42	10 o/all, 3rd GT
		Austin Healey 3000	P. Riley/A. Ambrose	SJB471	46	Ret – radiator
		Austin Healey 3000	D. Seigle-Morris/V. Elford	SMO744	66	5 o/all, 2nd GT
Sept	Viking Rally	Austin A40 Farina	Pat Moss/Ann Wisdom	947AOF	11	20 o/all, 1st Ladies, 4th class
		Wolseley 6/99	M. Chambers/D. Green	TBL698	4	Class award
Sept	German Rally	Austin Healey 3000	Pat Moss/Ann Wisdom	URX727	3	16 o/all, 3rd GT class
		Austin Healey 3000	D. Seigle-Morris/S. Turner	SMO745	2	1st GT class
		Austin Healey 3000	D. Morley/B. Hercock	SMO744	15	12 o/all, 2nd GT class
		MGA 1600	P. Riley/A. Ambrose	7EMK	8	2nd class
Nov	Tour de Corse	Austin Healey Sprite	Pat Moss/Ann Wisdom	WJB707	95	Ret–gearbox
Nov	RAC Rally	Morris Mini Minor	D. Seigle-Morris/V. Elford	TMO559	183	6 o/all, 2nd class
		Morris Mini Minor	T. Christie/N. Paterson	TMO560	174	Ret
		Morris Mini Minor	M. Sutcliffe/D. Astle	TMO561	170	8 o/all, 4th class
		Austin Healey Sprite	Pat Moss/Ann Wisdom	WJB727	60	2nd Ladies, 2nd class
		Austin Healey 3000	P. Riley/A. Ambrose	SMO745	9	10 o/all, 2nd class
		Austin Healey 3000	D. Morley/E. Morley	SJB471	1	3 o/all, 1st class
		Austin Healey 3000	R. Adams/J. Williamson	SMO744	11	39 o/all, 4th class

1961

Jan	Monte Carlo Rally	Austin A40 Farina	P. Riley/A. Ambrose	114COJ	60	28 o/all
		Austin A40 Farina	Pat Moss/Ann Wisdom	947AOF	96	61 o/all, 2nd Ladies, 2nd class
		Austin A40 Farina	D. Seigle-Morris/V. Elford	OGV285	90	39 o/all
		Austin FX3 Taxi	P. Dimmock/A. Brooks/W. Cave	UXX794	314	Ret – OTL
		Morris Mini Minor	P. Garnier/R. Jones	TMO559	254	Ret – accident
		Morris Mini Minor	T. Christie/N. Paterson	TMO560	227	Ret – illness
		Morris Mini Minor	D. Astle/S. Wooley	TMO561	226	Ret – accident
Mar	Sebring 12 Hr Race	MGA 1600 Coupé	J. Parkinson/J. Flaherty	Ch. No. 100148	44	14 o/all, 1st class
		MGA 1600 Coupé	P. Riley/J. Whitmore	100149	43	16 o/all, 2nd class
Mar	Lyons–Charbonnières Rally	Morris Mini Minor	Pat Moss/Ann Wisdom	TMO560		Ret – engine
May	Tulip Rally	Morris Mini Minor	D. Seigle-Morris/V. Elford	TMO559	135	23 o/all, 3rd class
		Morris Mini Minor	P. Riley/A. Ambrose	TMO561	136	12 o/all, 1st class
		Austin Healey 3000	Pat Moss/Ann Wisdom	XJB877	2	11 o/all, 1st Ladies, 1st class
		Austin Healey 3000	D. Morley/E. Morley	XJB876	4	14 o/all, 2nd class
May	Acropolis Rally	Austin Seven	D. Astle/M Sutcliffe	619AOG	115	Ret
		Austin Seven	D. Morley/Ann Wisdom	363DOC	117	Ret – accident
		Morris Mini Minor	D. Seigle-Morris/V. Elford	TMO560	125	Ret – suspension
		Austin Healey 3000	P. Riley/A. Ambrose	XJB871	3	3 o/all, 1st GT Cat.
June	Midnight Sun Rally	Austin Healey 3000	P. Riley/A. Ambrose	UJB143		12 o/all, 2nd class
June	Le Mans 24 Hr Race	Austin Healey 3000	R. Stoop/J. Bekaert (UJB143)	DD300	21	Ret
June	Alpine Rally	Austin Healey 3000	D. Seigle-Morris/V. Elford	XJB870	140	Ret – accident
		Austin Healey 3000	P. Riley/A. Ambrose	XJB871	143	Ret – accident
		Austin Healey 3000	J. Gott/W. Shepherd	XJB872	145	15 o/all, 7th GT Cat, 3rd class
		Austin Healey 3000	D. Morley/E. Morley	XJB876	146	1st o/all, 1st class
		Austin Healey 3000	Pat Moss/Ann Wisdom	XJB877	141	Ret – accident
Sept	Liège-Sofia-Liège Rally	Austin Healey 3000	D. Seigle-Morris/A. Ambrose	XJB870	64	6 o/all, 1st class
		Austin Healey 3000	J. Gott/W. Shepherd	XJB872	45	Ret – sump
		Austin Healey 3000	D. Grimshaw/R. Jones	XJB876	77	Ret – accident
		Austin Healey 3000	Pat Moss/Ann Wisdom	XJB877	41	Ret

1955 to 1980

Nov	Tour of Corsica	Austin Healey 3000	Pat Moss/Ann Wisdom	UJB143	101	2nd Ladies, 1st class
Nov	RAC Rally	Austin Healey 3000	D. Seigle-Morris/A. Ambrose	XJB870	5	5 o/all, 2nd class
		Austin Healey 3000	D. Morley/E. Morley	XJB876		Ret – rear hub brg.
		Austin Healey 3000	Pat Moss/Ann Wisdom	XJB877	4	2nd o/all, 1st ladies, 1st class
		MG Midget	D. Astle/P. Roberts	YRX727	31	8 o/all, 1st class
		MG Midget	M. Sutcliffe/R. Fidler	YRX723	21	2nd class
		MG Midget	T. Gold/M Hughes	473TEH	15	60 o/all

1962

Jan	Monte Carlo Rally	Austin A110	R. Glenton/D. Astle/M. Sutcliffe	516EOK	148	198 o/all, ret
		MG Midget	P. Riley/M. Hughes	YRX747	44	33 o/all, 1st class
		Morris Mini Cooper	Pat Moss/Ann Wisdom	737ABL	304	26 o/all, 1st Ladies, 7th class
		Austin Seven	R. Jones/P. Morgan	363DOC	97	77 o/all, 3rd class
		Morris Mini Cooper	R. Aaltonen/G. Mabbs	11NYB	100	Ret – accident
		MGA 1600 Coupé	D. Morley/E. Morley	151ABL	314	28 o/all, 1st class
		Austin Healey 3000	D. Seigle-Morris/A. Ambrose	XJB870	169	18 o/all, 1st class
		Riley 1.5	J. Cotter/A. Collinson	441MWL	153	
Mar	Sebring 12 Hr Race	MGA 1600 Mk2 Coupé	J. Sears/A. Hedges	Ch.no10607 351		16 o/all
		MGA 1600 Mk2 Coupé	J. Whitmore/R. Olthoff	Ch.no10607 452		20 o/all
		MGA 1600 Mk2 Coupé	J. Flaherty/J. Parkinson	Ch.no10607 553		17 o/all
May	Tulip Rally	Morris Mini Cooper	Pat Moss/Ann Riley	737ABL	104	1st o/all, 1st Ladies
		Austin Seven	D. Seigle-Morris/A. Ambrose	363DOC		Ret
		MGA 1600 Mk2 Coupé	R. Aaltonen/G. Palm	151ABL	11	15 o/all, 1st class
		Austin Healey 3000	D. Morley/E. Morley	37ARX	1	17 o/all, 1st class
		Austin Healey 3000	P. Riley/D. Astle	47ARX	5	18 o/all, 2nd class
		MG Midget	T. Gold/M. Hughes	YRX737	59	38 o/all, 3rd class
June	Le Mans 24 Hr Race	Austin Healey 3000	R. Olthoff/J. Whitmore	DD300	24	Ret–piston
June	Acropolis Rally	Austin Healey 3000	Pat Moss/Pauline Mayman	XJB877	9	8 o/all, 1st Ladies, 1st class
June	Alpine Rally	Morris Mini Cooper	R. Aaltonen/G. Palm	407ARX	63	Ret
		Austin Healey 3000	P. Riley/D. Astle	47ARX	2	Ret
		Austin Healey 3000	D. Morley/E. Morley	57ARX	5	1st o/all
		Austin Healey 3000	D. Seigle-Morris/A. Ambrose	67ARX	1	8 o/all
		Austin Healey 3000	Pat Moss/Pauline Mayman	77ARX	4	3 o/all, 1st Ladies, 1st class
		MG Midget	J. Williamson/D. Hiam	YRX737	23	
Aug	1000 Lakes Rally	Morris Mini Cooper	R. Aaltonen/A. Ambrose	407ARX		Ret
Aug	Polish Rally	Austin Healey 3000	Pat Moss/Pauline Mayman	77ARX		2nd o/all, 1st Ladies & class
Sept	Liége–Sofia–Liége Rally	Austin Healey 3000	L. Morrison/R. Jones	47ARX	56	5 o/all, 2nd class
		Austin Healey 3000	P. Hopkirk/J. Scott	57ARX	12	Ret–suspension
		Austin Healey 3000	D. Seigle-Morris/B. Hercock	67ARX	57	8 o/all, 3rd class
		Austin Healey 3000	R. Aaltonen/A. Ambrose	XJB877	22	Ret – lost roadbook
		MGA 1600 Mk2 Coupé	J. Gott/W. Shepherd	151ABL	49	Ret – fuel leak
		Morris 1100	Pat Moss/Pauline Mayman	677BRX	72	Ret – piston
		Morris 1100	P. Riley/H. A. R. Nash	877BRX	38	Ret – crankshaft
Sept	Baden-Baden German Rally	Morris Mini Cooper	Pat Moss/Pauline Mayman	737ABL		1st o/all, 1st Ladies & class
	Solitude GT Race	Austin Healey 3000	E. Bohringer	37ARX		3rd class
Oct	Geneva Rally	Morris Mini Cooper	Pat Moss/Pauline Mayman	737ABL	135	3rd o/all, 1st class
Nov	RAC Rally	Morris Mini Cooper	R. Aaltonen/A. Ambrose	977ARX	6	5th o/all, 1st class
		Morris Mini Cooper	T. Makinen/J. Steadman	407ARX	38	7th o/all, 1st class
		Morris Mini Cooper	L. Morrison/R. Finlay	477BBL	32	13th o/all, 3rd class
		Austin Healey 3000	P. Riley/H. Nash	XJB877	15	Ret – accident
		Austin Healey 3000	D. Morley/E. Morley	57ARX	3	Ret – accident
		Austin Healey 3000	P. Hopkirk/J. Scott	67ARX	19	2nd o/all, 1st class
		Austin Healey 3000	Pat Moss/Pauline Mayman	77ARX	5	3 o/all, 1st Ladies, 2nd class
		MG 1100	D. Seigle-Morris/R. Jones	977CBL	11	Ret – engine

European Ladies Rally Champions – Pat Moss/Ann Wisdom

Appendix C

1963

Month	Event	Car	Crew	Reg	No.	Result
Jan	Monte Carlo Rally	MG Midget	R. Jones/P. Morgan	YRX747	158	1st class
		Morris Mini Cooper	R. Aaltonen/A. Ambrose	977ARX	288	3rd o/all, 1st class
		Morris Mini Cooper	P. Hopkirk/J. Scott	407ARX	66	6th o/all, 2nd class
		Morris Mini Cooper	Pauline Mayman/Val Domleo	737ABL	58	28th o/all, 4th class
		Morris Mini Cooper	L. Morrison/B. Culcheth	477BBL	155	44th o/all, 1st class
		Austin Healey 3000	T. Makinen/Christabel Carlisle	77ARX	81	13th o/all, 1st class
		MG 1100	R. Baxter/E. McMillen	399CJB	268	4th class
		MG 1100	J. Cuff/Anderson		162	Ret – accident
Mar	Sebring 12 Hr Race	MGB	J. Parkinson/J. Flaherty	7DBL	47	Ret – engine
		MGB	Christabel Carlisle/Denise McCluggage	6DBL	48	Ret – engine
April	Tulip Rally	Morris Mini Cooper	P. Hopkirk/H. Liddon	17CRX	130	2nd o/all, 1st class
		Morris Mini Cooper	Pauline Mayman/Val Domleo	737ABL	129	21st o/all, 4th class
		Austin Healey 3000	D. Morley/E. Morley	37ARX	1	2nd GT Cat, 1st class
		Austin Healey 3000	L. Morrison/R. Finlay	47ARX		Ret – core plug
	Spa 500 kms Race	MGB	A. Hutcheson	8DBL		Ret – overheating
May	Trifels Rally	Morris Mini Cooper	Pauline Mayman/Val Domleo	737ABL		1st Ladies, 1st class
June	Le Mans 24 Hr Race	MGB	P. Hopkirk/A. Hutcheson	7DBL	31	1st class, 12 o/all
June	Midnight Sun Rally	Austin Healey 3000	T. Makinen/A. Ambrose	67ARX		Disqualified – no bumpers
	Acropolis Rally	MG 1100	B. Consten/J. Herbert	399CJB		
June	Scottish Rally	Morris Mini Cooper	L. Morrison/D. Brown			Ret – accident
June	Alpine Rally	Morris Mini Cooper S 1071	R. Aaltonen/A. Ambrose	277EBL	63	1st o/all, 1st class
		Morris Mini Cooper	Pauline Mayman/Val Domleo	18CRX	73	6th overall, 1st Ladies & class
		Morris Mini Cooper	J. Sprinzel/W. Cave	977ARX	24	Ret – steering
		Morris Mini Cooper	Denise McCluggage/Rosemary Sears	17CRX	64	Ret – transmission
		Austin Healey 3000	P. Hopkirk/J. Scott	XJB877		Ret – accident
		Austin Healey 3000	D. Morley/E. Morley	37ARX	4	Ret – axle
		Austin Healey 3000	L. Morrison/R. Finlay	47ARX		Ret – accident
		Austin Healey 3000	T. Makinen/M Wood	57ARX	7	Ret – stub axle
Aug	Spa–Sofia–Liège Rally	Austin Healey 3000	P. Hopkirk/H. Liddon	XJB877	120	6th o/all, 1st class
		Austin Healey 3000	T. Makinen/G. Mabbs	57ARX	2	Ret – accident
		Austin Healey 3000	L. Morrison/M. Wood	67ARX	14	Ret – accident
		Austin Healey 3000	R. Aaltonen/A. Ambrose	77ARX	104	Ret – accident
		MG 1100	Pauline Mayman/Val Domleo	399CJB	57	Ret – ball joint
Sept	Tour de France	MGB	A. Hedges/J. Sprinzel	7DBL	155	Ret – accident
		Morris Mini Cooper S 1071	P. Hopkirk/H. Liddon	33EJB	38	3rd o/all, 1st class
		Morris Mini Cooper	R. Aaltonen/A. Ambrose	477BBL	24	44th o/all
		Morris Mini Cooper	T. Makinen/L. Morrison	407ARX	27	Ret
		Morris Mini Cooper	Pauline Mayman/Elisabeth Jones	277EBL	39	Ret
Nov	RAC Rally	Morris Mini Cooper S 1071	P. Hopkirk/H. Liddon	8EMO	21	4th o/all, 2nd class
		Morris Mini Cooper	L. Morrison/R. Finlay	407ARX	36	19th o/all, 1st class
		Morris Mini Cooper S 1071	Pauline Mayman/Val Domleo	277EBL	38	30th o/all
		Austin Healey 3000	T. Makinen/M. Wood	47ARX	28	5th o/all, 1st class
		Austin Healey 3000	D. Morley/E. Morley	67ARX	5	9th o/all, 2nd class
		Austin Healey 3000	R. Aaltonen/A. Ambrose	37ARX	2	Ret – accident

1964

Month	Event	Car	Crew	Reg	No.	Result
Jan	Monte Carlo Rally	MGB	D. Morley/E. Morley	7DBL	83	17th o/all, 1st GT Cat
		Morris Mini Cooper S	P. Hopkirk/H. Liddon	33EJB	37	1st o/all, 1st class
		Morris Mini Cooper	T. Makinen/P. Vanson	570FMO	182	4th o/all, 2nd class
		Morris Mini Cooper	R. Aaltonen/A. Ambrose	569FMO	105	7th o/all, 3rd class
		Morris Mini Cooper	R. Baxter/E. McMillen	477BBL	39	43rd o/all, 2nd class
		Morris Mini Cooper S	Pauline Mayman/Val Domleo	277EBL	189	Ret – accident
		Morris Mini Cooper	J. Thompson/F. Heys	18CRX	187	Ret – accident
		MG 1100	T. Wisdom/J. Miles	399CJB	243	

1955 to 1980

Mar	Sebring 12 Hr Race	MGB	E. Leslie/J. Dalton		3rd class, 17th o/all
		MGB	J. Flaherty/J. Parkinson		Ret–oil seal
		MGB	F. Morrill/J. Adams/M. Brennan		22nd o/all
April	Tulip Rally	Morris Mini Cooper S 1275	T. Makinen/A. Ambrose	AJB66B 119	1st o/all, 1st class
		Austin Healey 3000	D. Morley/E. Morley	ARX92B 5	1st GT Cat, 1st class
May	Austrian Alpine Rally	Austin Healey 3000	P. Hopkirk/H. Liddon	ARX91B 2	1st o/all
May	Acropolis Rally	Austin Mini Cooper S 1275	P. Hopkirk/H. Liddon	AJB55B 67	Ret – battery
		Austin Mini Cooper S 1275	R. Aaltonen/Ambrose	AJB33B	Ret – steering
June	Scottish Rally	MGB	D. Morley/E. Morley	7DBL	Ret – accident
June	Le Mans 24 Hr Race	MGB	P. Hopkirk/A. Hedges	BMO541B 37	19 o/all, Motor Trophy, 2nd Class
June	Alpine Rally	Austin Mini Cooper S 1275	R. Aaltonen/A. Ambrose	AJB55B 70	4th Cat, 1st class, Coupe des Alpes
		Morris Mini Cooper S 970	Pauline Mayman/Val Domleo	AJB66B 8	6th Cat, 1st Ladies & class
		Morris Mini Cooper S 1275	P. Hopkirk/H. Liddon	AJB44B 18	Ret
		Morris Mini Cooper S 1275	T. Makinen/P. Vanson	BJB77B 19	Ret
		Austin Healey 3000	D. Morley/E. Morley	ARX92B 95	2nd GT Cat, 1st class, Coupe des Alpes
Aug	1000 Lakes Rally	Morris Mini Cooper S	T. Makinen/P. Keskitalo	AJB33B	4th o/all, 1st class
Aug	Spa–Sofia–Liège Rally	Morris Mini Cooper S	J. Wadsworth/M. Wood	570FMO 68	20th o/all
		MGB	Pauline Mayman/Val Domleo	BRX853B 78	Ret – clutch
		MGB	J. Vernaeve/	BRX854B	Ret – clutch
		Austin Healey 3000	T. Makinen/D. Barrow	ARX92B 53	Ret – punctures
		Austin Healey 3000	R. Aaltonen/A. Ambrose	BMO93B 3	1st o/all
		Austin Healey 3000	P. Hopkirk/H. Liddon	BRX852B 29	Ret-gearbox
		MGB	D. Hiam/R. Jones	8DBL 38	Ret-rear spring shackle
Sept	Tour de France	Morris Mini Cooper S 970	Pauline Mayman/Val Domleo	AJB66B 20	1st class
		Morris Mini Cooper S	P. Hopkirk/H. Liddon	AJB44B 19	Ret
		Austin Mini Cooper S	R. Aaltonen/A. Ambrose	AJB55B 30	Ret
		Morris Mini Cooper S 970	T. Makinen/P. Easter	BJB77B 18	Ret – accident
		MGB	A. Hedges/J. Sprinzel	BMO541B 153	Ret – engine
Nov	RAC Rally	Morris Mini Cooper S	P. Hopkirk/H. Liddon	CRX90B 1	Ret
		Austin Mini Cooper S	R. Aaltonen/A. Ambrose	CRX89B 2	Ret
		Morris Mini Cooper S	C. Orrenius/R. Dahlgren	AJB44B 37	Ret
		Austin Mini Cooper S	H. Kallstrom/R. Haakansson	AGU780B 42	Ret
		Austin Healey 3000	D. Morley/E. Morley	BMO93B 11	21st o/all
		Austin Healey 3000	T. Makinen/D. Barrow	BRX852B 14	2nd o/all, 1st class
		MGB	J. Fitzpatrick/J. Handley	BRX854B 177	Ret – accident
		MGB	Pauline Mayman/Val Domleo	BRX853B 39	Ret – clutch

1965

Jan	Monte Carlo Rally	Morris Mini Cooper S	T. Makinen/P. Easter	AJB44B 52	1st o/all, 1st class
		Morris Mini Cooper S	P. Hopkirk/H. Liddon	CRX91B 56	26th o/all, 1st class
		Morris Mini Cooper S	D. Morley/E. Morley	CRX90B 72	27th o/all, 2nd class
		Austin Mini Cooper S	R. Aaltonen/A. Ambrose	CRX88B 283	Ret
		Austin Mini Cooper S	H. Kallstrom/R. Haakansson	AGU780B 176	Ret
		Morris Mini Cooper S	R. Baxter/J. Scott	8EMO 91	Ret
		Austin 1800	T. Wisdom/C. Edwards/J. Sprinzel	AOB987B 138	31st o/all
		Austin 1800	R. Joss/J. Fitzpatrick	DJB94B 133	29th o/all, ret – accident
Feb	Swedish Rally	Austin Mini Cooper S	P. Hopkirk/H. Liddon	AJB33B 28	Ret – transmission
		Austin Mini Cooper S	R. Aaltonen/A. Ambrose	DJB93B 22	Ret – transmission
		Morris Mini Cooper S	T. Makinen/P. Easter	DJB92B 31	Ret – transmission
		Austin Mini Cooper S	H. Kallstrom/R. Haakansson	AGU780B	Ret – transmission

Appendix C

Mar	Sebring 12 Hr Race	MGB	M. Brennan/F. Morrell	BMO541B	49	25 o/all, 10 prot, 2nd class
		MGB	B. Pricard/A. Pease	DRX256C	48	32 o/all, 18 GT, 6th class
		MG Midget Coupé	C. Tannlund/J. Wagstaff	770BJB	82	Ret – engine
		MG Midget Coupé	R. Mac/A. Hedges	771BJB	68	12th GT, 1st class
Mar	Circuit of Ireland	Austin Mini Cooper S	P. Hopkirk/T. Harryman	CRX89B	2	1st o/all
April	Tulip Rally	Morris Mini Cooper S	T. Makinen/P. Easter	AJB33B	124	3rd Cat, 1st class
		Austin Healey 3000	D. Morley/E. Morley	DRX257C	4	8th o/all, 1st class
		MGB	K. Tubman/Stefanoff	BRX854B	12	
May	Luxembourg Slalom	Austin Mini Cooper S	P. Hopkirk	CRX89B	66	7th o/all, 1st class
May	Welsh Rally	MGB	T. Fall/R. Crellin	8DBL	7	34th o/all
May	Targa Florio	Austin Healey 3000	T. Makinen/P. Hawkins	ARX91B	108	20th o/all, 2nd class
		MG Midget Coupé	P. Hopkirk/A. Hedges	771BJB	44	11th o/all, 2nd class
May	Guards 1000 Race	MGB	J. Rhodes/W. Banks	8DBL	28	1st o/all
		Austin Healey 3000	P. Hopkirk/R. Mac		8	4th o/all, 2nd class
May	Acropolis Rally	Austin Mini Cooper S	T. Makinen/P. Easter	DJB93B	60	Ret – engine
May	1000 kms Nürburgring	MG Midget Coupé	A. Hedges/K. Greene	770BJB	98	
June	Le Mans 24 Hr Race	MGB	P. Hopkirk/A. Hedges	DRX255C	39	11th o/all, 2nd class
June	Scottish Rally	Austin Healey 3000	T. Makinen/P. Easter	DRX257C	2	Ret – pinion
		Austin Mini Cooper S	P. Hopkirk/H. Liddon	CRX89B	3	Ret – final drive
June	Geneva Rally	Austin Healey 3000	D. Morley/E. Morley	DRX258C	1	7th o/all, 1st class, 3rd GT
		Morris Mini Cooper S	R. Aaltonen/A. Ambrose	EBL55C	64	1st o/all, 1st class
July	Rallye Vltava Czechoslovakia	Austin Mini Cooper S	R. Aaltonen/A. Ambrose	EJB55C	102	1st o/all
		Morris Mini Cooper S	T. Makinen/P. Easter	AJB66B	100	Ret
July	Nordrhein-Westfalen Rally	Morris Mini Cooper S	P. Hopkirk/H. Liddon	DJB92B	58	6th o/all, 1st class
		MGB	A. Hedges/J. Scott	BRX853B	116	3rd GT Class, 11th o/all
July	Alpine Rally	Austin Mini Cooper S	T. Makinen/P. Easter	AJB33B	70	2nd Cat, 1st class
		Morris Mini Cooper S	P. Hopkirk/H. Liddon	EBL56C	60	4th Cat, 2nd class
		Morris Mini Cooper S	R. Aaltonen/A. Ambrose	EBL55C	56	14th Cat
		Austin Mini Cooper S	Pauline Mayman/Val Domleo	DJB93B	66	13th Cat, 1st Ladies
		Austin Healey 3000	D. Morley/E. Morley	DRX258C	137	2nd GT Cat, 1st class Man Team Prize
July	Polish Rally	Austin Mini Cooper S	R. Aaltonen/A. Ambrose	CRX89B	55	1st o/all, 1st class
	Bridgehampton 500	MGB	P. Hopkirk		48	4th o/all, 2nd GT class
		MG Midget	T. Makinen			11th o/all, 3rd class
		MG Midget	R. Aaltonen		50	6th o/all, 1st class
Aug	1000 Lakes Rally	Austin Mini Cooper S	T. Makinen/P. Keskitalo	AJB33B	28	1st o/all, 1st class
		Austin Mini Cooper S	R. Aaltonen/A. Jaervi	EBL55C	26	2nd o/all, 2nd class
		Morris Mini Cooper S	P. Hopkirk/K. Ruutsalo	EBL56C	22	6th o/all Man Team Prize
Oct	Munich–Vienna–Budapest Rally	Austin Mini Cooper S	R. Aaltonen/A. Ambrose	CRX89B	72	1st o/all
		Austin Mini Cooper S	A. Fall/R. Crellin	AJB55B	65	2nd class
		Morris Mini Cooper S	G. Halliwell/M. Wood	CRX90B	71	Ret – accident
Nov	RAC Rally	Austin Healey 3000	D. Morley/E. Morley	DRX258C	14	Ret – accident
		Austin Healey 3000	T. Makinen/P. Easter	EJB806C	2	2nd o/all
		Austin Mini Cooper S	R. Aaltonen/A. Ambrose	DJB93B	5	1st o/all
		Morris Mini Cooper S	J. Lusenius/M. Wood	DJB92B	44	6th o/all, 1st class
		Morris Mini Cooper S	P. Hopkirk/H. Liddon	EBL56C	8	13th o/all, 2nd class
		Austin Mini Cooper S	A. Fall/R. Crellin	CRX89B	36	15th o/all, 3rd class
		Morris Mini Cooper S	H. Kallstrom/N. Bjork	EJB55C	37	Ret – exhaust

1966
Jan	Monte Carlo Rally	Morris Mini Cooper S	T. Makinen/P. Easter	GRX555D	2	(1st o/all) disqualified
		Austin Mini Cooper S	R. Aaltonen/A. Ambrose	GRX55D	242	(2nd o/all) disqualified
		Austin Mini Cooper S	P. Hopkirk/H. Liddon	GRX5D	230	(3rd o/all) disqualified
		Morris Mini Cooper S	R. Baxter/J. Scott	GRX195D	87	Disqualified
		MGB	A. Fall/R. Crellin	GRX307D	183	Ret – oil pipe

1955 to 1980

Month	Event	Car	Crew	Reg	No	Result
Feb	Swedish Rally	Morris Mini Cooper S	R. Aaltonen/H. Liddon	GRX310D		Ret – transmission
		Morris Mini Cooper S	T. Makinen/P. Easter	DJB92B	35	Ret – transmission
Feb	San Remo 'Flowers' Rally	Austin Mini Cooper S	P. Hopkirk/R. Crellin	GRX309D	50	15th o/all, 6th class
		Austin Mini Cooper S	A. Fall/H. Liddon	GRX5D		Disqualified-air cleaner
Mar	Sebring 12 Hr Race	MGB	P. Manton/R. Mac/E. Brown	HBL129D	59	3rd GT Cat, 1st class
		MGB	P. Hopkirk/A. Hedges	8DBL	44	Ret – con rod
April	Circuit of Ireland	Morris Mini Cooper S	A. Fall/H. Liddon	DJB92B	4	1st o/all
		Austin Mini Cooper S	P. Hopkirk/T. Harryman	GRX55D	1	Ret – accident
April	Tulip Rally	Morris Mini Cooper S	R. Aaltonen/H. Liddon	GRX310D	89	1st o/all
		Austin Mini Cooper S	T. Makinen/P. Easter	GRX5D	100	9th o/all, 1st class / Man Team Prize
	Targa Florio	MGB	J. Handley/A. Hedges	JBL491D		2nd class
		MGB	T. Makinen/J. Rhodes	GRX307D	64	9th o/all, 1st class
		Austin Healey Sprite Coupé	R. Aaltonen/	EAC90C	208	
May	Austrian Alpine Rally	Morris Mini Cooper S	P. Hopkirk/R. Crellin	DJB93B	58	1st o/all
		Morris Mini Cooper S	A. Fall/M. Wood	GRX310D	97	Ret – steering
May	Acropolis Rally	Morris Mini Cooper S	P. Hopkirk/R. Crellin	GRX311D	67	3rd o/all, 1st class
		Morris Mini Cooper S	T. Makinen/P. Easter	HJB656D	82	10th o/all, 2nd class
		Austin Mini Cooper S	R. Aaltonen/H. Liddon	JBL172D	77	Ret – engine
June	Scottish Rally	Austin Mini Cooper S	A. Fall/M. Wood	DJB93B	2	1st o/all
June	Geneva Rally	Morris Mini Cooper S	A. Fall/H. Liddon	EBL56C	75	2nd o/all, 2nd class
		Austin Mini Cooper S	P. Hopkirk/T. Harryman	JBL495D	50	Ret / Man Team Prize
June	London Rally	Austin Mini Cooper S	P. Hopkirk/R. Crellin	JBL495D	6	Ret
		Austin Mini Cooper S	A. Fall/M. Wood	DJB93B	4	Ret
July	Vltava Rally Czechoslovakia	Austin Mini Cooper S	R. Aaltonen/H. Liddon	JBL495D	75	1st o/all
		Morris Mini Cooper S	T. Makinen/P. Easter	JBL493D	77	3rd o/all
		Morris Mini Cooper S	S. Zasada/Z. Leszczvk	EBL56C	16	4th o/all, 1st class / Man Team Prize
July	German Rally	Morris Mini Cooper S	P. Hopkirk/C. Nash	GRX311D	42	Ret – engine
		Austin Mini Cooper S	A. Fall/H. Liddon	JBL172D	49	Ret – engine
July	Mugello Race	MGB	A. Hedges/R. Widdows	GRX307D	92	3rd GT Cat
Aug	Polish Rally	Austin Mini Cooper S 970cc	A. Fall/A. Krauklis	GRX309D	56	1st o/all
		Morris Mini Cooper S	T. Makinen/P. Easter	GRX555D	37	2nd o/all, 1st class
		Morris Mini Cooper S	R. Aaltonen/H. Liddon	HJB656D	29	Ret
Aug	Marathon de la Route 84 Hrs	MGB	J. Vernaeve/A. Hedges	GRX307D	47	1st o/all
		MGB	R. Enever/A. Poole	BRX855B	46	Ret – axle shaft
Aug	Welsh Rally	Austin Mini Cooper S	A. Fall/M. Wood	GRX309D		Ret
Aug	1000 Lakes Rally	Morris Mini Cooper S	T. Makinen/P. Keskitalo	JBL493D	45	1st o/all
		Morris Mini Cooper S	R. Aaltonen/V. Numimaa	GRX310D	49	3rd o/all, 2nd class
		Austin Mini Cooper S	J. Lusenius/K. Lehto	JBL494D	27	6th o/all, 3rd class
Sept	Alpine Rally	Austin Mini Cooper S	R. Aaltonen/H Liddon	JBL495D	62	3rd o/all, 2nd class
		Morris Mini Cooper S	T. Makinen/P. Easter	JMO969D	68	Ret – engine
		Morris Mini Cooper S	P. Hopkirk/R. Crellin	GRX311D	67	Ret – transmission
		Morris Mini Cooper S	A. Fall/M. Wood	GRX195D	66	Ret – d/shaft
	1000 kms Nürburgring	MGB	A. Hedges/J. Vernaeve	JBL491D	107	Ret – head gasket
	1000 Kms Spa Race	MGB	A. Hedges/J. Vervaeve	GRX307D		1st GT Cat, 1st Class
Oct	Munich–Vienna–Budapest (Three Cities) Rally	Morris Mini Cooper S	T. Makinen/P. Easter	HJB656D	57	1st o/all
		Austin Mini Cooper S	A. Fall/H. Liddon	JBL494D		Ret
	1000 Kms Monthlhery	MGB	A. Hedges/J. Vernaeve	GRX307D		13th o/all, 3rd class
		MGB	R. Enever/A. Poole	BRX855B	33	12th o/all, 2nd class

Appendix C

Nov	RAC Rally	Austin Mini Cooper S	H. Kallstrom/R. Haakansson	JBL494D	66	2nd o/all, 1st class
		Morris Mini Cooper S	R. Aaltonen/H. Liddon	GRX310D	18	4th o/all, 2nd class
		Morris Mini Cooper S	A. Fall/M. Wood	GRX195D	21	5th o/all, 3rd class
		Moris Mini Cooper S	Marjatta Aaltonen/Caroline Tyler	EBL56C	117	37th o/all
		Morris Mini Cooper S	P. Hopkirk/R. Crellin	JMO969D	10	Ret – d/shaft coupling
		Austin Mini Cooper S	T. Makinen/P. Easter	GRX5D	12	Ret – engine
		Austin Mini Cooper S	S. Lampinen/A. Ambrose	JBL495D	29	Ret – accident
		Austin Mini Cooper S	G. Hill/M. Boyd	GRX309D	5	Ret – diff

1967

Jan	Monte Carlo Rally	Morris Mini Cooper S	R. Aaltonen/H. Liddon	LBL6D	177	1st o/all
		Austin Mini Cooper S	P. Hopkirk/R. Crellin	LBL666D	205	6th o/all, 5th class
		Austin Mini Cooper S	A. Fall/R. Joss	LBL606D	32	10th o/all
		Morris Mini Cooper S	S. Lampinen/M. Wood	HJB656D	178	15th o/all
		Morris Mini Cooper S	T. Makinen/P. Easter	LBL66D	144	41st o/all
Feb	Swedish Rally	Austin Mini Cooper S	R. Aaltonen/H. Liddon	JBL495D	26	3rd o/all, 1st class
		Morris Mini Cooper S	T. Makinen/P. Easter	JMO969D	22	Ret – brakes
Feb	Rally of the Flowers (San Remo)	Austin Mini Cooper S	P. Hopkirk/R. Crellin	LBL590E	67	2nd o/all, 2nd class
		Morris Mini Cooper S	A. Fall/M. Wood	GRX195D	82	4th o/all, 4th class
Mar	East African Safari	Morris Mini Cooper S	R. Aaltonen/H. Liddon	HJB656D	8	Ret – engine
Mar	Circuit of Ireland	Austin Mini Cooper S	P. Hopkirk/T. Harryman	GRX5D	1	1st overall
Mar	Sebring 3 Hr Race	Austin Mini Cooper S	P. Hopkirk/J. Rhodes	GRX309D	48	1st class
	Sebring 12 Hr Race	MGB	T. Makinen/J. Rhodes	GRX307D	48	12th o/all, 3rd class
		MGB GT	P. Hopkirk/A. Hedges	LBL591E	30	3rd Category, 1st class
April	Tulip Rally	Morris Mini Cooper S	T. Makinen/P. Easter	LRX827E	64	2nd o/all, 1st Cat
		Morris Mini Cooper S	R. Aaltonen/H. Liddon	LRX829E	65	3rd o/all, 2nd Cat
		Austin Mini Cooper S	D. Benzimra/T. Harryman	GRX5D	73	Ret – clutch Man Team Prize
May	Acropolis Rally	Austin Mini Cooper S	P. Hopkirk/R. Crellin	LRX830E	89	1st o/all
		Austin Mini Cooper S	R. Aaltonen/H. Liddon	LRX828E	92	Ret – accident
		Morris Mini Coooper S	T. Makinen/P. Easter	GRX195D	99	Ret – gearbox
	Targa Florio	MGB GTS	P. Hopkirk/T. Makinen	MBL546E	230	9th o/all, 3rd class
		MGB	A. Hedges/A. Poole	MBL547E		Ret – accident
June	Scottish Rally	Morris Mini Cooper S	L. Ytterbring/L. Persson	GRX311D	1	2nd o/all
		Austin Mini Cooper S	A. Fall/M. Wood			Ret
June	Geneva Rally	Morris Mini Cooper S	A. Fall/M. Wood	LRX827E	79	1st o/all
	Criterium de Crans-sur-Sierre	Morris Mini Cooper S	J. Vernaeve/H. Liddon	LRX829E	80	2nd o/all, 2nd class
July	London Rally	Austin Mini Cooper S	A. Fall/M. Wood	GRX5D	8	Ret – accident
July	Danube Rally	Austin Mini Cooper S	R. Aaltonen/H. Liddon	LRX828E		Ret – no visa
		Austin 1800	A. Fall/M. Wood	LRX824E	5	1st o/all
Aug	1000 Lakes Rally	Morris Mini Cooper S	T. Makinen/P. Keskitalo	GRX195D	29	1st o/all
Aug	Marathon de La Route	Austin Mini Cooper S 970 cc	A. Fall/J. Vernaeve/A. Hedges	GRX5D	39	2nd o/all, 1st class
		Austin Mini Cooper S 970 cc	A. Poole/R. Enever/C. Baker	LRX830E	40	Ret – accident
Sept	Alpine Rally	Morris Mini Cooper S	P. Hopkirk/R. Crellin	LRX827E	107	1st o/all
		Austin Mini Cooper S	R. Aaltonen/H. Liddon	JBL172D	106	Ret – gearbox
		Morris Mini Cooper S	T. Makinen/P. Easter	GRX311D	103	Ret – engine
		Morris Mini Cooper S	A. Fall/M. Wood	GRX310D	40	Ret – accident
		Austin 1800	B. Culcheth/J. Syer	LRX824E	66	11th o/all, 1st class
Sept	Monza Record Run Int Class E Records	Morris 1800	A. Poole/R. Enever/C. Baker/ J. Vernaeve/R. Aaltonen/A. Fall	LBL416E		4 days – 93.90 mph 5 days – 93.42 mph 6 days – 93.24 mph 7 days – 92.80 mph 15,000 miles – 92.64 mph 20,000 km – 93.38 mph 25,000 km – 92.78 mph

Nov	Tour of Corsica	Austin Mini Cooper S	P. Hopkirk/R. Crellin	GRX5D	79	Ret – fan belt
		Austin Mini Cooper S	R. Aaltonen/H. Liddon	JBL172D	73	Ret – fan belt
Nov	RAC Rally Cancelled – Foot & Mouth Disease	Morris Mini Cooper S Fuel Injection	T. Makinen/P. Easter	GRX311D	24	
		Austin Healey 3000	R. Aaltonen/H. Liddon (ARX92B)	PWB57	22	
		Mini Cooper S	T. Fall/M. Wood		27	
		Mini Cooper S	P. Hopkirk/R. Crellin		26	
		Mini Cooper S	L. Ytterbring/L. Persson		80	
		Austin 1800	B. Culcheth/J. Syer		33	

1968

Jan	Monte Carlo Rally	Morris Mini Cooper S	R. Aaltonen/H. Liddon	ORX7F	18	3rd o/all, 1st Category
		Austin Mini Cooper S	A. Fall/M. Wood	ORX707F	185	4th o/all, 2nd Category
		Austin Mini Cooper S	P. Hopkirk/R. Crellin	ORX777F	87	5th o/all, 3rd Category
		Morris Mini Cooper S	T. Makinen/P. Easter	ORX77F	7	55th o/all
		Morris 1800	B. Culcheth/J. Syer	KOC391E	172	24th o/all, 2nd class
Feb	Flowers Rally	Morris Mini Cooper S	R. Aaltonen/H. Liddon	ORX77F	40	Ret
		Morris Mini Cooper S	A. Fall/M. Wood	ORX777F	44	Ret
Mar	Sebring 12 Hr Race	MGC GT	P. Hopkirk/A. Hedges	MBL546E	44	10th o/all, 1st class
		MGB GT	G. Rodrigues/R. McDaniel/B. Brack	LBL591E	66	18th o/all, 5th class
April	Tulip Rally	Austin Mini Cooper S	J. Vernaeve/M. Wood	ORX707F	74	3rd o/all, 1st Category
		Morris Mini Cooper S	T. Makinen/P. Easter	LBL66D	73	41st o/all
April	Circuit of Ireland	Morris Mini Cooper S	P. Hopkirk/T. Harryman	JMO969D	1	Ret diff
		Austin Mini Cooper S	L. Ytterbring/L. Persson	OBL46F	3	Ret accident
April	East African Safari	Morris 1800	R. Aaltonen/H. Liddon	KOC391E	6	Ret – OTL
		Austin 1800	A. Fall/L. Drews	ORX662F	14	Ret – OTL
		Morris 1800	T. Makinen/D. Benzimra	ORX661F	11	Ret – oil cooler
April	Canadian Shell 4000 Rally	Austin Mini Cooper S	P. Hopkirk/M. Kerry	GRX5D	119	Disqualified
		Austin 1800	A. Fall/D. Johnson	ORX663F	110	8th o/all, 2nd class
May	Targa Florio	MGB GT	P. Hopkirk/A. Hedges	LBL591E	130	12th o/all, 2nd cat
May	Acropolis Rally	Morris Mini Cooper S	R. Aaltonen/H. Liddon	RBL450F	46	5th o/all, 1st class
		Morris Mini Cooper S	T. Makinen/P. Easter	GRX310D	49	Ret – head gasket
		Morris 1800	B. Culcheth/M. Wood	RBL448F	16	10th o/all, 2nd class
June	Scottish Rally	Morris Mini Cooper S	L. Ytterbring/L. Persson	JMO969D	3	2nd o/all, 1st class
	Marathon de La Route	MGC GT	A. Fall/A. Hedges/J. Vernaeve	MBL546E	4	6th o/all
		MGC GT	C. Baker/R. Enever/A. Poole	RMO699F		Ret
Oct	TAP Rally	Austin Mini Cooper S	P. Hopkirk/A. Nash	LBL606D	71	2nd o/all, 2nd class
Dec	London–Sydney–Marathon	Austin 1800 Mk2	T. Kingsley/P. Evans/D. Bell	ORX663F	64	19th o/all
		Austin 1800 Mk2	P. Hopkirk/A. Nash/A. Poole	SMO226G	51	2nd o/all
		Morris 1800 Mk2	R. Aaltonen/H. Liddon/P. Easter	SMO225G	61	5th o/all
		Morris 1800 Mk2	A. Fall/M. Wood/B. Culcheth	SMO974G	4	23rd o/all
		1800 Mk2	E. Green/J. Murray/G. Shepherd	SMO227G	31	21st o/all
Dec	ITV Rallycross	Mini Cooper S	J. Rhodes			3rd o/all
	Croft	Mini Cooper S	J. Handley			6th o/all

1969

Jan	BBC Rallycross Lydden Hill	Mini Cooper S	J. Rhodes			Ret – diff
		Morris 1300 PI	P. Hopkirk			6th o/all
Feb	BBC Rallycross Lydden Hill	Triumph 1300 4 × 4	B. Culcheth		35	1st o/all
		Mini Cooper S	G. Mabbs			Ret – accident
Feb	ITV Rallycross Croft	Mini Cooper S PI	J. Rhodes			2nd o/all + FTD
		Mini Cooper S PI	J. Handley			5th o/all
Mar	ITV Rallycross Croft	Morris 1300 PI	J. Rhodes			2nd o/all
		Mini Cooper S PI	J. Handley			4th o/all
		Rover 3500	G. Mabbs			
		Triumph 1300 4 × 4	B. Culcheth		76	1st-Demo Race

Appendix C

Month	Event	Car	Driver	Reg	No	Result
April	ITV Rallycross Croft Final	Mini Cooper S PI	J. Rhodes			4th o/all, 2nd Championship
		Morris 1300	J. Handley			7th o/all
		Rover 3500	G. Mabbs			Not placed
		Triumph 1300 4 × 4	B. Culcheth			Not placed
April	High Egborough Rallycross	Triumph 1300 4 × 4	B. Culcheth			Ret – accident
		Mini Cooper S PI	J. Handley			1st in Heat
		Mini Cooper S PI	G. Mabbs			
		Morris 1300 PI	J. Rhodes			1st in Heat
Mar	Sebring 12 Hr Race	MGC GT	C. Hill/W. Brack	MBL546E	36	34th o/all, 15th Prototype Cat
		MGC GT	P. Hopkirk/A. Hedges	RMO699F	35	15th o/all, 9th Prototype Cat
		MGB GT	J. Truitt/L. Blackburn	LBL591E	62	28th o/all, 8th GT Cat
Mar	Brands Hatch Saloon Car Race	Mini Cooper S	J. Rhodes	OBL45F		Ret – accident
		Austin Mini Cooper S	J. Handley	OBL46F		Ret – accident
Mar	Silverstone Daily Express Meeting	Morris Mini Cooper S	J. Handley	LRX827E	15	10th o/all, 4th class
		Morris Mini Cooper S	J. Rhodes	GRX310D	14	11th o/all, 5th class
April	Snetterton Guards Trophy Meeting	Morris Mini Cooper S	J. Rhodes	GRX310D		12th overall, 4th class
April	Thruxton Easter Monday Meeting	Morris Mini Cooper S	J. Handley	LRX827E		9th o/all, 4th class
		Morris Mini Cooper S	J. Rhodes			22nd o/all
April	Circuit of Ireland	Morris Mini Cooper S	P. Hopkirk/A. Nash	GRX311D	2	2nd o/all, 2nd class
May	Austrian Alpine Rally	Triumph 2.5 PI Mk1	P. Hopkirk/A. Nash	UJB643G		Ret – clutch
May	Silverstone Martini Race Meeting	Austin Mini Cooper S	J. Rhodes	LBL666D	17	6th o/all, 2nd class
		Morris Mini Cooper S	J. Handley	LRX827E	16	7th o/all, 3rd class
May	Crystal Palace Annerley Trophy	Austin Mini Cooper S	J. Rhodes	LBL666D	134	4th o/all, 4th class
		Morris Mini Cooper S	J. Handley	LRX827E	135	3rd o/all, 3rd class
June	Hockenheim Race Meeting	Morris Mini Cooper S	J. Rhodes	URX560G		6th o/all, 3rd class
		Morris Mini Cooper S	J. Handley	URX550G		5th class
June	Brands Hatch 6 Hr Race	Morris Mini Cooper S	J. Handley/R. Enever	RBL450F		4th o/all, 2nd class
		Morris Mini Cooper S	J. Rhodes/P. Hopkirk	GRX310D		7th o/all, 3rd class
June	Mallory Park Guards International	Austin Mini Cooper S	J. Rhodes	LBL666D	118	8th o/all, 4th class
		Morris Mini Cooper S	J. Handley	LRX827E		Ret – engine
June	Scottish Rally	Triumph 2.5 PI Mk1	B. Culcheth/J. Syer	UJB643G	9	24th o/all, 2nd class
July	Nürburgring 6 Hr Race	Morris Mini Cooper S	J. Handley/R. Enever	RBL450F	74	Ret – rear suspension
		Morris Mini Cooper S	J. Rhodes/G. Mabbs	GRX310D	73	Ret – rear suspension
July	Silverstone British GP Meeting	Austin Mini Cooper S	J. Rhodes	LBL666D	16	8th o/all, 4th class
		Morris Mini Cooper S	J. Handley	LRX827E	15	10th o/all, 6th class
July	Spa 24 Hour Race	Morris Mini Cooper S	J. Handley/R. Enever	RBL450F	78	Ret – engine
		Morris Mini Cooper S	J. Rhodes/G. Mabbs	RJB327F	79	Ret – engine
Aug	Thruxton Race Meeting	Morris Mini Cooper S	G. Mabbs	RJB327F		BBC Camera Car
Aug	Oulton Park Race Meeting	Austin Mini Cooper S	J. Rhodes	LBL666D		12th o/all, 4th class
		Morris Mini Cooper S	J. Handley	RJB327F		15th o/all
Sept	Tour de France	Austin Mini Cooper S	P. Hopkirk/A. Nash	OBL45F	57	14th o/all, 1st class
		Morris Mini Cooper S	J. Handley/P. Easter	URX560G	56	Ret – accident
		Morris Mini Cooper S	B. Culcheth/J. Syer	URX550G	12	5th Trg Cat, 2nd class
Sept	Brands Hatch Guards Trophy	Austin Mini Cooper S	J. Rhodes	LBL666D	244	10th o/all, 4th class
		Morris Mini Cooper S	J. Handley	LRX827E	245	Ret
Oct	Salzburgring Saloon Car Race	Austin Mini Cooper S	J. Rhodes	LBL666D	30	1st o/all
		Morris Mini Cooper S	J. Handley	LRX827E	31	2nd o/all
Nov	RAC Rally	Triumph 2.5 PI Mk1	A. Cowan/B. Coyle	VBL195H	1	11th o/all, 1st class
		Triumph 2.5 PI Mk1	B. Culcheth/J. Syer	VBL196H	23	17th o/all, 3rd class
		Triump 2.5 PI Mk1	P. Hopkirk/A. Nash	VBL197H	8	15th o/all, 2nd class
	Cadwell Park Rallycross	Triumph 2.5 PI Mk1	A. Cowan	VBL195H		Not classified

1955 to 1980

1970						
Feb	BBC TV Rallycross Lydden Hill	Austin Maxi Triumph 2.5 PI Mk1	Rosemary Smith R. Chapman			
April	Circuit of Ireland	Austin Maxi 1500	Rosemary Smith/Alice Watson	UJB646G	6	1st Ladies, 21st o/all
April	London/Mexico World Cup Rally	Mini Clubman 1275	J. Handley/P. Easter	XJB308H	59	Ret – engine
		Austin Maxi 1500	Rosemary Smith/Alice Watson/ Ginette Derolland	XJB306H	74	10th o/all, 1st Ladies
		Austin Maxi 1500	T. Kingsley/P. Evans/M. Scarlett	XJB307H	96	22nd o/all, 1st class
		Triumph 2.5 PI Mk2	E. Green/J. Murray/H. Cardno	XJB303H	92	Ret –engine
		Triumph 2.5 PI Mk2	A. Cowan/B. Coyle/U. Ossio	XJB304II	43	Ret – accident
		Triumph 2.5 PI Mk2	B. Culcheth/J. Syer	XJB305H	88	2nd o/all, 1st class
		Triumph 2.5 PI Mk2	P. Hopkirk/A. Nash/N. Johnston	XJB302H	98	4th o/all, 2nd class
June	Scottish Rally	Triumph 2.5 PI Mk2	B. Culcheth/J. Syer	WRX902H	4	1st o/all
		Mini Clubman 1275 GT	P. Hopkirk/A. Nash	XJB308H	14	2nd o/all, 1st class
Sept	Marathon de La Route	Mini Clubman 1275 GT	J. Handley/A. Poole/J. Vernaeve	SOH878H	20	Ret – Head gasket
		Rover V8 4.3 Litre	R. Pierpoint/C. Baker/R. Enever	JXC806D	21	Ret – propshaft
Oct	Southern Cross Rally	Mini Clubman 1275 GT	A. Cowan/R. Forsyth	YMO881H		Ret – accident
		Morris Mini Cooper S	B. Culcheth/R. Bonhomme	RJB327F	12	Ret – OTL
Nov	Rally of the Hills	Morris Mini Cooper S	B. Culcheth/R. Bonhomme	RJB327F		4th o/all
1971						
May	Welsh Rally	Triumph 2.5 PI Mk2	B. Culcheth/J. Syer	XJB305H	4	14th o/all
June	Scottish Rally	Triumph 2.5 PI Mk2	B. Culcheth/J. Syer	XJB305H	1	10th o/all, 2nd class
Sept	Cyprus Rally	Triumph 2.5 PI Mk2	B. Culcheth/J. Syer	XJB305H	1	2nd o/all
Nov	RAC Rally	Morris Marina 1.3 Coupé	B. Culcheth/W. Cave	AOX705K	23	1st class, 20th o/all
1972						
April	East African Safari	Triumph 2.5 PI Mk2	B. Culcheth/L. Drews	KNW798	23	13th o/all, 1st class
June	Scottish Rally	Triumph Dolomite	B. Culcheth/J. Syer	CKV2K	2	19th o/all, 2nd class
Sept	Cyprus Rally	Morris Marina 1.3	B. Culcheth/J. Syer	NBL786L	3	2nd o/all
	TAP Rally	Triumph Dolomite	B. Culcheth/J. Syer	CKV2K	78	Ret – axle tie-rod
Nov	RAC Rally	Morris Marina 1.3	B. Culcheth/J. Syer	AOH609K	28	Ret – engine
1973						
May	24 Hrs of Ypres Rally	Morris Marina 1.3	B. Culcheth/J. Syer	NBL786L		10th o/all, 1st class
	Semeprit Rally	Morris Marina 1.8	B. Culcheth/J. Syer	NBL786L	8	11th o/all, 3rd class
Aug	1000 Lakes Rally	Morris Marina 1.3	B. Culcheth/J. Syer	NBL786L	7	16th o/all, 2nd class
	Cyprus Rally	Morris Marina 1.3	B. Culcheth/J. Syer	NBL786L	3	6th o/all, 1st class
1974						
	TAP Rally	Triumph Dolomite Sprint	B. Culcheth/J. Syer	FRW812L		Ret – steering
	Burmah Rally	Triumph Dolomite Sprint	B. Culcheth/J. Syer	FRW812L	5	Ret – ball joint
June	24 Hrs of Ypres Rally	Triumph Dolomite Sprint	B. Culcheth/J. Syer	FRW812L	1	Ret – brakes
	Tour of Britain	Triumph Dolomite Sprint	B. Culcheth/R. Hutton	RDU983M	24	Ret – carb. fire
	Criterium Antibes– Grasse Rally	Triumph Dolomite Sprint	B. Culcheth/J. Syer	FRW812L		Ret – radiator
Aug	1000 Lakes Rally	Morris Marina 1.3	B. Culcheth/J. Syer	NBL782M	21	24th o/all, 1st class
Oct	Rideau Lakes Rally	Austin Marina 1.8 Coupé	B. Culcheth/J. Syer	NBL782M	109	Ret – gear box
Nov	POR Rally	Austin Marina 1.8 Coupé	B. Culcheth/J. Syer	NBL782M	15	Ret – gearbox

Appendix C

Nov	RAC Rally	Triumph Dolomite Sprint	B. Culcheth/J. Syer	FRW812L	22	Ret – accident
		Morris Marina 1.3 Coupé	P. Cooper/E. Bamford	NBL786L	117	

1975

Jan	Tour of Dean Rally	Austin Allegro 1.3	R. Brookes/A. Bodman	NOJ946M	13	Ret – transmission
		Triumph Dolomite Sprint	B. Culcheth/J. Syer	FRW812L	6	Ret – accident
Feb	Mintex Rally	Triumph Dolomite Sprint	B. Culcheth/J. Syer	FRW812L	14	7th o/all
		Morris Marina 1.3	P. Ryan/J. Gittins	NBL782M	33	1st class
Mar	Hackle Rally	Triumph Dolomite Sprint	B. Culcheth/J. Syer	FRW812L	4	1st o/all
April	Granite City Rally	Triumph Dolomite Sprint	B. Culcheth/J. Syer	FRW812L	10	4th o/all
		Morris Marina 1.3	P. Ryan/J. Gittins	NBL782M	23	1st class
May	Welsh Rally	Triumph Dolomite Sprint	B. Culcheth/J. Syer	FRW812L	18	11th o/all
		Morris Marina 1.3	P. Ryan/J. Gittins	NBL782M	38	1st class
May	Scottish Rally	Triumph Dolomite Sprint	B. Culcheth/J. Syer	SOE8M	7	Ret – accident
		Morris Marina 1.3	P. Ryan/J. Gittins	NBL782M	30	Ret – accident
July	Jim Clark Rally	Triumph Dolomite Sprint	B. Culcheth/J. Syer	FRW812L	10	3rd o/all
Aug	Avon Tour of Britain	Triumph Dolomite Sprint	B. Culcheth/R. Hutton	RDU983M	24	2nd o/all
Aug	Burmah Rally	Triumph Dolomite Sprint	B. Culcheth/J. Syer	FRW812L	5	Ret – steering
		Morris Marina 1.3	P. Ryan/J. Gittins	NBL782M	21	
Sept	Manx Trophy Rally	Triumph Dolomite Sprint	B. Culcheth/J. Syer	FRW812L	6	Ret – axle
Oct	Lindisfarne Rally	Triumph Dolomite Sprint	B. Culcheth/J. Syer	FRW812L		3rd o/all
		Morris Marina 1.3	P. Ryan/J. Gittins	NBL782M		1st class
Nov	RAC Rally	Triumph Dolomite Sprint	B. Culcheth/J. Syer	RDU983M	28	16th o/all, 1st Group 1, 1st class
		Austin Allegro 1.3	P. Ryan/M. Nicholson	NOJ946M	50	Ret – transmission
		Morris Marina 1.3	P. Cooper/A. Marriott	NBL782M	86	4th class, 43rd o/all

1976

Jan	Shellsport Tour of Dean Rally	Triumph Dolomite Sprint	T. Pond/D. Richards	RDU983M	16	13th o/all, 1st Group 1
		Austin Allegro 1.3	P. Ryan/M. Nicholson	NOJ946M		1st class
Jan	Snowman Rally	Triumph Dolomite Sprint	T. Pond/D. Richards	RDU983M		Ret – engine
		Triumph Dolomite Sprint	B. Culcheth/J. Syer	FRW812L	9	5th o/all
		Austin Allegro 1.3	P. Ryan/M. Nicholson	NOJ946M		Ret – electrical
Feb	Mintex Rally	Triumph Dolomite Sprint	B. Culcheth/J. Syer	FRW812L	20	7th o/all
		Triumph Dolomite Sprint	T. Pond/D. Richards	RDU983M	9	10th overall, 1st Group 1
		Austin Allegro 1.3	P. Ryan/M. Nicholson	NOJ946M	29	Ret – transmission
Mar	Granite City Rally	Triumph Dolomite Sprint	B. Culcheth/J. Syer	FRW812L		Ret – brakes
		Triumph Dolomite Sprint	T. Pond/D. Richards	RDU983M	10	4th o/all, 1st Group 1
		Austin Allegro 1.3	P. Ryan/M. Nicholson	NOJ946M	30	Ret – transmission

1955 to 1980

May	Welsh Rally	Triumph TR7	T. Pond/D. Richards	KDU498N	8	Ret – engine
		Triumph TR7	B. Culcheth/J. Syer	KDU497N	18	Ret – head gasket
		Triumph Dolomite Sprint	P. Ryan/M. Nicholson	RDU983M	46	3rd class
May	Lucien Bianchi Rally	Triumph Dolomite Sprint	B. Culcheth/J. Syer	MYX175P	1	Ret – head gasket
June	Scottish Rally	Triumph TR7	T. Pond/D. Richards	KDU498N		Ret – engine
		Triumph TR7	B. Culcheth/J. Syer	KDU497N		Ret – engine
		Triumph Dolomite Sprint	P. Ryan/M. Nicholson	RDU983M	31	5th class
June	Texaco Tour of Britain	Triumph Dolomite Sprint	B. Culcheth/R. Hutton	MYX175P	6	2nd o/all
		Triumph Dolomite Sprint	T. Pond/D. Richards	RDU983M		Ret – engine
Aug	Int Caravan Rally	Triumph 2500/Monza	T. Pond/D. Richards	JHP368N	13	Disqualified
Aug	Burmah Rally	Triumph TR7	T. Pond/D. Richards	KDU498N	8	Ret – accident
		Triumph TR7	B. Culcheth/J. Syer	KDU497N	11	15th o/all
		Triumph Dolomite Sprint	P. Ryan/M. Nicholson	RDU983M	35	1st Group 1, 7th o/all
Aug	Manx Trophy Rally	Triumph TR7	T. Pond/D. Richards	KDU498N	11	3rd o/all
		Triumph TR7	B. Culcheth/J. Syer	KDU497N	15	5th o/all
		Triumph Dolomite Sprint	P. Ryan/F. Gallagher	RDU983M	30	9th o/all Man Team Prize
Oct	Lindisfarne Rally	Triumph TR7	T. Pond/D. Richards	KDU498N	15	9th o/all
		Triumph TR7	B. Culcheth/J. Syer	KDU497N		Ret – electrical
		Triumph Dolomite Sprint	P. Ryan/M. Nicholson	RDU983M		1st Group 1
Oct	Castrol Rally 76	Triumph TR7	T. Pond/D. Richards	KDU498N	8	3rd o/all
		Triumph TR7	B. Culcheth/J. Syer	KDU497N	10	8th o/all
		Triumph Dolomite Sprint	P. Ryan/M. Nicholson	RDU983M	24	2nd Group 1
Oct	Raylor Rally	Triumph TR7	T. Pond/M. Nicholson	KDU498N	2	1st o/all
Nov	RAC Rally	Triumph TR7	T. Pond/D. Richards	OOE938R	21	Ret – suspension
		Triumph TR7	B. Culcheth/J. Syer	OOE937R	12	9th o/all
		Triumph Dolomite Sprint	P. Ryan/M. Nicholson	RDU983M	24	Ret – engine

1977

Jan	Tour of Dean	Triumph Dolomite Sprint	P. Ryan/M. Nicholson	RDU983M	18	Ret – accident
Feb	Boucles de Spa Rally	Triumph TR7	T. Pond/F. Gallagher	KDU498N	3	1st overall
Feb	Mintex Rally	Triumph TR7	T. Pond/F. Gallagher	OOE938R	7	3rd o/all
		Triumph TR7	B. Culcheth/J. Syer	OOE937R	12	17th o/all
		Triumph Dolomite Sprint	P. Ryan/M. Nicholson	RDU983M	17	35th o/all
April	Circuit of Ireland	Triumph Dolomite Sprint	P. Ryan/D. Gillespie	MYX175P	23	Ret – accident
April	Tour of Elba	Triumph TR7	T. Pond/F. Gallagher	OOE938R	5	3rd o/all
		Triumph TR7	B. Culcheth/J. Syer	KDU497N	12	Ret – throttle linkage
April	Granite City Rally	Triumph Dolomite Sprint	P. Ryan/M. Nicholson	RDU983M		8th o/all, 1st Group 1
May	Welsh Rally	Triumph TR7	T. Pond/F. Gallagher	OOE938R	8	Ret – accident
		Triumph TR7	B. Culcheth/J. Syer	OOE937R	18	Ret – oil pipe
		Triumph Dolomite Sprint	P. Ryan/M. Nicholson	RDU983M	26	2nd Group 1, 9th o/all
June	Scottish Rally	Triumph TR7	T. Pond/F. Gallagher	OOE938R	11	2nd o/all
		Triumph TR7	B. Culcheth/J. Syer	KDU497N	15	9th o/all
		Triumph Dolomite Sprint	P. Ryan/M. Nicholson	RDU983M	20	12th o/all, 3rd class Man Team Prize
June	24 Hr of Ypres Rally	Triumph TR7	T. Pond/F. Gallagher	OOM513R		Ret – engine
		Triumph TR7	B. Culcheth/J. Syer	OOE937R		Ret – accident
July	Jim Clark Rally	Triumph Dolomite Sprint	P. Ryan/M. Nicholson	MYX175P		Ret – engine

Appendix C

Month	Event	Car	Crew	Reg	No	Result
July	Milles Pistes Rally	Triumph TR7	T. Pond/F. Gallagher	OOE938R		Ret – axle
		Triumph TR7	B. Culcheth/J. Syer	KDU497N	11	4th o/all
July	Hunsruck Rally	Triumph TR7	T. Pond/F. Gallagher	OOM513R	6	Ret – accident
		Triumph TR7	B. Culcheth/J. Syer	OOE937R	12	Ret – axle
Sept	Manx Trophy Rally	Triumph TR7	T. Pond/F. Gallagher	OOM513R	6	Ret – engine
		Triumph TR7	B. Culcheth/J. Syer	OOM512R	11	2nd o/all
		Triumph Dolomite Sprint	P. Ryan/M. Nicholson	MYX175P	19	7th o/all, 1st Group 1
Nov	Tour de Corse	Triumph TR7	T. Pond/F. Gallagher	OOM513R		Ret – gearbox
		Triumph TR7	B. Culcheth/J. Syer	KDU497N	17	11th o/all
Nov	RAC Rally	Triumph TR7	B. Culcheth/J. Syer	OOM512R	29	Ret – wheel studs
		Triumph TR7	T. Pond/F. Gallagher	OOM514R	24	8th o/all
		Triumph TR7	M. Saaristo/I. Grindrod	SCE645S	57	37th o/all
		Triumph TR7	P. Ryan/M. Nicholson	OOM513R	42	Ret – gearbox

1978

Month	Event	Car	Crew	Reg	No	Result
Feb	Mintex Rally	Triumph TR7	T. Pond/F. Gallagher	OOM513R	6	17th o/all
Mar	Circuit of Ireland	Triumph TR7	T. Pond/F. Gallagher	SJW533S	11	Ret – overheating
April	Texaco Rallysprint	Triumph TR7 V8	T. Pond	OOM512R	6	2nd o/all
April	Granite City Rally	Triumph TR7 V8	T. Pond/F. Gallagher	OOM512R	3	1st o/all
May	Welsh Rally	Triumph TR7 V8	T. Pond/F. Gallagher	SJW533S	6	Ret – alternator
June	Scottish Rally	Triumph TR7 V8	T. Pond/F. Gallagher	SJW533S	7	Ret-accident
June	24 Hours of Ypres	Triumph TR7 V8	T. Pond/F. Gallagher	SJW540S	2	1st o/all
July	Border Counties	Triumph TR7 V8	T. Pond/F. Gallagher	OOM512R	11	4th o/all
Aug	Burmah Rally	Triumph TR7 V8	T. Pond/F. Gallagher	SJW533S	5	Ret – suspension
		Triumph TR7 V8	J. Buffum/N. Wilson	OOM512R	12	8th o/all
Sept	Ulster Rally	Triumph TR7 V8	D. Boyd/F. Gallagher	KDU497N		Ret – engine
Sept	Manx Trophy Rally	Triumph TR7 V8	T. Pond/F. Gallagher	SJW540S	5	1st o/all
		Triumph TR7 V8	D. Boyd/R. Kernaghan	KDU497N		Ret – oil pump belt
Sept	Lindisfarne Rally	Triumph TR7 V8	T. Pond/F. Gallagher	SJW533S		Ret – engine
Oct	Cork Rally	Triumph TR7 V8	D. Boyd/R. Cole	KDU497N		Ret – gearbox
Oct	Texaco Rallysprint	Triumph TR7 V8	J. Watson	OOM512R	6	3rd o/all
Nov	Tour de Corse	Triumph TR7 V8	T. Pond/F. Gallagher	SJW540S		Ret–gearbox
		Triumph TR7 V8	J. L. Therier/M. Vial	SJW548S		Ret–gearbox
Nov	Wyedean Stages Rally	Triumph TR7 V8	G. Elsmore/S. Harrold	OOM512R	1	2nd o/all
Nov	RAC Rally	Triumph TR7 V8	T. Pond/F. Gallagher	SJW540S	7	4th o/all
		Triumph TR7 V8	S. Lampinen/M. Broad	SJW548S	15	Ret – clutch
		Triumph TR7 V8	J. Haughland/I. Grindrod	SJW533S	24	12th o/all
Nov	Hitachi Rallysprint	Triumph TR7 V8	D. Boyd/F. Gallagher	KDU497N		Not classified

1979

Month	Event	Car	Crew	Reg	No	Result
Feb	Boucles of Spa Rally	Triumph TR7 V8	J. L. Therier/M. Vial	SJW548S	2	Ret – distributor
Feb	Galway Rally	Triumph TR7 V8	G. Elsmore/S. Harrold	UYH863S	8	Ret – accident
		Triumph TR7 V8	D. Boyd/F. Gallagher	SJW533S	2	Ret – accident
Feb	Mintex Rally	Triumph TR7 V8	P. Eklund/M. Broad	SJW548S	5	2nd o/all
		Triumph TR7 V8	G. Elsmore/S. Harrold	SJW540S	7	Ret–engine
April	Circuit of Ireland	Triumph TR7 V8	G. Elsmore/S. Harrold	SJW546S	12	Ret – accident
		Triumph TR7 V8	P. Eklund/H. Sylvan	TUD682T	3	Ret – engine
		Triumph TR7 V8	D. Boyd/R. Kernaghan	SJW533S	11	Ret – accident
May	Welsh Rally	Triumph TR7 V8	G. Elsmore/S. Harrold	SJW540S	19	Ret – accident
		Triumph TR7 V8	P. Eklund/H. Sylvan	TUD682T	5	Ret
		Triumph TR7 V8	S. Lampinen/I. Grindrod	SJW548S	8	12th o/all
June	BP Rallysprint	Triumph TR7 V8	G. Elsmore	SJW533S		8th o/all
		Triumph TR7 V8	P. Eklund	TUD683T	7	1st o/all

1955 to 1980

June	Scottish Rally	Triumph TR7 V8	G. Elsmore/S. Harrold	SJW540S	21	Ret – head gasket
		Triumph TR7 V8	S. Lampinen/F. Gallagher	SJW548S	10	13th o/all
		Triumph TR7 V8	P. Eklund/H. Sylvan	TUD682T	7	3rd o/all
Aug	Peter Russek Manuals Rally	Triumph TR7 V8	G. Elsmore/F. Gallagher	OOM514R	7	1st o/all
Aug	1000 Lakes Rally	Triumph TR7 V8	P. Eklund/H. Sylvan	TUD682T	4	8th o/all
		Triumph TR7 V8	S. Lampinen/J. Markkanen	TUD683T		Ret – distributor
Sept	Lindisfarne Rally	Triumph TR7 V8	G. Elsmore/S. Harrold	OOM514R		8th o/all
Sept	Mopar Manx Rally	Triumph TR7 V8	G. Elsmore/F. Gallagher	SJW546S	14	3rd o/all
Sept	San Remo Rally	Triumph TR7 V8	P. Eklund/H. Sylvan	XJO414V	10	Ret – engine
		Triumph TR7 V8	S. Lampinen/F. Gallagher	TUD683T		Ret – suspension
Oct	Eaton Yale Rallysprint	Triumph TR7 V8	P. Eklund	TUD682T		
Oct	Castrol 79 Rally	Triumph TR7 V8	G. Elsmore/S. Harrold	OOM514R		Ret
Oct	Scarborough Stages Rally	Triumph TR7 V8	G. Elsmore/H. Sylvan	OOM514R		
Nov	RAC Rally	Triumph TR7 V8	P. Eklund/H. Sylvan	XJO414V	9	13th o/all
		Triumph TR7 V8	S. Lampinen/F. Gallagher	TUD683T	15	17th o/all
		Triumph TR7 V8	G. Elsmore/S. Harrold	SJW546S	32	16th o/all
		Triumph TR7 V8	T. Kaby/B. Rainbow	UYH863S	34	Ret – engine

1980

Feb	Henley Forklift Galway Rally	Triumph TR7 V8	R. Clark/J. Porter	SJW546S	2	Ret – engine
Feb	Mintex Rally	Triumph TR7 V8	R. Clark/J. Porter	SJW546S	5	Ret – engine
Mar	Rally of Portugal	Triumph TR7 V8	P. Eklund/H. Sylvan	HRW251V	14	Ret – fuel pump
		Triumph TR7 V8	T. Pond/F. Gallagher	HRW250V		Ret – engine
April	Circuit of Ireland	Triumph TR7 V8	R. Clark/J. Porter	XJO414V	9	Ret – engine
April	Daily Mirror Rallysprint	Triumph TR7 V8	T. Pond	UYH863S	12	Ret – accident
		Triumph TR7 V8	P. Eklund	HRW251V	1	2nd o/all
May	Criterium Alpin Rally	Triumph TR7 V8	T. Pond/F. Gallagher	TUD683T	9	Ret – engine
		Triumph TR7 V8	P. Eklund/H. Sylvan	TUD686T	6	Ret – alternator
May	Welsh Rally	Triumph TR7 V8	R. Clark/J. Porter	XJO414V	8	Ret – fuel pump
May	Rothmans Manx Stages	Triumph TR7 V8	T. Pond/F. Gallagher	UYH863S	2	1st o/all
June	Scottish Rally	Triumph TR7 V8	T. Pond/F. Gallagher	HRW250V	8	4th o/all
		Triumph TR7 V8	P. Eklund/H. Sylvan	HRW251V	10	Ret – engine
		Triumph TR7 V8	R. Clark/J. Porter	XJO414V	14	9th o/all
June	24 Hours of Ypres	Triumph TR7 V8	T. Pond/F. Gallagher	TUD683T	11	1st o/all
		Triumph TR7 V8	P. Eklund/H. Sylvan	TUD686T	7	Ret – engine
Aug	1000 Lakes Rally	Triumph TR7 V8	P. Eklund/H. Sylvan	TUD686T	15	3rd o/all
		Triumph TR7 V8	T. Makinen/E. Salonen	HRW251V	11	Ret – fuel
Sept	Rothmans Manx Trophy Rally	Triumph TR7 V8	T. Pond/F. Gallagher	TUD683T	4	1st o/all
		Triumph TR7 V8	R. Clark/J. Porter	XJO414V	6	Ret – axle shaft
Sept	Tour of Cumbria	Triumph TR7 V8	T. Pond/F. Gallagher	UYH863S	2	2nd o/all
Oct	Castrol 80 Rally	Triumph TR7 V8	T. Pond/F. Gallagher	UYH863S	2	Ret – OTL
Oct	Eaton Yale Rallysprint	Triumph TR7 V8	T. Pond/A. Jones	HRW250V	1&5	1st o/all
Nov	RAC Rally	Triumph TR7 V8	T. Pond/F. Gallagher	JJO931W	15	7th o/all
		Triumph TR7 V8	P. Eklund/H. Sylvan	TUD686T	9	Ret – engine
		Triumph TR7 V8	R. Clark/N. Wilson	XJO414V	20	Ret – engine
		Triumph TR7 V8	J. Buffum/I. Grindrod	HRW251V	22	Ret – axle

1981

April	L & S British Rallycross–Lydden	Unipart Metro	T. Reeves		5	1st in Heat 2nd in Heat

INDEX

Aaltonen, Marjatta, 171.
Aaltonen, Rauno, 79, 85, 86, 90, 92, 94, 101, 104, 113, 120, 123, 127, 128, 131, 133, 134, 145, 146, 147, 148, 150, 155, 160, 163, 167, 169, 170, 174, 185, 187, 188, 190, 194, 196, 206, 211, 217, 218, 219, 221.
Adams, Ronnie, 17, 62, 70.
Aldon Automotive, 284.
Aley, John, 27.
Alford & Alder, 312.
Allison, Joe, 264, 266.
Ambrose, Tony, 57, 58, 75, 92, 127, 128, 130, 169, 201, 273.
Andersson, Ove, 174.
A. P. Racing, 305, 339.
Appleby, W. V, 17.
Appleyard, Ian, 11, 90.
Astle, Derek, 73, 84, 85, 92, 102.
Austin Motor Co, 9, 17.
Autocar, 286, 308, 348.
Autosport, 16, 308, 348.

Backus, Jim, 276.
Baker, Clive, 131, 194, 196, 197, 199, 210, 214.
Bamford, J. C, 277.
Banks, Warwick, 130, 143.
Barber, John, 282, 289.
Barrow, Don, 127, 130.
Bartram, Peter, 142, 149, 150, 153.
Bastos, Henry, 153, 174.
Battam, Peter, 280, 282, 285.
Baxter, Raymond, 20, 101, 134, 135, 153, 202.
BBC, 278, 308, 309.
Beaumont, Marie-Claude, 235.
Bell, Roger, 163.
Bellis, John, 357.
Bengry, Bill, 262, 266.
Bensted-Smith, R, 22.
Bentley, Ian. 305.
Benzimra, David, 188, 204.
Bertaut, Alain, 157.
Best, Ken, 26, 282.
Best, Kevin, 282, 287, 288, 295, 296, 305, 315, 330, 332.
B. R. Goodrich, 364.
Bianchi, Lucien, 167, 217, 218, 221.
Bibb, Bert, 58.
Bilstein, 288, 303, 330.
Birtwistle, Gordon, 281, 333.
Bishop, Reg, 9, 34.
Blake, Alan, 291.
Blake, Eric, 265.
Blenkhorn, Phil, 333.
BLI, 278, 282, 286, 287, 288, 295, 302, 315, 337.
Blomqvist, Stig, 315.
Bloxham, John, 284, 286, 287.
Bodman, Andy, 296.
Bohringer, Eugen, 79, 92, 96, 114, 127, 131.
Bolton, Cyril, 340.
Bowman, Les, 284.
Boyd, Adrian, 187, 207, 227.
Boyd, Derek, 341, 342, 345, 346, 347, 348, 352.
Boyd, Maxwell, 169.
Brabham, Jack, 15.
Brack, Bill, 227.

Bradford, Stan, 157, 194, 201.
Bray, Cliff, 13.
Broad, Mike, 342, 346.
Broadspeed, 284, 296, 309, 310, 315, 337, 341.
Brockhurst, Roy, 30, 92.
Brooks, Tony, 71.
Brookes, J, 22.
Brookes, R, 23, 26.
Brookes, Russell, 278, 291, 296, 301, 317.
Brown, Emmett, 161.
Brown, Peter, 207.
Brown, Roy, 173, 192.
Browning, Peter, 102, 122, 138, 142, 161, 163, 165, 167, 172, 174, 185, 186, 187, 189, 190, 193, 196, 198, 201, 203, 204, 211, 214, 218, 219, 223, 227, 232, 234, 237, 239, 240, 247, 254, 258, 263, 264, 266, 271, 276.
Buffum, John, 340, 341, 352, 353, 364.
Burgess, Gerry, 11, 17, 20, 30, 52, 54.
Burnell, Eddie, 213, 217, 255, 268, 272, 281, 282, 288, 289, 291, 297.
Burrows, Bill, 203, 275, 276, 281, 282, 304, 312, 345, 348.
Burt, Patsy, 22.

Car & Car Conversions, 348.
Cardell, Dennis, 297.
Cardew, Basil, 92.
Cardno, Hamish, 253, 261.
Carlisle, Christabel, 80, 83, 87, 100, 101, 102.
Carlsson, Erik, 29, 52, 54, 58, 64, 70, 73, 79, 83, 84, 95, 127, 148.
Carpenter, Mac, 92.
Carello, Tony, 339.
Castrol, 17, 23, 26, 32, 57, 135, 140, 142, 148, 153, 174, 191, 192, 196, 214, 218, 227, 268, 278, 286, 289, 295, 296, 300, 312, 354.
Cave, Willy, 71, 276, 278.
Challis, Neville, 68, 80, 126, 172, 214, 221, 262, 275.
Chambers, Marcus, 9, 10, 18, 20, 21, 22, 25, 26, 30, 33, 37, 38, 40, 51, 54, 55, 58, 66, 70, 73, 75, 76, 78, 80, 122, 147, 161, 172, 271, 273.
Champion, 57.
Chapman, Rod, 250.
Chatfield, Brian, 249, 282.
Chequered Flag, 345, 346, 348, 352.
Choules, Roy, 299.
Christie, Tom, 70, 73.
Clark, Jim, 169.
Clark, John, 33.
Clark, Roger, 155, 157, 169, 207, 217, 218, 219, 227, 282, 297, 354, 355, 358, 363, 364.
Clayton, Ann, 76.
Clegg, John, 299.
Consten, Bernard, 115.
Cooper Car Co, 224.
Cooper, Charles, 80.
Cooper, John, 80, 172.
Cooper, Phil, 276, 282, 296, 297, 302.
Cooper, Sheilagh, 11.
Couper, Mike, 20.
Coyle, Brian, 233, 249.
Cousins, Cecil, 9.

Index

Cowan, Andrew, 221, 232, 233, 237, 239, 247, 253, 256, 260, 264, 265, 266, 272.
Cox, Jimmy, 13, 18.
Crellin, Liz, 276.
Crellin, Ron, 148, 160, 163, 206, 211.
Crisp, Peter, 267.
Croft-Pearson, S, 18.
Cross, Betty, 293.
Cuff, John, 101.
Culcheth, Brian, 101, 122, 194, 201, 207, 208, 217, 218, 223, 224, 225, 229, 231, 232, 233, 234, 235, 239, 240, 247, 256, 258, 260, 264, 266, 267, 268, 271, 272, 278, 280, 281, 284, 286, 288, 289, 295, 298, 300, 301, 305, 308, 310, 313, 315, 318, 320, 329, 330, 332, 333, 334, 337, 338.

Daley, Dan, 135.
Dalton, John, 38.
Daniels, Jack, 128, 130, 161.
Davenport, John, 125, 185, 289, 315, 317, 318, 329, 330, 332, 333, 334, 337, 339, 340, 341, 342, 344, 346, 351, 355, 358, 361, 363, 364, 365.
Davis, Bill, 278, 281.
Davis, SCH, 9.
Dawson, Andy, 291, 297.
Delamont, Dean, 203.
Denton, Jean, 265, 276.
Denovo, 281.
Derrington, Jane, 58.
Dickin, Mike, 276.
Dimmock, Peter, 71.
Dixon, David, 83.
Domei, Bob, 64.
Domleo, Val, 99, 102, 113, 119, 125, 131.
Donald Healey Motor Co, 9, 13, 27, 29, 57, 59, 138, 140, 203.
Drake, Paul, 365.
Drews, Lofty, 206, 278, 280.
Dron, Tony, 337.
Drummond, Tony, 299.
Dundrod, 17.
Dunlop, 26, 33, 40, 57, 58, 59, 68, 72, 92, 114, 115, 133, 135, 163, 173, 192, 196, 202, 214, 217, 218, 224, 281, 299, 310, 330, 339.
Dwyer, Christine, 299.
Dymar Electronics, 333.

Eales, Tommy, 127, 155, 196, 208, 217, 218, 250, 253.
Easter, Paul, 122, 130, 133, 135, 137, 142, 143, 145, 148, 150, 153, 154, 163, 172, 203, 204, 211, 212, 219, 235, 240.
Edis, Alan, 315, 334, 337.
Eklund, Per, 346, 348, 350, 352, 354, 355, 357, 361, 364.
Elford, Vic, 64, 75, 138, 150, 174, 194.
Elkins, Ron, 259, 275, 276, 281, 301, 338, 363.
Elmhorn, Bo, 131.
Elsmore, Graham, 342, 345, 346, 347, 350, 351, 352.
Emde, Hugo, 288.
Emmott, Jack, 9.
Enever, Roger, 167, 194, 196, 210, 231, 232.
Enever, Syd, 9, 16, 17, 27, 30, 34, 90, 102, 138, 213, 276.
English, Mike, 145.
Equipe Arden, 284.
Esso, 354.
Evans, Glynn, 140, 275.
Evans, John, 155, 174, 189, 190, 260.
Evans, Peter, 233.

Eyston, George, 17, 32.

Faichney, Pat, 10, 21.
Fairman, Jack, 18.
Fall, Tony, 147, 148, 149, 153, 154, 160, 161, 163, 164, 166, 167, 170, 172, 174, 176, 185, 191, 192, 194, 196, 199, 202, 204, 207, 208, 210, 217, 218, 221, 273, 276.
Fangio, Juan Manuel, 247.
Ferguson, Jeremy, 204, 217, 263.
Ferodo, 57, 64.
Firth, Harry, 217.
Fitzpatrick, John, 130, 131, 135, 215.
Flaherty, Jack, 73, 89.
Flockhart, Ron, 15, 18, 19.
Flynn, Joe, 13.
Foden, John, 291.
Folley, Malcolm, 357.
Fordham, Morva, 340.
Forsyth, Bruce, 120.
Foster, Alan, 12, 26.
Freeborough, Bob, 191, 201, 282.
Friswell, David, 125.
Frost, Derek, 84.

Gallagher, Fred, 310, 315, 317, 337, 341, 344, 345, 346, 348, 350, 351, 352, 354, 364.
Garbett, Ernie, 264.
Garnett, Alf, 219.
Garnier, Peter, 73.
Garot, Maurice, 17.
Garton, Mike, 275.
Garrard, Norman, 92.
Gill, Barrie, 169.
Gillespie, Drexel, 318.
Gillibrand, Brian, 172.
Girling, 286, 288, 303.
Glenton, Robert, 85, 86.
Gold, Tommy, 62, 70, 75, 83, 84.
Goodyear, 340, 352.
Gott, John, 10, 15, 16, 17, 19, 20, 23, 26, 27, 28, 29, 30, 37, 78, 79, 84, 90, 92, 94, 96, 114, 203, 217, 273.
Grace, Harold, 12, 26.
Grace, HRH Princess, 137.
Green, Dickie, 13.
Green, Den, 54, 58, 59, 66, 85, 119, 122, 130, 135, 147, 148, 167, 187, 201, 203, 212, 218, 219, 223, 258, 263, 265, 266, 267, 271, 272, 304, 308, 310, 312, 318, 333, 337, 351, 364.
Green, Evan, 218, 219, 221, 233, 260, 261, 262, 264, 265.
Grice, Bob, 9.
Griffin, Charles, 64, 282.
Grimshaw, Don, 79.
Grindrod, Ian, 333, 340, 342.
Grounds, Frank, 30.
Groves, Richard, 172.

Haakansson, Ragnvald, 169.
Hacquin, G, 26.
Hall, Anne, 26.
Hall, Margaret, 26.
Hall, Nobby, 74, 122, 134, 135, 155, 161, 199, 213.
Haig, Tom, 21.
Hamblin, Doug, 33, 64, 70, 78, 80, 84, 90, 115, 119.
Hambro Automotive, 38.
Hancock, Brian, 165.
Handley, John, 161, 221, 224, 225, 227, 231, 232, 233, 235, 237, 240, 250, 252, 253, 260, 299.

Index

Hans-Hamilton, Capt, 276.
Harper, Peter, 139, 237.
Harper, Richard, 284, 287.
Harriman, Sir George, 9, 16, 18, 29, 120, 135, 169.
Harris, G; 26.
Harrison, E, 27.
Harrold, Stuart, 342, 345.
Harryman, Terry, 138, 187.
Hartto, Raimo, 351.
Haugland, John, 342, 345.
Hawkins, Paul, 140.
Hayter, Don, 30, 196.
Healey, Donald, 70.
Healey, Geoff, 27, 138, 172.
Hedges, Andrew, 89, 115, 122, 130, 140, 142, 146, 161, 190, 194, 203, 207, 210, 211, 225.
Helmsley, Maj John, 282.
Henderson, Ray, 223, 227, 280, 300.
Henson, Sid, 22, 23.
Heys, Jack, 119.
Hiam, David, 73, 127.
Higgins, Norman, 57, 119, 135, 137, 197, 262, 268, 277, 284.
Hill, Craig, 225.
Hill, Graham, 169, 170, 215, 217.
Hine, Bill, 282.
Hockley, Harry, 363.
Holt, Bros, 10, 12.
Hopkins, Keith, 215, 284, 286, 299.
Hopkirk, Paddy, 92, 96, 99, 100, 101, 102, 104, 113, 114, 115, 116, 119, 122, 123, 130, 131, 133, 134, 135, 137, 138, 140, 142, 143, 146, 148, 149, 155, 156, 157, 160, 161, 163, 165, 169, 174, 176, 185, 186, 187, 190, 191, 194, 199, 201, 202, 203, 206, 207, 208, 211, 215, 217, 218, 219, 221, 223, 225, 226, 227, 231, 232, 233, 234, 235, 239, 240, 247, 253, 256, 260, 264, 266, 267, 268, 271, 272.
Horrocks, Gyde, 27, 32.
Hounslow, Alec, 9, 12, 13, 17, 21, 23, 26.
Howells of Cardiff, 297.
Howlett, John, 339, 346, 348, 354, 365.
Humphries, Cliff, 84, 85, 147, 165, 170, 172, 194, 203, 213, 233, 240, 250, 255, 272, 345, 348, 350, 355.
Hunt, Sir David, 264.
Hunter, Terry, 104, 114.
Hurdwell, Richard, 348, 352, 355, 357, 361, 363, 365.
Hutcheson, Alan, 102.
Hutchinson, Glen, 297, 317, 339.
Hutton, Ray, 286, 299.

Ickx, Jacky, 139.
Issigonis, Sir Alec, 120, 135, 192.

Jackson, Eric, 219.
Jacobs, Dick, 12, 13, 138, 140.
Jacquin, Madame, 85.
James, Ken, 54.
Janspeed, 299, 354.
Jinks, Gillian, 10, 26.
Johns, Douglas, 20, 114.
Johns, Joan, 10, 11, 20, 22, 27, 30.
Johnston, Neville, 227, 267.
Jones, Alan, 352, 363.
Jones, Johnny, 284.
Jones, Liz, 83, 100.
Jones, Rupert, 33, 52, 62, 79, 84, 192.
Jopp, Peter, 276.
Joss, Raymond, 174.

Kaby, Terry, 352, 353.
Kallstrom, Harry, 131, 133, 134, 135, 169.
Keller, J, 16.
Kemsley, Jack, 203.
Kernaghan, Roy, 348.
Kerswill, John, 286, 288, 292, 299, 304, 320, 334, 348.
Keskitalo, Pekka, 192.
Key, Neville, 310.
King, Dr, 13.
Kingsley, Terry, 219, 233.
Kirkby, Diana, 130, 201.
Knight, Laurie, 310.
Kyle, Mike, 348, 357, 363, 365.

Lambourne, Les, 135, 276, 277.
Lampinen, Simo, 169, 170, 174, 176, 193, 221, 340, 343, 346, 350, 352.
Lane, Bill, 15, 275, 276.
Lawrence, Chris, 143.
Lawson, Sandy, 214, 271.
Lay, John, 94, 113, 119.
Learoyd, Rob, 74.
Le Mans, 11, 17, 102.
Levegh, Pierre, 13.
Levy, Wolfgang, 54.
Liddon, Henry, 120, 121, 123, 133, 145, 148, 160, 169, 190, 204, 208, 211, 282.
Lines, Del, 358.
Lloyd, John, 281.
Loake, Murray, 203.
Lockett, John, 13, 18.
Longman, Richard, 233.
Lord, Leonard, 9, 30.
Lowe, Derek, 33.
Lowrey, Joe, 26, 30.
Lucas Racing, 196, 297, 320.
Lund, Ted, 13, 17, 18.
Lungfeldt, Bo, 119.
Lusenius, Jorma, 169.
Lyons, Sir William, 169.

Mabbs, Geoff, 85, 86, 113, 115, 134, 135, 172, 190, 201, 224, 225, 232, 233, 240, 247.
Mac, Roger, 143, 161.
Maher, Eddie, 17, 18, 32, 38, 84.
Makinen, Timo, 97, 99, 100, 101, 102, 104, 113, 115, 116, 120, 122, 125, 126, 127, 128, 130, 133, 135, 138, 139, 140, 145, 147, 146, 148, 149, 153, 154, 155, 160, 161, 163, 165, 169, 170, 174, 185, 186, 188, 192, 193, 199, 201, 203, 206, 207, 211, 361.
Malkin, Colin, 291.
Manton, Peter, 161.
Markkanen, Juhani, 351.
Marnat, Jean-Louis, 276.
Marriott, Andy, 302.
Mason, Tony, 364.
Mayman, Pauline, 90, 92, 96, 99, 100, 102, 104, 113, 115, 119, 123, 125, 130, 131, 133, 146.
McComb, Wilson, 80, 92, 119, 123, 149, 163.
McLuggage, Denise, 104.
McMillen, Ernie, 119.
Menadue, Roger, 135.
MG Car Co Ltd, 9.
Michael, HRH Prince, 256, 268.
Michelin, 357, 358, 361, 363, 364.
Mikkola, Hannu, 125, 267, 338.
Miles, Ken, 13.

Index

Millard, Peter, 38.
Milne, John, 16, 23, 25, 26, 51, 58, 59.
Mitchell, Nancy, 15, 20, 21, 22, 23, 25, 26, 27, 28, 29, 30, 54, 55, 57.
Mitchell, Terry, 30, 173.
Montlhéry, 18, 26, 32.
Moore, Bobby, 253.
Moore, Don, 80, 128, 143, 172, 234, 309, 312, 315, 320, 329, 350, 352.
Moore, John, 132.
Moore, Sam, 30.
Morgan, Phillip, 84.
Morley, Brothers, 40, 54, 58, 62, 69, 70, 75, 84, 99, 102, 104, 116, 119, 120, 122, 123, 125, 130, 131, 135, 139, 145, 147, 150, 161, 201, 259.
Morley, Val, 201.
Morrell, Peter, 17.
Morris Bodies, 11, 17.
Morris Engines, 17, 18, 29, 32, 38, 90, 92, 197.
Morris-Goodall, M, 9.
Morrison, Logan, 96, 99, 101, 102, 104, 113, 115.
Moss, Alf, 10.
Moss, Pat, 10, 12, 20, 26, 27, 28, 30, 34, 37, 40, 51, 52, 55, 57, 64, 69, 70, 73, 75, 76, 78, 79, 83, 85, 87, 89, 90, 92, 94, 95, 96, 99, 101, 148, 197.
Moss, Stirling, 10, 75, 89.
Motor, 22, 30, 308, 348.
Motoring News, 308, 348.
Motospeed, 364.
Moulton developments, 291.
Moylan, Brian, 14, 26, 55, 92, 114, 115, 125, 137, 147, 163, 175, 217, 267, 272, 342, 364.
Murray, Jack, 215, 217, 259, 262.
Mylchreest, Brian, 310, 330.
Mylchreest Motors, 310, 330, 341.

Nash, Ralph, 247.
Nash, Tony, 211, 215, 221, 227, 233, 239, 240, 258, 272.
Needham, Les, 196, 223, 237, 263.
Nelson, Brian, 310.
Nicholson, Mike, 302, 308, 315, 320.

Oakley, Jed, 221.
Oates, Jim, 292, 363.
Olthoff, Bob, 73, 83, 89.
Organ, Johnny, 15, 40, 134, 190.
Orrenius, Carl, 131.
Owen, Rubery, 68.
Ossio, Ulrico, 240, 247.
Ozanne, Tish, 54, 57, 58, 260, 273.

Palm, Gunnar, 90.
Parkes, Mike, 315.
Parkinson, Jim, 38, 73, 89.
Pascal, Madame, 85.
Pearce, Fred, 276.
Pearson, Simon, 278, 280, 281, 282, 284, 296, 301, 315.
Pease, Al, 138.
Penny, Dr, 28.
Persson, Lars, 191.
Phillips, Gordon, 275.
Phillips, Reg, 20.
Pianta, Giorgio, 145.
Pierburg, 346, 350.
Pierpoint, Roy, 143, 268, 271.
Pike, Dudley, 194, 234, 264, 304.
Piranha Ignition, 296.
Pitts, Alec, 54, 57, 58.

Pond, Tony, 299, 301, 304, 305, 308, 309, 310, 312, 314, 315, 317, 318, 320, 329, 330, 337, 338, 339, 342, 345, 352, 354, 355, 357, 363, 364.
Poole, Alec, 167, 192, 196, 198, 212.
Poole, Arne, 227.
Porter, Bob, 18, 19.
Porter, Bob, 354, 355.
Pye Radio, 33.
Pyle, Laurie, 14.

Rainier, HRH Prince, 135.
Rallysport, 348.
Ramsey, Sir Alf, 259.
Reade, Martin, 267, 276, 301, 350.
Red Arrows, 219, 221, 264.
Redgrave, Reg, 276.
Reece, Doreen, 20, 22.
Reece, Peter, 17.
Reeves, Trevor, 363, 364.
Rhodes, J, 70.
Rhodes, John, 143, 161, 172, 186, 221, 223, 224, 225, 227, 231, 232, 233, 235, 250.
Rich, Doreen, 21.
Richards, David, 291, 304, 312, 317.
Richardson, Clive, 203.
Richmond, Daniel, 172, 276.
Riley, Ann, 89, 90.
Riley, Peter, 52, 54, 57, 58, 64, 69, 70, 73, 75, 76, 89, 90, 92, 94, 96.
Riviere, Peter, 27.
Rosqvist, Ewy, 52, 69, 70, 131.
Rudman, Frank, 217.
Ruutsalo, Kauko, 192.
Ryan, Pat, 295, 297, 301, 302, 308, 310, 312, 315, 318, 320, 329, 330, 334, 337.

Saaristo, Markku, 282, 333, 334.
Safety Devices, 301, 333, 339, 341, 363, 364.
Salonen, Erkki, 361.
Saviola, Charles, 140.
Scarlett, Michael, 253.
Schmarje, Christian, 231.
Sclater, Chris, 282.
Schock, W, 51.
Scott, Dennis, 17.
Scott, Jack, 92, 99.
Scott-Russell, P, 20, 21.
Seager, Stuart, 122, 165.
Sears, Jack, 20, 23, 26, 40, 51, 54, 59, 89, 215, 273.
Seigle-Morris, David, 64, 69, 70, 76, 79, 80, 84, 90, 96, 99.
Seth-Smith, Richard, 286, 288, 289, 293, 294, 296, 298, 299, 301, 304, 309, 310, 312.
Shaw, Anthony, 264.
Shaw, Bill, 240, 268, 271, 272, 296.
Shaw, J, 10.
Shillabeer, Harry, 101, 146.
Shepherd, Barry, 364.
Shepherd, Bill, 15, 16, 17, 20, 23, 25, 26, 27, 51, 84.
Shepherd, Richard, 165.
Silberman, Eric, 333.
Silver City Airways, 16, 20, 75.
Simpson, Cyril, 75.
Simpson, Jim, 127, 142, 163, 197.
Simpson, Ray, 27, 174.
Slotemaker, Rob, 207.
Smith, A. E, 57.
Smith, Mary, 201, 214.

391

Index

Smith, Derek, 308.
Smith, John, 350.
Smith, Rosemary, 157, 233, 250, 254, 260, 264.
Smiths Industries, 72.
Soderstrom, Bengt, 170, 192.
Soisbault, Annie, 54.
Sopwith, Tom, 203, 217.
Sparkrite, 354.
Sparrow, Will, 301.
Speight, Oliver, 73, 114.
Spouse, John, 254, 259.
Sprinzel, John, 27, 28, 30, 40, 62, 75, 87, 104, 233.
Staepalaere, Gilbert, 217, 339.
Stead, Jerry, 264, 266.
Steadman, John, 99.
Stewart, Jacky, 131.
Stokes, Lord, 215, 221, 232, 259, 268, 271, 337.
Stone, Henry, 9, 14, 17.
Stoop, Dickie, 18.
Stoter, Jean, 58.
SU Carburettors, 196.
Summers, Bill, 33.
Surgey, Frank, 264.
Sutcliffe, Mike, 58, 59, 70, 84, 85.
Syer, Johnstone, 229, 233, 247, 272, 278, 284, 286, 289, 290, 296, 297, 298, 332.
Sylvan, Hans, 348, 352.

Tarbuck, Jimmy, 157.
Targa Florio, 161, 186, 199.
Taylor, Anita, 143.
Taylor, Henry, 153.
Taylor, John, 27.
Taylor, Trevor, 143.
Therier, Jean-Luc, 342, 245.
Thompson, Gavin, 256, 268.
Thompson, Jack, 119.
Thornley, John, 9, 10, 13, 14, 15, 18, 20, 25, 34, 38, 84, 92, 135, 140, 157, 172, 275.
Threlfall, Tom, 27.
Toivonen, Pauli, 157.
Tomlinson, Ken, 310.
Torlay, Morris, 92.
Trana, Tom, 131, 133.
Trautmann, Rene, 145, 148.
Triplex, 119.
Tubman, Ken, 266.
Turnbull, George, 215, 271, 276.
Turner, Stuart, 52, 58, 78, 82, 85, 89, 90, 92, 99, 113, 115, 116, 119, 120, 122, 123, 125, 126, 130, 133, 134, 137, 138, 142, 146, 147, 149, 150, 153, 157, 165, 172, 173, 174, 176, 185, 187, 192, 266, 275, 361.
Tutt, Ron, 219.
Tyler, Carolyn, 169.
Tyrell, Ken, 131.

Unipart, 286, 288, 295, 300.

Valance, Peter, 282.
Valentyne, John, 26.
Van Damm, Sheila, 10.
Vandermeersch, 329, 361.
Vanson, Patrick, 122.
Vatanen, Ari, 310, 318.
Vernaeve, Julien, 122, 139, 140, 145, 167, 191, 194, 196, 201, 207, 210, 234, 235.
Vial, Michel, 342.

Vokins, Robin, 125, 146, 157, 190, 201, 227, 259.
Von Bayern, Prince
Leopold, 235.

Wachowski, Marek, 148, 166.
Wadsworth, John, 127, 128, 130.
Waldegaard, Bjorn, 237.
Wales, Basil, 140, 164, 203, 272, 275, 276, 277, 278, 281, 282, 284, 286, 292.
Waeffler, H, 13.
Walker, Ian, 83.
Walton, Jeremy, 333.
Warner, Graham, 348.
Watson, Alice, 233, 254.
Watson, John, 340, 363.
Watts, Doug, 11, 13, 15, 17, 18, 21, 28, 33, 38, 62, 73, 78, 83, 84, 104, 119, 122, 126, 135, 140, 143, 153, 161, 165, 172, 173, 189, 206, 223, 250, 264, 268, 271, 272.
Webster, Harry, 223.
Welch, David, 282, 289, 295, 296.
Wellman, Tommy, 11, 14, 15, 17, 18, 26, 72, 78, 92, 104, 113, 126, 138, 145, 146, 172, 190, 191, 196, 208, 210, 223, 225, 227, 250, 251, 254, 271, 272, 275.
Weslake, Harry, 17.
West, John, 276, 289, 357, 365.
Wharton, Ken, 12, 15, 16, 20, 22.
White, Derek, 240.
White, Doc, 15.
Whitehouse, Jim, 276.
Whitmore, John, 73, 89.
Whittington, Bob, 192, 214, 217, 218, 304.
Wiffen, Gerald, 12, 33, 78, 90, 114, 145, 190, 201, 272, 275, 284.
Wiggins, Harold, 11.
Wilkins, Bill, 139.
Wilkinson, Brian, 364.
Wilks, Peter, 247.
Williams, Barrie, 130.
Williams, Engineering, 365.
Williams, George, 17.
Williams, Ken, 299.
Williamson, Jeff, 247.
Williamson, John, 15, 16, 26, 27, 30.
Willis, Roger, 278.
Wilson, Neil, 341.
Wilson, Peter, 18, 22.
Wisdom, Ann, 27, 28, 34, 40, 52, 57, 58, 66, 69, 70, 73, 75, 76, 85, 89.
Wisdom, Tommy, 27, 28.
Wisdom, Mrs T, 10.
Wood, David, 329, 330, 333, 337, 339, 340, 341, 346, 348, 350, 351, 352, 354, 365.
Wood, Mike, 127, 164, 194, 207, 212, 218, 276.
Wood, Joe, 233.
Wood, Ray, 320, 346.
Woodcock, G, 14.
Wooding, Don, 235.
Woolley, Saville, 73.
Wootton, Derek, 240, 288.
Worswick, Ted, 191.
Wright, Pat, 726.

Ytterbring, Lars, 191, 206, 207, 208, 276.

Zafer, Alan, 214, 215, 223, 234, 237, 250, 253, 263, 302.
Zasada, Sobieslaw, 148, 165.
Zweifel, H, 16.